STO

ACPL ITEM
DISCARDED

Y0-AAB-658

2.20.79

ECONOMIC ISSUES AND NATIONAL SECURITY

NATIONAL SECURITY STUDIES SERIES

Sponsored by the National Security Education Program of New York University, in cooperation with The National Strategy Information Center.

Editorial Board

Donald G. Brennan, Hudson Institute
Klaus Knorr, Princeton University
Laurence W. Martin, University of London
Ernest R. May, Harvard University
Charles C. Moskos, Jr., Northwestern University
Fred A. Sondermann, Colorado College
Frank N. Trager, New York University

ECONOMIC ISSUES AND
NATIONAL SECURITY

edited by

Klaus Knorr and Frank N. Trager

Published for the
NATIONAL SECURITY EDUCATION PROGRAM
BY THE REGENTS PRESS OF KANSAS

QC 047

79 7991 7

© Copyright 1977
by the National Security Education Program
of New York University

Standard Book Number 0-7006-167-8
Library of Congress Catalog Card Number 77-91836

Printed in the United States of America
by Allen Press, Inc., Lawrence, Kansas

Foreword

Survival values, particularly of people, political independence, and territorial integrity, have long served as the traditional focus of American national security concerns for which the Constitution imposes on the Congress and the President the obligation "to provide for the[ir] common defense." Concern for these values arises whenever they are perceived as being threatened by adverse foreign action or events. Threat perception—and the state-actor's response—is "strategically easy when societies are prepared to see a threat in any state whose military strength is either great or growing relative to their own." It is especially so when such a state is regarded by the perceiving state as an actual or potential adversary.[1]

The list of survival or vital national values—used here as interchangeable terms—is not confined to those cited above. Shortly after World War II, American leadership recognized the need to undertake a vast economic aid program to war-devastated Europe—The Marshall Plan—not only to help repair war damages but also to assist the recipient countries to regain important elements of their security. Later, on a smaller scale, similar economic assistance was extended to former enemy countries such as Japan and to the newly independent developing countries of Asia and Africa. This was done for several reasons including the assumption that economic benefits were translatable into security benefits. Conversely, deprivation of economic assets, such as water resources, food grains, fossil fuels, trade, and other goods and services may come to be perceived as threats to the security of the deprived state-actor. Though the character and intensity of each such threat may be difficult to assess, it is clear that an aggravated economic threat, e.g., deprivation of oil, could initiate coercive behavior.

The relation of economic values to the concern for national security values has been a somewhat neglected area of study. This volume attempts in part to repair that neglect.

The editors indicate elsewhere in this volume that the subjects treated in the several chapters do not exhaust all aspects of the relation between economics and national security. However, the several authors herein deal with what seem to us to be key aspects at this juncture in history. It is hoped that this book will contribute to a better understanding and stimulate further study of the circumstances that have generated widespread anxiety about an advanced degree of international economic interdependence, its consequences, and its relation to national security. This rarely explored view of national security should be of interest to the general reader as well as to the student.

v

This volume is the seventh in the National Security Studies Series sponsored by the National Security Education Program of New York University in cooperation with the National Strategy Information Center, Inc. Under the general editorship of Professor Frank N. Trager of New York University, the Series has attempted to provide the academic community with texts, bibliographies, and other materials suitable for research and classroom use.

Other volumes in the National Security Studies Series include:

1. *National Security and American Society: Theory, Process, and Policy*, edited by Frank N. Trager and Philip S. Kronenberg (1973).

2. *American Defense Policy Since 1945: A Preliminary Bibliography*, compiled by John Greenwood and Robin Higham, edited by Geoffrey Kemp, Clark Murdock, and Frank L. Simonie (1973).

3. *Congressional Hearings in American Defense Policy, 1947–1971: An Annotated Bibliography*, edited by Richard Burt and Geoffrey Kemp (1974).

4. *Nuclear Proliferation: Phase II*, edited by Robert M. Lawrence and Joel Larus (1974).

5. *Modules in Security Studies*, edited by Alden Williams and David W. Tarr (1974).

6. *Historical Dimensions of National Security Problems*, edited by Klaus Knorr (1976).

Note

1. For national security values and interests, see F. N. Trager and F. L. Simonie, "An Introduction to the Study of National Security," in *National Security and American Society*, ed. F. N. Trager and P. Kronenberg (Lawrence, Kansas: University Press of Kansas, 1973), pp. 35–48. For "threat perception," see Klaus Knorr, "Threat Perception," in *Historical Dimensions of National Security*, ed. Klaus Knorr (Lawrence, Kansas: University Press of Kansas, 1976), pp. 78–119.

Acknowledgments

The editors' task was greatly lightened by the special contribution of Professor Janet Kelly. Hila Cohen Rosen, Editorial Assistant, National Security Education Program, New York University, had the onerous responsibility of steering the manuscript through the publishing process.

F.N.T.

Contents

Part I

Part II

Part I

CHAPTER 1

Economic Interdependence and National Security

Klaus Knorr

I

Following World War II, the major trading countries created a new international economic order designed to stimulate international trade and investment. The principal institutions of this order were the General Agreement on Tariffs and Trade, the International Monetary Fund, and the World Bank. The first of this triad was to facilitate the diminution of national trade barriers; the second set up an international monetary regime centered on fixed and freely convertible exchange rates among national currencies; and the third provided for the international flow of capital to meet economic recovery and development projects that private investors were unable to support.

It was the United States—by far the world's richest state and, until the late 1960s, the world's premier military power—which was primarily responsible for establishing this new economic order. Moreover, the other important trading countries were also highly developed economically, capitalist, and democratic. The congruent interests of this entire set of societies were seen by the bulk of their elites, guided by the vast majority of economic experts, as best served by a liberal, that is, open international economic system in which private enterprise could operate across national boundaries with a minimum of national regulation and interference. The benefits expected were primarily economic: broad, progressive advancement in terms of rising productivity and incomes for all participating nations. Furthermore, it was assumed that this order would benefit not only the advanced capitalist societies but also the undeveloped or less developed countries. Expanding international trade and investment was seen as a powerful engine that would gradually transform backward economies into national systems capable of self-sustained growth.

The sponsors of the new system were aware that liberating international economic life from the restraints of national control might hurt national groups that had been protected by these restraints. When threatened groups were large and influential, liberalization would proceed cautiously, permitting time for adjustment and even some compromise. It was generally believed, however, that persistent economic expansion along economically efficient lines would make it easy to reallocate the economic factors involved (labor and capital) for more efficient employment and, if necessary, to compensate their owners for any transitional losses and costs. Governments in the capitalist states were expected to be strong enough domestically to enforce an economic order that promised far more gain than loss to the majority of populations and to populations as a whole.

The new world economic order was also perceived as a potent source of political benefit. According to one underlying conception of governments and elites, a system producing continuous, massive, and pervasive improvements in the material foundations of human life would make possible a politically peaceful and stable world in which nations would be capable of solving disputes by judicious bargaining and compromise. Moreover, newly emerging countries in the less developed part of the world would be attracted to democratic and capitalist constitutions.

In this view, the communist countries were regarded, on the economic level, as an awkward anomaly that was, in terms of the volume of communist trade with non-communist states, fortunately on too small a scale to cause much worry. However, the communist military and political challenge was believed to be significant and dangerous. The Soviet Union had emerged from World War II as indubitably the world's second largest military power. Its perceived threat to Europe and the Middle East was regarded as a serious security problem. But it was felt that the United States alone was capable of deterring or coping with any communist aggression as long as other capitalist nations were still weakened by the ravages of World War II. In the longer run, recovery from war damages and the economic progress that the new economic order was to generate would augment the national bases of military strength in all capitalist societies and would also make them immune to political appeals of communism. In the short run, however, the United States not only gave large-scale economic support to the economic and political rehabilitation of western Europe and Japan through the Marshall Plan, but it also tolerated significant deviations from the newly installed international economic order in the form of trade restrictions and postponement of currency convertibilities.

International trade and investment flourished under the new economic world order, and the dependence of national economies on each other grew accordingly. This spectacular increase of economic interdependence was not, however, evenly spread. It grew primarily among the capitalist economies which, as a group, were most open economically and who formed a customs union of the European Economic Community (EC) and became engaged in building other components of an economic union. Eco-

2

nomic interdependence increased less among the Less Developed Countries (LDCs) as a group and less between LDCs and the capitalist advanced societies. Economic interdependence also remained comparatively limited among the communist states and between them and the rest of the world.[1]

The new economic order produced several of the benefits anticipated by its sponsors. The twenty-year period beginning in 1950 was one of vigorous economic growth in the capitalist countries, with Japan and West Germany turning in spectacular performances. When cyclical downturns set in, Keynesian remedies worked, and recessions remained short and mild. Inflation was moderate. The LDCs as a group experienced a rate of economic growth that was high by historical standards, even if it did not measure up to expectations and, in view of explosive population growth and the distributive policy of many LDC governments, to the needs of poor people.

By the middle 1960s, these developments had precipitated various academic speculations about actual or impending structural changes in the international system. One view saw countries becoming more and more preoccupied with economic and, ultimately, domestic issues. Another line of argument predicted the increasing importance of international economic power in settling international conflicts and even its progressive substitution for military power as a determinant of international order and behavior. Another hypothesis, focusing on the globally spreading operations of multinational corporations and other transnational activities, foresaw the international decline of the nation-state and of what has been called the state-centric system. A related thesis, reminiscent of the free-trade doctrines of mid-19th-century England—doctrines that were meant to root out the vestiges of mercantilist thought and practice—asserted that growing international economic enmeshment had become irreversible and was going to make international war irrelevant and unfeasible.

Yet, during the late 1960s and 1970s, the open international economic system introduced after World War II suddenly showed signs of disintegration and came under increasing critical challenge. A number of events marked this change. With the American dollar losing its dominance as the key international currency, the dollar's convertibility into gold (1971), and the abandonment of fixed foreign-exchange rates, the monetary system set up at Bretton Woods was essentially dead. Its tentative replacement remained in a state of flux. The surge of heavy inflation throughout the capitalist world and the subsequent persistence of strong inflationary pressures, even when the capitalist economies experienced a sharp business slump in 1975, caused national governments to show a renewed interest in national economic controls. Within the regional context of the EC, the process of economic integration first ground to a halt and then suffered considerable setbacks. The OPEC countries used their monopoly power in 1973 to quadruple the price of oil, and Arab members imposed a partial

3

embargo on oil exports in order to coerce the capitalist importing states into modifying their policy posture toward the Arab-Israeli conflict. Encouraged by this show of strength, the countries of the Third World intensified their pressure toward negotiation of a new world economic order. By the end of 1976, with economic recovery faltering in the main capitalist states, Great Britain and Italy in the grips of fundamental international disequilibrium, and another increase in oil prices administered by OPEC, widespread pessimistic expectations were voiced about the prospects of continued economic growth.

What principally concerns us here are the accompanying changes in perception on the merits of the liberal economic order and the degree and kind of international economic interdependence it had brought about. LDC leaders had been complaining throughout the 1960s that the established order worked against them in terms of the growth, distribution, and stability of national incomes in favor of the industrial states. The doubts that were now expressed questioned the value of the benefits derived by the capitalist countries, not in terms of their economic relations with the LDCs, but in terms of their economic transactions among themselves.

Of course, it had always been understood that substantial gains in economic efficiency and income generated by free trade and investment would also subject each national economy to frequent market changes occurring in the outside world. These changes would affect particular branches of production, as when foreign competitors became more efficient, or would affect the entire economy, as when key national economies abroad fell victim to inflation or deflation. Participation in an open international system thus required societies to be highly flexible in adapting themselves to incessant dynamic processes initiated elsewhere. It was generally concluded, however, that the economic advantages greatly outweighed the social disadvantages. This conclusion rested on the assumption that societies in the aggregate and in their various parts were able and willing to tolerate the strains and stresses involved. In other words, the case for the free international movement of goods and capital rested on the expectation that a compatible social, cultural, and political infrastructure would prevail.

This assumption might have been or might have remained secure, if participating societies had been able to do more domestically to make painful adjustments to external economic impacts a public responsibility. As it was, adjustments were absorbed primarily by unfortunate groups of workers, owners, and entrepreneurs, often concentrated in particular localities. But such public provision was made only seldom and inadequately.[2] Moreover, for reasons to be discussed shortly, democratic capitalist societies have apparently become less willing to accept painful adjustments in terms of employment, income, and their social precipitates. How a society weights the disutility of painful instabilities and adjustments for

4

some against long-term income gains for society as a whole is ultimately a subjective valuation and, as a practical matter, depends upon the structure and mobilization of political influence. But there is another normative consideration. Once all the advantages and disadvantages are fully taken into account, it is rational for a society to determine through the political process the trade-offs between the benefits of additional productivity and income and the costs of more subjection to disruptions emanating from abroad. In principle there will be an optimum level and structure of economic interdependence with the outside world; the location of the optimum depending on the relative strengths of effective preferences.

Growing economic interdependence brings with it increased vulnerability to normal economic changes in the comparative national production and investment advantages governing the flow of transactions on which the case for free trade rests. For example, witness the impact of Japanese and West German producers having succeeded in recent decades in competing with American producers of a variety of manufactured products. Growing interdependence also entails vulnerability to the inability of foreign governments to avoid inflationary or deflationary bouts. Growing interdependence naturally increases national vulnerability to economic disruptions caused by natural adversities such as crop failures or military conflicts abroad. Vulnerability is increased further by attempts by external actors, especially governments but also private business firms, to exploit dependencies to their advantage deliberately. Notable among these are, first, government actions designed to mitigate or solve domestic economic problems (e.g., unemployment or inflation) by means of policies that are, in effect, at the expense of employment and price stability in the outside world (e.g., "beggar-my-neighbor policies"); and second, the formation of monopolies by foreign governments or business corporations to extract monopolist prices and profits (e.g., OPEC). Beyond these types of manipulation, increasing international economic interdependence also tends to augment vulnerability to foreign attempts to use economic leverage for politically coercive purposes (e.g., OAPEC's oil embargo in 1973). In various ways, these vulnerabilities threaten the income and stability of productive activity of either specific producer groups or of entire nations.

National reactions to these undesirable impacts, which represent the costs of international economic interdependence, have been sharpened by basic changes in the cultural dispositions, political structures, and social preferences of the democratic capitalist countries. Although these recent changes are not yet fully understood, two major developments seem to be at work. First, the cultural infrastructure that had made capitalism such an immensely effective engine of technological and economic progress is apparently in serious disrepair. The hold of the Protestant ethic that extolled hard work, saving, and personal responsibility for material success and welfare has weakened. This transformation has evidently been more profound in some societies (e.g., Great Britain) than in others (e.g., West Germany). But to the extent it has taken effect, the ability and willingness of societies to adjust to disruptive economic change emanating from abroad has been reduced. Public demands that the government intervene in order to avert these disruptions or compensate their victims have increased. There is now a strong expectation in all segments of society that one is entitled to annual improvements in income, conditions of work, and welfare benefits regardless of whether they are manageable in view of increases in labor productivity or national real output. The advanced and rich capitalist societies have become habituated to ever-expanding economic growth. They have acquired a tendency to live collectively beyond their means, thereby—among other things—causing investment in further economic growth to lag.

Second, most of these societies have become more democratic in real, as distinct from formal, terms than they were prior to World War II. Population segments previously more or less underprivileged in terms of influence on government—ethnic and religious minorities, women, and youths—have gained more political influence in exerting their rights and making public welfare claims. At the same time, labor unions and farmers' associations have become strengthened vis-à-vis employers and are using their power more readily to defend or increase the economic welfare of their members. Although these tendencies are not equally strong in all advanced capitalist countries, they do seem to be characteristic of the group as a whole.

These developments in the cultural and political infrastructure have entailed three important consequences. First, economic problems, both domestic and international, have become more widely politicized than before, and have apparently risen in salience relative to other national problems. There have, of course, always been interest groups that politicized economic issues of special concern to them. Recently, however, such politicization has increased, because economic issues are regarded as more vital, nationally or sectionally, by members of society, and because more segments of society share this regard and can exercise political influence on government in these matters. Second, the increased ability of various interest groups in these pluralistic societies to advance their preferences and their greater willingness to do so in competition with other groups—which in itself signifies a weakening of national solidarity and of support for national rather than sectional interests—has tended to enfeeble government authority and weaken the great political parties in these societies. Popular government support based on trust in the disposition of authorities to cultivate the general public good has diminished, and support has now become more conditional, focusing on the satisfaction of particularist demands.

Third, these interest groups are making increasingly effective demands on the state for new or larger public benefits—even if benefits can only be realized in considerable part by public deficits. In any case, new tasks are being imposed on states at the same time as government ability to formulate effective programs and to mobilize resources for the effective discharge of these new obligations has declined.

Given these developments in capitalist nations, increased economic interdependence and its consequences can be appreciated from a new perspective. The more open the national economy, the greater the need to absorb and adapt to disruptive impacts received from the external environment. These impacts now become more readily politicized and elicit stronger public demands for government protection. Vulnerability to disturbing impacts is thus not only a function of their intensity and breadth but also of the receiving economy's and society's resilience and desire to adjust. The more unwilling and unable domestic groups are to undertake adjustments and submit to this burden, the more sensitive they become to economic disruption. Under this circumstance, disruptions lead to three major demands on government: (a) demands for direct public action to reduce or eliminate adverse foreign economic impacts (e.g., curtail the import of foreign shoes, specialty steels, textiles), (b) demands for a redistribution of the perceived burden of adjusting to foreign events or for toleration of direct redistributive action by interest groups (e.g., strong labor unions pressing for wage increases to offset inflation caused, in part, by the higher costs of imported oil, thereby shifting the burden onto less powerful segments of society), and (c) demands for a redistribution of the perceived burden of national measures designed to cope with adverse foreign impacts (e.g., when the government raises taxes on consumer goods in order to decrease imports). These reactions describe one side of vulnerability in an open international system. Individuals and groups are less willing to bear the costs and want relief through public action. At the same time, as we have seen, governments have become less capable of managing the effects of international economic disturbances. That is the other side. The new demands come at a time when economic government agendas have already been expanded by other economic demands and when governments enjoy less authority than they did before. The costs of operating at a high level of international interdependence have thus tended to rise, and the desire to diminish these impacts has naturally grown.

In this context, we can see why certain international economic problems arising from interdependence should now be regarded as "security" problems. Of course, national security considerations naturally arise when a country faces the use of economic leverage by another state for coercive purposes in matters of high diplomacy. The Arab oil embargo was an act of economic aggression. Any dependence on the outside world for supplies

7

that are vital to national economic life and that can be exploited in coercive attempts is a vulnerability raising security concerns. Similarly, throughout history any foreign dependence for essential defense supplies has raised security considerations, particularly in times of war. But what about other adverse economic impacts arising from an advanced stage of international economic interdependence? Why raise the resulting problems to the level of concern that national security problems usually occupy?

Political and territorial integrity has long served as the traditional focus of national security concerns. It is presumably still paramount. However, with the decline in the intensity of the prolonged Cold War confrontation, the perception of external military threats has diminished in capitalist societies. This may well be a temporary phenomenon, especially since the rest of the world expects no shrinkage in the use and utility of international military force.[3] Yet, the weakening of the perception of military threat in the capitalist states has also encouraged a growing sense of insecurity on other accounts.

National security concerns arise when vital national values (i.e., core values) are perceived as being threatened by adverse foreign actions or events. What is regarded as "vital" is a matter of subjective judgment depending on a nation's hierarchy of values. There is no reason why economic values and particular patterns of economic life cannot be regarded as vital. Once these values are perceived as being vulnerable to external events, they naturally inspire security concerns and the desire to minimize these concerns. It then becomes important to avert or curtail serious risks in this functional area. This does not mean, of course, that security concerns are generated whenever foreign competitors cut into national production of a particular commodity or service, or when mild deflationary or inflationary impulses are received from abroad. Economic threats are a matter of more or less, and so is threat recognition.[4] Economic threats to national security are more apt to be perceived when adverse impacts are massive and continuous. Even then, threat perception still depends on the degree of sensitivity to the loss of threatened values and on the keenness of relevant threat perception.

If a high degree of international economic interdependence is now perceived by many in the capitalist countries as something that is not necessarily benign, and by others as more deeply troublesome and even dangerous to national welfare and security, it is not surprising that one sees references to a "crisis of interdependence" and hears talk of neo-mercantilism. The question of how much and what structure of interdependence should be selected by a nation has become a serious and legitimate political issue. The practical choices available for such selection are, of course, limited by the unwillingness to absorb serious losses of productive efficiency and income. Indeed, it is very unlikely that capitalist countries will move far toward protecting their economies by insulating them from the outside world. To do so would be far too costly, if not impracticable. The benefits that economists have taught us to expect from expanding international economic transactions are not, of course, illusory. They are quite real. But economists have narrowly focused on efficiency of resource employment to the exclusion of other values associated with economic life. Indeed, the case for free trade as an arrangement bringing universal benefits has always been something of a myth, even when everything other than efficiency has been ignored.[5] In any case, the gains to be expected from such efficiency may be incrementally less once a fairly high degree of interdependence has already been reached and societies have become more conscious of the price they have to pay for gains. The critical question relates to sacrificing what may be moderate income gains from foreign trade and investment in order to diminish national vulnerability to externally produced disruptions. In the interest of stability, some nations will be willing to pay a price for giving some protection to particular producers, including labor and local communities, or, at the macroeconomic level, for choosing a pattern of unemployment and inflation that suits political demands.

Whatever the choices to be considered and exercised, they will almost certainly push the governments in capitalist and democratic societies in the direction of assuming greater control of economic life, including international economic transactions and, quite contrary to expectations of the waning utility of national governments, into expanding government activities. Whether national governments in this set of democratic societies can recover enough authority to discharge these new functions effectively remains a serious question. The problem is whether or not these countries can muster enough "political will" to enable their governments to discharge these tasks effectively. As we have seen, weakness of will adds a great deal to a nation's economic vulnerability in a highly interdependent world. (For a conceptualization of "national will" see the Appendix to this chapter.) In highly developed capitalist countries, advancing democratization has apparently impaired national unity and encouraged weak governments. National will suffers from division and resists mobilization for the purposes with which we are concerned. The political consequences could be grave if they do. Certainly, there does not seem to be much margin for surviving failure in, say, present-day Italy and Britain. If central government in these societies fails to recover sufficient authority and competence, they will court the sort of disaster that has befallen Argentina where, during the late 1960s and early 1970s, government control collapsed, and political and economic chaos came to prevail. This condition is apt to endanger the survival of democracy.

Assuming that the capitalist societies manage to solve their internal problems, the question arises of what sort of international economic regime would suit the new attitudes and policy criteria in the capitalist states. After all, instead of avoiding or reducing disruptive economic impacts generated abroad strictly by uncoordinated national measures, substantial progress could be made through cooperation and multilateral programs and institutions. In principle, states could lessen present risks and costs of advanced interdependence by giving up only a minimum of income gains that can be derived from international trade and investment. In terms of the values involved, the best solution lies in the direction of more multilateral diplomacy and institutionalization. The problem is whether, or to what extent, this is a politically feasible solution. Part of the problem arises from the challenges advanced by the communist states and the Third World countries to the liberal world economic order.

For the communist countries, international economic interdependence also results in disadvantages as well as benefits. Soviet exports decline when business in the capitalist world is depressed, and Yugoslavia must pay the oil price fixed by OPEC. However, these countries as a group have kept their economic interdependence with capitalist countries and LDCs at a distinctly limited level, even though it has recently increased. Close control of foreign economic transactions has always been a government responsibility in communist states. The principal reasons for giving such control a high priority are to avoid risky dependence on the outside world for vital requirements and to insulate planned economies from external economic forces to a great extent. Communist ruling groups dislike vulnerability to the outside world. However, they accepted a somewhat higher level of economic interdependence among themselves (within COMECON) under conditions of careful planning and regulation by state authorities. These societies, then, have deliberately sacrificed many international trade gains in order to preserve competing values.

The fact that the Soviet Union, like most communist countries, has recently displayed a keen interest in expanding trade with the capitalist countries—especially in order to import the advanced technologies it is not now capable of producing and grain when crop failures threaten consumer diets—cannot be currently regarded as a new communist eagerness to enhance permanent participation in a liberal system of economic transactions. It is more likely that these approaches are meant to serve pragmatic and temporary state interests. Moreover, on the ideological and rhetorical level, communist governments continue to predict the collapse of capitalist systems and to support the attack of the Third World against the old liberal economic order.

The challenge of the Third World reveals two major concerns. One is basically in line with the sensitivity to the costs and risks of international economic interdependence recently experienced in the capitalist so-

10

cieties. This concern is focused in particular on the cyclical instabilities to which capitalist economies are subject, and which tend to make LDC earnings from the export of raw materials and foodstuffs fluctuate extremely in response to changing prices and volumes of demand. The other concern centers on the injustice of the established order which is alleged to be so structured that the capitalist countries exploit the poor and prevent their proper development. The specific demands of the Third World are mainly that prices of the raw materials and foodstuffs they export be raised substantially above the level generated by the play of supply and demand in unregulated markets and be indexed at this higher level relative to the prices of manufactured goods imported by LDCs; that LDC industrial exports be granted special access to markets in capitalist states; that past LDC debts be cut back and refunded; and that wealthy societies grant larger funds, without strings attached, for the development of LDC economies.

If met, these demands have the following implications for capitalist countries and the evolving international economic system. To the extent that they require a continuous redistribution of world income from the capitalist societies to the LDCs, the former must be willing to accept the transfer and to deal with the difficult political problems of distributing the resulting burden among income recipients within them—a task that would hardly be easy in view of the recent proclivity of these societies to spend more than they produce. In the capitalist countries, privileged access for LDC industrial exports would increase disruptive and costly economic impacts from abroad in terms of economic and social adjustment. Virtually all proposals would serve to augment the role of government in the capitalist states. For example, the establishment and operation of international commodity agreements and buffer stocks for stabilizing and elevating the prices of LDC raw materials and foodstuffs demand close intergovernmental cooperation and regulation. Indeed, in most instances, these schemes would be viable only if capitalist governments would support them by means of finance and regulatory action, even though the chief purpose of the arrangement is to make the commodities more expensive to capitalist consumers.

Third World demands regarding the operations of capitalist multinational corporations have become more muted of late than they were a decade ago. The fact is that the conditions under which these enterprises operate in the LDCs have been transformed dramatically over the last ten years. Not only have foreign private investments been nationalized in many LDCs[6]—the oil companies representing the most spectacular instance—but the activities of the remaining multinational corporations are being regulated in various ways by national governments to confer greater benefits on the host countries.[7] Raymond Vernon's book on the multinationals, published in 1971, bore the title *Sovereignty at Bay*. It posed the question of

11

whether multinationals were too powerful to be regulated by LDC governments.[8] Only a few years later, it is clear that national sovereignty is winning out nearly everywhere, and private corporations are more and more threatened, not only in Third World host countries, but also in the capitalist home states themselves. This includes the United States where congressional criticism of and attacks on private corporate power have grown remarkably.

In view of all these changes on the world scene, it is difficult to foresee what sort of economic order will eventually emerge. One thing which is clear is that the shape of things to come can no longer be solely determined by the United States, which was the case right after World War II. Its military power, political influence, and economic preeminence have declined vis-à-vis other states. Of course, capitalist countries as a group can decide on the framework within which their own economic intercourse with one another will take place, and this accounts for the large bulk of international economic transactions. But they are less able than before to determine the order within which their economic relations with the rest of the world will take place. Here some sort of compromise is evidently in the making. What the components of this compromise will be remains to be seen. Compared with the period from 1945 to the early 1970s, however, the following major changes are likely to prevail.

The future system will be less open than its predecessor. The movement of goods and capital will be less free, and the play of market forces will be subjected to more government control. The new order will be more, not less, state-centric. As a result, the system will be more politicized than before, especially in the sense that governments will be involved in shaping transactions that were previously left to private enterprise. The evolving order will also be less stable in response to changing government concerns, and influence over how the order will change will be more fragmented internationally than has been the case. Nevertheless, international economic interdependence is apt to expand beyond current levels. It is unlikely to grow, however, at the pace characteristic of the 1950s and 1960s, and its structure will be less determined by market forces and private initiatives than by government involvement and fiat. The considerations governments will bring to bear on these decisions will be governed less by the efficiency and income gains that can be derived from the free movement of goods and capital and more by other concerns with national welfare to which publics are sensitive, and more by their own concerns over national economic security and economic vulnerabilities that jeopardize such security.

To what extent and by which means the developing world economic order will be institutionalized is also unclear, both on the global level and within regional confines. On the global level, a substantial degree of institutionalization is obviously in the interest of all states, because it makes

12

economic events more predictable. This is important to governments as well as private enterprise. The critical question is whether there will be enough international consensus on the purpose and operation of institutions to sustain a high level of institutionalization. This question is interconnected with the future structure of international influence wielded by the great trading countries and by other groupings inspired by conflicting ideologies and objectives.

As we have remarked above, the democratic capitalist countries could attempt to reach an international economic order among themselves that is institutionally more advanced than what is feasible on the global level. The purpose would be to minimize resort to purely nationalist measures for regulating international economic transactions in response to politically effective domestic welfare concerns and to considerations of national economic security. Nationalist measures tend to safeguard national values at the expense of other countries. Multilateral regulation will often offer a solution that, over the longer run, is superior in the net. But it is presently doubtful whether or not capitalist governments will be able to muster the vision to opt for multinational solutions. What has been recently happening to the integration of economic policy in the European Community does not support an optimistic outlook. The inability of the European nations to proceed with the establishment of a monetary union disclosed the strength of reservations when it comes to surrendering or greatly curtailing national economic control.

Two interrelated problems seem to obstruct the establishment of international rather than national remedies to the instabilities coursing through international economic life. First, and most fundamental, is that although the capitalist countries and many others share a common concern about the drawbacks of a very high level of international economic interdependence, this concern does not necessarily lead to consensus about exactly what needs to be done. Neither their economies nor their politics are sufficiently compatible to insure common interests even among highly industrialized states. Differences in domestic conditions will tend to entail conflicting policy preferences.[9] The differences are even greater between highly developed and less developed countries.

The other problem is more contingent. If forecasters prove right that the economic future of the world will not be like the 1950s and 1960s, with continuous and rapid economic expansion, but rather a world of slow growth, at best, and possibly stagnation, international agreement on new institutions to mitigate the disadvantages of a high degree of international interdependence is unlikely.[10] This is true primarily because domestic problems of resource adjustment are easier to endure and manage within vigorously expanding economies where attractive opportunities exist and where there is more real income to be shared. Such adjustments are harder to

13

undertake and adjust to when there is little or no economic growth. Moreover, recourse to national remedies is more likely if international solutions are hard to come by or fail.

However, in this area as in others on which we have touched, what is at issue is a question of more or less rather than of either-or. The economic world is unlikely to fall into the kind of chaos that bedevilled the 1930s, even if it does not recover the degree of order established after World War II. It is the balance between national and international solutions that is in question.

II

The following chapters deal with the issues raised above in more factual and analytical detail.

Chapter 2 reminds us that the pros and cons of an open or a more state-regulated international economic order are not essentially new but have long engaged statesmen and experts. Robert Gilpin analyzes the historical conditions that led to different kinds of systems in the past: the rise of mercantilism; the development of capitalist market economies interlinked in a fairly open international economic system; the subsequent revolt against this form and degree of interdependence fueled by economic nationalism, Marxists critics of capitalist imperialism, and the breakdown of the system in the 1930s; the establishment of an American-centered economic order after World War II, and its gradual weakening in recent years. In presenting his interpretation, Gilpin relates the changes in economic order to changes in the domestic politics and relative power and wealth of the capitalist societies.

In Chapter 3, Clark Murdock examines in some detail the national vulnerabilities that a high degree of international economic interdependence engenders. He discusses the circumstances under which national sensitivity to these vulnerabilities generates concern over national economic security.

Chapter 4 presents a conceptualization of various uses of international economic leverage in support of national objectives, with particular emphasis on attempts at coercion. The forms of such leverage are examined systematically in terms of their bases, opportunity costs, and conditions of success. Economic power is shown to consist of active and passive economic power. The interchangeability of economic and military power is analyzed, and the prospects of the international use of economic leverage in the contemporary world are briefly discussed.

In Chapter 5, Cheryl Christensen addresses herself to the kinds of power and influence that enable states to determine the international order within which international economic transactions take place—a subject that has so far received little systematic attention. This structure is shown to

14

impinge on the distribution of advantages and disadvantages that participating countries derive from economic interdependence. The capacity to establish and maintain such an order rests on several bases of influence. The author illustrates these phenomena by discussing three cases: recent transformations in the international monetary system, changes in the structure of world oil production, and the demand of Third World countries for a new international economic order.

The ability of states to exercise economic power against others by using economic leverage depends, among other things, on the domestic economic system they maintain and on the domestic strength of central authorities in directing the flow of economic transactions on behalf of state objectives. Capitalist countries obviously differ in these respects from the command economies of communist countries. But, as Stephen Krasner makes clear in Chapter 6, there are also relevant differences among capitalist nations. These problems are illustrated in considerable detail with reference to American trade and oil policies since the 1940s.

Chapter 7 deals with the economic bases of international military power—the traditional concern in political economy that linked economic factors to the conditions of national security. Special attention is paid to the impact of modern technology on the ability of various countries to sustain effective military postures. In order to avoid an overemphasis on the economic foundation of national military strength, other equally important bases are carefully analyzed, i.e., military statecraft and the national will to support military force and its international employment.

In Chapter 8, Ronald Meltzer explores the development of international trade relationships under conditions of growing economic interdependence and the national problems—especially problems of economic security—to which this development has given rise. The author emphasizes the desirability and feasibility of collective international solutions to these national problems.

Chapter 9 by Janet Kelly focuses on international monetary relations as a factor in the national economic security of different kinds of states. It is her thesis that monetary relations can neither be understood outside the context of international and national politics, nor be given an orderly structure without taking these political realities into account.

Hanns Maull presents in Chapter 10 a factually detailed and conceptually sophisticated case study of the use of oil power for purposes of coercive political leverage as well as the administering of high monopolist prices. The foundations of this economic power and the constraints on its exercise are examined with painstaking care.

The use of the oil weapon by Arab members of OPEC in 1973–74 has prompted a search for other commodity markets that offer the opportunity to assemble and exploit economic leverage. A number of Americans have wondered whether the United States' food power might not be organized in order to rival OPEC's oil power. In Chapter 11, Cheryl Christensen critically examines the bases of American food power, the opportunity costs of employing it, and the probable results of its use.

The editors are aware that the subjects treated in these chapters do not exhaust all aspects of international economic security. However, they deal with what seemed to be key aspects at this juncture in history. It is hoped that this book will contribute to a better understanding and stimulate further study of the circumstances that have generated widespread anxiety about an advanced degree of international economic interdependence and its consequences.

Appendix
National Will and National Security

National security, whether military or economic, can be diminished both by events in the outside world and by domestic failures to provide the means of coping with any external threats, whether actual or potential. Strictly speaking, this failure is not a failure of threat perception but of realistically acting upon such perception. However, any unwillingness to bear the opportunity costs of providing for security often leads to a wishful underestimate of external threats.[11] In any case, this sort of failure can be regarded as a deficiency of "national will." Since this failure of will is referred to as such in this chapter and in Chapter 4 and in other chapters, especially Chapters 3 and 6, it seems useful to present a brief statement on the nature of national will.

Dictionaries tell us that "will" is the power of choosing and of acting in accordance with one's choice. National will is an aggregative configuration of individual wills exerted toward influencing national action. In our context, national will is the ability of national authorities to commit regulatory and allocative powers to national programs of action designed to cope with external events that affect national security, whether economic or military. A strong ability to do so will bolster national security, provided, of course, that the chosen programs are designed realistically, that is, are capable of coping effectively and efficiently with perceived threats to national security. Effectiveness, however, depends not only on will but also on the magnitude of suitable resources that are nationally available and can be nationally mobilized. Efficiency is important when such resources are scarce in relation to program needs. Waste can be afforded only when capabilities exceed needs. Furthermore, there is a dynamic relationship between will and resources available for commitment. A high level of will tends to augment capabilities over time, just as ample capabilities tend to increase will.

16

In these terms, national will is stronger when the people with influence on national decision-making are motivated to support action intended to cope with problems of national economic security. Conversely, national will tends to be weaker when the more influential groups are divided on the use of national resources and are motivated by a priorities structure that favors withholding resources from all national programs or, among national programs, favors those that compete with national security action. Although security programs attract strong potential support, national will also tends to be weak when influentials are divided on the nature of specific courses of action because of differences in threat perception or different expectations on the various pros and cons of particular programs.

Using this concept of national will, specific ranges of determinants can be readily identified, e.g., the nature of political and economic systems; culturally embedded attitudes and belief systems; the strength, skill, and bureaucratic unity of governments; and historical experience. Thus, political systems determine the distribution of political influence and the mechanisms for its exercise. The nature of economic systems facilitates or impedes resource mobilization for national purposes. For example, private ownership of economic assets is apt to make it more difficult for governments to direct flows of goods, money, and technology than is the case in authoritarian socialist systems. Effective culture tends to shape the relative emphasis citizens place on personal welfare as opposed to the production of collective goods, the legitimacy bestowed on government and its actions, and ideological dispositions toward the outside world. In parliamentary systems government strength depends on the size of the majority the executive commands in the legislature and, in authoritarian systems, on whether top leaders are united or divided. But strength of government also depends on the degree to which leaders can overcome bureaucratic friction and make administrators respond to chosen policies. Moreover, strength of government also depends on the skill of leaders in organizing support for their policies. Historical experience is a factor to the extent governments and publics have learned from previous threats to national security and from previous responses to these threats.

The foregoing chapter has dealt at some length with the ability of highly developed democratic countries to cope with threats to economic security. Is there a problem about national will that is specific to democratic societies? A number of observers have posed the question whether democratization tends to reduce the ability of governments to mobilize resources for dealing with problems of national security. There seem to be two crucial problems in this respect: first, the degree to which all groups are integrated in the national political system and support the national authorities which they regard as representative of their interests; and, second, the degree to which people resist the mobilization of resources for national security pro-

17

grams, when they have a lesser interest in and knowledge about international affairs and a greater disposition to discount future as against present benefits. The extent to which these conditions operate in particular countries is an empirical question. Moreover, it is also clear that the other factors we have identified above are at work.

Footnotes

1. For an interesting analysis of the growth of economic interdependence and the differences among countries in this respect, see Peter J. Katzenstein, "International Interdependence: Some Long-Term Trends and Recent Changes," *International Organization, 29* (Autumn 1975):1021–34.

2. In the United States, for example, although the Trade Expansion Act of 1962 provided for adjustment assistance, virtually no effective compensation was enacted over the five-year duration of this law.

3. Relative to the wealthy capitalist states, military expenditures and manpower and arms imports have recently increased greatly in the rest of the world.

4. The fact that both economic threats to national security and relevant threat perception are matters of more or less causes a lot of conceptual uneasiness, because we prefer a clean cutoff point between mere sensitivity and threat recognition that touches off national security concerns. We do so because *military* threats to national security are usually (not necessarily correctly) perceived as *discrete* things. Economic threats *can* be discrete (e.g., the oil embargo), but often they are not. We may "import" inflationary pressures. But, if it is very mild, we do not worry. If it is heavy, we do. Thus, there are often no discontinuities. But this is the way it is. Whether sensitivity leads to threat perception is a subjective thing. It is also an empirical thing. It exists when it happens.

   When threat recognition does occur, it tends to generate demands for government action. But there are always demands for government action. They also are a matter of more or less. They increase in volume, intensity, and persistence as external economic threats are perceived to have increased or are increasingly perceived.

5. See Fred Hirsch, "Is There a New International Economic Order?" *International Organization, 30* (Summer 1976):527–30.

6. For a description of recent expropriations, see Department of State, Bureau of Public Affairs, GIST (Washington, D.C.: April 1976).

7. For an illuminating case study, see Theodore H. Moran, *Multinational Corporations and the Politics of Dependence: Copper in Chile* (Princeton: Princeton University Press, 1975). On the problems that multinational corporations present to their home countries, see Robert Gilpin, *U.S. Power and the Multinational Corporation* (New York: Basic Books, 1975).

8. However, in a recent article, Raymond Vernon suggests more of a balance between national and corporate power than is asserted here. Raymond Vernon, "Storm over the Multinationals: Problems and Prospects," *Foreign Affairs, 55* (January 1977):243–62.

9. See Peter J. Katzenstein, "International Relations and Domestic Structures: Foreign Economic Policies of Advanced Industrial States," *International Organization, 30* (Winter 1976):1–34.

10. See Lawrence A. Veit, "Troubled World Economy," *Foreign Affairs, 55* (January 1977):263–79.

11. See Klaus Knorr, "Threat Perception," in *Historical Dimensions of National Security Problems,* ed. Klaus Knorr (Lawrence, Kansas: University Press of Kansas, 1976), pp. 78–119.

CHAPTER 2

Economic Interdependence and National Security in Historical Perspective

Robert Gilpin

Roy Harrod, as quoted in William Baumol's *Welfare Economics and the Theory of the State,* has characterized the originality of economic theory propositions as "subject to the eroding effects of the researcher into the history of economic thought."[1] Harrod's admonition that one should be skeptical regarding claims to originality in economic matters and theory comes to mind in connection with the current discussion of international economic interdependence and its implications for international relations. In particular, as this chapter will show, the important issue of the relationship of economic interdependence and national security is an old one and has engaged the attention of many thinkers and conflicting schools of thought over the past three centuries.

This chapter will place the current controversy over economic interdependence in a larger historical perspective. Specifically, the chapter seeks to analyze the relationship of economic interdependence and national security as it has been conceived by theorists of earlier ages and as it has changed during successive historical periods. In carrying out this task, an attempt will be made to overcome serious limitations in much contemporary theorizing about economic interdependence and its political implications.

Both scholars and popularizers of interdependence have tended to overemphasize the uniqueness of contemporary developments[2] and regard the past as irrelevant. Indeed, we are said to live in an age characterized by major discontinuities and unprecedented changes—an age where the experience and theorizing of previous historical periods are not significant. For these reasons, the discussion of economic interdependence and related issues has often lacked an historical dimension.

In two important senses, the discussion and theorizing about economic interdependence have frequently had a distinctly unhistorical quality. In the first place, contemporary developments have seldom been discussed in the context of a long tradition of theorizing about the political economy of international relations. Secondly, the historical record itself has been insufficiently examined for the insights it can provide regarding the nature,

19

causes, and consequences of economic interdependence. Too much of the literature on interdependence has focused on the period since World War II. Consequently, there is a deficiency in comparative analyses, and an inordinate amount of the theorizing on interdependence has rested on a narrow empirical base.

Another major limitation in the contemporary interdependence literature has been its neglect of national security concerns and issues. The reason for this myopia is instructive in itself. In general, writers on interdependence have shared the nineteenth-century faith of John Bright, Richard Cobden, and other representatives of the so-called Manchester School who believed that economic intercourse is a force for peace. Almost by definition, numerous theorists have regarded increasing economic interdependence as eliminating traditional national security concerns. Moreover, they have too frequently viewed economic interdependence as symmetrical in nature, equally binding on all parties. They have not recognized that economic or political advantage can accrue to particular groups or nations. Thus, by focusing overwhelmingly upon the beneficial and mutually constraining aspects of interdependence, theorists of interdependence have insufficiently analyzed its negative consequences for the core values and interests of nation-states and their constituent members.

This chapter argues that international economic interdependence is a consequence of one of the most distinctive features of modern history, namely, the emergence of a market exchange system for organizing economic relations. Markets, of course, have long existed, and commercial exchange has taken place in every civilization. Moreover, certain geographical areas and historical periods have been characterized by highly sophisticated trading systems. Yet, economic relations within and among societies in the modern period have a distinctive character due to the prevalence of markets in both the domestic and international spheres. The rise of a market economy on a global scale over the past 300 years and its profound importance for the security of states constitute the subject matter of this chapter.[3]

The Rise of an International Market Economy

Prior to the emergence of the market exchange system in the early modern period, three types of exchange systems have tended to prevail in different eras and civilizations.[4] In truth, all societies have had a mixture of systems, yet one or another exchange type has always dominated. By way of contrast, we will briefly consider the other systems before entering upon a more detailed analysis of the market exchange system.

The most elementary exchange system is *reciprocity*. Such a system is principally characterized by gift-giving and barter within and between primitive societies. This type of exchange is rigidly controlled by social mores and is highly circumscribed by custom. In other words, the reciproc-

20

ity system is largely subordinated to the social needs of the group, particularly the maintenance of close intergroup bonds and relations. Thus, the preservation of society's core values takes precedence over the efficient organization of economic relations.

A more advanced form of economic exchange is that of *redistribution*. This type of exchange was characteristic of the early irrigation and storehouse civilizations. It tends to involve a central institution or bureaucracy which organizes the production, storage, and distribution of produce. Societies with this type of exchange tend to be highly stratified and dominated by a bureaucracy. Produce is allocated according to status and occupation. In contrast to the system of reciprocity, redistributive societies are characterized by powerful state governments to which the economy is subordinate. However, like the reciprocity system, the primary goal of economic activity is to enhance the security of the society and particularly to reduce its vulnerability to the vicissitudes of nature.

Closely related to but distinct from the redistributive type is *mobilization* exchange. Like the redistributive economy, this type of economy involves state control and disposition of a society's goods and services. However, the economy's primary function is to advance the security and power of the dominant elite. As in the case of the redistributive system, the economy is subordinate to perceived state security interests. The primary goal of exchange is to enhance the war-making capability of the state. The Assyrians of antiquity and perhaps the Soviets of the modern world exemplify this type of economy.

A *market economy* constitutes a radical departure from these three traditional types of exchange. It involves a market place wherein goods and services are exchanged to maximize the returns to individual buyers and sellers. While markets can exist with respect to all types of commodities (goods, labor, capital, etc.), the nature of the market depends on two characteristics: openness and competition. This is to say, markets may differ with respect to the freedom of individuals to enter them and to the extent to which particular buyers or sellers can influence the terms of the exchange. A perfect or self-regulating market is open to all potential buyers and sellers, and no individuals can determine the terms of the exchange.

In contrast to the other types of exchange, a market system (at least in theory) is not subordinate to society or the state. The terms of exchange are not determined by the society's larger goals or needs or by the state's political and strategic goals. The market is composed of individuals seeking to enhance their own objectives. The outcome of exchange in a self-regulating market is determined by economic "laws," such as those of comparative advantage and of supply and demand rather than by the society's core values and state security interests. Thus, under a market system, the economy constitutes a more or less autonomous sphere.

21

Although Adam Smith—the first great theorist and proponent of the market exchange system—recognized defense to be "of much more importance than opulence," the rationale for a market system is that it increases economic efficiency and maximizes economic growth. The objective of economic activity is not to enhance the power and security of the state (though it may well do so nevertheless) but ultimately to benefit consumers. It holds, if you will, that it is more blessed to consume than to produce. As such, Smith and the other market system proponents have tended to deemphasize the security and other costs of the market system. However, as the other contributers to this volume point out, the costs of increasing market interdependence among national economies frequently entails disrupting the society's core values and increasing vulnerability to external influence.

From this analysis it should be apparent that a market system of exchange is a radical departure from the ways in which societies have traditionally organized their economies. Prior to the modern period, self-regulating markets have been associated almost exclusively with city-states with ready access to the sea.[5] The city-state systems of classical Greece and the Hellenistic Mediterranean, for example, incorporated a peculiar set of conditions which enabled markets to break free from social and political constraints, at least partially. Other than in a few such exceptional circumstances, societies throughout history have placed much greater emphasis on security values such as social stability or self-sufficiency than on income gains from the free operation of markets. For these reasons, it should be apparent that societies freely enter into extensive market relations only when the perceived gains are much greater than the perceived costs or when market relations are forced upon them by a superior society. Nor should it be surprising that the champions of an interdependent world market economy have been politically the most powerful and economically the most efficient nations. Both elements, hegemony and efficiency, are necessary. Hegemony without efficiency tends toward mobilization or imperial types of economies. Efficiency without a corresponding political-military strength cannot induce more powerful societies to assume the costs of a market system. It should not be surprising, therefore, that market systems have seldom existed in the past and that the two great champions of market systems in the modern world have been Great Britain in the nineteenth century and the United States in the twentieth.

The association of the global market system with the political and economic fortunes first of Great Britain and then of the United States provides one clue to the reason why the market system of exchange emerged in the modern era and ultimately became the predominant mode of organizing international economic relations.[6] However, it is not enough to focus on these two economies and their interests. The market system (or what today we call international economic interdependence) runs so counter to the great bulk of human experience that only extraordinary changes and circumstances could have led to its innovation. In seeking to understand this development, we can gain an insight into the political and security issues associated with economic interdependence in the past and increasingly in the contemporary world. But these concerns will be discussed later. For the moment, what was the extraordinary set of economic, sociological, and political changes which led to the rise of a market economy and increasing economic interdependence?

Monetization of Economies

Although markets may be characterized by simple barter, and frequently have been, such markets have obvious and serious limitations. For this reason the emergence of large and complex markets has necessitated monetization of the economy. The monetization of the economy has been a precondition for both pre-modern and modern self-regulating economies. The reason for this is that money in the form of gold or silver coins (or as we shall see, their functional equivalents) performs several critical functions, and these tasks immensely enhance the efficient operation of the market.

In the first place, money performs as a medium of exchange, whereas a barter system allows for only the direct exchange of goods or services. Secondly, money serves as a measure of value and as a unit of account. Thirdly, money (in contrast to perishable barter goods) provides a store of value; it is divisible, portable, and storable. And, finally, money is a standard by which payment can be deferred. Together, these four functions of money have radical implications for organizing economic relations.

The most obvious implication of the monetized economy is that it greatly extends the geographical scope of markets, the range of goods traded, and therefore, market efficiency. Motivation for entering the market is not immediate gratification with respect to a particular good, as in a barter system, but to obtain money which can be accumulated and eventually exchanged for a wide range of goods at home and abroad. Monetized markets have a dynamic quality in that they tend to expand both geographically and with respect to goods traded, as more and more buyers and sellers enter the market to obtain a particular universal medium of exchange. Because of its efficiency, a monetized market tends to drive out other forms of exchange and to draw an increasing number of sellers and buyers into its nexus of relations.

The implications for security of a monetized economy are profound and far reaching. The advent of a monetized economy tends to dissolve existing forms of social relations and to undercut traditional values; it leads to the creation of more complex forms of social relations. For example, as Max Weber has argued, a basic factor in European feudalism was the lack of adequate supplies of money; its eventual demise was related to the monetization of the European economy.[7] Moreover, once introduced into a society, money encourages the accumulation of wealth, both domestically and internationally, thus transforming the power relation among groups and states.

For all these reasons the introduction of money into an economy usually has a profound impact on security relations. As a universal medium of exchange which can be accumulated, money tends to have far-reaching consequences for political and military, as well as economic relations. The monetization of the ancient Greek economy, for example, transformed all aspects of international relations, as revealed in the following observation:

> The consequences of the spread of money and markets are, clearly, enormous. Even warfare is affected. The Greeks who fought the Trojan War took ten years to do so, because their forces had to scatter and live off the countryside. By the time of the great Peloponnesian War, however, the market and its sutlers (merchants following an army to buy up booty for resale elsewhere) had coped with the logistical problems of servicing major concentrations of manpower. The scope and scale of warfare changed in consequence.[8]

In a similar fashion the flow into Europe of New World gold and silver in the sixteenth and seventeenth centuries had profound economic, political, and security impact. The vast expansion of the money supply facilitated the monetization of the economy and the development of the market exchange system. The demand for money grew apace, and the accumulation of bullion became a major preoccupation of the state. The rapid growth of a monetized market system brought important political and military changes in its train.

In particular, the monetization of the European economy financed and made possible what Michael Roberts has characterized as the Military Revolution of the seventeenth century.[9] By this term, he is referring to the rise of professional armies and the creation of supporting national bureaucracies. Both of these developments required money, and lots of it. The nature of war was transformed from a clash of societies into an instrument of the national policies of emergent nation-states in pursuit of their respective national interests. As such, the monetization of economies and the rise of the nation-state as essentially a war-making machine went hand in hand. As we shall see below, the increasing importance of money for national security, in turn, had a profound impact on the behavior of nation-states.

The Rise of the Middle Classes

In addition to the economic and political changes associated with monetization, the emergence of a market exchange system and the nation-state was due to sociological developments associated with the rise of the

24

European bourgeoisie. The seeming ease with which this aggressive class achieved ascendancy in both domestic and international society in the Western world obscures how extraordinary a development this was. In no other civilizations have the so-called middle classes enjoyed an equivalent prominence in economic and political affairs. In only a very few civilizations, in fact, have what we would regard as middle classes had any influence at all. The prominent role of the middle class is indeed a distinctive feature of Western civilization and a fundamental cause of the emergence of a market system and of the character of modern international relations.

As Henri Pirenne,[10] Fernand Braudel,[11] and John Hicks[12] among others have argued, the uniqueness of European civilization is due in large measure to the fact that it passed through a city-state phase; this difference is a key to the divergence of the history of Europe from that of other civilizations. The reasons for this difference are largely geographical, particularly the role of the Mediterranean as a commercial highway among culturally different peoples with widely differing productive capacities. In Europe north of the Alps, the river systems, the North Sea, and the Baltic Sea similarly encouraged the rise of commercial centers in which middle classes could achieve a high degree of independence and political influence.

In contrast to the cities of Asia and other continents, European cities have tended to be commercial centers rather than administrative capitals of great states and empires. As a consequence, the commercial and trading cities of Renaissance Italy, the Hanseatic League, the Low Lands, and Rhineland Germany enjoyed a degree of autonomy unknown to non-European cities. They became the stronghold of merchants and bankers and protected this rising class against predatory feudal aristocracies. In time, the middle classes of Western European countries made alliances with their respective kings or became completely independent, as in the case of the Dutch Republic. In exchange for their services and taxes, they received the King's protection. This alliance gave rise initially to that form of an interdependent international economy known as mercantilism.

The modern European nation-state was founded on this alliance between the sovereign or ruling elite and the rising middle class. On the part of the monarch, it was based on the growing recognition of the importance of trade and money for national power. The money income generated and the taxes paid by the middle classes financed the Military Revolution and expanding national bureaucracies. The monarch for his part protected and guaranteed the property rights of the middle classes both at home and abroad. Although this alliance was rife with tension, state extension and recognition of middle class property rights were critical factors in the evolution of the nation-state and the development of the mercantile empires of the seventeenth and eighteenth centuries.[13] These empires constituted the initial type of an interdependent international economy on a global scale.

The European Balance of Power System

In addition to the extensive monetization of its economy and the rise to economic and political supremacy of its middle classes, the third unique feature of European civilization which contributed greatly to the emergence of an interdependent market economy was the European balance of power system.[14] Other international political systems have, of course, been characterized by balances of power. As David Hume long ago pointed out, the balancing of power by power has always been a universal principle of prudent policy.[15] But, as numerous commentators have observed, European civilization is unique in the systemic character of its balancing mechanism.[16] As a consequence, Europe was able to avoid (or at least postpone) the fate of other civilizations: unification by a universal empire.

The reasons why the European state system was able to avoid imperial unification and to preserve a balance of power are not of concern here. They relate to the geographical, technological, and cultural characteristics of Europe and European civilization.[17] What is important is that the inability of the Hapsburgs and subsequently of other powers to unify the European state system under a universal imperium was a fundamental precondition for the creation of a world market economy.[18] The fragmented state system and the competition for wealth and power among the several nation-states provided a political framework within which the rising middle classes could develop a global trading economy. Thus, paradoxically, the necessary condition for the emergence of an interdependent international economy was a system of independent states. Let us consider why.

As we have already suggested, market exchange systems have been extremely rare in world history. They have been largely restricted to the exchange of a few luxury goods or a highly prized commodity: salt, silk, spices, etc. Or, they have been confined to certain geographical areas, particularly to the Mediterranean basin. The low degree of monetization and the absence of an independent commercial class have been partially responsible for this situation. But, an equally important factor has been the prevalence of imperial economies.

Imperial economies tend to be redistributive or mobilization exchange systems. Empires, after all, are created by warrior elites and aristocracies for their own interests. Although markets and trade can and do flourish in imperial systems, the empire's economic rationale is the exacting of tribute for the benefit of the imperial elite. Imperial economies are what we today would label as command economies rather than as self-regulating market systems.

The empires created by the European nation-states in the sixteenth and seventeenth centuries were initially tribute empires.[19] The empires of Spain and Portugal hardly passed beyond this stage. But, in the cases of the Dutch and the British, particularly, a different evolution took place. Under the protection of the state, merchant adventurers organized in a Dutch East India Company or a Virginia Company and laid the foundations of a new type of mercantile empire. These European states with their strong commercial middle classes were guided by a theory of empire vastly different from that of the Assyrians, Persians, or Romans. Adam Smith in his *Wealth of Nations* pinned a label on this new theory of empire: mercantilism.[20]

Mercantilism and the theory or set of practices it embodied constituted the first attempt to create an international market economy. Mercantilism reflected the economic and political conditions of the period between the emergence of the European state system in the sixteenth century and the establishment of the *Pax Britannica* in the early decades of the nineteenth century. It represented the modern world's first effort to organize a world market economy among the several components of the world's economy. In terms of our classification of economies above, mercantilism represents a halfway house between a mobilization and a liberal market economy. In other words, the state attempts to influence and channel emerging market forces in directions which will enhance its security and other national interests.

Subsequently, as we shall see, mercantilism was displaced by the doctrines of economic liberalism which were first given cogent expression by Smith. But liberalism's victory was never complete, either in the land of its birth or elsewhere in the world, especially on the continent of Europe. Moreover, liberalism has also reflected a peculiar set of economic and political circumstances. When these conditions have been challenged, mercantilism has always revived in a new guise. This is no less true today.

Liberalism and mercantilism, then, represent two different ways of organizing an interdependent world economy. Though they differ profoundly in theory, in reality they exist at opposite ends of a continuum. Whereas the one emphasizes the organization of a world economy through self-regulating markets, the other emphasizes state intervention and manipulation of market forces. Both doctrines depart from the non-market systems of reciprocity, redistribution, and mobilization exchanges. As economic doctrines, liberalism and mercantilism also differ from Marxism which in theory is a revival of redistribution and, as practiced in the Soviet bloc, is akin to mobilization exchange. In this chapter, however, we will consider Marxism primarily as a doctrine which arose in the nineteenth century as a rejection of both liberalism and mercantilism.[21]

The Age of Mercantilism

Ever since Adam Smith's scornful attack on what he called the mercantile system, mercantilism has generally had a "poor press," except in a few continental European countries. Neither Smith nor subsequent critics, however, have succeeded in destroying its appeal. Throughout the past two

27

centuries, the mercantilist heresy has been revived in one form or another to attack economic orthodoxy. This fundamental tenacity of mercantilism at least suggests that it meets the economic and security needs of particular groups and nations regardless of its intrinsic merits as a scientific theory.

The common thread that runs through the several varieties of mercantilist thought and practice is the partial subordination of the economy to the perceived security and welfare needs of the state and society.[22] The measures and practices advocated by mercantilist writers and statesmen were those which would lead to the creation and maintenance of a strong nation-state and national economy. In effect, mercantilism can be described as the striving after security through economic means. As we shall see in a moment, under the conditions of the times, this meant the encouragement of trade and manufacture through protectionism and what we today would label monetarist policies.[23]

It would be a mistake, however, to claim a high degree of coherence and systemization for mercantilist thought and practice. The precise objectives and policies advocated and practiced have differed in time and place. Yet, as Jacob Viner has convincingly argued in an oft-quoted passage, mercantilist writers did share a set of convictions concerning the relationship of wealth and power:

> I believe that practically all mercantilists, whatever the period, country, or status of the particular individual, would have subscribed to all of the following propositions: (1) wealth is an absolutely essential means to power, whether for security or for aggression; (2) power is essential or valuable as a means to the acquisition or retention of wealth; (3) wealth and power are each proper ultimate ends of national policy; (4) there is long-run harmony between these ends, although in particular circumstances it may be necessary for a time to make economic sacrifices in the interest of military security and therefore also of long-run prosperity.[24]

Mercantilism reflected and was a response to the political, economic, and military developments of the sixteenth, seventeenth, and eighteenth centuries. It represented the emergence of strong national states in constant competition; the rise of a middle class devoted at first to commerce and increasingly to manufacture; and the quickening of economic activities due to internal changes within Europe and the discovery of the New World. Of critical importance, however, were the evolution of a monetized market economy and the wide range of changes in the nature of warfare that have been characterized as the Military Revolution. It was not without good reason that mercantilists tended to identify a favorable balance of trade with national security. And concern about national security can be linked to the transformation in warfare. The beginning of transfor-

28

mation in warfare was the innovation of gunpowder and the rise of professional armies.[25] Other developments were also important, but these military innovations greatly enhanced the role of manufacturing as an element of national power. Increasingly, as mercantilists appreciated, manufacturing was beginning to displace agriculture as the basis of wealth and power.

With the rise of standing professional armies, warfare increasingly became an instrument of national policy. Armies became more costly and required new bureaucracies to support them. In this new environment of warfare, nation-states required large quantities of bullion to finance their newly formed professional armies and the balance of payments drain of foreign campaigns. The acquisition of money or bullion became the *sine qua non* of national power.

A related and paradoxical consequence of the Military Revolution in terms of national security was that the great European powers became decreasingly self-sufficient and increasingly dependent on the world economy. The rise of professional armies and the new technology of warfare required vital war materials, such as naval stores or saltpeter for gunpowder. These war materials could frequently be acquired only through trade or the export of bullion. Mercantilists appreciated that the international economy had become an important source of both the financial and material sinews of national power. The frequent and seemingly petty commercial wars of the mercantilist era were really conflicts over access to or control over the sources of treasure, markets, and raw materials upon which national security increasingly depended. This loss of self-sufficiency and new vulnerability contributed greatly to the insecurity of states.

The mercantile empires characteristic of this age were established by the northern European powers and reflected this new insecurity and dependence upon trade and markets for treasure and war materials. In contrast to the mobilization empires of the Assyrians or the Romans, they were primarily trading rather than tribute empires.[26] The European states regarded their colonial possessions as secure sources of raw materials—gold, furs, timber, sugar, tobacco, etc.—and as consumers of their expanding output of manufactured goods.[27] The purpose of the Navigation Acts and other acts governing trade was to "regulate colonial trade so that raw materials were produced for the mother country and manufactured goods were purchased from her."[28]

While several mercantile empires dominated the world economy, trade among the European states also increased. In truth, as Klaus Knorr has noted, prior to the Industrial Revolution, international economic integration was proceeding at a more rapid pace than national economic integration. It was primarily in the nineteenth century with improvements in land communications (particularly the railroad) and the advent of stronger nation-states that national integration caught up.[29]

Under mercantilism, then, the world economy was increasingly interdependent. This fact and its political significance were at the same time gaining recognition by theorists of international relations. Despite the outbreak of frequent commercial conflict, this era gave currency to the theme which became prominent in the nineteenth century that "peace is the natural effect of trade."[30] In fact, no contemporary writer has stated better than Jean Jacques Rousseau the argument that economic interdependence creates bonds of mutual interest and restraint which have a moderating influence upon the struggle for power and advantage among nation-states:

> It would be easy for me to draw the same lesson from a study of the special interests of all the Courts of Europe; to show that those interests are so cunningly interwoven as to hold their respective forces mutually in check. But current theories of commerce and money have bred a political bigotry which works such rapid changes in the apparent interests of princes that it is impossible to arrive at any firm conclusion as to their real interests, seeing that everything now depends upon the economic systems, for the most part thoroughly crazy, which chance to flit through a minister's brain. For all that, commerce tends more and more to establish a balance between State and State; and by depriving certain Powers of the exclusive advantages they once drew from it, deprives them at the same time of one of the chief weapons they once employed for imposing their will upon the rest.[31]

Alas! As we shall see, it hasn't turned out quite this way. The extension of markets and the growth of economic interdependence among societies have wrought high costs in the form of personal and national insecurity as well as immense benefits from an enlarged international division of labor.

In the last analysis, mercantilism was the first attempt to organize an interdependent world economy. The organization of this economy in terms of mercantile empires reflected the balance of power among the metropolitan European states and their respective economic-security interests. Following the rapid industrialization of Great Britain after 1750 and Britain's victory in the Napoleonic Wars, however, the interdependent world economy would be re-established in the form we recognize today, that is, a multilateral system of relatively free trade. As we shall see, its implications for the security of states were different from but no less than those of mercantilism.

The Rise of Liberalism[32]

Throughout the mercantilist era the major powers of Western Europe had fought for control of Asia and of the New World and had struggled over the European balance of power. One by one these contenders for empire and dominance had been eliminated until only France and Great Britain remained locked in combat. Although both were growing in wealth and power, after 1750 British power began a more rapid advance, due to the accelerating pace of the Industrial Revolution. Endowed with rich resources and an enterprising population, Great Britain was gaining an economic and technological lead which would take her to a commanding position over other nations following her victory in the Napoleonic Wars.

The defeat of Napoleon and the French ushered in a new era of international politics and economics which has been rightly identified as the *Pax Britannica.* Great Britain was supreme on the seas and controlled access to Asia and the New World for her European rivals. On the continent of Europe a balance had been established at the Congress of Vienna which kept the European powers in check. Until the unification of Germany and the rise of the United States in the latter part of the century, no nation or group of nations would be in a position to challenge British world hegemony.

The *Pax Britannica,* which was to provide the general structure of international relations until the collapse of the system under the impact of the First World War, transformed the conduct and general features of international economic relations. In place of the mercantilistic emphasis on the control and possession of colonies, the *Pax Britannica* at its height (1849–1880) emphasized an open, interdependent world economy based on free trade, non-discrimination, and equal treatment. Although Great Britain and several other European powers retained the remnants of colonial empires, the conquest of territory and colonies declined in importance. Behind the shield of British sea command, nations had relatively open and free access to the world's markets and sources of raw materials. In short, the *Pax Britannica* provided the political framework for the emergence of a liberal international economy.

The Nature of Economic Interdependence

Following the Industrial Revolution and the emergence of an industrial center in Great Britain, an essentially new type of international economy was organized, one which was based on specialization, multilateral free trade, and an international division of labor. Initially, this international division of labor was composed of the British industrial center and the non-industrial periphery; the former exporting manufactured goods in exchange for the food and raw materials of the latter. Subsequently, as other industrial centers arose in Western Europe, North America, and elsewhere, there evolved among the industrial countries themselves a division of labor based on industrial specialization. These essential features of interdependence continue to characterize the world economy in the twentieth century.

Prior to the industrialization of England and its emergence as the world's dominant economy, one must be careful in speaking of an interdependent

31

world economy. Certainly there had been sophisticated international trading arrangements in the past. But these systems have been limited with respect to geographical extent, the range of goods traded, and the complexity of the interdependence which resulted. On the whole, the great bulk of mankind lived in relatively isolated and self-contained economic systems, generally severed from economic intercourse except with their immediate neighbors. What constituted the international economy until the late eighteenth century were the mercantile empires of the European littoral states with their colonial possessions in the New World and the periphery of Asia. There was, indeed, a type of interdependence between the metropolitan power and its colonies and among the European powers themselves, but it was rudimentary compared to the type of interdependence which developed in the nineteenth century under the impact of industrialism. Moreover, the mercantile empires were exclusive and preferential systems; there was relatively little trade or other commerce among the empires themselves, though it was increasing. Trade tended to be governed by monopolies and confined to exclusive spheres defined by imperial and mercantilist policies.

Subsequent to the Industrial Revolution, however, the world economy must be viewed increasingly in terms of the dominant British economy and its global trading partners. Under the influence of British industrial and later financial centers, the world economy became more and more integrated, as shown in Figure 1. Although England did retain much of her First Empire, the bulk of world trade was increasingly carried on between Great Britain and independent nations. While force was occasionally used to gain economic advantage and to open economic intercourse, the major inducements for integrating the world economy became the benefits which could be derived from participation in the developing world.

As a consequence of the Industrial Revolution, there began an "[i]rreversible increase in the internal and external interdependence of economic systems."[33] Domestically and internationally, the Industrial Revolution increased the interlocking of economic activities within and among nations through increasing functional and geographical specialization of production. This economic interdependence, in turn, stimulated a process of political consolidation on the national level and the decline of barriers across national boundaries. Let us take a closer look at this development.

The Causes of the Interdependent World Economy

The causes of the interdependent world economy as it developed in the nineteenth century must be separated into necessary and sufficient causes. The necessary causes were the military and territorial consequences of the Napoleonic Wars discussed above and the revolution in transport produced by the Industrial Revolution. The sufficient conditions for the rise of the

32

Mercantilism:

European Economies

Colonies

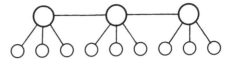

Interdependence (Early phase):

European Economies

Less developed

Interdependence (Latter phase):

Advanced Economies

Less developed

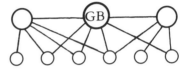

Figure 1

Diagram of Mercantilistic and Interdependent World Economies

interdependent world economy were the changes in the British economy and British economic thinking due to the Industrial Revolution.

A necessary condition for the creation of an interdependent world economy was the technological revolution in production and transportation. The Industrial Revolution and rapid economic growth based on new production methods undercut the static mercantilist conception of wealth. The invention of the separate condenser steam engine by Issac Watt in the same year that Adam Smith wrote *The Wealth of Nations* symbolized this profound transformation. The harnessing of steam power meant a vast expansion of mankind's productive capabilities. With this change, global economic relations became a decreasing source of conflict. One nation's economic gain was not necessarily another's loss; everyone could gain from international trade; albeit not in equal measure. The appreciation of this novel situation was a major factor in the expansion of the market system.[34]

Another factor associated with rapid technological advance was that communications and transportation by land and by sea were revolutionized with the invention of cheap steel and the application of steam power to sea and land transport. The steamship decreased the time, cost, and risk of marine transportation, thereby having a profound effect on economic relations as well as on the exercise of military power. Economically, it made possible specialization and an international division of labor on an unprecedented global scale. As a result, the revolution in oceanic transportation which followed the Industrial Revolution made possible British economic expansion throughout the entire world.

The coming of the railroad, on the other hand, had a more ambiguous impact. On the one hand, the railroad opened up the interior of the continents and connected hitherto inaccessible lands to the world economy. As the only country to industrialize prior to the railroad, Great Britain profited greatly from this. On the other hand, the railroad also made possible the uniting of great land masses under single political and economic regimes and made large sections of the world less dependent on access to the seas. Thus, the railroads caused growth to spread inward, even as the development of the major seaboard cities and their immediate hinterlands expanded. This would eventually lessen the dependence of land powers on the good will of England. Therefore, the railroad eventually permitted and encouraged the rise of economic entities and markets large enough not only to challenge British economic supremacy but also to isolate themselves from the British-dominated global economy through tariffs and other autarkic devices. But, it is the global unifying effects of technological developments with which we are concerned at the moment.

The Revolution in the British Economy and Economic Thought

Underlying the development of an interdependent nineteenth-century world economy was Great Britain's redefinition of her national security interests based on the precepts of liberalism. The essence of the teaching of Adam Smith and of later free traders was that wealth from overseas trade was due to the exchange of goods and not to territorial possession. Economic growth, Smith had argued in *The Wealth of Nations* (1776), is primarily a function of the extent of the division of labor which, in turn, is dependent upon the scale of the market. For an economy to grow, it must continually expand its territorial base and integrate a larger and larger market. Herein, Smith argued, lay the true security interests of Great Britain.

The free trade ideas of Smith, especially as they were developed by David Ricardo, became the ideology of the increasingly important British middle class. What this class and the liberal theoreticians appreciated was that the costs and disadvantages of empire and territorial control outweighed its benefits. By the end of the eighteenth century, they pointed out that ideals of imperial self-sufficiency and of exclusive economic spheres were impeding the natural flow of trade and handicapping growth. British supremacy and security, they argued, rested on her manufacturing and naval supremacy and not on the Empire. With only half the population of France,

England was turning out two-thirds of the world's coal, half of its iron and cloth. Technologically more advanced than her competitors, Britain could capture world markets with cheaper goods. Why should Britain restrict her trade to a closed empire, when the whole world lay open and desired her goods? Her interest resided with univeral free trade and the removal of all barriers to the exchange of goods. Through concentration on industrial efficiency, Great Britain could be the first power to create an empire of trade rather than one of colonies.

The objective of British foreign economic policy was to create complementary economic relations between industrial Britain and an overseas periphery which would supply cheap food and raw materials.[35] Through the migration of labor and the export of capital to developing lands (e.g., the United States, Canada, Australia, etc.), Britain could both acquire cheap imports and gain a market for her growing industrial exports. In this way, not only would the profit rate of capital remain high, but through the importation of cheap food and the concentration on her comparative advantage in industrial goods, Great Britain could out-compete the rest of the globe and thereby ensure her security.

Prior to the emergence of strong nationalistic sentiments in Europe and the rest of the world and before the rise of industrial competitors, Great Britain was able to extend her trade and influence without encountering much resistance. Throughout the early and middle portions of the nineteenth century, the primary mechanisms for integrating the periphery into the emerging world economy were largely economic in nature. Economic growth and industrialization at the British core stimulated a great volume of foreign trade and the spread of the network of international trade and investment to previously isolated areas.

The incorporation of the periphery into the world economy frequently meant imposition on these areas of numerous restrictions, such as extraterritoriality privileges for Western businessmen and denial of tariff autonomy. Where local rulers opposed the opening of trade and investment, or where they were unable to guarantee the security necessary for stable trading and investment relations, Great Britain (and subsequently other industrial powers) felt little reluctance to force them and to establish "law and order." The use of gunboat diplomacy, informal rule, and, where necessary, actual political control were frequent occurrences during the era of "free" trade. In the words of Lord Palmerston, the government's business is to "open and secure the roads for the merchant."[36] Kuznets wryly understates the point when he writes that "the greater power of the developed nations imposed upon the reluctant partners the opportunities of international trade and division of labor."[37] But, the primary nexus of the interdependent world economy created by Great Britain and the essential ingredients of British power were trade, investment, and the international monetary system.

Trade and Investment: The era of free trade was initiated unilaterally by the British with the repeal of the Corn Laws in 1846, which had restricted the importation of grain into Great Britain. Following the British example, the free trade movement spread to other countries through such instruments as the Anglo-French Treaty of 1860. The immediate results were spectacular. In the period 1870–1913, the introduction of free trade led to an impressive four-fold expansion of world trade. Although confined principally to the nations of Northern and Western Europe, the free trade movement gave rise to the dream of a world-wide trading system where national boundaries would be of little economic significance. Increasing trade was enmeshing domestic economies into an interdependent world economy.

Under mercantilism, international trade had tended to be based on the absolute advantages of the trading partners. The mother country exported manufactures and the colonies raw materials, because these were the goods available for exchange. Under free trade and a liberal international economy, however, trade was increasingly influenced by considerations of comparative advantage. Comparative costs of production and prices became more and more the determinants of trade. Moreover, whereas mercantilism was based on a static conception of wealth, liberalism reflected the dynamic growth possibilities inherent in the Industrial Revolution. Wealth was expandable, provided economic relations were based on the efficient use of resources. For these reasons, free trade was regarded as providing mutual benefits for both trading partners.

Prior to 1870, that other nexus of an international economy, investment, played a very small part in creating an interdependent world economy. Though the export of British capital began after the conclusion of the Napoleonic Wars, this movement was initially of little consequence. The scale, character, and importance of foreign investment began to change after 1850 with the development of railroads, the discovery of gold in California, and, after the Civil War, the opening of the American West. But it was really after 1870, due to the great accumulation of capital from trade, that foreign investment of capital became an important factor in world economic development and interdependence. In the four decades preceding the First World War, Great Britain, followed by other European countries as they industrialized, exported great quantities of capital.

While the great accumulation of capital had made this investment surge possible, there were several underlying motives. In part, it was a response to the discovery abroad of valuable natural resources. Additionally, and more importantly, it was due to the intense development of the British, and later the European, economies. With the expansion of production and urban population growth, there was a great need for raw materials and food imports to feed factories and people. Moreover, while Marxists have distorted

36

its role in imperialism, a third factor was the existence of "surplus" savings looking for profitable investment outlets. And, in the latter part of the century, foreign investment was stimulated by the economic and strategic conflicts among nation-states for new markets, sources of raw materials, and diplomatic leverage.

The changing character of British investment after 1870 reflected these new demands of the British economy. Previously, British foreign investment had taken the form of loans to European governments to support railroad and banking development. Subsequently, British and European capital went to primary producing countries for investment in port facilities, railroads, plantations, and mines all over the globe. By 1913, over 88% of British foreign investment was in primary product-exporting nations.[38] Although a part of this investment went to the empire, the larger share went to the white-settled dominions (Canada, South Africa, Australia), the United States, and South America (Argentina, Brazil). Together with the great migration of European peoples it stimulated, this investment was a major factor in the development of these new lands.

In summary, trade and investment reinforced one another in creating an interdependent world economy. The income from trade was invested abroad to develop the production of primary products on a vast scale and to create there a market for European, especially British, manufacturers. Foreign investment opened up a vast market for machines, railroads, and other capital goods. In exchange for these goods, Britain obtained industrial metals (Nigeria, Northern Rhodesia, Malaya), meat (Argentina), rubber (Ceylon, Malaya), etc.[39] Thus, the expansion of trade in the latter part of the nineteenth century was largely dependent upon the flow of investment.

The Gold Standard and Hierarchy of Markets: Underlying the crucial role that capital export played in the expansion of trade and the creation of economic interdependence was the evolution and commanding position of the London money market and the City of London.[40] In the early part of the century, the capital market and banking in England and elsewhere had had very little to do with capital accumulation and investment. The capital for industrialization had come primarily from corporate profits and savings. After 1850, however, a sharp increase in capital supplies took place, particularly in England, due to its leadership in trade. Capital accumulation, foreign investment, and trade worked together to make England and the London financial market the dominant integrating factor of the interdependent world economy.

In the latter part of the nineteenth century, the City of London, that is, the financial and commercial district of London, was the locus of the three great markets which held the world economy together. In the first place, there was the *capital or money market* which provided the bulk of the world's short-term credit to finance the expanding volume of trade and organized long-term investment for economic development throughout the world. Secondly, London was the middleman in the *international commodity exchange*. There, American wheat, Argentine beef, and Malayan rubber entered world markets and ultimately found their way to the consumer. And, thirdly, London became the international *currency market* and, by virtue of this fact, the guardian of the Gold Standard. Through its adjustment of the interest rate on sterling, which was the world's principal medium of account, the Bank of England held powerful leverage over the international economy. In short, London had not only a commanding position with respect to trade and investment, but it managed the international monetary system as well. International payments were ultimately cleared in London, and delinquent nations could be forced through one device or another to bring their accounts into balance. As long as nations played the gold standard game, London could exercise a powerful role over international finance and, by implication, over the entire system.[41]

The interdependent world economy upon which the *Pax Britannica* ultimately rested meant three things in the era prior to the First World War. In the first place, it meant an elaborate division of labor among industrial and non-industrial economies based on specialization. Secondly, interdependence involved unprecedented flows of goods and factors of production (capital, technology, and labor) among national economies. In truth, there was more free movement of goods, money, and especially people than at any time in previous history. And, most significant of all, international economic interdependence was based on a hierarchy of world markets which ultimately culminated in London. The major decisions affecting the world's trade and investment were taken by those individuals and institutions in control of the London markets for investment capital, currencies, and commodities. This centralization of decision-making in the hands of a relatively few private persons was the high point of economic interdependence. In exaggerated acknowledgment of the political importance of what today we would call the transnational actors who dominated this age, J. A. Hobson in his book on imperialism asks rhetorically whether "a great war could be undertaken by any European state, or a great loan subscribed, if the house of Rothschild and its connections set their face against it."[42]

The exercise of such power by private financiers rested, however, on a peculiar set of circumstances. The City of London was able to run the system effectively as long as economic nationalism had not yet triumphed as a predominant force in the world and as long as the other elements of the *Pax Britannica* remained intact. But, with the emergence after 1870 of new industrial powers interested in revising the balance of economic and industrial power, economic nationalism and the struggle for empire came increasingly into conflict with a British-centered, interdependent world economy. Until the First World War, however, international interdependence based

38

on British power continued to predominate, and the latter part of the nineteenth century was the great age of world economic interdependence. Under the impact of the War, however, interdependence was greatly weakened and was not to be revived until the emergence of the United States as the world's dominant economy following the Second World War.

The Revolt Against Liberalism: Economic Nationalism and Marxism

For the British in the nineteenth century, a liberal international economy was the natural order of things, founded on the laws of economics themselves: the laws of comparative advantage, of supply and demand, etc. While the market system was to Britain's own advantage, others also gained through trade and the maximization of global wealth. In an era of rapid economic growth, international economic relations ceased to be regarded as a zero sum game. Moreover, during these years of peace and prosperity, the identification of trade and peace achieved its foremost expression in the writings of the Manchester School. Trade, investment, and increasing ties of economic interdependence were held to be creating the preconditions of peace. Nations, it was said, could achieve security and welfare through trade and peaceful economic intercourse rather than through military conflict.

The defenders of economic liberalism, however, saw only one side of the picture. As spokesmen of the emergent middle class in England, they saw only its benefits. They overlooked the costs that a market system imposed, at least in the short run, on the welfare and security of other groups and classes within Great Britain and other societies. Nor were they sufficiently aware of the reaction of lesser developed economies to the impact of unregulated market forces. The evident costs of the free market system in the nineteenth century gave rise, therefore, to two major revolts against the British conception of a liberal economic order. One—the growth of economic nationalism—was, in effect, a revival of mercantilism, with its emphasis on the subordination of the market to the security objectives of the state. The other—Marxism and other forms of socialism—entailed a total rejection of the market exchange system in the interest of dispossessed classes and in effect advocated a return to the earlier emphasis on redistribution. Of the two, economic nationalism was by far the more serious challenge, at least in the nineteenth century.

Economic Nationalism

The intellectual origin of economic nationalism and the classic defense of economic protectionism was Alexander Hamilton's *Report on the Subject of Manufactures* presented to the House of Representatives in December 1791.[43] Like the mercantilists before him, Hamilton's defense of protectionism was based on the so-called infant industry argument. But, he went

39

further in contesting the basic assumption of liberalism: the static nature of comparative advantage. In doing so, Hamilton modernized the mercantilist thesis and, in effect, fostered a dynamic theory of economic development based on the superiority of manufacturing over agriculture.

The liberal theory of international trade as subsequently developed by David Ricardo was based on a static view of comparative advantage. Trade originated and was mutually profitable, because nations were endowed differently with respect to resources, labor, and other factors of production. Such factors were considered to be fixed attributes of individual countries. As Ricardo had demonstrated in his famous example, Portugal's advantage lay in the production of wine and Great Britain's in the production of cloth. Such an immutable international division of labor was determined by natural endowments and beyond the power of humans to change.

Contrary to both the earlier mercantilists and later liberals, Hamilton emphasized the transferability of factors between national economic systems. An economy's position in the international division of labor was not determined by unalterable endowments. The government, through national economic policies, could transform the nature of its economy and international economic position. For example, the encouragement of migration, especially of skilled labor, constituted "a much more powerful means of augmenting the fund of national industry than may at first sight appear."[44] In addition, the nation should encourage the importation of foreign capital and should establish a banking system to provide investment capital. In short, Hamilton's *Report* set against the classical liberal theory of static comparative advantage a dynamic theory of comparative advantage based on economic development.

Like the mercantilists before him, Hamilton identified national security with the development of manufactures and argued that the state had a principal role in guiding economic activities. Like them as well, he regarded economics as subordinate to the fundamental task of state-making. Although his ideas on protectionism were not to achieve full force until the victory of the rapidly industrializing North in the Civil War, his ideas were to exert a powerful influence at home and abroad. The developing nations today, with their emphasis on protectionism, industrialization, and state intervention, owe more than they may appreciate to Hamilton's conception of economic development.

Economic nationalism, both in the nineteenth century and today, is a response to the tendency of markets to concentrate wealth and power as well as to establish dependency relations between strong and weak economies. Although markets over time stimulate the diffusion of economic activities and industries, the tendency in the short run is for the concentration of wealth in the advanced economies to take place faster than the spread of economic activities in the developing economies. In order to

40

protect its nascent industries and safeguard domestic interests against external market forces, the government of the developing economy tends to pursue protectionist and related nationalistic policies. As Harry Johnson and other liberal economists have noted, economic nationalism represents an alliance of producer interests and the state.[45] For these reasons, Hamilton's ideas favoring autarky continue to have a broad appeal among developing economies.

In the nineteenth century, Hamilton's ideas had their greatest impact on Germany. The ground had already been prepared there by Johann Fichte and Georg Hegel, who had enunciated the theme of economic nationalism in the early decades of the century.[46] The seeds of these ideas were planted by Friedrich List, who had spent a number of years in the United States and carried Hamilton's ideas back to Germany. Along with Wilhelm Roscher, Gustav Schmoller, and others, List helped found the German Historical School of economic analysis.[47] Their systematic and fierce attack on liberalism had a powerful influence on the development of Germany and on the world economy generally.

The thrust of List's argument in his influential *National System of Political Economy* was that liberalism was the economic policy of the strong.[48] The British, List argued, had used the power of the state to protect their own infant industries against foreign competition. But, once having achieved technological and industrial supremacy over their rivals, they had reversed themselves to become the champions of free trade. In advocating free trade, they were seeking to advance their own national economic interests in achieving unimpeded access to foreign markets. What we today would call an interdependent world economy List regarded as an expression of Britain's national interests. A true cosmopolitan world economy, he believed, would be possible only when other nations ranked equal with Great Britain in industrial power. In order to achieve this goal, the German economic nationalists advocated German unification and the erection of high tariff barriers to protect the development of German industry.

Following the unification and proclamation of the German Empire in January 1871, the ideas of the German Historical School became the official policy of Germany. In 1879, Bismarck negotiated the "compact of iron and rye" between the grain-growing Junkers east of the Elbe and the rising industrialists of the Rhineland. Tariff protection was extended both to grains and manufactures. The unification of Germany with its high tariff walls reversed the free trade movement and, as one writer has put it, "set every continental power on the search for security and self-sufficiency."[49] The sweep of economic nationalism across Europe meant that commercial policy became increasingly subordinate to diplomatic and balance of power considerations. The extension of these economic and political rivalries beyond the boundaries of Europe, in turn, led to the revival of intense imperialistic struggles.

41

In effect, Europe had reverted to the mercantilistic conflicts characteristic of its earlier centuries.

In retrospect, the neo-mercantilists of the German Historical School may be seen as having identified a major security issue associated with the rise of a world market economy. Nineteenth-century liberals were quite right in emphasizing that never before in history had the world enjoyed a comparable era of peace and unprecedented prosperity. While England gained the most, others gained as well.

The expansion of trade, the flow of investment, and the efficiency of the international monetary system ushered in a period of economic growth which spread from England throughout the system. Perhaps never before or since has the cosmopolitan interest been so well joined to the national interest of the dominant power as under the *Pax Britannica*. But, while all may have gained, the neo-mercantilists emphasized that some gained more than others. In a world of competing states unequal gain is frequently more important than mutual gain. In order to increase their own relative gains, other nations seek to change the rules which tend to benefit the dominant industrial power(s). In the face of this neo-mercantilistic spirit which is never far from the surface, a liberal international economy cannot come into existence and be maintained unless it has behind it the most powerful state(s) in the system. A liberal economic system is not self-sustaining but is maintained only through the actions of the dominant power(s)—initiatives, bargaining, and sanctions. As Condliffe has put it, "[l]eadership in establishing the rule of law lay . . . as it always lies, in the hands of the great trading nations. . . ."[50] As a consequence, as British power waned in the latter part of the century, so did the fortunes of a liberal world economy.

The Marxist and Socialist Critique of a Market System

Economic nationalism was not the only attack delivered against classical liberalism. A more fundamental critique was that of Marxism. Although the founders of this school of thought—Karl Marx and Friedrich Engels—wrote relatively little on international economics, they fully appreciated the political implications of the development of an interdependent world economy. But, in contrast to many modern scholars who hold this development as conducive to peaceful international relations, they regarded it as the prelude to world revolution:

> The bourgeoisie has through its exploitation of the world market given a cosmopolitan character to production and consumption in every country. To the great chagrin of Reactionists, it has drawn from under the feet of industry the national ground on which it stood. All old-established national industries have been destroyed or are daily being destroyed. They are dislodged by new industries, whose introduction

42

becomes a life and death question for all civilized nations, by industries that no longer work up indigenous raw material, but raw material drawn from the remotest zones; industries whose products are consumed, not only at home, but in every quarter of the globe. In place of the old wants, satisfied by the productions of the country, we find new wants, requiring for their satisfaction the products of distant lands and climes. In place of the old local and national seclusion and self-sufficiency, we have intercourse in every direction, universal *interdependence of nations*. And as in material, so also in intellectual production. The intellectual creations of individual nations become common property. National one-sidedness and narrow-mindedness become more and more impossible, and from the numerous national and local literatures, there arises a world literature. (Italics mine.)

The bourgeoisie, by the rapid improvement of all instruments of production, by the immensely facilitated means of communication, draws all, even the most barbarian, nations into civilization. The cheap prices of its commodities are the heavy artillery with which it batters down all Chinese walls with which it forces the barbarians' intensely obstinate hatred of foreigners to capitulate. It compels all nations, on pain of extinction, to adopt the bourgeois mode of production; it compels them to introduce what it calls civilization into their midst, i.e., to become bourgeois themselves. In one word, it creates a world after its own image.[51]

For Marx and Engels, the rise and spread of an interdependent global market economy was progressive. Contrary to contemporary neo-Marxist denunciations of capitalistic imperialism, they believed that the extension of the market system was a step forward for humanity. The historic mission of the bourgeoisie and imperialism, they believed, was to smash the feudalistic and Asiatic mode of production which held back the modernization of what we would today call the Third World. In an essay, *The Future Results of British Rule in India (1853),* which contemporary dependency theorists might read with profit, Marx argued that British imperialism was necessary for the modernization of India and that the establishment of a railroad system by the British was "the forerunner of modern industry."[52]

Marx's ambivalent view of imperialism is well expressed in the following passage:

England, it is true, in causing a social revolution in Hindostan was actuated only by the vilest interests, and was stupid in her manner of enforcing them. But that is not the question. The question is, can mankind fulfill its destiny without a fundamental revolution in the social state of Asia? If not, whatever may have been the crimes of England, she was the unconscious tool of history in bringing about that revolution.[53]

In brief, Marx believed the root cause of the underdevelopment of the Third World lay within these societies themselves, and that the outside "hammer" of western imperialism was necessary to smash social and cultural conditions inhibiting economic development.

Marx and Engels wrote in the belief that the maturing of capitalism in Europe and the drawing of the whole globe into the market economy had set the stage for the proletarian revolution and with it the end of the market exchange economy. That this development had not come to pass and that nationalism had proven to be a far more powerful force than proletarian internationalism were the primary concerns of Lenin's classic *Imperialism*.[54] Written during the First World War, *Imperialism* was both a polemic and a synthesis of socialist and communist critiques of a capitalist world economy.

The task which Lenin set for himself was to explain why economic nationalism had triumphed over proletarian internationalism. Why, in particular, had the socialist parties of the several European powers supported their respective bourgeoisies? Of equal importance, why had the impoverishment of the proletarian not taken place as Marx and Engels had predicted? The reason, he argued, was that capitalism had saved itself through overseas territorial imperialism. Through the export of surplus capital to their colonies, European nations had inhibited the operation of the law of the falling rate of profit. Moreover, super-profits from colonial exploitation had enabled the European capitalists to co-opt and deradicalize what Lenin called the labor aristocracy. In short, the tendency of profits to fall in a mature capital economy and the desire for secure outlets for surplus capital led inevitably to territorial imperialism.

Although Lenin's primary concern was the seizure of colonies by capitalist powers, Lenin recognized the existence of what today is called neo-colonialism: "The extraction of unequal gain from the domination of one society over another on the basis of power" rather than than through formal territorial control.[55]

Imperialism must be credited, therefore, as one of the forerunners of modern dependency theory:

The division of the world into two main groups—of colony-owning countries on the one hand and colonies on the other—is not the only typical feature of this period; there is also a variety of forms of dependent countries; countries which, officially, are politically independent, but which are, in fact, enmeshed in the net of financial and diplomatic dependence. We have already referred to one form of dependence—the semi-colony. Another example is provided by Argentina.[56]

However, like Marx and unlike contemporary neo-Marxist theorists of imperialism and dependency theorists, Lenin regarded colonialism and neo-colonialism as progressive and necessary for the eventual modernization of lesser developed countries. The export of capital, technology, and know-how to colonies and dependencies, he argued, would "pave the way for the economic, and later, the political emancipation of the coloured races."[57] But, as we know from contemporary experience, both Marx and Lenin oversimplified the problems of economic development and of escape from dependency status.

The "Achilles Heel" of a capitalist international economy, Lenin argued, was what he called the law of uneven development. As capitalist economies mature, as capital accumulates, and as profit rates fall, the capitalist economies seize colonies and dependencies as investment outlets. In competition with one another, they divide up the colonial world in accordance with their relative strengths; the most advanced capitalist economy, namely Great Britain, appropriates the largest share of colonies. As other capitalist economies advance, they seek a redivision of colonies which inevitably leads to armed conflict among the rising and declining imperial powers. World War I, according to Lenin, was a war of territorial redivision between a declining Great Britain and rising continental capitalist powers. Such wars of redivision would continue until the industrializing colonies and dependencies revolted against the war-enfeebled capitalist powers.

In summary, Lenin argued that the inherent contradiction of capitalism was that it develops rather than exploits the world. The dominant capitalist economy plants the seeds of its own destruction in that it diffuses technology and industry, thereby undermining its own position. It raises up against itself foreign competitors which have lower wages and standards of living and can out-compete it in world markets. The intensification of the economic competition between the declining and rising capitalist powers leads to economic conflicts and imperial rivalries. Such was the fate of the British-centered liberal world economy of the nineteenth century. Today, he would undoubtedly argue, as the American economy is increasingly pressed by rising foreign competitors, a similar fate threatens the U.S.-centered twentieth-century liberal world economy.

A critique of Lenin's theory lies outside the scope of this chapter. But in one sense, Lenin was correct in attributing World War I to the uneven growth of power among industrial states and to a conflict among them over the division of territory. There can be little doubt that the uneven growth of the several European powers and the consequent effects on the balance of power contributed to their collective insecurity. Moreover, the competition

45

for markets and empires aggravated interstate relations. Of significance as well was a growing awareness on the part of the common man of the effects of the vicissitudes of the world market on his personal welfare and security. For both nations and individuals alike, the growth of economic interdependence brought with it a new sense of insecurity and vulnerability.

Lenin was wrong, however, in attributing World War I to the logic of capitalism and the market system. In the first place, the territorial disputes among the European powers which brought on the war were not concerned with overseas colonies but lay within Europe itself; the conflict involved principally the redistribution of the Balkan possessions of the decaying Ottoman Empire. The three major imperial rivals—Great Britain, France, and Russia—were, in fact, on the same side. Secondly, he was wrong in tracing the basic motive force to the internal workings of the capitalistic system. More insightful is the analysis of Simon Kuznets who interrupts his detailed economic analysis in *Modern Economic Growth* to inquire whether there is a connection between the phenomenon of economic growth and the two great world wars of the twentieth century. He restricts himself to three highly pertinent comments.

In the first place, Kuznets emphasizes the great growth in power that preceded the outbreak of World War I. "[T]he growing productive power of developed nations, derived from the science-oriented technology that played an increasing role in modern economic growth, has meant also greater power in armed conflict and greater capacity for protracted struggle . . ."[58] Together, accumulated capital and modern technology have enabled nations to conduct wars of unprecedented magnitude.

Secondly, Kuznets regards such great wars as the "ultimate tests of changes in relative power among nations, tests to resolve disagreements as to whether such shifts have indeed occurred and whether the political adjustments pressed for are really warranted."[59] In other words, the role of war is to test whether the redistribution of power in the system has operated to change the fundamental balance of power in the system, and if the balance has shifted, then appropriate political and territorial adjustments reflecting the new distribution will be made. In an age of rapid and continuous economic growth, there will be frequent and significant shifts of relative economic and thus of military power among nations. "If wars are needed to confirm or deny such shifts, the rapidity and frequency with which shifts occur may be the reason for the frequent conflicts that serve as tests."

And, lastly, Kuznets argues that "major wars were associated with the emergence in the course of modern economic growth of several large and developed nations."[60] The century of uneasy peace that had followed the Napoleonic wars had been relatively peaceful primarily because during much of the period there was only one large advanced country in the world generating economic growth. The emergence of other industrialized and growing societies, especially Germany after 1870, eventually led to hegemonic war. The emergence of several large economically developed countries is the necessary, if not sufficient, condition for the occurrence of world wars. "In this sense it was a century of *Pax Britannica* that ended when the leading country could no longer lead and impose its peace on such a large part of the world."[61]

The rise of new powers and the relative decline of the others had undermined the foundations of the European balance of power and of the British-centered liberal international economy. But, though the war destroyed the existing international political and economic order based on the hegemony of Great Britain, it did not give rise immediately to a stable, new international system. The victors were either unable or unwilling to impose a new and durable structure. It was only following the Second World War that the United States emerged as the dominant power and reordered international economic and political relations in accordance with its primary interests. The interwar period was the transition from the regime of the *Pax Britannica* to that of the *Pax Americana.* In the absence of strong political and economic leadership, the period was marked by intense political insecurity and economic anarchy.

Economic Interdependence and Security in the Interwar Period

The dominant motif of the interwar period was the spread of economic insecurity and national responses to the untoward effects of increasing economic interdependence. It was during this period that the United States redefined its own international economic and security interests. Like Great Britain in the early part of the nineteenth century, the United States came to regard its interests in terms of an open-world economy. As this change in national perception took place, the United States used its influence to reestablish a liberal interdependent world economy.

The First World War dealt a crippling blow to what in many respects was the Golden Age of an interdependent global market economy. The intensity and duration of the war revolutionized both domestic and international economies. The economic burden of the war had greatly weakened Great Britain and had forced her to liquidate much of her overseas investments. International markets had been disrupted and in many cases destroyed. The demands of the war effort on the major combatant had necessitated extensive government intervention in the economy; even in Great Britain the market economy gave way to a command economy. Outside of Europe, the demand for war material and the cutoff of European goods stimulated industrialization. In short, the war profoundly altered the role of the state in the economy and the international distribution of economic power.

Following the war, Great Britain sought to resume her role of economic leadership and to restore an interdependent market economy to working order. The international distribution of power had shifted decisively in favor of the United States, however, and it emerged from the war as a creditor nation and the foremost industrial power of the world. The United States was unwilling or unable to take over from the British the reins of international economic leadership, at least until late in the interwar period. The story of the interwar international economy, therefore, is essentially one of increasing American leadership in the face of steadily mounting challenges to the international economic order.

These challenges and the rise of the United States to world economic leadership constitute four major developments of the interwar period which profoundly altered the nature of global economic interdependence. As these developments continue to influence the evolution of the world economy, it is important to understand them.

The first major development was the Bolshevik Revolution and the subsequent withdrawal of the Soviet Union from the world market economy. In theory, as we have already suggested, Marxism rejects the market exchange system in favor of a redistributive exchange system. But in practice, and particularly following the victory of Stalin and the decision to emphasize rapid, heavy industrialization, the Soviet Union's economy can rightfully be characterized as a mobilization economy; the economy has been subordinated to the maximization of state power and self-sufficiency.

The Bolshevik Revolution in Russia led initially to the nearly complete isolation of Russia from the world economy and subsequently to the forced-draft industrialization of the country. On the foundations put down by Czarist Russia and borrowing technology heavily from the West, the communists industrialized the country largely outside the framework of the international economy. Hostile to the liberal emphasis on free trade, specialization, and the international division of labor, the communist ideal in practice was that of the most extreme economic nationalist: economic autarky, political independence, and industrial power.

Although a major power at the outbreak of the First World War, Russia ranked far behind the other European nations and the United States as an industrial power. Under the ruthless leadership of Stalin, the country was rapidly industrialized and, according to one estimate, by 1937 Russia's manufacturing production represented over 18% of the world's total [Table 1]. In the post-war period, the Soviet Union would use this great and expanding industrial base to cause the greatest breach ever in the interdependent world economy and, eventually, to challenge America's global hegemony.

The communization of the Soviet Union meant a profound rupture and fragmentation of the interdependent world economy. This fissure was greatly extended following the Second World War; the Soviet ideals of

48

Table 1
Percentage Distribution of the World's Manufacturing Production, 1913–38

Period	U.S.	Ger-many	U.K.	France	Rus-sia	Swe-den	Japan	India	Rest of World	World
1913	35.8	14.3	14.1	7.0	4.4	1.0	1.2	1.1	21.1	100.0
1926–29	42.2	11.6	9.4	6.6	4.3	1.0	2.5	1.2	21.2	100.0
1936–38	32.2	10.7	9.2	4.5	18.5	1.3	3.5	1.4	18.7	100.0

Note: The 1913 percentages represent the distribution according to the frontier established after the 1914–18 war.

Source: League of Nations, *Industrialization and Foreign Trade* (Geneva, 1945). Table 1, p. 13.

autarky and a command economy were expanded to include the economies of East Europe, which fell under the domination of the Red Army. The communization of China in 1948 meant a further extension of the mobilization exchange system. As a consequence, whereas the interdependent world economy of the nineteenth century incorporated most of the globe, the twentieth century has witnessed a major contraction. Economic interdependence has become nearly synonymous with the non-communist economies.

The second major transformation of the modern world economy has been the emergence of several major concentrations of economic power. In the nineteenth century, Britain, until the last two or three decades, stood alone as an economic power. Moreover, the units engaged in international commerce tended to be relatively small; they were either individual entrepreneurs or small firms. In the twentieth century, both aspects have changed. The world economy is composed not only of several powerful industrial economies but of large corporations whose resources dwarf those of the great majority of nation-states.

This transformation in the distribution of economic power has profoundly affected the nature of economic interdependence. In the nineteenth century the scale of markets relative to the scale of national economies or individual firms contributed to the automaticity of financial, commodity, and other markets. Domestic economies were subordinate to the international economy, and few producers were powerful enough to control international markets. The spread of industrialization, the rise of large corporations, and the intervention of the state into domestic economies triggered by World War I and the Great Depression have changed this situation dramatically.

As John Condliffe has argued, the world economy in the twentieth century has been transformed from an "international economy" to a "commerce of nations."[62] The presence of large concentrations of economic power in nations and corporations has made adjustments more difficult and less automatic. Moreover, the rise of welfare states committed to full employment has made nation-states less willing to subordinate their domestic economies to international discipline. Corporations which can exercise monopoly or monopsony power can easily resist market forces. As a consequence, the world economy has become increasingly characterized by bargaining and negotiations among large concentrations of state and corporate economic power.

The third major development of the interwar period was the rapid spread of economic nationalism. The origins of this economic nationalism are to be found in the war itself. Because of its totality and the demands imposed on the economy, one aspect after another of economic life was nationalized and brought into the service of the war effort. The role of the state in the economy was further enhanced in the post-war period by the disruptions caused by the war and its aftermath. Thus, whereas in the past balance of payments adjustment had been the major objective of economic policy, after the war price stability and full employment became major concerns of national policy. And with the rise of organized labor and mass movements of the Left and Right, national planning in the interest of internal stability became more important than external stability and adherence to international norms.

In part the spread of economic nationalism was a reaction to a strengthened sensitivity within governments to the dangers of becoming overly dependent on the world market. Interdependence brings with it the benefits of specialization, but it also brings with it new insecurities and vulnerabilities. Of equal importance, the lower classes in all European states had won new power due to the war. Governments and middle classes had had to make concessions to win their support. Whereas in the past the European working class had accepted the personal insecurity and other costs of a market system with resignation, they were now less willing to do so. The ultimate response of Western government to this new militancy on the part of the lower classes was to be the innovation of the welfare state and the adoption of Keynesian instruments of economic policy.

Prior to the war, only Japan and Germany had intervened decisively in their economies. After the war, state intervention became widespread, particularly with the onset of the Depression. In the first place, there was a "nationalization" of the balance of payments adjustment mechanism. Under the pre-war system, London and the mechanism of the gold standard had enforced the adjustment of exchange rates. In the post-war period, all transactions became subordinated to national controls. Secondly, in response to rising unemployment in the 1930s, protectionism became widespread with

50

the imposition by all trading nations of quantitative and other restrictions on imports. And, thirdly, in place of non-discrimination and the multilateralism of the pre-war period, bilateralism, tariff bargaining, and economic warfare came to characterize trading relations.

As has already been mentioned, underlying this rise of economic nationalism and weakening of interdependence was the emergence of several large markets under unified political control. The existence of several powerful industrial nations with monopoly or monopsony power in world markets had increased the importance of economic power and bargaining in international economic relations. These changes meant that the larger economies could manipulate tariffs and other protective devices in order to maximize their own trade gains. It also meant that henceforth the exercise of economic power would be a more prominent feature of international relations.

With the collapse of British leadership and the rise of powerful economies, economic nationalism took a still more virulent form in the 1930s with the rise of rival economic blocs and intensification of national insecurities. A decision which symbolized the final collapse of multilateral free trade was the British move in 1931 to go off the gold standard, which, along with the Ottawa Agreements of 1932, created the sterling area and the Commonwealth trading system (Imperial Preference). Although the intellectual origins of such a preference system composed of Britain and the Commonwealth nations are to be found in late nineteenth-centur' writers seeking an answer to the German and American trade challenge, the immediate cause for these decisions was the onset of the Depression, the contraction of world trade, and the breakdown of the multilateral system.

The fragmentation of the world economy into relatively isolated trading blocs and the retreat from global interdependence proceeded at a rapid pace. Already the United States had passed the high Smoot-Hawley Tariff (1930), and in 1933, on the eve of the London Economic Conference, President Franklin Roosevelt decided to leave the gold standard and thereby further isolate the United States from the world economy. But the two most ominous developments were taking place in Central Europe and the Far East, where Germany and Japan were organizing their own neighboring areas of strategic and economic importance under their respective hegemonies. Under the leadership of Adolph Hitler, defeated and revisionist Germany took advantage of the collapse of the Austro-Hungarian Empire and the divisions among her more powerful neighbors to create the greater Reich denied her by World War I. And in the Far East a rapidly industrializing Japan expanded into a crumbling China and sought to create a self-sufficient territorial base for Japanese industrial and military power.

A primary factor in the expansionist policies of these mobilization economies was the intensification of national insecurity. As advanced indus-

51

trialized countries with large populations, highly dependent on export trade, these countries, along with Italy, believed it essential to ensure the security of the supply of foodstuffs and raw materials. Both Germany and Japan, for example, faced powerful neighbors; neither, however, had a large and secure territorial base which could provide them access to essential food and raw materials as did the United States, the Soviet Union, and the British Empire. As one writer describes the policies of Germany, Japan, and Italy, "so long as countries have reason to fear the recurrence of war, no emphasis on the economic benefits of international trade will induce them to forego such a measure of economic self-sufficiency as their Governments consider feasible and desirable for their military security."[63]

The creation of exclusive economic blocs under the hegemony of the great industrial powers was one of the most significant international developments of the interwar period. It was a response to the breakdown of the international economic order and the global balance of power. With the collapse of the *Pax Britannica,* the competing industrial powers sought to enhance their security through the creation of exclusive spheres of economic influence; commerical relations became instruments of economic warfare. Through bilateral negotiations, competitive currency depreciation, and trade restrictions of various types, the large powers attempted to manipulate interdependence and to achieve economic and political advantages over each other and their weaker neighbors.

After the spread of economic nationalism, the fourth major development of the interwar period was the rise of the United States to a position of global economic leadership. Although America's meteoric rise to economic and industrial preeminence had begun in the latter part of the nineteenth century, it was only following the First World War that the United States really began to challenge British world leadership in trade, investment, and monetary affairs. As a consequence of the war, the American industrial plant had greatly expanded, and the nation had shifted from the status of debtor to creditor. A major force in world markets since the 1890s, American interest and concern over the international trading system expanded throughout the interwar period, with two major protectionist aberrations in 1930 and 1933. By the end of the Second World War, the United States had reached a point where it desired to see a major reformation of the world economy in a direction more in line with its own interests as the world's dominant economy.

The growth of American economic and industrial power was reflected in changing American attitudes and policies with regard to investment, trade, and the international monetary system. With respect to investment, at the same time that Great Britain had had to liquidate over $4 billion in overseas investment, the United States had become the major lending country of the world. American foreign investment, which had operated on

52

a modest scale since the 1890s, now expanded rapidly. It contrasted markedly, however, with traditional British practice in both scale and significance and did not have the same dynamic impact on the international economy. Whereas British investment had gone mainly to underdeveloped countries for the tapping of natural resources, American capital expense was primarily in manufacturing, with the major exception of petroleum, and it took the form of direct investment. Nearly 70% of American investment went to Europe and Canada, and only 22% went to Latin America. Initially on a modest scale compared with British investment, only after the Second World War would American foreign investment (and foreign aid) become a major factor in international economic relations.

Almost from the initial thrust of American business abroad, foreign direct investment, i.e., the establishment of foreign subsidiaries, has been an important mechanism to penetrate markets protected by tariffs, cartels, or other barriers; to gain control of valuable sources of raw materials; and to protect technological leads which American enterprise had established over foreign competitors. In the decades following the Second World War, the overseas expansion of what we today call multinational corporations would become a predominant feature of the interdependent world economy.

A second major change in America's world economic role was in trade. Traditionally a highly protectionist nation, America's industrial maturity and changing interests were reflected after World War I in the evolution of her tariff policy toward free trade. Although the Smoot-Hawley Tariff of 1930 and the 1933 decision to go off the gold standard were clear cases of backsliding, the passage of the Reciprocal Trade Agreements in 1934 signaled the conversion of the United States to free trade. Enacted as a solution to the Depression and reflecting America's industrial supremacy, the purpose of the Act was to negotiate mutual reductions in tariff barriers. As had been the case with Great Britain, with the maturing of its industrial strength and expanded productive capacity, the United States became the opponent of exclusive economic spheres and the proponent of the "open door" on a global scale.

But whereas Great Britain had originally established free trade primarily through a unilateral reduction of her own tariff barriers, this approach was no longer possible. In a world of large industrial powers and trading blocks, such an action would have brought immediate disaster. The existence of competing industrial powers meant that the international division of labor had come to be determined far more by government policies and international bargaining than by static comparative advantage. More than market-oriented economists are prone to admit, these great industrial powers seek to structure their international economic relations in order to foster the development of high technology industry and to protect domestic employment levels. In recognition of this new world, the Reciprocal Trade

Agreement was a bargaining device. Though the immediate success of this economic weapon was limited, the potential of bilateral negotiations was demonstrated as a method to achieve the expansion of multilateral trade; the Act was the forerunner of the post-war General Agreements on Tariffs and Trade (GATT).

In international monetary affairs a similar devolution of leadership from Great Britain to the United States was taking place. Whereas in the pre-war period, the City of London had, in effect, managed the international monetary system, during the interwar period, the system was initially divided into two spheres of influence. On the one hand, there was a loose sterling-dollar condominium under the joint management of London and New York, and, on the other, a European gold bloc, largely dominated by France.[64] While the Tripartite Agreement of 1936 foreshadowed the re-emergence of a global system and the supremacy of the dollar, the United States was not yet powerful enough to impose its will on the international monetary system. As a result, the centers of economic power were too divided to provide the central direction and coordination which had existed in the pre-war period.

The depth and scope of the Great Depression of the 1930s, as Charles Kindleberger has argued, was a direct consequence of this faltering of economic leadership. The world was in transition between the sterling standard and the dollar standard. "[T]he leading country must provide a market for distress goods, sustain capital exports on a counter-cyclical basis, or at least be stable and be prepared to rediscount in a crisis."[65] Unfortunately, in 1929–1931, Great Britain no longer had the capacity to assume these responsibilities, and the United States would not. As was argued earlier, unless the dominant economic power organizes the international system, it will collapse into bickering fragments.

In short, although the United States had become the dominant economic power in the world, it was not yet powerful enough militarily, or sufficiently willing politically, to restructure the international system in accordance with its economic and security interests. It was not yet prepared to supplant the *Pax Britannica* with a *Pax Americana* and to recreate an interdependent world economy centered on the American economy. But, the United States was determined to change what it believed to be the discriminatory features of the existing international economy. The reorganization of the world economy was to be the keynote of American post-war planning during the Second World War.[66]

The American-Centered World Economy

The United States emerged from the Second World War as the champion of a liberal international economy.[67] Like Britain in the nineteenth century, the United States hoped to create an international economy which

54

would guarantee its economic and security interests. American economic interests on the whole lay with free trade and free investment. As the world's leading industrial power, the United States had no need for an exclusive imperial system. It looked to the whole world for its markets, outlets for investment, sources of raw materials. It demanded "equal treatment," though one can argue that in the case of the strong, equal treatment may mean unequal advantage.

But, in addition to these considerations of economic self-interest, the American desire for a return to an interdependent world economy was based on a redefinition of America's security interests. American leadership believed that economic nationalism and the competition for markets and resources had been at the root of the Second World War. The basis of American opposition to trade discrimination and bilateralism, therefore, was not merely that they harmed American economic interests, but President Roosevelt and other American leaders believed colonial empires, exclusive economic blocs, and "beggar-thy-neighbor" policies, exemplified particularly by the British empire, had been responsible for the Second World War. The Germans and the Japanese, for example, were excluded from colonial markets and sources of raw materials in the interwar years, and they were regarded as having been driven to create exclusive blocs of their own. The achievement of America's post-war goal of a lasting peace was impossible in the absence of free trade, security, and an open world. From the American perspective, a renewal of the competition between "have" and "have-not" states for exclusive economic spheres of trade, investment, and especially for raw materials would lead to a third world war. The American intention was to lessen the economic importance of political boundaries and enhance the security of all states by giving every state equal opportunity for access to markets and raw materials and thereby to defuse the issue that had led to the economic struggles of the 1930s. Economic interdependence and security would replace competition for exclusive economic spheres.

Under American leadership, economic interdependence in the contemporary world has had three distinguishing characteristics. In the first place (and this is perhaps the most significant innovation of the American post-war planners), international institutions were created to perform certain of the essential functions formerly lodged in the institutions of the City of London. Collectively known as the Bretton Woods System, after the conference held in 1944 to re-establish the international monetary system, these organizations provide the broader framework for multilateralism today. While it is not our intention to discuss these organizations, their history, or their functions here, the more important ones should be noted: the International Monetary Fund (IMF); the General Agreement on Tariffs and Trade (GATT); the International Bank for Reconstruction and Development (World Bank); the stillborn International Trade Organization; and, from an earlier era, the Bank for International Settlements.[68] In addition to the principles of free trade and free investment, the system governed itself through three key rules of the game: fixed exchange rates, currency convertibility, and the IMF as overseer of the international monetary system.[69] (See Chapter 9 for a discussion of this "money" system.)

In reality, however, and behind the facade of these institutions, the United States has run the international economy.[70] While American pressure played a large part in establishing the system, the major contribution of the United States was in providing its psychological underpinnings and in exercising leadership. Throughout the industrial non-communist world, with its memory of the disastrous experience of the interwar period, there was a general recognition of the need to eliminate discrimination. But the prevailing circumstances at the end of World War II made bilateralism, discrimination, and inconvertibility of currencies the most rational courses of action. No country could risk removing currency and trade restriction unless everyone else did so simultaneously; to do otherwise would have meant a hemorrhage of currency and commercial disaster.[71] "The restoration of an international system of trade and payments after the war was thus recognized at an early stage as a problem whose solution would require international negotiation and agreement rather than unilateral uncoordinated decisions by several scores of sovereign countries."[72] Together with Great Britain, the United States provided the necessary leadership and fostered an atmosphere of mutual confidence which would make the transition to multilateral free trade possible.[73]

Under the umbrella of these institutions, the market economies led by the United States have determined the rules of the game of international economic relations. Neither the Soviet bloc nor the nations of the so-called Third World, with their strong commitment to state intervention, have exercised much influence. The rules governing trade, investment, and monetary relations have been set by nations, corporations, and international organizations committed, at least in principle, to a market exchange system.

As a consequence of these institutional and policy initiatives, the second feature of economic interdependence over the past several decades has been the increased sensitivity of national economies to foreign trade flows, particularly the exchange of manufactures for manufactures.[74] Decreases in transportation costs, improved communications, and lower trade barriers have all operated to stimulate the exchange of goods. Moreover, the accumulation of capital and the international transmission of technical knowledge have caused a convergence in industrial structure. Comparative advantages have become more dynamic and less a consequence of national endowments. As a result, national economies are more intensely subjected to the insecurities of foreign competition and external disruptions.

The third and most controversial aspect of economic interdependence today has been the extensive integration of national economies by the large multinational corporations. These enterprises, most of which are American, have taken interdependence beyond the realm of trade, finance, and money to that of production itself. This internationalization of production has carried to its ultimate conclusion the logic of a market exchange system. The increased mobility of capital, technology, and managerial know-how associated with the multinational corporation has greatly benefited national economies. But the implantation of foreign-owned and managed enterprises in national economies has also threatened the core values of host societies. As a result, the threat of the multinational corporation to the economic, political, and cultural autonomy of states has led to a resurgence of economic nationalism on the part of host governments.[75]

A New International Economic Order?

Since the early 1970s, and particularly since the announcement of President Richard Nixon's New Economic Policy of August 15, 1971, nations have become increasingly concerned over the costs of economic interdependence. As Klaus Knorr points out in Chapter 1, this resurgence of concern over national security and vulnerability to external market forces does not mean the end of an open-world economy. But economic interdependence is unlikely to expand at the rapid rate with which it has over the past several decades. More importantly, the nature of economic interdependence is changing. In the areas of trade, investment, and international currencies, government intervention in markets greatly accelerated in the early 1970s. International economic relations, in fact, became increasingly politicized as nations sought to enhance their own individual benefits and protect their particular security interests from the harmful effects of an open-world economy. Behind these developments lie more fundamental changes in domestic and international society.

A major theme of this chapter has been that the rise of a highly interdependent global market economy in the modern world was due to a peculiar set of political, sociological, and technological factors. Among the factors we have emphasized in explaining the success of this form of economic exchange were the development of the modern nation-state system, the political supremacy of the middle class, and the technological revolution in communications and transportation. We have also stressed that successive dominant world powers—Great Britain in the nineteenth and the United States in the twentieth century—have regarded an open, liberal world economy to be in their economic and security interests and have used their power positions in its support.

In recent years, the several supports of a liberal interdependent world economy have weakened. In the first place, the political foundations of an interdependent world economy have greatly eroded. The United States no longer enjoys an unchallenged position in the world economy. As its relative power has declined, the United States has become more sensitive to the costs of an open economy and has become less willing or able to enforce the rules of a free market. Moreover, the economic and political bonds between the United States and the other market economies have weakened as these economies have become strong competitors and the policy of détente with the Soviet Union—a uniform name for an ambiguously held policy—has weakened the previously overriding importance of security ties. For both economic and security reasons, the preservation of an open, liberal economic order has declined as a foreign policy priority of the world's leading economy.

In addition, as Knorr argues in Chapter 1, a major set of changes has taken place in the nature and disposition of the market economies themselves. Taken together, these changes have transformed the attitudes of society in the capitalist economies with respect to the benefits and costs of an open-world economy. On the one hand, for the middle and laboring classes in many of these economies, the marginal utility of additional income appears to have declined in an age of high affluence. On the other hand, there is less willingness to pay the costs associated with an open economy and rapid economic growth. In effect, the "good life" and economic security are being given a higher priority than marginal increments to national income.

Several changes internal to the capitalist economies appear to be responsible for this reordering of national priorities. In the first place, a redistribution of power among social groups and classes has undermined the socio-political framework essential for a free market system.[76] In the past the middle classes could, in effect, shift the cost of rapid economic growth and interdependence to the working class and powerless groups. Since the First World War and increasingly over the past several decades, the power of the underprivileged groups which have borne a disproportionate share of the costs of a market system (i.e., loss of income and employment) has grown. As their bargaining strength has grown, these groups have become less willing to make the adjustments imposed on them by economic changes, and they are more able to resist such adjustments through unionization or political action. Society has thus become less flexible with respect to its ability and willingness to adapt to external dynamic processes.

The rise of the market and the toleration of the relatively free play of market forces in the early modern period was due to a depoliticization of economic activities. Market forces were permitted to work themselves out regardless of the consequences for particular groups—labor, peasants, farmers, etc. In part, this was because the holders of power were the ones most benefited by the unregulated market. In part, it was due to a belief that market forces were beyond the control of government and that government

58

intervention would only make things worse. Today, these supports of an unregulated market no longer hold, and disadvantaged groups seek by every means available to protect themselves against the undesirable consequences of market forces. The result of this change is a repoliticization of economies at both the domestic and international levels.[77]

The repoliticization of economic relations is having a profound effect on people's loyalties and the integrity of nation-states. However, contrary to the oft-repeated view that increasing interdependence, modernization, and the emergence of transnational processes are leading to a sense of world community, the very opposite may, in fact, be the case. As Robert Nisbet has argued, the dissolution of the central state and the gradual erosion of allegiance and trust in the national state is strengthening intermediate social groups.[78] People's loyalties are being transferred to labor unions, ethnic groups, and separatist movements rather than to mankind as a whole. The rise of these particularisms with their narrow definitions of security is not conducive to an open-world economy.

In addition to these changes, there is the mounting evidence that a profound transformation of the ethos and cultural disposition of the middle class itself is taking place.[79] As this essay has argued, the victory of the market system over its rivals was due in large measure to an alliance between the emergent nation-state and the rise of an aggressive middle class. Today, as many perceptive observers suggest, a decay of the bourgeois ethic is taking place; the prevalent ethic of hard work, savings, and sense of social responsibility which once characterized the middle classes has weakened. A higher value seems to be placed on security and the pleasures of consumption rather than on entrepreneural risk-taking and the work ethic. This apparent change in middle class mentality, in turn, has decreased the willingness and ability of societies to accept the disruptive economic changes and insecurities inherent in an open-world economy.

One finds, even among its middle class champions, greater hostility toward the market as arbiter of social values and allocator of economic values. In the words of one distinguished economist, "when people become prosperous they think they can afford to be hostile to the market—or at least to what they regard as the blind forces of the market."[80] Thus, an historic shift in middle class values is undercutting commitment to the market exchange system.

Finally, and perhaps as a consequence of the above-mentioned changes, there appears to be a weakening of governmental authority and capacity to govern taking place.[81] The importance of this change lies in the fact that a well-functioning market system requires a strong state; this paradox is explained by the fact that the state must be strong enough to resist the pressures of special interests. The reality of the present situation in many democratic, capitalist socieites is that at the same time that society, in general, and particular groups are increasing their demands on the state, loyalty to the state has declined, and its authority has suffered. As a consequence, many societies are "governed" by minority or weak governments, and a political *immobilisme* prevents the resolution of pressing social and economic problems. The overall result is a chipping away of the supports of the market system.

The third set of challenges to the survival of an open-world economy relates to a global shift of power in favor of non-market economies. The market exchange economies are on the defensive and find themselves in an increasingly hostile environment. Over the past several decades, communist and Third World countries have grown in economic power and importance, although this growth has been extremely uneven, particularly in the developing countries. These essentially mobilization economies harbor antagonisms and, in many cases, hostility toward market economies and the rules of the game of an international market economy. The prevalence of the middle classes and the respect for property rights which were critical factors in the rise of a market economy seldom characterize these societies. But, what is most important for the future of an open-world market economy is that these economies give precedence to national security, political independence, and other non-market values. In the light of the increasingly important role of these non-market economies in the world economic balance, their commitment to non-market values will have a profound impact on the character of global economic interdependence and on the character of the market economies themselves.

The most dramatic illustration of the nature of this new international environment is, of course, the action of the Organization of Petroleum Exporting Countries (OPEC) of raising by manyfold the price of petroleum. The success of this cartel, in turn, has stimulated other efforts to organize commodity cartels. (OPEC and related cartelization issues are treated in Chapters 6 and 11.) As a consequence of these developments, the market economies and their conception of an interdependent, international economy are confronted by the so-called "Group of 77" developing countries (the Group at this writing has spawned additional members) and their demands for a "new international economic order." These developments have triggered an increased concern over the costs of interdependence and greater attention to matters of security in all societies.

As a consequence of the global redistribution of economic power and of strong dissatisfaction on the part of particular domestic groups with respect to the effects of economic interdependence, powerful tensions have developed in the world economy. No aspect of the contemporary international economic order has gone unchallenged, as states and groups seek to maximize and safeguard their own interests. Several developments may be discerned. In the first place, the international economic institutions and

60

rules established under American leadership are increasingly being challenged. New sets of rules are being demanded. The reform of established institutions is being demanded. Rival institutions have come into existence. Secondly, individual nations are emphasizing security values and are seeking to protect themselves from the destabilizing effects of economic interdependence. In particular, the decision taken in 1973 to shift from a system of fixed to flexible exchange rates was a response to the desires of statesmen to isolate their domestic economies from international economic disturbances. And, finally, the dominance of the multinational corporation over the world economy is being eroded as nation-states seek to reassert control over their domestic economies.

Much as it happened in the latter part of the nineteenth century and the interwar period, the relative decline of the dominant economy and the emergence of new centers of economic power have led to increasing economic conflicts. During such periods of weak international leadership, international economic relations tend to be characterized by a reversion to mercantilism (economic nationalism), intense competition and bargaining among economic powers, and the fragmentation of the liberal interdependent world economy into exclusive blocs, rival nationalisms, and economic alliances.

Drawing parallels between the contemporary period and past eras is obviously a risky undertaking. The United States in the last quarter of the twentieth century is not Great Britain in the last quarter of the ninteenth. Despite economic and military challenges, the United States has the resources and industrial base to maintain its position of global leadership for a long time to come. The advent of nuclear weapons appears to have moderated conflicts, at least among developed countries, and makes unlikely a resort to war to resolve economic and political differences. The mutual benefits from economic interdependence continue to be a strong cement holding together the international economic order. These contrasts between past and present are real.

Yet, the strains and tensions of the present are there, and the experience and lessons of the past indicate cause for concern over the future of the international economic order in an era of weakened international and domestic leadership. In particular, there are three major challenges to global economic interdependence and the market exchange system.

The first issue is the adjustment of relations among advanced noncommunist industrial powers, particularly the United States, Western Europe, and Japan. Since the end of the Second World War, the relationship among these industrial powers has been one in which the United States has taken the lead with respect to trade, investment, money, and energy. While the United States must continue to exercise this leadership role, the United States must also, of necessity, come to terms with stronger and more

61

independently minded economic partners. Both the ties and strains of economic interdependence are leading to demands on all sides for greater coordination of domestic and international economic policies. Cases in point are the American initiatives which led to the International Energy Agency and the European demand for the economic summit of mid-November 1975. If the non-communist powers are to avoid what West German Chancellor Helmut Schmidt has called "the struggle for the world product" and an individualistic pursuit of security concerns, there will undoubtedly have to take place a great institutionalization of policy coordination among the United States, Western Europe, and Japan.

The second issue is what, for lack of a better term, one may call the reintegration of Russia and China into the world economy. A basic premise of America's détente policy toward the Soviet Union and America's rapprochement with China is that the development of economic ties with these communist powers will moderate their policies and provide the best hope for peace over the long term. This notion that the creation of a "web of interdependencies" can establish the basis for a lasting peaceful coexistence and mutual security harkens back to the position that "peace is the natural effect of trade." As such, it may easily mislead one to believe that the sources of great power conflict have been eliminated.

Another danger or challenge arises out of the mere fact that these non-market economies will have an increased importance in international economic relations. As Jacob Viner pointed out long ago, extensive economic intercourse between market and state-controlled economies will have profound implications—not necessarily salutory—for the free market economies themselves and for the world economy.[82] As witnessed in the recent wheat deal between the United States and the Soviet Union, the consequence of this development will be greater intervention into the market by the United States Government. The ironic consequence of the reintegration of the major communist economies into the world economy may well be greater state intervention in the market economies rather than the lessening of state intervention in the communist economies. In short, the reintegration of communist economies into the world economies has important implications for the American economy itself and the nature of the emergent international economic order.

The third significant issue is what the lesser developed countries call the creation of a New International Economic Order. For the Third World this means the transformation of the international division of labor and the terms of trade and investment in a manner which will bring about a massive redistribution of world wealth. As already pointed out, these Third World economies tend to reject the market exchange system and espouse socialism of one sort or another; their economies are more akin to the redistributive and mobilization models than to the market model of exchange. Few have strong middle classes, and most reject middle-class, capitalistic values as inimical to independence and development.[83] The essence of their demands is a global redistributive economy to replace the present market exchange system.

The implications of the increasing role of the Third World in the international order and of its demands for a new international economic order could be profound for the American economy and the organization of the world economy. Thus, as counter-measures to OPEC, the United States, in its striving for a national energy policy and in proposals for a massive government funding of energy development, has already moved in the direction of government management of a vital sector of the American economy. In the future, Third World initiatives for a new international order and American responses could thrust the United States Government further into the economic arena in order to protect its core interests.

The growing importance of the economic factor in international relations and the specific policy issues which loom ahead suggest the increasing politicization of international economic relations. In the decades ahead, economic power and economic competition could become an increasingly important factor in the relations and competition among nation-states.

This situation, if carried to its logical extreme, would be the transformation of all economies into mobilization economies. But, whereas the mobilization economies of the past were organized for military conflict, those of the future would be organized for economic conflict. In an age of economic interdependence and of mutual military restraint, international economic relations—to paraphrase Clausewitz—could well become the pursuit of policy by other means.

Footnotes

1. William Baumol, *Welfare Economics and the Theory of the State,* 2nd ed. (Cambridge, Mass.: Harvard University Press, 1965), pp. 182–83.
2. For an excellent review of the literature, see Peter Katzenstein, "International Interdependence: Some Long-Term Trends and Recent Changes," *International Organization,* XXIX, 4 (Autumn 1975):1021–35.
3. For a superb analysis of the evolution of the market economy, see John Hicks, *A Theory of Economic History* (London: Oxford University Press, 1969). The classic study of the impact of a market economy on international relations is, of course, Karl Polanyi, *The Great Transformation: The Political and Economic Origins of Our Time* (New York: Farrar and Rinehart, Inc., 1944).
4. The following discussion is based principally upon T.F. Carney, *The Economics of Antiquity: Controls, Gifts and Trade* (Lawrence, Kansas: Coronado Press, 1973), especially Ch. 1.
5. Ibid., p. 22.
6. In addition to Hicks, contrasting explanations of the rise of a market system are provided by Immanuel Wallerstein, *The Modern World System: Capitalist Agriculture and the Origins of the European World Economy in the Sixteenth Century* (New York: Academic Press, 1974) and especially, Jean Baechler, *The Origins of Capitalism* (New York: St. Martin's Press, 1975); French ed. published in 1971. Though ideologically at odds, Baechler and Waller-

stein argue the identical thesis, namely, that the rise of capitalism and a world market required a pluralistic international political system as a precondition.

7. Max Weber, *Economy and Society: An Outline of Interpretative Sociology*, ed. Guether Roth and Claus Wittich (New York: Bedminster Press, 1968).
8. Carney, *Economics of Antiquity*, p. 25.
9. Michael Roberts, *The Military Revolution 1560–1660*. An Inaugural Lecture delivered before the Queen's University of Belfast (Belfast, Boyd, 1956); see also George Clark, *War and Society in the Seventeenth Century* (Cambridge: Cambridge University Press, 1958).
10. Henri Pirenne, *Economic and Social History of Medieval Europe* (New York: Harcourt, Brace and World, Inc., 1937).
11. Fernand Braudel, *Capitalism and Material Life 1400–1800* (New York: Harper and Row, 1973).
12. Hicks, *Theory of Economic History*.
13. Douglass C. North and Robert Thomas, *The Rise of the Western World: A New Economic History* (Cambridge: Cambridge University Press, 1973), Ch. 3.
14. Wallerstein, *Modern World System*; Baechler, *Origins*.
15. David Hume, "Of the Balance of Power," in *Balance of Power*, ed. Paul Seabury (San Francisco: Chandler Publishing Company, 1965), pp. 32–36.
16. Edward Gulick, *Europe's Classical Balance of Power* (New York: W.W. Norton, 1955).
17. For several contrasting interpretations, see Ludwig Dehio, *The Precarious Balance* (New York: Alfred A. Knopf, 1962); Felix Gilbert, *To The Farewell Address* (Princeton: Princeton University Press, 1961); and Charles Tilley, *The Formation of National States in Western Europe* (Princeton: Princeton University Press, 1975).
18. Wallerstein, *Modern World System*; Baechler, *Origins*.
19. A neglected but excellent discussion of imperial systems is John Strachey, *The End of Empire* (New York: Praeger, 1964), Part 3.
20. Adam Smith, *An Inquiry into the Wealth of Nations* (New York: The Modern Library, 1937), Book IV, Ch. 1; first published 1776.
21. Actually the term "mercantilism" itself was not coined until the latter part of the nineteenth century by representatives of the German History School. See Walter E. Minchinton, *Mercantilism: System or Expediency* (New York: D.C. Heath, 1969), p. VII.
22. See, for example, Eli Heckscher, *Mercantilism* (London: G. Allen and Unwin, 1935).
23. This point is made by John Maynard Keynes, *The General Theory of Employment Interest, and Money* (New York: Harcourt, Brace and World, 1936).
24. Jacob Viner, "Power versus Plenty as Objectives of Foreign Policy in the Seventeenth and Eighteenth Centuries," *World Politics, 1,* (1948–49):59.
25. This discussion is based primarily on Clark, *War and Society*.
26. Strachey, *End of Empire*.
27. James Adams, *Epic of America* (Boston: Little, Brown, and Company, 1931), p. 73.
28. Edmund S. Morgan, *The Birth of the Republic 1763–1789* (Chicago: University of Chicago Press, 1956), pp. 8–9.
29. Klaus Knorr, *The Power of Nations: The Political Economy of International Relations* (New York: Basic Books, Inc., 1975), p. 210.
30. Baron de Montesquieu, *Spirit of the Laws*, trans. Thomas Nugent (New York: Harper Press, 1949), p. 316; first published in 1748.
31. Jean Jacques Rousseau, "Abstract of the Abbé de Saint-Pierre's Project for Perpetual Peace," in *The Theory of International Relations*, ed. M.G. Gorsyth, H.M.A. Keens-Saper, and P. Savigear (New York: Atherton Press, 1970), p. 140.
32. The following discussion draws heavily upon my book, *U.S. Power and the Multinational Corporation: The Political Economy of Foreign Direct Investment* (New York: Basic Books, Inc., 1975).

33. Gunnar Myrdal, *An International Economy* (New York: Harper and Row, 1956), p. 32.
34. Klaus Knorr, *British Colonial Theories 1570–1850* (Toronto: University of Toronto Press, 1944), p. 248.
35. For a more detailed analysis, see Gilpin, *U.S. Power*.
36. Quoted in Donald Gordon, *The Moment of Power: Britain's Imperial Epoch* (Englewood: Prentice-Hall, 1970), p. 87.
37. Simon Kuznets, *Modern Economic Growth* (New Haven: Yale University Press, 1966), p. 335.
38. Gerald Meier and Robert Baldwin, *Economic Development* (New York: John Wiley and Sons, Inc.), p. 212.
39. Ibid.
40. John Condliffe, *The Commerce of Nations* (New York: W.W. Norton, 1950), pp. 238–43.
41. Ibid., p. 342.
42. J.A. Hobson, *Imperialism: A Study*, 3rd ed. rev. (London: G. Allen and Unwin, 1938), p. 57.
43. Discussed in Condliffe, *Commerce of Nations*, p. 240.
44. Ibid., p. 246.
45. Harry Johnson, *Economic Nationalism in Old and New States* (Chicago: University of Chicago Press, 1967).
46. On Fichte, see Knorr, *The Power of Nations*, p. 235.
47. List's classic defense of economic nationalism is *National System of Political Economy* (London: Longmans, Green and Co., 1928).
48. The views of this school are discussed by Condliffe, *Commerce of Nations*, Ch. 9.
49. Ibid., p. 233.
50. Ibid., p. 219.
51. Karl Marx and Friedrich Engels, *The Communist Manifesto, The Marx-Engels Reader*, ed. Robert C. Tucker (New York: W.W. Norton, 1972), pp. 338–39.
52. Karl Marx, "The Future Results of British Rule in India," *Karl Marx on Colonialism and Modernization*, ed. Shlomo Avineri (Garden City, New York: Doubleday and Company, 1969), p. 136.
53. Cited in Solomon F. Bloom, *The World of Nations: A Study of the National Implications in the Work of Karl Marx* (New York: 1941), p. 53.
54. V. I. Lenin, *Imperialism, The Highest Stage of Capitalism* (New York: International Publishers, 1939).
55. Knorr, *The Power of Nations*, p. 57.
56. Lenin, *Imperialism*, p. 85.
57. Ibid., p. 125.
58. Kuznets, *Modern Economic Growth*, p. 344.
59. Ibid., p. 345.
60. Ibid.
61. Ibid.
62. Condliffe, *Commerce of Nations*.
63. Heinz Arndt, *The Economic Lessons of the Nineteen-Thirties* (Oxford: Oxford University Press, 1944), p. 274.
64. Susan Strange, *Sterling and British Policy* (Oxford: Oxford University Press, 1971), p. 55.
65. Charles Kindleberger, "Needed World Monetary Leadership," *New York Times*, 4 June 1972.
66. Condliffe, *Commerce of Nations*, pp. 417–18.
67. An excellent analysis of this period is Richard Gardner, *Sterling-Dollar Diplomacy: Anglo-American Collaboration in the Reconstruction of Multilateral Trade* (Oxford: Clarendon Press, 1966), p. XLII.

68. Ibid., LVIII, pp. 42–44, 282, 313.
69. Ibid., p. 261.
70. Peter Kenen, *Giant Among Nations* (New York: Rand McNally, 1963), p. 87.
71. Ibid., p. 91.
72. Robert Triffin, *Europe and the Money Muddle* (New Haven: Yale University Press, 1957), p. 91.
73. Ibid., p. 93.
74. Richard Cooper, *The Economics of Interdependence: Economic Policy in the Atlantic Community* (New York: McGraw-Hill Book Company, 1968), p. 80.
75. See Gilpin, *U.S. Power,* Ch. 9.
76. See, for example, Morris Janowitz, "Toward a Redefinition of Military Strategy in International Relations," *World Politics*, Vol. XXVI (4), July 1974, esp. pp. 473–78.
77. The nature of these changes and their implications are treated by Richard Erb, "National Security and Economic Policies," American Enterprise Institute, Washington, D.C., Reprint Number 41, May 1976.
78. Nisbet's views are discussed in *Business Week*, 30 August 1976, p. 8.
79. This thesis is developed by Daniel Bell, *The Cultural Contradictions of Capitalism* (New York: Basic Books, Inc., 1976).
80. Goran Ohlin as quoted in *New York Times*, 13 June 1976, p. F9.
81. Samuel Huntington, "The Democratic Discontent," *The Public Interest, 41,* Fall 1975: 9–38.
82. Jacob Viner, "International Relations Between State-Controlled National Economies," (1944). Reprinted in Jacob Viner, *International Economic Studies* (Glencoe, Illinois: The Free Press, 1951).
83. Knorr, *The Power of Nations,* p. 230.

CHAPTER 3

Economic Factors as Objects of Security: Economics, Security and Vulnerability[1]

Clark A. Murdock

This chapter begins by stressing two general, although commonplace, characteristics of the current economic environment. First, governments must now answer more often to their domestic publics for the satisfactory achievement of national objectives, particularly economic ones.[2] Indeed, not only has the policy agenda of governments increased, but even the number of groups demanding satisfaction has grown. As Assar Lindbeck observes, "the target of full employment increasingly refers not only to the economy as a whole, but to specific regions, branches, and subsets of the labor force such as married women, handicapped, ethnic minority groups, the young, the old, etc."[3] In essence, this trend represents the politicization of economic issues as various groups within the society recognize how their interests are affected by the economic system and have turned to the political system to promote their interests.[4] Thus, the political system now often replaces free economic markets in determining how the benefits and costs of the national economy are distributed.

Secondly, global economic interdependence—which implies that economic conditions within a nation are sensitive to external economic factors—has clearly grown as well.[5] This has meant that at the same time that governments are asked to do more, their policy instruments—particularly monetary and fiscal policy which assume the existence of a fairly autonomous national economy—are less effective, since domestic economic conditions are increasingly influenced by external factors. The politicization of economic issues has consequently extended to international economic issues, resulting in a blurring of the distinction between domestic policy and foreign policy. As Peter Katzenstein has observed, international relations have been "internalized" and the domestic political system "externalized," since "the primary constraints on governmental policy have shifted away from the international and towards the domestic level."[6]

Authors describing the increased politicization of domestic and international economic issues also cite the decreasing salience of traditional security issues in the industrialized world as enhancing these trends. Fred

67

Bergsten, for example, notes that "security concerns will decreasingly determine overall relations among political allies," and many have noted that there has been a breakdown of the traditional hierarchy of policy objectives headed by national security objectives.[7] While it is the case that the end of the Cold War has lessened the fear of military attack in the industrialized world, it might be more accurate to state that security concerns have not waned but have changed to include economic issues. In the short run, Western European countries are much less concerned now about whether the U.S. will keep its commitment to attack the Soviet Union if the latter should invade Germany. Instead, these countries worry more about whether the U.S., in an effort to increase its domestic employment, restricts access to the large American market, thus causing unemployment in the export-oriented economies of Western Europe. The problem we shall now discuss is the relationship between economic issues and security issues in a world characterized by growing interdependence and increased politicization of economic issues.

Traditionally, in line with mercantilist philosophy, economic and security considerations have been analyzed as if economic factors were a means to security ends. There have been essentially two principal concerns (both the subjects of chapters by Klaus Knorr in this volume): (1) the use of economic means as leverage—that is, the utilization of a state's control over an economic resource needed by another state to induce behavior changes in the "dependent" state; and (2) the economic base of military power—that is, the limiting factors placed upon a nation's ability to deploy military capabilities by its economic capacity. States have always been concerned about the security implications of the lack of economic self-sufficiency. Robert Gilpin argues in Chapter 2 that German and Japanese imperialism in the 1930s was partially inspired by their lack of secure access to vital raw materials—an access that the U.S., U.K., and the Soviet Union all had. States have also frequently "linked" economic and security issues. Former Secretary of State Kissinger's policy of detente with the Soviet Union attempted to forge a "link" between economic issues and security issues, so that the Soviet Union's interest in increased economic interaction with the U.S. could be exploited for concessions with respect to security issues such as the SALT negotiations.[8] In February 1974, when the 13-nation Washington Energy conference was convened for the purpose of creating a common energy program for oil-consuming nations, President Nixon stated that "security and economic considerations are inevitably linked, and energy cannot be separated from either" and that European nations could not expect U.S. cooperation in security matters, if Europe did not cooperate in economic matters.[9] Other examples of linkage include U.S. troops in Germany and German economic policy, Japanese textile quotas and mutual security arrangements, and so forth.

Implicit in the concept of linkages, however, as in the notion of a hierarchy of policy objectives, or the "high" politics of security and the "low" politics of economics, is the separation or divisibility of economic issues and security issues. The focus in this chapter is on the treatment by governments and domestic publics of economic issues as security issues themselves. As President Ford's statement (in the 1975 State of the Union message) indicated, the line separating economic from security issues is not clear at all:

> Americans are no longer in full control of their own national destiny when that destiny depends on uncertain foreign fuel at high prices fixed by others. Higher energy costs compound both inflation and recession. And dependence on others for future energy supplies is intolerable to our national security.[10]

As shall be argued later, the treatment of an economic issue as an economic security issue is a significant departure, because governments and their publics perceive security issues in a different manner and will react differently than they would with an economic issue that is merely politicized. First, however, the nature of security concerns and the manner in which economic concerns are included must be discussed.

Frank N. Trager and Frank L. Simonie define the purpose of national security policy as "the creation of national and international political conditions favorable to the protection or extension of vital national values against existing and potential adversaries."[11] The notion of security appears to have two critical connotations—a "we-they" notion and a sense of threat to core values—which tend to elevate issues of security over other issues. *Someone or something is threatening to take or deprive us of someone or something we value highly.*

As countless discussions of the concept have indicated, the idea of "security" is hardly precise. Lawrence B. Krause and Joseph S. Nye, Jr. accurately observe that security usually involves much more than mere survival (since what people really want is security for the continued enjoyment of a number of other basic values) and that the operational definition of security for a particular nation is highly situational, and its content varies over time.[12] Krause and Nye define security as "the absence of acute threats to the minimal acceptable levels of the basic values that a people consider essential to its survival" and identify three basic clusters of values: welfare (including a minimal level of economic welfare), independence, and prestige or political status.[13]

As these definitions make clear, the precise content of security will vary from state to state and will change for a particular state as its circumstances and leaders change. Operationally, governmental elites determine what is a "core value" and, indeed, when a "core value" is threatened. The relationship between governmental policy and domestic public opinion depends, of course, on the nature of the political system within a particular state. The aforementioned trends—increased interdependence and increased politicization of economic issues—certainly make it likely that both governments and domestic publics will increasingly perceive and react to economic issues as security issues.

Krause and Nye define economic security as the "absence of threat of severe deprivation of economic welfare" and go on to state that "economic security as a goal becomes visible when a country consciously chooses to accept economic inefficiency to avoid becoming more vulnerable to economic impulses from abroad or when a country stresses national approaches at the expense of integration gains."[14] This concept of a severe deprivation of economic welfare is clearly a part of any definition of economic security, primarily because it is so closely analogous to traditional definitions of military security—that is, the existence of a discrete military threat to the core values of a society. In this context, what constitutes a serious deprivation of economic welfare is frequently viewed as a supply problem involving security of access to various essential material goods for which a state is dependent on external sources. The question often posed is how vulnerable a particular state would be if there were an embargo or boycott. These are economic security issues in the narrowest sense: what are the security implications of a lack of economic self-sufficiency, or how does a nation ensure its viability in a state of war or near-war?

One could argue, however, that there is a broader range of economic issues which have become security issues and have evoked a sense of being threatened by outside actors and forces for different nations at different times. Increased economic interdependence has greatly increased the number of ways in which external forces and actors may affect national economic conditions. In addition to limiting access to supply or markets, the levels of employment, degree of inflation, return to various productive factors, distribution of income, and so forth may also be affected by external forces. These are all highly politicized domestic policy objectives and to the extent they are perceived as being threatened by external actors, they may be perceived as security issues.

In addition, economic interdependence offers the possibility of both international conflict and international cooperation. And, increasingly it appears that it is only through the activist intervention of the government that a nation-state can ensure a successful outcome in either a conflictual or a cooperative situation. National security policy has always been differentiated from other policy areas because it is the sole province of the central government. The central government has a monopoly on the legitimate use of force and has the sole responsibility to provide security, a true public good, for all its citizens. It is here contended that many economic issues are now perceived by political elites and domestic publics as being either too important to be left to non-governmental actors (who will pursue interests other than the national interest) or beyond the capability of non-governmental actors. As the following quotation by the Japanese Industry Minister almost a half-year before the oil embargo illustrates, the economic welfare of the nation necessitates governmental intervention:

> I have become strongly aware of the need to approach Middle East oil not simply as tradeable merchandise but something more deeply politically involved. Oil is a critical resource for Japan and dealings in oil cannot be handled by the individual Japanese enterprises or traders alone without the support of the Japanese Government and its people. The Japanese Government will involve itself in strong and continuous petroleum diplomacy in the future.[15]

Even a superficial reading of the literature on international political economy after the oil embargo reveals significant and generalized concurrence with this Japanese view. National efforts to combat or cope with OPEC-determined prices and oil supply almost invariably emphasize the government's role in encouraging shifts in consumption and production patterns in addition to influencing OPEC behavior by other means.[16] More significantly, however, was the realization by many analysts that national means were not the best way to cope with problems stemming from resource dependence by the industrialized countries and the instability of the international monetary system. Only international agreements would provide optimal economic gains for all the parties affected, and in many cases, they were the only way nations could avoid significant losses in national economic welfare. Multilateral solutions to economic problems stemming from interdependence also necessitate the involvement of governmental actors though not necessarily to the exclusion of non-governmental actors.

Seen in this context, the perception that governments must pursue economic ends abroad (in the same sense that governments are held responsible for military security) makes the policy system in economic issues more similar to that in national security affairs. Yet, it is also clear that not all politicized economic issues are economic security issues. During the oil embargo, for example, the issue of access to petroleum products was a supply problem with heavy security implications as well as serious economic costs that necessitated governmental action (such as Project Independence). Currently, the security implications for most oil-dependent countries have receded as the oil issue has become largely a question of price and global income transfers, though it may again become a security issue either as a result of new embargo threats or the threat implied by accumulated income transfers. Certainly, the Carter Administration accepts the need for a more

71

active governmental role in formulating and implementating a national energy policy.

The distinction between politicized economic issues and economic security issues will never be precise, since what societies and their governments perceive as central values—and threats to central values—are both subjective and highly variable. In addition, most military threats are relatively discrete phenomena, while many potential economic threats are not. A small amount of imported unemployment or inflation will not be disturbing but larger amounts will. Therefore, with the exception of discrete economic threats (e.g., potential embargoes), there can be no *a priori* definition of what constitutes an economic security issue. An analyst can project what should be viewed in security terms, but what makes an economic issue an economic security issue is defined by whether a government behaves as if an economic issue is a security issue.

A nation will behave differently if it is pursuing an objective that it might like to have (it is unlikely that there are any inherent limitations to a nation's appetite), or if it is defending or pursuing a value or objective that it perceives it *must have* in order to preserve its present state of being. In the latter case, a threat to these values will evoke similar states of mind as do military threats—"we are being threatened by them"—and will compel a particular regime to act or to recognize that failure to act imposes high costs both to central values and to regime stability. Security issues have invariably involved a greater sense of urgency, more nationalistic sentiment, and more ethnocentrism than have issues of comparable magnitude in other issue areas. Thus, most economic security issues will be identified according to the manner in which nations deal with economic issues. The threat of a serious deprivation of economic welfare, as discussed earlier, is certainly the minimal component of economic security. Yet, economic interdependence has also spawned a welter of other issues that affect levels of national economic welfare and whose successful management, either on a national or international level, requires governmental intervention. To the extent that political elites or domestic publics perceive this, economic issues not limited to specific threats of economic deprivation may also be perceived and treated as security issues.

Types and Sources of Economic Threats

As was discussed above, it is the elite perception and the actual, even potential, behavior of a nation's domestic political system that determines whether or not an economic security problem exists. Economic interdependence by definition means that a national economy is sensitive to external forces. Whether a particular sensitivity is perceived and responded to as an economic threat will depend largely on the nature of the domestic political-economic system. This is why it is so important to discern which groups experience potential or actual harm. A threat to overall levels of national income may be ignored by a state, if elites controlling the political system benefit by the economic relationship (this is essentially the structure of exploitation described by dependency theorists). Conversely, external economic forces that promise generalized benefits may be viewed as economic threats, because they adversely affect the sectoral interests of politically important subgroups. Thus, threat recognition will be variable within and between states, reflecting the many different domestic structures and their changeable nature. We will return to this subject when discussing the various factors affecting a nation's capacity to cope with economic threats.

Following Klaus Knorr's analysis in Chapter 1, we can usefully differentiate among the following types of threats:

to income—the amount and distribution of income and wealth;

to stability—usually the levels of employment and inflation; denial to sources of supply, markets, capital, aid, technology, and so forth;

to economic sovereignty—defined by John A. Holsen and Jean L. Waelboeck as the "power to control a full range of policy instruments," states may well perceive economic security threats when their ability to influence national economic levels are undermined, even if there are no discernible economic losses.[17]

In practice, it is often difficult to discriminate among these types of economic threats, since they may all exist simultaneously in the same relationship; certainly the oil embargo involved all four types of threats to the heavily dependent oil-consuming nations. There are, however, other external forces whose effects do fall largely in one of the categories—for example, the effects of a specific export subsidy or a fall in the international price of a particular commodity.

It is also useful to differentiate between different sources of economic threats, although again it is often difficult to separate the effects of different sources in a concrete relationship. The principal sources of economic threats are:

governmental actors—national and international, intentional and unintentional acts;

non-governmental actors—principally multinational companies;

systemic factors—in the sense of the cumulative impact of the actions of many actors, including government, systemic threats would include the impact of international business cycle fluctuations on a particular nation (e.g., the impact of falling demand for export goods) or the impact of the flows of hot money in the Eurocurrency market on a nation's monetary policy.

73

Different coping mechanisms or strategies will be appropriate for different threats emerging from different sources, and a state's perception of the source and type of threat will be extremely important in determining the efficacy of its attempts to deal with a vulnerability. Frequently, a nation will attempt to blame one discrete actor (e.g., OPEC countries for domestic inflation or the U.S. for a series of offenses), when the influences are actually systemic in nature. Furthermore, it is difficult to differentiate between "external" threats and the effect of largely domestic conditions, since the international economic system often reflects or reacts to a state's domestic policy. For example, the recent fall in the price of a French franc (government officials estimate that a drop of 1% in the price of a French franc costs the economy $100–110 million since it increases inflation, and France has already saturated its export markets) has largely been caused by the market's response to France's inability to slow the wage-price spiral and bring inflation below 10%.[18] Although French officials tend to castigate the Eurocurrency market and particularly American MNCs, this "external" threat is more appropriately analyzed as the system's response to internal conditions. Economic interdependence has grown sufficiently so that clear delineations between domestic and foreign effects, as well as domestic and foreign policy itself, are impossible to make.

Interdependence and Vulnerability

Increasing interdependence and the concomitant erosion of the autonomy of national economies have clearly increased national vulnerability to external economic factors. Any attempts to classify states according to economic vulnerability, however, brings one directly to the question of the variable national ability to cope with external impacts. If a state has national means or can arrange for international coping mechanisms to deal with a potential vulnerability at relatively low cost, by definition that state is sensitive rather than vulnerable. Often this determination can be made only by examining the relative coping capability of all parties involved in a particular conflict. It is only after considering *the costs of utilizing different responses (including calculations for other actors as well) that one can make statements about a state's vulnerability to a particular economic threat*. (See Klaus Knorr's chapter on International Economic Leverage [Chapter 4] for a thorough analysis of the factors affecting the use of economic power.) Thus, measures of economic vulnerability—such as the ratio of imports to consumption for various commodities, the ratio of imported capital to domestic capital, the ratio of exports to production—represent some variable mixture of a nation's susceptibility to external impacts and its internal ability to reduce its potential weakness. In addition, a nation's ability to dissuade external actors from exploiting its economic vulnerability is also relevant for any comparisons of national vulnerability; a powerful country will be less vulnerable than a weak country, even if their economic positions are similar.

Thus, any discussion of national vulnerability will have two principal aspects: the varying economic capability of the relevant actors and the variable ability of nations to cope or respond to external economic forces. Clearly, the size and diversity of a nation's economy is a principal determinant; other things being equal, a country that has few natural resources will be more vulnerable than one that has many. But, of great significance is the varying ability of nations to create or allocate economic resources, shift patterns of economic activity, and the like, and this appears to be a function of the different domestic political-economic systems of nations, the subject to which we shall now turn.

Factors Affecting National Coping Capability

The difference between a state's economic sensitivity and its actual vulnerability depends upon its abilities to cope with sensitivities to external factors. The literature emerging after the oil embargo on how to cope with higher prices and uncertainty of supply indicates that the range and variety of coping mechanisms and strategies are virtually limitless. National coping mechanisms would include, among others, supply diversification, alteration of consumption and production patterns, the sacrifice of other economic goals (slower rates of growth mean lower rates of energy consumption), export promotion for the OPEC market, accomodations in foreign policy to satisfy or influence suppliers, and the creation of stockpiles. International coping mechanisms include the negotiation of common energy programs, creation of international stockpiles, agreement on commodity indexing, alterations in international economic institutions to allow new representation, as well as the creation of new monetary institutions to ensure recycling of petrodollars, and the like.

Richard N. Cooper provides a typology of governmental responses to increasing economic interdependence which is useful for categorizing coping mechanisms:

(1) a passive response—acceptance of loss of economic autonomy, because the costs of independence are too high and the benefits of dependence high;

(2) an exploitative response—a nation "attempts to take advantage of growing interdependence in ways which are successful if pursued by only a few countries, but which cannot be generalized for the world economy" (examples include special tax advantages or facilities for multinationals, flags of convenience, and so forth);

(3) a defensive response—nations attempt to reduce vulnerability by restoring economic autonomy and retarding economic interdepen-

dence (e.g., the use of currency controls to isolate the domestic monetary system, import and export restrictions);

(4) an aggressive response—a nation attempts "to extend national control to the mobile factors wherever they be" (extra-territorial extension of laws and regulations);

(5) a constructive or multilateral response—nations reduce their vulnerability by creating international responses which reduce or limit the consequences of their vulnerability.[19]

In terms of coping with economic capabilities, national coping mechanisms could be characterized as defensive (reducing sensitivity by internal adjustments) or aggressive (use of national capabilities to prevent external actors from exploiting vulnerabilities). In addition, international coping strategies could be characterized as "aggressive" (as in the creation of rival trading blocs which interact in a conflictual manner) or "cooperative" (the negotiation of mutually beneficial solutions in a multilateral framework).

What type of response a nation may choose will depend largely on its effective power capabilities (that is, its power sources and its ability to use them). A state with little power and a vulnerable economy will undoubtedly choose a relatively passive nationalistic response and a cooperative international strategy. Bergsten suggests a distinction among types of power that is relevant here: "negative power, based largely on the ability of a country to resist external pressure for changes in its own policies; veto power, through which a country can block efforts of others to achieve their own policy objectives, including systemic changes; and positive power, by which a country can compel others to change their own policy objectives."[20] Many states (such as China) really only have negative power with the attendant costs of foregone development and the benefits of national economic autonomy. The largest industrialized states, as well as the oil-rich nations, have effective veto power. Perhaps only the U.S., with respect to some issues, and the OPEC countries, with respect to one issue, have positive power. Again it must be stressed, however, that any analysis of the efficacy of national coping mechanisms must include an accounting of the cost distribution for all relevant actors.

Turning from the subject of coping mechanisms to that of the factors affecting the coping capability of nations, aside from the size, diversity, and technological level of the national economy, a nation's political-economic structure and a nation's social culture should be stressed as the two principal independent factors. An exhaustive attempt to characterize the world's economies is clearly beyond the scope of this chapter, but a few comments are certainly in order.

Little research has been done in the comparative analysis of the independent impact of a nation's political-economic system on a nation's performance. Peter J. Katzenstein, in a recent and important article, provides a comparative analysis of domestic structures in France and the United States (noting that many observers have characterized the two countries as having similar political and economic systems). He traces the differential impact of their domestic structures on foreign economic policies in three issue-areas. He finds that the society-centered policy network in the U.S. (weak, decentralized political system, pluralistic society with strong, independent units) makes "policies which are 'rational' in the sense of mutual adjustment and muddling through, and in the role they assign to private power." In contrast, the state-centered policy network in France (strong, centralized state in an atomistic and stalemate society) produces "policies which are 'rational' in the sense of comprehensive review and conscious planning, and in the emphasis they accord to public power."[21] Katzenstein finds the differences in performance particularly striking in the area of energy policy, with extensive French governmental involvement in the operation of French oil companies and promotion of national purposes, and a virtual abdication of power by the U.S. government to the oil companies with little consistent policy to promote public as opposed to private purposes.

While one may disagree with his paradigm of U.S. domestic structures, this kind of research is extremely important for determining the relative coping capabilities of states. The mechanisms for national economic planning vary widely in the large capitalist democracies, ranging from very little, if any, in the United States to indicative planning in France. The nature of government-business-labor relations varies greatly as well: the special government-business-domestic structure in Japan (company rather than trade labor unions, life-time employment, high debt-equity ratios with the government accepting the financial risk, the extensive network of formal and informal communication lines between business and government, and so forth) contrasts sharply with the more antagonistic nature of relations between the U.S. government, business, and labor organizations. Germany falls somewhere in between with its stress on voluntary agreements among government officials, central bankers, companies, and unions on income distribution.[22] These factors certainly influence a nation's coping capability in different, although not very predictable ways, since they reflect variations in the ability of a state to reallocate resources or shift patterns of economic activity. That these differences among industrialized, capitalist democracies are significant does not detract from the more sizable differences between market economies and planned economies, nor the significant differences among the capabilities of planned systems as well. Stephen Krasner pursues these questions further in Chapter 6, comparing the capabilities of command economies, LDCs, and various capitalist states.

In addition to the impact of domestic political-economic structures, the independent impact of a nation's social culture is also important. Certainly, much has been made of the differences in work ethics of various capitalist countries: then-Secretary of the Treasury Connally contrasted worker attitudes in Japan and Germany with those in the U.S. and called for a "renaissance of responsibility in this country . . . a resurgence of spirit, a rededication of will:"

> When you walk into the plants and see the assembly lines in Japan and Germany or any of these industrial nations and see what these people are doing, you see the manifest pride that they have. They are not working for just the buck in their pocket or to buy beer on Saturday night, they are working not only for themselves, they are working for Japan, they are working for Germany. They have a national pride in what they are doing.[23]

This is certainly difficult to operationalize, but it did contribute to the fact that in the 1960s, productivity in Germany grew twice as fast as in the U.S. and in Japan over three times as fast.[24] A nation's social and cultural heritage is reflected in many economically relevant forms. For example, rates of personal saving vary greatly (for 1965–72, they averaged 6.5% in the U.S., 19.1% in Japan, 13% in Germany, and 8.8% in the United Kingdom) as do the number of days lost to strikes each year (the ratio for Germany, U.K., and Italy is 1:5:20).[25] These kinds of factors affect a government's ability to obtain economic sacrifices from its citizens in any defensive nationalistic response to economic vulnerability and thus are important determinants of national coping capability.

Economic Vulnerability and Economic Power

As discussed earlier, measurement of nation-state vulnerability is complicated because economic statistics of necessity represent some aggregation of both the "objective" sensitivity of the society and the efforts, or lack thereof, of the society to cope with the sensitivity. Statistics implying a heavy mineral dependence, for example, could actually reflect a nation's efforts to stockpile or conserve its own supplies. Measurement of vulnerability is further complicated by two additional factors: interaction among different vulnerability measures and the simultaneous existence of both economic power and economic vulnerability in most economic relationships.

The first factor simply reflects the interconnectedness among different types of economic relations and the ability of states to form linkages around different issues. A state's potential vulnerability (e.g., dependence on raw material imports) may greatly exceed its actual vulnerability, because it has a diversified economy capable of earning considerable amounts of foreign exchange enabling it to alter domestic consumption patterns drastically. Or, again, a nation may prefer importing a material cheaply to producing it at

78

higher costs at home. In that case, its vulnerability is limited by the possibility of switching to somewhat higher domestic production. Moreover, that state will have considerable bargaining leverage if it, in turn, supplies imports that are needed by the raw material source, or if it represents a large market for other exports from the supplier. Thus, any general measure of overall vulnerability would involve weighing many different measures as well as making many complex judgments about the political capabilities of the involved actors.

Secondly, most economic relationships usually involve the simultaneous existence of both economic vulnerability and economic power for the involved actors—the precise balance depends on the relative costs in changing the relationship for the involved parties. Dependence on imported raw materials is a vulnerability, but it is also a source of economic power over an exporting country that may depend upon its foreign exchange earnings from the sale of raw materials to purchase necessary imports. The actual vulnerability of the importing nation will depend not only upon its own ability to cope with its dependence but also on the ability of the exporting nation to cope with *its* dependence.

There are many examples of this simultaneous existence of both economic power and economic vulnerability. A creditor has influence over a debtor but is also vulnerable to the possibilities of debtor default. The flow of petrodollars into the foreign branches of U.S. banks—between 1972 and 1975 the total assets and liabilities of American banks' foreign branches rose from $78 to $176 billion—proved both a source of power (in granting loans) and a potential vulnerability. In search for new investment outlets necessary to cover interest payments to the oil-rich nations, these banks have made many suspect loans, particularly to non-oil-producing developing countries such as Zaire, Peru, Argentina, and so on.[26] As Christensen's analysis of food power in Chapter 11 indicates, U.S. domination of world agricultural exports is often touted as a source of economic power, but its utility is affected by the costs to the U.S. of restricting food supply. Table 1 shows that the U.S. does dominate the export market but also that U.S. agriculture is quite dependent upon export markets. Although exports account for only about 15% of cash farm income (non-crop food production is almost all consumed domestically), it is estimated that between one-fourth and one-third of the land being cropped by U.S. farmers is for the export market.[27] Furthermore, the percentages represented by U.S. exports as a share of foreign consumption indicate less dependence on the part of importers than that of U.S. exporters. Other than Japan for some products (and Japan earns sufficient foreign exchange to buy elsewhere), the countries most dependent upon U.S. agricultural exports are the poorest countries, such as Bangladesh, for whom supply restriction would have political costs for the U.S. In the light of the domestic political power of U.S.

79

Table 1

	Wheat	Feedgrains	Oilseeds	Cotton
U.S. Exports as a Share of World Exports, 72–73	43.9%	43.9%	58.1%	27.4%
U.S. Exports as a Share of Foreign Consumption, 72–73	9.7	9.2	33.0	11.3
Share of U.S. Production Exported, 72–73	72.3	20.5	51.9	42.3

Source: *International Economic Report of the President*, Feb. 1974, pp. 54–55.

farmers—Presidential candidates Ford and Carter quickly foreswore any future export embargoes except in national emergencies—the costs to the U.S., which earns more than $20 billion in foreign agricultural exports, would seem to outweigh the advantages in any supply restrictions.

As a final example of the simultaneous existence of both economic power and economic vulnerability, U.S. direct investment abroad is often viewed as both a source of American influence (frequently cited as the main agent of American economic hegemony) and a potential vulnerability in the "hostages" that it provides other countries in the form of fixed assets which may be expropriated in some sense. U.S. direct investment abroad has grown rapidly from $31.9 billion in 1960 to $118.6 billion in 1974, and in 1970, sales of U.S.-owned foreign manufacturing affiliates totaled $76.8 billion, while U.S. exports of manufactured goods totaled only $29.3 billion.[28]

This investment imposes both costs and benefits on both host and home countries. While providing a source of considerable capital flows back to the U.S. (investment income receipts in 1974 totaled $17.7 billion), foreign earnings as a percentage of domestic profits have risen consistently since World War II, reaching 28% ($9.5 billion) in 1969.[29] American corporations, particularly the largest 75 which account for about 70% of all direct foreign investment, (IBM, Coca-Cola, and Xerox all derive at least half of their earnings from overseas operations) are certainly going to inhibit any governmental action which might interfere with this profit flow. In fact, they pressure the government for more liberalized rules governing capital flows, thus raising the possibility of the U.S. exporting more jobs from the U.S. From a broader perspective, Gilpin argues persuasively that the U.S. has overinvested abroad; that the balance of payments benefits do not compensate either for the costs to domestic capital formation or the distribution of income away from labor to capital.[30] For host countries, U.S. investments represent both intrusions into national economic autonomy and potential hostages. However, the hostages are usually too costly to capture. American investment represents capital, technology, and employment that all serve

80

the national economic policy objectives of the host country. In addition, U.S. MNCs account to an astonishing extent for both world export growth (69% of total export growth for 1966–70) and host nations' exports (in 1970, 42% of Canada's exports, 36% of Latin America's, and 10% of the EECs).[31] This investment relationship clearly contains both sources of power or leverage and potential vulnerabilities for both host and home country. The actual vulnerability for any particular country will depend upon the particular situation and on the opportunity costs attached to any rupture of the relationship (more will be said on investment relations later).

National Vulnerability

In the final section of this chapter, three aspects of economic vulnerability will be discussed: trade, investment, and finance in particular. As we shall see, in addition to the previously discussed problems of measuring vulnerability, there is a difficulty in disaggregating the date sufficiently. It was pointed out above that for many kinds of vulnerabilities there are corresponding strengths. The United States may appear vulnerable to OPEC decisions about the price of oil, but as an important buyer of oil, the U.S. also carries a good deal of weight, particularly in Venezuela. Below, we shall see that there are many kinds of vulnerabilities, and it is crucial to distinguish which are more important and under what conditions. Measurements of vulnerability must be evaluated with care. One can make fairly precise statements about vulnerabilities with respect to raw materials, agricultural exports, or financial pressures, but it is more difficult to make general statements ranking states by overall vulnerability.

Trade Relations

The most frequently mentioned measure of vulnerability, and a measure of economic interdependence as well, is the proportion of a state's GNP represented by exports and imports. Growth in the proportion of a nation's production devoted to exports increases the proportion of the labor force dependent on export markets, thus making domestic welfare and employment more vulnerable to changes abroad. Under such conditions, market access becomes a question of importance in national policy. Equally, economic slumps abroad may spread to the home economy as foreigners cut back on their consumption. Because so many of their exports go to the United States, Canada and Mexico find themselves in an endangered position when economic activity in the United States slows down.

Obviously, the problem of export ratios works in two directions. My exports are your imports. High export ratios may also indicate the extent to which *importing* nations are dependent upon the exporters for vital resources. No nation wishes to find itself subject to the leverage of its suppliers. For this reason, many countries make efforts to diversify their

Table 2

World Gross National Product, Exports, Imports

(in billions of U.S. dollars)

	1960					1970					1975				
	GNP	Ex's	(% GNP)	Im's	(% GNP)	GNP	Ex's	(% GNP)	Im's	(% GNP)	GNP	Ex's	(% GNP)	Im's	(% GNP)
United States	506	20.6	(4.1)	16.3	(3.2)	982	43.2	(4.4)	42.4	(4.3)	1,499	107.7	(7.2)	103.4	(6.9)
Canada	36	5.8	(16.1)	6.2	(17.2)	80	16.8	(21.0)	14.4	(18.0)	154	32.2	(20.9)	35.4	(23.0)
Japan	39	4.2	(10.8)	4.5	(11.5)	197	19.3	(9.8)	18.9	(9.6)	556	54.6	(9.8)	52.5	(9.4)
United Kingdom	71	10.2	(14.4)	12.6	(17.8)	121	19.4	(16.0)	21.7	(17.9)	224	41.4	(18.5)	53.3	(23.8)
West Germany	70	11.4	(16.3)	10.1	(14.4)	186	34.2	(18.4)	29.8	(16.0)	411	90.1	(21.9)	74.7	(18.3)

Source: *International Economic Report of the President*, March 1976, pp. 137, 146, 147.

Table 3
Exports in Relationship to Production*

	1950	1960	1972
United States	9.1	11.6	14.4
Japan	20.7	30.3	31.9
West Germany	17.3	31.7	41.8
United Kingdom	42.9	37.9	46.1
Canada	42.5	43.0	71.3

* Including agriculture, forestry, fishing, mining, quarrying, and manufacturing.
Source: *International Economic Report of the President*, February 1974, p. 5.

supply sources, even at the cost of higher prices. In some cases not much diversification is possible—the accidents of geography did not distribute resources evenly across the earth. And, even for the most self-sufficient countries, the costs of reducing vulnerabilities beyond a certain point are high. The example of modern China shows that a large country with a good range of natural resources can choose to avoid trade almost altogether, but it does so at the cost of doing without many goods available abroad and accepting a slower growth rate. What information we have from The People's Republic indicates that the government itself has been carrying on a long internal argument about the wisdom of maintaining China's position of autarky.

The ideal position for a state to be in with regard to trade vulnerabilities would be for the trade it carries on to be relatively unimportant to the domestic economy while at the same time to be relatively important to its trading partners. That way the trading partners will not be able to affect the functioning of the economy seriously, and the home state's bargaining power will be strong. We can observe in Table 2 how some countries stand in terms of their dependence on trade. The U.S. depends less on trade than the other states, even though American exports and imports are the world's highest in absolute terms. By this crude measure, it would appear that the United States approaches the ideal position of relatively limited dependence and relatively large importance to others. Yet, since 1960, exports and imports have grown in relation to the American economy as a whole, with most of the growth since 1970. This trend toward increasing trade applies equally to the European countries and Canada. Only Japan decreased her trade dependence after 1960.

While Table 2 provides a gross measure of the vulnerabilities involved, more refined statements about national security require additional disaggregation. On the export side, the figures do not reveal the extent to which specific industries are dependent upon foreign markets. In addition,

Table 4

| | Composition of U.S. Trade, 1975 | | | U.S. Trading Partners, 1975 | |
	Exports	Imports		Exports	Imports
Agric. goods	21%	10%	Canada	20%	23%
Raw materials			European Comm.	21%	17%
(non-agric.)	5%	7%	Japan	9%	12%
Fuel	4%	28%	Other develop.	10%	6%
Capital Goods	43%	24%	OPEC	10%	18%
Other mfgs.	27%	31%	Other Less		
			Develop.	27%	23%
			Communist	3%	1%

Source: *International Economic Report of the President*, March 1976, pp. 26–27.

the use of the GNP as the base of our analysis is somewhat misleading. GNP includes government expenditures, income on foreign investment, and service industry income, none of which are directly affected by foreign trade. In Table 3, exports are related instead to domestic production totals (that is, GNP minus government expenditures and income from services). Here is appears that Japan and Canada are even more dependent on external trade than Table 2 had indicated. The United States and other European countries, meanwhile, appear to remain in the same relation as they did in Table 2. Yet, even the relative insensitivity of the U.S. may understate the political importance of export markets (as in the example of U.S. agricultural markets). It is estimated that currently two million Americans depend upon export production for employment.[32] While it is true that this represents only 2% of the labor force, this does not remove its importance to any administration.

The natural question which follows is "trade with whom?" A high level of exports to a friendly ally surely creates less vulnerability than extensive relationships with unfriendly states. Western European countries clearly differentiate between intra-EEC trade, U.S.-EEC trade, Japan-EEC trade, and East European-EEC trade. Even though the security aspects of these relationships vary, the most salient feature in conflictual terms would appear to be the magnitude of trade deficits. Japanese trade surpluses with Europe have increased rapidly from about $300 million in 1970 to approximately $4 billion in 1976.[33] Currently, Japan is under heavy pressure from her trading partners to reduce her exports and desist from anticompetitive practices (principally "dumping" goods abroad or extensive government subsidies to export-oriented industries such as ship-building) or risk a trade war. At this time, Japan has made some unilateral concessions with respect

84

Table 5

Energy Sources, 1973[1]

[In percent]

Country	Domestic					Total imported	Imported			
	Total domestic	Coal	Natural gas	Crude oil	Hydro and nuclear		Coal	Arab oil	Non-Arab oil	Other
United States	83	18	31	29	5	17	—	4	13	Negl.
Japan	10	4	1	Negl.	5	90	12	34	44	Negl.
European Community	40	23	12	1	4	60	Negl.	42	18	Negl.
United Kingdom	53	38	11	Negl.	4	47	—	30	16	1
France	23	11	4	1	7	77	6	53	12	6
West Germany	41	30	6	2	3	59	—	38	15	6
Italy	17	Negl.	10	Negl.	7	83	6	60	16	1

[1] Based on metric tons coal equivalent.

Table 6
World Oil Trade and Consumption[1]
[Thousand barrels/day and percent of consumption]

	Total consumption	Total imports	Origin of imports — Arab countries — Total Arab	Saudi Arabia	Kuwait	Libya	Iraq	Abu Dhabi	Algeria	Other Arab	Iran	Venezuela	Indonesia	Canada	Nigeria	Others
1973																
Total	58,000	33,000	17,850	7,500	3,000	2,100	1,800	1,300	1,000	1,150	5,600	3,100	1,200	1,100	1,900	2,250
Percent	100.0	56.9	30.8	12.9	5.2	3.6	3.1	2.2	1.7	2.0	9.7	5.3	2.1	1.9	3.3	3.9
United States	17,300	6,200	1,590	590	160	350	50	160	140	140	420	1,810	250	1,100	550	450
Percent	100.0	35.8	9.2	3.4	0.9	3.0	0.3	0.9	0.8	0.8	2.4	10.6	1.4	6.4	3.2	2.6
Western Europe	15,400	15,200	10,000	4,000	1,750	1,500	1,220	600	670	770	1,900	410	Negl.	Negl.	1,130	1,130
Percent	100.0	98.7	68.8	26.0	11.4	10.3	7.9	3.9	4.4	5.0	12.3	2.9	Negl.	Negl.	7.3	7.3
Japan	5,400	5,400	2,390	1,240	540	20	Negl.	430	—	160	1,730	10	840	—	100	330
Percent	100.0	100.0	44.3	23.0	10.0	0.4	Negl.	8.0	—	3.0	32.0	0.2	15.6	—	1.9	6.1
Canada	1,800	1,000	220	80	Negl.	40	20	60	—	20	180	470	Negl.	—	80	50
Percent	100.0	55.6	12.2	4.4	Negl.	2.2	1.1	3.3	—	1.1	10.0	26.1	Negl.	—	4.4	2.8
Communist area	9,100	500	400	—	—	100	200	Negl.	50	50	100	—	—	—	—	—
Percent	100.0	5.5	4.4	—	—	1.1	2.2	Negl.	0.5	0.5	1.1	—	—	—	—	—
Others	9,000	4,700	2,650	1,590	550	Negl.	310	50	140	10	1,270	310	110	—	40	290
Percent	100.0	52.2	29.4	17.7	6.1	Negl.	3.4	0.6	1.6	0.1	14.1	3.8	1.2	—	0.4	3.2

[1] This table allocates imports on a direct and indirect basis—i.e. refined products from export refineries are traced to the source of the crude oil.
Source: *International Economic Report of the President*, March 1975, pp. 154-55.

Table 7
Dependence on Selected Imported Industrial Raw Materials, 1974
[Imports as a percent of consumption]

	United States	European Community	Japan		United States	European Community	Japan
Aluminum (ore and				Manganese	98	99	87
metal)	88	31	93	Natural rubber	100	100	100
Chromium	90	100	90	Nickel	72	100	100
Cobalt	99	100	100	Phosphates	(^{1})	100	100
Copper	20	76	93	Tin	92	87	90
Iron (ore and metal)	17	59	100	Tungsten	64	100	100
Lead	19	70	67	Zinc	59	73	74

^{1} Net exporter.
Source: *International Economic Report of the President*, March 1975, pp. 154–55.

to television and steel exports as well as shipbuilding. But, negotiations are far from over.

Thus, precise statements about the effective vulnerability of a state with respect to overseas markets requires further disaggregation to permit some estimates of the bilateral relationships that exist. Table 4 presents a more detailed picture of U.S. exposure to external forces by identifying the composition and sources of U.S. exports and imports.

A more definitive statement about actual vulnerability would require even more information; in particular, an industry breakdown of the percentage of production exported and where it is exported as well as the importance of this production for the importing country (proportion of U.S. imports to amount consumed, alternative sources, and so on). In addition to these aspects affecting the bilateral bargaining relationships with respect to a particular product area, we would still have to know how important economically and politically each product would be. How crucial are the exporters (or importers) to government support, and how crucial are those exports (or imports) to domestic production? In France, for instance, foreign sales of military items play a determining role in the cost of weapons production. Therefore, for France to be able to include certain weapons in her own inventory, she must also find buyers abroad. Thus, the implications for national vulnerability stemming from any potential export dependence are many, and any overall gauge of national vulnerability must aggregate these implications for all the separate relationships.

On the import side, there is considerably more information about the exact nature of particular vulnerabilities with respect to specific com-

Table 8
Sources of U.S. Imports of Industrial Raw Materials, 1974
[Percent of total]

	Developed					Less developed		
	Canada	Australia, New Zealand	South Africa, Rhodesia	Other	Africa	Latin American	Other	Communist
Aluminum (ore and metal)	8	18	Negl.	1	8	65	Negl.	Negl.
Chromium	—	—	44	5	—	1	26	24
Cobalt	1	—	—	51	48	—	—	—
Columbium	2	—	—	2	5	88	3	—
Copper	25	Negl.	6	18	1	44	3	3
Fluorspar	Negl.	—	Negl.	17	3	80	—	—
Iron (ore, metal, and scrap)	42	2	—	1	6	49	—	Negl.
Lead	29	10	—	—	4	57	Negl.	Negl.
Manganese	1	12	14	19	22	23	2	7
Mercury	33	—	—	15	20	23	1	8
Natural rubber	—	—	—	—	12	—	88	—
Nickel	58	11	3	15	—	8	Negl.	5
Platinum group	2	Negl.	31	35[1]	Negl.	1	Negl.	31
Tin	Negl.	1	—	5	1	18	68	7
Titanium[2]	38	51	—	7	1	1	3	1
Tungsten	15	—	1	19	5	37	20	3
Vanadium	—	—	51	14	—	21	—	14
Zinc	52	6	Negl.	19	3	17	Negl.	3

[1] Includes materials from South Africa, Canada, and the U.S.S.R. refined in the United Kingdom.

[2] Rutile, ilmenite, slag, and sponge.

Source: *International Economic Report of the President*, March 1975, pp. 154–55.

modities. Tables 5, 6, 7, and 8 on the next pages reveal useful information about relative dependencies on imported fuels and minerals. The two important factors in assessing vulnerability are: the proportion imported in relation to domestic consumption and the diversity of supply sources. The U.S. appears far less vulnerable than European countries and Japan (but more so than "communist areas") in most respects; Japan's supply sources are more diversified than Europe's, and so forth.

As with exports, precise statements about overall vulnerability are difficult to make. Is the U.S. more vulnerable with respect to aluminum, which it buys mostly in the somewhat unstable Caribbean (but in amounts difficult

Table 9

Economic and Export Growth in Less
Developed Countries, 1960–69

	Average Rate of Growth			
	8% or more	6–7%	5%	4% or less
Average Annual Export Growth	18%	8%	4%	3%

Source: Peter G. Peterson, "U.S. in the Changing World Economy—Volume II: Statistical Background Material," Dec. 1971, pp. 53–55.

to stockpile) or with respect to chromium, which it buys in South Africa, Rhodesia, and even from communist countries (25%)? The case of chromium is particularly illustrative with the recent repeal of the Byrd Amendment (which lifted the ban on Rhodesian chrome as long as the U.S. imported chrome from the Soviet Union). Although it stockpiles a considerable amount of chrome, the U.S. imports virtually all of its current consumption but has greatly reduced its dependence on Rhodesia (from whom it once imported half of its consumption). Advances in technology (which permit increased smelting of high-grade ore from low-grade ore rather than importing high-grade ore from Rhodesia, which has two-thirds of the world's reserves of metallurgical-grade ore) and expansion of the mining and smelting capacity of Brazil, Turkey, and South Africa has permitted the U.S. to decrease its dependency on Rhodesia greatly (importing in 1976 only 19% of high-grade and 2.7% of low-grade ore) and the Soviet Union (imports in 1976 dropped about 45%).[34] The U.S., however, may have simply traded one politically costly dependency for another: U.S. imports from South Africa increased about 40%. In the case of chrome, the U.S. has maintained the same general dependency (it imports all it consumes), but the character of the dependency as well as its political implications have changed. The United States is more free to put direct pressure on Rhodesia (witness the repeal of the Byrd Amendment) but less able to apply indirect pressure; that is, influencing South Africa to put direct pressure on Rhodesia. The existence of chromium stockpiles, of course, reduces the immediate consequences of U.S. vulnerability.

Further complicating the problem of assessing precise vulnerability with respect to imports is the lack of knowledge about which materials and commodities will prove most necessary. It is dangerous to predict the next crisis from the last. Natural rubber used to be a strategic good but can now be replaced. No one has either found a substitute for coffee or insisted that coffee is a strategic import, yet, to date, demand for coffee appears to be as inelastic as that for other presumably more vital goods. There are, however,

89

strategic goods which can only be replaced at high cost and which are controlled by a few suppliers. The oil crisis of 1973–74 brought this point forcefully home.

We have been discussing trade relations within a national security context which stresses the dangers of vulnerability to one's enemies or susceptibility to external pressures through economic relations. Trade relations, as well as investment and financial relations, which will be discussed shortly, also affect diffuse national goals like welfare, employment, and growth. States often seek export growth to enhance the overall rate of growth in the domestic economy. In some countries, achieving economic growth may be a prerequisite for social or governmental stability. Economic well-being does much to bolster regime support, and for many countries trade lies at the heart of economic concerns. For some countries, exports may contribute to GNP expansion and employment. For others, exports may provide foreign exchange earnings for the purchase of essential capital goods or raw materials needed for development. In the last analysis, providing these collective goods may be critical to government survival.

Both developed and lesser developed countries seek exports to achieve positive domestic effects—even at the cost of increasing strategic vulnerabilities to foreign markets. The statistical effects of increased exports can be dramatic. Even for the U.S., which as we have seen is relatively less vulnerable with respect to export markets, export growth is terribly important. Marina Whitman noted that export growth from the fourth quarter of 1972 to the fourth quarter of 1973 accounted for 38% of the total increase in real GNP for that period.[35]

In economic terms, the connection between growing exports and a robust domestic economy is somewhat complex. If imports also rise, the stimulus will be less. If export prices are falling, the increased sales might bring a low return to the country. But whatever the *causal* effects, most countries, especially less developed countries, think that exports will help them escape the cycle of poverty. It is true that the fastest growing LDCs also experience the fastest growing exports, as can be clearly seen in Table 9. Countries which have grown by 8% or more a year have had export growth of 18% on the average.

Table 10 shows, however, while exports may be helpful, they are not a simple answer to development. Brazil, with the second highest growth rate in GNP, exports a relatively small proportion of its products. Chile, with a high export/GNP ratio, experienced a negative rate of growth. Thus, growing exports may help stimulate growth, but export dependence or a constant high export level simply tends to create dependence. Table 11 also shows that those countries which have managed to raise per capita income above $375 have somewhat lower dependence on exports and somewhat lower export growth rates than those with per capita incomes between $200 and

Table 10

An Overview of the 10 Largest Economies in Latin America

Country	1975 GNP Bil. $	Average Annual Real Growth 1971–5 (%)	1975 Inflation (%)	1975 Exports Bil. $	(% GNP)	Foreign Public Debt at yearend 1975 (Bil. $)	(% Exports)	Principal Exports
Brazil	$100	9.3%	31%	$ 8.7	(8.7%)	$12.0	(138%)	Soybeans, coffee, iron ore, mfg. products
Mexico	78.7	5.6	17	3.4	(4.3%)	10.2	(300%)	Oil, sugar, minerals, steel, mfg. products
Argentina	37	3.2	184	3.0	(8.1%)	4.0	(133%)	Grains, meat
Venezuela	27	4.7	8	11.2	(42%)	0.4	(3.6%)	Oil, iron ore
Colombia	12.7	6.5	24	1.7	(13.4%)	2.5	(147%)	Coffee, cotton, textiles
Peru	8.8	6.0	23	1.4	(15.9%)	2.6	(186%)	Minerals, fishmeal
Chile	6.8	–1.4	375	1.5	(22.1%)	5.0	(333%)	Copper, agricultural products, cellulose
Ecuador	4.3	8.0	16	1.0	(23.3%)	0.4	(40%)	Oil, bananas
Dominican Republic	3.8	9.9	14	0.9	(23.7%)	0.5	(55.5%)	Sugar, bauxite
Guatemala	3.6	5.5	18	0.6	(10.9%)	0.2	(33.3%)	Coffee, sugar, cotton, bananas

Source: *Business Week*, 9 August 1976, pp. 34–35.

$375. The poorest countries, on the other hand, have neither high exports nor high export growth rates. They tend to be import-dependent as well. Considering the general lack of economic leverage possessed by non-oil exporting nations, there is little the poorest developing countries can do in terms of coping with their vulnerability, even through export-oriented growth.

Investment Relations

Earlier we discussed U.S. direct foreign investment as a case of the simultaneous existence of both economic vulnerability (as hostages to be threatened by host countries) and economic power (as leverage stemming from the benefits conferred on host countries). The actual vulnerability of either the investing or host country depends on the costs involved in the rupture of the relationship. Examination of Table 12 reveals the extent to which the United States tends to invest rather than export (only the United Kingdom, with its past history of economic dominance, and Switzerland even approach the U.S.) and the U.S. domination of world foreign direct investment.

As mentioned earlier, foreign earnings as a percent of total corporate earnings have been steadily increasing (reaching 28% in 1969), and for many of the largest corporations, foreign earnings account for half or more of total earnings. While Gilpin argues persuasively that in the long run the United States has been harmed by overinvestment abroad, it is certainly clear that in the short run the United States has very high stakes in maintaining its present investment.[36]

While direct foreign investment in the U.S. is growing over twice as fast as U.S. direct foreign investment, U.S. investments abroad outstripped foreign direct investment in the U.S. by a ratio of five to one (approximately $127 billion to $25 billion in 1975).[37]

Yet, this potential vulnerability of the U.S. is extremely costly to exploit. The Senate Committee on Finance analyzed the impact of U.S. MNCs on the economies of the principal host countries (the eight countries below account for about two-thirds of all U.S. D.F.I.) and, as Table 13 indicates, U.S. direct foreign investment accounts for a major share of total capital formation. The Committee report goes on to conclude:

> In the absence of the Americans, these countries might be hard-pressed to maintain capital formation at "normal" rates consistent with the pace of economic growth to which they have become accustomed. Furthermore, the sectoral distribution of U.S. affiliates' capital spending—which is concentrated in the more dynamic industrial branches—suggests (but does not prove) that the affiliates' input may be an important, perhaps indispensable, source of change and innovation in the key industries of these countries.[38]

92

Table 11
Principal Economic Characteristics of Three Groups
of Developing Countries,[a] 1968–72

Group of countries	1972 population as percentage of total	Average annual percentage growth of GDP 1968–72	Exports as percentage of GDP in 1972	Average annual growth of exports,[b] 1968–72, in percentage	Outstanding public debt per capita, 31 December 1972, in dollars
Oil-exporting countries	15.8	9.6	26.9	5.0	62
Other minerals exporters	3.7	4.8	21.9	4.6	119
Other developing countries according to per capita income:					
Above $375	21.2	7.1	11.1	7.5	94
$200–$375	9.3	6.6	19.9	10.2	95
Below $200	50.0	3.5	6.7	1.8	25
Total or average	100.0	6.2	14.2	6.4	55

Source: IBRD staff studies.

[a] Data by group of countries in this and subsequent tables are based on a sample of forty-seven countries: the sample countries in each group, taken together, represent 90 percent or more of the entire group when it is measured according to population, GNP, capital inflows, and indebtedness. The number of sample countries in each group is given in parentheses.

Oil-exporting countries (7): Iran, Iraq, Venezuela, Nigeria, Algeria, Ecuador, Indonesia.

Other minerals exporters (7): Chile, Bolivia, Jamaica, Liberia, Morocco, Zaire, Zambia.

Countries with per capita income above $375 (12): Greece, Tunisia, Yugoslavia, Argentina, Brazil, Colombia, Dominican Republic, Guatemala, Mexico, Peru, Uruguay, Malaysia.

Countries with per capita income between $200 and $375 (11): Egypt, Syria, Turkey, Korea, Philippines, Thailand, Cameroon, Ghana, Ivory Coast, Senegal, Sierra Leone.

Countries with per capita income below $200 (10): Ethiopia, Kenya, Mali, Sudan, Tanzania, Uganda, Bangladesh, India, Pakistan, Sri Lanka.

[b] In constant 1967–69 prices.

Source: Wouter Tims, "The Developing Countries" in Edward R. Fried and Charles L. Schultz, eds. *Higher Oil Prices and the World Economy: The Adjustment Problem* (Washington, D.C.: The Brookings Institution, 1975), p. 176.

The rather significant extent to which U.S. investments account for domestic capital formation in these countries suggests that their vulnerability (in terms of potential losses in growth and employment) might exceed U.S. vulnerability (in terms of losses to particular firms). Clearly this is not always the case; host countries' control of raw materials, particularly oil, has frequently led them to "capture the hostage" of U.S. foreign investments, since their control over supply dissuades effective reprisals. Thus, as was the

93

Table 12
Major Countries' International Production and Exports, 1971
[Millions of dollars]

	Stock of Foreign Direct Investment (Book Value)	Estimated International Production	Exports	International Production as Percentage of Exports
United States	86,000	172,000	43,492	395.5
United Kingdom	24,020	48,000	22,367	214.6
France	9,540	19,100	20,420	93.5
Federal Republic of Germany	7,270	14,600	39,040	37.4
Switzerland	6,760	13,500	5,728	235.7
Canada	5,930	11,900	17,582	67.7
Japan	4,480	9,000	24,019	37.5
Netherlands	3,580	7,200	13,927	51.7
Sweden	3,450	6,900	7,465	92.4
Italy	3,350	6,700	15,111	44.3
Belgium	3,250	6,500	12,392	52.4
Australia	610	1,200	5,070	23.7
Portugal	320	600	1,052	57.0
Denmark	310	600	3,685	16.3
Norway	90	200	2,563	7.8
Austria	40	100	3,169	3.2
Total of above	159,000	318,000	237,082	133.7
Other market economies	6,000	12,000	74,818	16.0
Total	165,000	330,000	311,900	105.8

Source: United Nations, Department of Economic and Social Affairs, *Multinational Corporations in World Development* (New York, 1973), p. 159.

Source: Robert Gilpin, *U.S. Power and the Multinational Corporation: The Political Economy of Foreign Direct Investment* (New York: Basic Books, Inc.), p. 15.

case with trade relations, many factors affect the actual vulnerabilities of the various actors in any relationship, and it is only through the careful examination of cost and benefit distribution that any meaningful statements about vulnerability are possible.

Financial Vulnerability

When turning to the question of financial vulnerability, it is clear that financial relationships both affect and stem from trade and investment relationships. Currency devaluations and revaluations are of utmost importance to any country. In the case of France above but also in Italy and the U.K., falling currency values usually reflect an inability to control domestic inflation. Yet, depreciation may cause increases in import bills thereby exacer-

94

Table 13
Plant and Equipment Spending by MNCs as Percent
of Gross Fixed Capital Formation

Industry Description	United King-dom	France	W. Germany	Belgium-Luxem-bourg	Canada	Mexico	Brazil
All Manufacturing	20.9	5.8	12.3	14.1	32.2	9.3	18.3
Food	4.4	0.9	2.0	n.a.	23.5	3.1	11.1
Chemicals	17.9	2.1	10.4	24.9	68.1	10.7	27.4
Primary and Fabricated Mat.	21.1	1.0	8.4			8.3	11.9
Machinery	29.0	23.3	27.8	12.0	57.8	13.9	57.1
Transportation Equipment	45.5	9.8	27.8			17.9	25.6
All Other Mfg.	18.2	2.8	2.7	10.8	20.5	13.0	5.9

Source: "Implications of Multinational Firms for World Trade and Investment and for U.S. Trade and Labor," *Report to the Committee on Finance of the U.S. Senate*, Feb. 1973, p. 411.

bating inflation, and often because of market saturation, depreciation does not stimulate concomitant increase in exports. Both West Germany, in the somewhat truncated European float, and Japan, particularly with respect to the dollar, resist currency revaluations because of the impact on domestic employment through export curtailment. In fact, West Germany's successful management of domestic inflation invites external inflationary pressure, since the mark is strengthened and inflation is imported through the additional demand for marks. As Janet Kelly demonstrates in Chapter 9, however, West Germany gained leverage through her strong position in the international monetary system.

The financial vulnerability implicit in a weak currency often increases national dependence on external actors: the United Kingdom, in its attempt to bolster a steadily weakening pound, has had to obtain both additional IMF loans and a "safety net" of $3 billion worth of credit through the Bank of International Settlements (pledged by the major central bankers, the U.S. contributing $1 billion). The United Kingdom, however, was particularly vulnerable to external currency pressures because of the pound's former role as a reserve currency. Britain's domestic inflation was increased by the instability stemming from foreign holdings of sterling; in 1975–76, they dropped from $7 to $4 billion as the pound lost almost 40% of its value.[39]

In addition to varying degrees of vulnerability with respect to currency values, another measure of financial vulnerability is found in assessing na-

95

tional indebtedness, particularly for less developed countries. Table 10 provided one measure of financial vulnerability for the Latin American countries by calculating public debt owed to foreigners as a percentage of exports. We compare debt to exports since countries must use earnings of foreign exchange from exports to pay off their foreign debts. The contrast between oil-rich Venezuela (3.6%), Mexico (300%), Peru (186%), and Chile (333%) is quite startling. In fact, Peru, which was unable to make $318 million in interest payments in early 1976 and wanted to avoid the stringent economic conditions involved in an IMF loan, went to a consortium of New York banks and found that it had first to adopt a new stabilization program before the loan would be considered.[40] The intrusion into national economic sovereignty was completed, when it was announced that the private loans would be monitored in the same fashion as are the IMF loans.

The financial vulnerability of the LDCs is often counteracted, however, by the vulnerability of the lending agents. Between 1970 and 1976, the debt of LDCs tripled to a total of $250 billion (largely as a result of financing inflating fuel and commodity bills). At the same time, the portion of debt held by commercial banks has increased eightfold to $100 billion (part of the recycling of petrodollars) with U.S. banks holding over half of it. This overexposure by the banks has made loan foreclosure difficult, and a number of "debt renegotiations" have occurred (e.g., Zaire, Peru, and Indonesia).

Again, as was the case with trade and investment relationships, precise statements about financial vulnerability demand a careful analysis of the costs involved in any change in the relationship. Moreover, no particular relationship exists in isolation and must be examined in the context of the entire web of trade, investment, and financial relationships.

Summary

This chapter has argued that increasing economic interdependence and the increased politicization of economic issues has created a new range of economic vulnerabilities for nation-states. It has also discussed a number of different types of vulnerabilities and the manner in which they interact. These vulnerabilities may often be perceived by governmental elites and domestic publics as security threats, because of the magnitude of their impact upon national and sectoral conditions. Whether they do so or not depends upon the particular circumstance involved. Domestic political-economic structures largely determine the nature of economic vulnerability, the types of vulnerabilities that will be perceived as economic security issues, and the ability of a nation to cope or respond to an economic security threat.

Footnotes

1. The author wishes to thank all the contributors to this volume for their suggestions, for this was truly a collective project, but special thanks are due to Janet Kelly and, of course, the editors.
2. See C. Fred Bergsten, "The Future of the International Economic Order: An Agenda for Research," and Robert O. Keohane and Joseph S. Nye, "World Politics and the International Economic System," in *The Future of the International Economic Order: An Agenda for Research*, ed. C. Fred Bergsten (Lexington, Mass.: Lexington Books, 1973); Bergsten, Keohane and Nye, "International Economics and International Politics: A Framework for Analysis," and Lawrence B. Krause and Nye, "Reflections on the Economics and Politics of International Economic Organizations," in *World Politics and International Economics*, ed. C. Fred Bergsten and Lawrence B. Krause (Washington, D.C.: The Brookings Institution, 1975).
3. Assar Lindbeck, "Research on Internal Adjustment to External Disturbances: A European View," in Bergsten, *Future*, p. 62.
4. As Klaus Knorr points out in Chapter 1, there have always been politicized economic issues with some interest groups seeking the political resolution of "economic" issues. What is notable now, however, is the tremendous increase in the number of segments of society involved—particularly in capitalist democratic societies—and in the number of such issues.
5. See Richard Rosecrance and Arthur Stein, "Interdependence: Myth or Reality?" *World Politics*, XXVI, *1* (October 1973), and Peter J. Katzenstein, "International Interdependence: Some Long-Term Trends and Recent Changes," *International Organization*, XXIX, *4* (Autumn 1975) for a fairly conclusive demonstration of the validity of this observation.
6. Peter J. Katzenstein, "International Relations and Domestic Structures: Foreign Economic Policies of Advanced Industrial States," *International Organization*, XXX, *1* (Winter 1976).
7. Bergsten, "Future," p. 5.
8. See Franklyn D. Holzman and Robert Legvold, "The Economics and Politics of East-West Relations," in Bergsten and Krause, *World Politics*, for a good analysis of this issue.
9. Warner J. Feld, "Atlantic Interdependence and Competition for Raw Materials in the Third World" (paper presented at the ISA Convention, Toronto, February 1976), p. 21.
10. Robert B. Krueger, *The United States and International Oil: A Report for the Federal Energy Administration on U.S. Firms and Government Policy* (New York: Praeger Publishers, 1975), p. 92.
11. Frank N. Trager and Frank L. Simonie, "An Introduction to the Study of National Security," in *National Security and American Society: Theory, Process and Policy*, ed. Frank N. Trager and Philip S. Kronenberg (Lawrence, Kansas: University Press of Kansas, 1973), p. 36.
12. Krause and Nye, "Reflections," p. 330.
13. Ibid.
14. Krause and Nye, "Reflections," pp. 330–31.
15. Philip Connelly and Robert Perlman, *The Politics of Scarcity: Resource Conflicts in International Relations* (London: Oxford University Press, 1975), p. 103.
16. See, in particular, Krueger, *U.S. and International Oil*, and Edward R. Fried and Charles L. Schultz, eds., *Higher Oil Prices and the World Economy: The Adjustment Problem* (Washington, D.C.: The Brookings Institution, 1975) as well as innumerable articles in *Foreign Affairs* and *Foreign Policy*.
17. John A. Holsen and Jean L. Waelbroeck, "The Less Developed Countries and the International Monetary Mechanism," *Proceedings of the American Economic Association*, LXVI, *2* (May 1976): p. 172.
18. *New York Times*, 14 August 1976, pp. 26–27.

19. Richard N. Cooper, "Economic Interdependence and Foreign Policy in the Seventies," *World Politics*, XXIV, 2 (Jan. 1972): 168–70.

20. Bergsten, "Future," p. 32.

21. Katzenstein, "Domestic Structures," p. 20.

22. Peter G. Peterson, *U.S. in the Changing World Economy*, Volume II: *Statistical Background Material* (Washington, D.C.: Government Printing Office: Dec. 1971), pp. 57–73; *Business Week*, 26 July 1976, pp. 62–68; *New York Times*, 22 July 1976, pp. 1, 4.

23. Keohane and Nye, "World Politics," pp. 138–39.

24. Robert Gilpin, *U.S. Power and the Multinational Corporation: The Political Economy of Foreign Direct Investment* (New York: Basic Books, Inc., 1975), p. 196.

25. *International Economic Report of the President, March 1976* (Washington, D.C.: Government Printing Office, 1976), p. 5; *New York Times*, 14 May 1976, p. 16.

26. *New York Times*, 5 July 1976, pp. 24, 25.

27. *International Economic Report of the President, Feb. 1974* (Washington, D.C.: Government Printing Office, 1974), p. 53.

28. Peterson, *Changing World Economy*, p. 47.

29. Rosecrance and Stein, "Interdependence," p. 26; *International Report*, 1976, p. 165.

30. See Gilpin, *U.S. Power*, particularly Chapter 7.

31. U.S., Congress, Senate, Senate Finance Committee, "Implications of Multinational Firms for World Trade and Investment and for U.S. Trade and Labor," Feb. 1973, p. 354.

32. Marina v. N. Whitman, "The Current and Future Role of the Dollar: How Much Symmetry?" *Brookings Papers on Economic Activity*, 3 (1974):553.

33. *Time*, 3 Jan. 1977, p. 61.

34. *Business Week*, 21 Feb. 1977, p. 29.

35. Whitman, "Role of the Dollar," p. 544.

36. Gilpin, *U.S. Power*.

37. *Business Week*, 12 April 1976, pp. 50, 51.

38. U.S., Senate, "Implications," pp. 410, 412.

39. *New York Times*, 12 Jan. 1977, pp. D1, D10.

40. *New York Times*, 24 July 1976, pp. 29, 33.

41. *Newsweek*, 29 Nov. 1976, p. 49.

CHAPTER 4

International Economic Leverage and its Uses

Klaus Knorr

In Chapter 3 we saw how economic factors function internationally *as objects* in the national security and welfare of societies, as when external economic disturbances impact broadly and deeply on the national economy. To protect the national economy from such dislocation is often a state policy objective. In this chapter we will observe how economic factors figure internationally *as means* to achieving state policy.[1] Economic valuables can be used as direct leverage over the outside world. They can also be transformed into non-economic means of leverage, particularly military power (see Chapter 7). Of course, when economic capabilities are used *as means*, the objective can, but need not be, the promotion of economic interests. And in any case, such use by one country impinges on the *objectives* of national security and welfare of another country or countries.

Leverage means one actor using a lever to gain advantage over another actor. National economic capabilities that afford international leverage can be used for four distinct purposes. The first is coercion. A can withhold or threaten to withhold something of value to B in order to make B comply with some specified form of behavior. Thus, A may deny or threaten denial of a supply of a commodity, access to a market, or economic aid to B, in an attempt to make B modify a trade policy, pay compensation for foreign nationalized investments, or drop out of an alliance with a third state. Successful coercion is a form of influence and constitutes "behavioral power."

The second purpose is to extract monopoly profit from market control over a highly valued product. Thus, A announces to all states that they can buy a particular commodity only at high prices substantially exceeding marginal production costs. A then exploits monopoly power to derive a special economic advantage. A is not attempting to influence other actors to do anything beyond paying a fixed price, if they do not want to do without the commodity.

This purpose of wielding economic power has a great deal in common with applying coercive economic power. Indeed, on a high level of abstraction, the two actions can be regarded as identical. Both essentially depend on

99

monopoly power. In the second case, a high monetary price is demanded in a commercial market. In the first case, the price is some other compliance with the coercer's demand outside commercial markets. It is possible, in fact, for a monopolist to threaten price hikes if certain customer countries fail to comply with his demands on other matters. Some members of OPEC, for example, announced in 1976 that OPEC might raise oil prices substantially if the leading capitalist states refused to meet the demands of the Less Developed Countries (LDCs) for the establishment of a new "World Economic Order." This threat clearly amounted to an attempt at coercion. Because coercive threats are directed against specific countries, while all customers are normally required to pay a price designed to yield monopolist profit, we can speak of the difference between a discriminating and a non-discriminating exercise of monopoly power. This distinction of purposes is recognized in the real world. Since they raise different normative responses, they should be kept separate as forms of economic leverage.[2]

The third purpose aims at direct impact on another state's economic security, welfare, and capabilities without any attempt at compelling it to behave in a specified way. The desired impact can be harmful or beneficial. A may withhold certain commodities, financial aid, or his market from B in order to weaken him economically or in some other way. Thus, in times of military conflict, belligerents often also engage in economic warfare by interfering with one another's supply of food or essential raw materials. Or, as the United States still does vis-à-vis the Soviet Union, A may refuse to export to B certain goods that are expected to enhance B's military capabilities. On the other hand, A may give financial aid or other economic valuables to B in order to strengthen him economically or in some other way. Thus, during the 5th century B.C., the Persian king gave money to Greek city-states in order to strengthen them against Greek opponents that threatened or were capable of threatening Persian interests. Throughout history, governments have granted subsidies to strengthen allies. The United States gave Lend-Lease to Britain and the Soviet Union in World War II and, after that war, extended vast economic aid under the Marshall Plan to war-ravaged West European countries (although such aid was initially offered but then rejected by Soviet-dominated countries) in order to boost their ability to cope with domestic communist threats.

The fourth purpose is being pursued when a government gives economic valuables to another country in order to gain a position of general influence over it. For example, beginning in 1956, the Soviet Union gave economic aid to Egypt and other Arab countries to achieve influence over them. Similarly, the United States has extended aid to Latin American countries in order to maintain or increase its regional influence. And, as in India, the United States and the Soviet Union have provided aid in order to compete with one another for influence. Once achieved, such influence may be exploited coercively, as when the extension of further aid is made conditional. In that event, we have a case of the first purpose—applying economic leverage. Yet, influence may also be sought in terms of generating in the receiving society voluntary identification with the influential country and its policies or, more generally, generating an attitude of friendship. It is precisely this non-exploitative objective that makes up our fourth purpose.

The four purposes of using economic leverage are, of course, analytical distinctions. In the real world, some of these purposes may be combined in a particular policy. For instance, something of value may be withheld from a country in order both to weaken and to coerce it; or a position of influence may be cultivated by economic means for the purpose of generating friendship and, should this objective fail, for developing a basis for economic coercion. What all four purposes have in common is the achievement of preferred outcomes in relationships with the outside world. As we shall see, national economic wealth affords international economic leverage only to the extent that it has appropriate structural characteristics. For the sake of analytical completion, however, one must add that such wealth also affords the ability to buy things of value from other countries—not only commercial goods and services but also other objects such as naval bases, port facilities, airfields, votes in the U.N. These items are bought as *pure exchanges* and are not exercises of economic *power*. In a pure exchange, two parties *voluntarily* trade things regarded as *equivalent* in value. No influence is brought to bear, no side is meant to be supported or injured, and no general influence is established. For example, in a recent treaty between the United States and Spain (1976), the former exchanged $1.2 billion in economic aid and other benefits for the use of military bases in Spain over a five-year period. This important use of wealth—that is, the use of international "purchasing power"—is not discussed below, because it does not represent the employment of leverage as previously defined.

Economic Leverage Between States

Coercive Economic Power

At war with Napoleon's France, Britain established a naval blockade on much of Western Europe's coast. Beginning in 1807, the United States had serious quarrels with the British government because this blockade interfered with the trade of neutral countries (and also because of other British practices, especially the impressment of American sailors). Since negotiations failed to solve the issue, the United States retaliated by imposing a partial embargo on British trade in July 1807. This economic sanction proved to be ineffective, and it caused substantial economic hardships at home, since American exports fell from $108 million in 1807 to $22 million in 1808. The embargo was repealed in March 1809. After further experimentation with lesser and likewise ineffective economic warfare measures, an embargo on British trade was again established in March 1811. Gradually, American leaders persuaded themselves that the country had to go to war unless the embargo proved effective in compelling the British government to revoke the Orders-in-Council on which blockade policy was based. This time, economic coercion proved effective. In June 1812 Foreign Secretary Castlereagh declared the Orders-in-Council suspended. Unfortunately, unaware of the British concession, the United States declared war two days later.

When Yugoslavia asserted its independence from Soviet control in 1948, the Soviet government cut off trade and aid in order to bring her to heel. Other communist countries in Eastern Europe followed suit. At the time, more than half of Yugoslavia's trade was affected, and she was completely dependent on these communist states for credits and technical assistance. This attempt at economic coercion failed, however, because Yugoslavia was able to expand trade with the capitalist countries which were also ready to furnish her with aid.

The Peruvian government announced in 1968 its intention to buy sophisticated military aircraft from France. Washington was displeased, curtailed grant commitments, and suspended credits to Peru in order to make it desist from this transaction. The Peruvians were infuriated by this refusal and went through with the purchase without hesitation.

In order to evaluate these instances of international economic pressure, we must clarify the meaning, bases, effectiveness, and utility of economic coercive power. The purpose of all coercion is to establish influence on the intentions and behavior of an actor by threatening him with, or placing him under, some form of damage or punishment. The ability to effect economic coercion arises from an economic interdependence between two actors. If B is highly dependent on A for something of great economic value to him, and A is not similarly dependent on B, the latter is vulnerable to the threat of having the receipt of the valued object suspended. He is subject to the coercive exertion of economic leverage. Power arises from an asymmetrical interdependence. It does not matter whether the coercing actor uses the carrot or the stick. In either case, he threatens or actually withholds something of value.

To threaten to inflict economic deprivation is not the only way through which coercive economic power can become internationally effective. Power is also a matter of perception and anticipation. B may be careful not to adopt courses of action to which A might object, because he expects that if he does, A might well resort to a threat. If B takes such care, his freedom of choice is restricted, and A's power has become effective without having been brought into play. This effectiveness stems from A's reputation for making coercive use of his power whenever important interests are frustrated by the actions of weak actors. It is highly likely that power becomes effective more often through this silent mechanism than as a result of deliberate threats and their execution. We cannot verify this hypothesis statistically. While the execution of international threats is always a matter of record, and making threats is also frequently made public (always in cases involving important stakes), the cautious act of rejecting, let alone not even considering, policies that might lead to unwelcome trouble, requires no communication between actors, usually occurs in private, and often remains unrecorded.

The coercive power that actor A can derive from asymmetrical economic interdependence over actor B depends upon three factors: First, A must have a high degree of control over the supply of something B values, be it a market, a source of goods, or economic aid, including credits and gifts. Second, B's need for this supply must be intensive. Third, B's costs of compliance must be less than the costs of doing without the supply. In discussing these three conditions, we will initially assume an extreme asymmetry of interdependence, that is, that A does not depend on B for anything he needs urgently.

Control over Supply: A's coercive economic power over B tends to be the stronger, the greater his control over supply, and hence his ability to damage B by means of denial. Below a very high threshold, however, his control is of little or no coercive worth. Yet, possession of a high degree of control is extremely rare, because foreign markets, sources of commodity supply, and aid are usually dispersed internationally. There are virtually always other suppliers than A. Even though Yugoslavia in 1948 was very dependent on trade with and aid from the Soviet Union and the East European communist countries, her government was able to switch to other export markets, sources of goods, and aid. Similarly, the trade and aid embargo which the United States established against Cuba following Fidel Castro's revolution achieved no coercive power, because the Soviet Union and its allies were ready to substitute as trade partners and aid providers. The American embargo of 1811 against the United Kingdom was effective only owing to an extraordinary combination of circumstances. Although trade between Britain and the United States was substantial, it was not by itself important enough to coerce the British government, as was in fact demonstrated by the ineffectiveness of earlier acts of economic warfare by the United States. The 1811 embargo was superimposed on Napoleon's Continental Blockade that cut off Britain from its major trading area. Moreover, in 1811 Britain suffered one of the worst crop years in its history. It was the joint consequences of all these adversities that made economic dislocations—especially unemployment and food scarcities—unusually severe and led to much political unrest. The British government was compelled to seek relief by making

103

concessions to American demands. The Arab embargo on oil exports in 1973, another successful case discussed in Chapter 10, proved effective, at least vis-à-vis some industrial oil-importing countries, because of the unavailability of sufficient alternative oil sources. Since 1973, Israel has become isolated as a result of Arab pressures, leaving the United States as the only major source of economic aid and arms. The United States is genuinely supporting Israel's security and independence (an example of our third purpose of using economic leverage) but also derives substantial coercive power from its singular position as a source of vital supply; it has used this leverage to push Israel toward negotiating a settlement with the Arab countries.

The historical record shows very few cases in which control over supply by a single state was sufficient to produce effective economic coercion when the conflictual issues at stake were important to both actors. The international market for goods and services is composed of many national markets, and even though some are much larger than others, even the largest for any one good seldom controls an overwhelming share. The international supply of goods is also rarely concentrated in one or a very few countries. Special dependencies do arise when a country accepts privileged access to a particular large market (e.g., at lower tariff duties), a source of commodity supply (e.g., on easy credit terms), or a source of aid. Such special arrangements are apt to create a patron-client relationship that will offer the patron country a degree of leverage, unless the client has countervailing political leverage because his viability is important to the patron, because he can threaten to shift to a rival patron, or for some other reason. However, such special relationships seldom create an inescapable dependence. The client state may be able to switch to alternative suppliers, even at the cost of losing a privileged economic benefit. In most instances, the state that is subjected to economic pressure readily finds such alternatives. Countries that are economic competitors of the state resorting to economic coercion are usually eager to offer their goods and markets, because it is profitable to do so. As in the Yugoslav and Cuban cases, political rivals of the country attempting coercion see an opportunity to increase their relative influence by substituting for the sanctioning state. Finally, when coercion is attempted through military threats or war, most third countries are unlikely to intervene in support of the coercion target, because to do so is both costly and risky. This is not true when intervention involves trade and aid. The reluctance of some countries to support Israel with arms sales in the face of Arab displeasure is exceptional.

As the partial success of the oil embargo shows, a high degree of control over supply is more easily mustered by a coalition of countries than by a single state. If Libya or even Saudi Arabia alone had imposed an oil embargo, the attempt at coercion would have failed. A group of countries

104

with high aggregate control over the supply of an economic valuable may readily coalesce to charge monopoly prices. They are far less likely to agree politically, however, about the purposes of economic coercion against the target state or states. Here again, the case of the Arab oil embargo was exceptional. A high collective control over oil exports coincided with a strong determination to force international action against Israel. This gave the coercing states sufficient cohesion for joint action. On the other hand, although Moscow was able to induce other communist countries to agree with its policy of putting Yugoslavia under economic pressure, their joint leverage proved insufficient. Indeed, the history of collective economic sanctions demonstrates the obstacles to assembling a crushing degree of monopoly power. The League of Nations applied such sanctions against Italy when she attacked Ethiopa (1935–1936). The action proved abortive because enough states failed to cooperate for political or economic reasons. Similarly, the economic embargo imposed on Rhodesia by a U.N. resolution in 1966 certainly did not succeed in its aims for many years, in large part again because some states, in particular South Africa, refused to cooperate.

The evident obstacles to the command of sufficient power over the supply of some economic value necessary to the coercion of other states when the conflictual issues at stake are very high, and often dramatic, apply less when the issues are less important and conflicts less salient. We will discuss this problem in connection with the costs of compliance as a factor in determining the efficiency of international economic coercion.

Intensity of Demand: Not even an extremely high degree of control over supply will afford coercive leverage unless the target state strongly needs the economic value that can be withheld. The two factors are complementary: the more intensive B's demand for the value in question, the greater A's coercive power. Vital dependence on oil imports rendered Japan and the West European industrial countries highly vulnerable to the Arab oil embargo of 1973. Even a partial but substantial fall in imports would have entailed cumulative disruptions in the economic life of these societies. Similarly, from 1973 to the present, Israeli governments, keenly aware of the contingency of another war with Arab countries, have been in urgent need of American weapons and economic support for maintaining a high state of military readiness. The combination of a high control over supply and an inelastic demand yielded effective leverage in both cases.

On the other hand, in the Peruvian case, American leverage failed to achieve the desired results, because Peru was not vitally dependent on the continuation of American aid, and the volume of credits was not very large. To cite another example, in October 1972, the governments of the Soviet Union and the United States came to an agreement on expanding mutual trade, in part through the extension of American credits. The Soviet leaders had expressed a keen interest in this move, in part as means towards infusing modern western technology into their technologically backward civilian economy. Yet in January 1975, they quashed the agreement because Congress had passed an enabling act that required the Soviet Union to liberalize its emigration policy. This stipulation was clearly an attempt at economic coercion on the part of the United States. However, the Soviet government did not want expanded trade with the United States badly enough to be coerced, at least openly, into revising its policy in a different issue area. The Soviet Union had been able to do without greatly expanded trade with the United States before, and it could do so again. To Soviet leaders, the Trade Act of 1974 was an intolerable interference in the domestic affairs of their country. Alluding to the Jackson amendment in December 1976, Leonid Brezhnev stated: "Those who believe that discrimination in economic relations can influence our policy or arrest our economic development are deeply mistaken. The Soviet Union has never made itself dependent in these matters on the benevolence of Western partners."[3] In 1948 Yugoslavia was, of course, vitally dependent on foreign trade and aid. But even the most urgent need will not produce great vulnerability unless it is associated with a high degree of control over supply on the part of the country attempting coercion.

The Costs of Compliance: Attempts at international economic coercion often fail. The possession of economic leverage is only a base of *putative* power. *Actual* economic power arises only when, and to the extent that, the coercive attempt controls the behavior of the target state. A state that is subjected to an attempt at economic coercion will not submit unless the economic punishment involved exceeds the costs of complying with the demand of the coercing country. As we have seen, this is one reason why the historical record shows few cases of effective economic coercion when the stakes were high; the other reasons are that the coercing state usually lacks adequate control over the supply of the economic values involved or that the need of the states under pressure is not vital enough. What was at stake for Yugoslavia in 1948 was its independence and autonomy. When the United States imposed an embargo on all exports to Cuba (except for food and medicine) in October 1960, it put the integrity of the revolution at stake for Cuban leaders. In both cases, the costs of compliance were unacceptable. On the other hand, when Japan and a number of West European countries were faced by the Arab oil embargo in 1973, they submitted, in part, because the cost of complying with Arab demands was relatively low. All they needed to do was to declare support of United Nations Resolution 242 requiring Israel to return territories seized in the 1967 war. The costs of compliance were not nil, for it is always costly to be compelled to do something, and this additional cost often figures in the choice of the target state. But the costs were not very high.

Of course, the target country of an attempt at economic coercion will suffer, even though it can turn to alternative markets and supply sources or decide to do without whatever is involved. Even when other supplying countries are available, the terms may be less favorable, and temporary shortages and other disruptions occur because switching to other suppliers and markets takes time. Yugoslavia suffered grievously in 1958 and again in 1959, when the Soviet Union once more cut off trade in order to compel Yugoslav submission. To give another example, in June 1960, the Albanian government displeased the Soviet Union when it openly backed communist China against Moscow. At the time, 56% of Albania's imports came from the USSR, which also took 45% of her exports. Most of the rest of Albanian trade was with East European communist countries, and her plans for economic development rested overwhelmingly on Soviet loans. The Soviet Union began to apply pressure by cutting back on loans and technical assistance and delaying trade negotiations in the hope that Albania's leadership would split and the country would return to the fold. In April 1961, China obligated herself to give Albania a credit of $123 million for industrial development. Five days later, Moscow canceled all aid to Albania and by the end of the year, all Soviet trade with Albania had been suspended. Chinese deliveries were slow, and Albania suffered acute economic distress for a long time. But the Albanian government chose not to yield to Soviet pressure.

Evidently, the costs of compliance and hence effective leverage by the denying state may be different over the shorter and the longer run. As indicated, time affords opportunity for remedial adjustments. Yet, it is possible that the costs of compliance can grow over time. This can occur when the denying state has a high degree of control over supply, and the effects of denial are cushioned for a time by reserve stocks in the target country. (This could happen in the case of an oil embargo.)

Defiance will occur when the economic burden falls short of the costs of compliance. There may be international costs, as when the target country defies a patron state that has also provided military security; but these may be offset wholly or in part by international gains resulting from the refusal to be coerced. There is also the domestic public on which the costs of defiance and the costs of compliance would fall. At this point, foreign policy becomes domestic politics. The distribution of the expected costs of compliance is apt to differ markedly from that of the costs of defiance. To side with Peking rather than Moscow may have been important to an Albanian ideologue, but an Albanian worker who faced unemployment may have been indifferent to this issue.

Most of the influential public may agree with the choice of the government or may have forced its choice on the government in the first place. But much of the public will not react until after the decision has been made, and its painful consequences have become apparent. In order to choose defiance and stick with it, a government—whatever the political system—must remain strong internally. And this factor is important when the respective costs of compliance and defiance are compared. There is considerable evidence from a number of cases, including those of collective economic sanctions against Italy and Rhodesia, that attempts at economic coercion tend to increase rather than diminish national political unity and cohesion. Many governments can appeal to the public need to stand together in solidarity, when foreign aggression is economic as when it is military. It is even possible that some societies regard a yielding to economic pressure as more ignominious than yielding to military pressure.

Government and public response to economic coercion attempts is, of course, in large part situational. Much depends upon relative opportunity costs, on how the burdens of compliance and defiance compare in particular situations, and on how they are distributed over the domestic public. Beyond this, it is difficult to generalize in the absence of more empirical work. We can suggest, however, that—everything else being equal—defiance of external economic pressure is more likely, the greater the general support of and trust in government, the more the political culture demands solidarity in the face of foreign aggression, and the less the public prefers immediate private economic welfare to other social goals and goods.

Economic pressure is not, of course, used only in conflicts of "high" policy. Undramatic employment in conflicts of "low" policy is more frequent. While we do not know this statistically, for reasons that will shortly become apparent, we suspect that in most cases of attempted economic coercion, the costs of compliance are small, and the attempt then often succeeds. The costs of compliance are small, first, when the demands of the coercing state are minor, touching on things of little importance to the country under mild pressure, and second, when the coercive threat is made ambiguously and in private and receives little or no publicity. It is, indeed, because so many attempts are in this range that we know little about them, and statistical measurement is impossible. This is especially true when the threat is a mere hint and, if made in public at all, is ambiguously inferential. The public threat as a hint occurs, when an aid-giving government reminds an aid-receiving one with which it has a slight policy conflict of the large volume of aid that it is giving. The mild threat in private occurs, for example, when the official of a donor country mentions to an official of the recipient countries that it would be easier to get more aid granted next year if the receiving government were to modify a certain economic policy.

There is, finally, a range of relationships in which the unspectacular exertion of economic power is routine, recognized, and accepted as such. This practice characterizes bilateral and multilateral bargaining on import tariffs and other trade regulations. Most such bargaining involves a voluntary exchange of concessions that the parties regard as having equivalent value. Economic threats are commonly introduced in such negotiations and are often effective. While the use of economic leverage for extracting *economic* gain is often unsurprising, its use—across issue areas—for securing *political* gain is not commonly expected. The linkage is regarded as artificial and likely to be resisted by the target state.

To conclude: we hypothesize that attempts at coercion by the use of economic leverage are more likely to succeed in conflicts of low policy than in conflicts of high policy. Low-policy attempts at coercion have one or more of the following characteristics: (1) the threat has low salience, because it is vague or made in private; (2) the stake and hence the costs of compliance are small, often close to nil; (3) threats and stakes are located in the same issue area, i.e., economic, and mild threats in the issue area are employed so frequently, almost routinely, that they have gained a degree of international legitimacy. In these cases, the degree of control over supply need not be high, and many countries can engage in this game. Cases of high-policy coercion attempts have one or more of the following characteristics: (1) the threat is public, dramatic, and hence has high salience; (2) the stakes are high and the costs of compliance large; (3) threats and stakes typically cut across issue areas. In these cases, the required degree of control over supply is high.

When distinguishing between cases of high and low policy, a dichotomy is not suggested. Of course, there can be cases of pressure that fall in between these types. There are also cases in which the stakes are uneven to the two parties, low to one and high to the other. When this happens, it usually means that the stake is low to the country applying economic leverage (e.g., a big donor state such as the United States) and of high value to the target country (e.g., a small aid-receiving state).

International Economic Power Reconsidered: The historical record makes it clear that attempts at economic coercion often fail, and our analysis has explained that this happens when the coercer's control over supply proves inadequate, when the target state's demand for the economic value in question is not urgent enough, or when it estimates the costs of compliance to exceed the costs of defiance. It is, therefore, conceptually important that we distinguish between the means to power and the achievement of power, as theorists of power have done. Coercive power exists only if, or only to the extent that, the instruments of power have been applied effectively in making an actor comply with the coercer's demand. This means that power is achieved only in particular situations with reference to particular actors. The instruments that can be used to achieve coercion are not power in themselves. A powerful country can be said to possess putative military or economic power (perhaps better called military or economic strength), if its use of the instruments of power would prove effective in various situations of conflict. Yet the achievement of power requires this putative power to be actualized, and a number of factors we have identified will determine whether or not the attempt to do so will succeed. The outcome is context-determined, because it depends upon a particular degree of monopoly power, a particular intensity of demand, etc., that operate in a particular situation.

Like other forms of power, economic power is variable in amount and range. Amount varies with the degree of coercion achieved. Range varies with the range of coercive effects achieved over the behavior of the target state. As already observed, amount varies with degree of control over supply, elasticity of demand, and the costs of compliance. Range varies with whether economic coercion becomes effective within or across issue areas.

The Bases of Economic Power: To equate national economic power and national wealth is a frequently encountered gross misconception. In the late 1960s and early 1970s, many people talked about world power becoming less bipolar as, in addition to China, Japan and "Western Europe" were becoming great powers based on economic strength rather than military power. And in international dealings concerned with trade and monetary arrangements and with foreign investment and aid, they have, indeed, become increasingly influential. This is a result of the growing wealth and high dependence on foreign trade that gives them associated bargaining power in conflicts over matters of economic policy. But they have gained influence in this issue area largely at the expense of the United States, whose wealth and trade have been expanding less than theirs. The Soviet Union and China have never been important actors in these contexts. In any case, speculations about an emerging pentagon of international power rested on the premises that economic power could function as a substitute for military power across issue areas and that increasing wealth gave such power to Japan and the major West European states. The extent to which national economic power can substitute for national military strength is a question we will take up below. The illusion that these rich trading countries had vast economic power was shattered by the Arab oil embargo of 1973. It was a number of militarily weak oil-producing states that displayed economic coercive power and demonstrated that the wealthy industrial countries are extremely vulnerable. There was nothing in their wealth that would have permitted them to mount an effective economic counter-threat against the Arab oil-exporting states.

As the preceding analysis made clear, economic coercive power can be derived only from a very high control over the supply of an economic valuable that can be withheld from others who cannot do without it. Wealth gives the highly developed industrial states one basis for extending economic aid. They also export goods containing advanced technology that are

110

in demand in the outside world, and they can offer capacious markets to countries eager to export their products. Yet none of them can singly muster a high degree of control over any of these things. The members of the European Community could not even do so collectively. They do enjoy bargaining power when it comes to negotiating international trade, aid, and monetary arrangements, but they lack the means to sufficient economic coercive power that can be engaged in conflicts of high policy. Indeed, as is shown by the recent challenge of the less developed countries to the international trade and monetary order supported by the rich capitalist countries, the latter's economic power is even circumscribed in economic issue areas. An example is what has been happening recently to multinational corporations of highly advanced countries that operate in the so-called Third World. Over the past ten years, these business firms have become increasingly subject to nationalization and to regulations enforced by governments of less developed countries that limit their operational freedom and profits. Indeed, foreign investments often represent hostage capital over which the host state exercises sovereign control. It tends to give the debtor leverage that can be exerted against the creditor. Wealth is not the same as economic coercive power, which depends on highly concentrated control over something of extreme value to others.

Moreover, close control over such precious economic assets is only one base of coercive economic power. Another base is the political will[4] and ability to turn these assets to coercive employment. Such determination is crucial, because, as we will see below, wielding economic coercive power involves opportunity costs that must be borne. Capitalist countries, furthermore, are handicapped, because suitable economic assets are frequently under private control, usually dispersed, rather than concentrated under public control. And to establish government control for purposes of exercising national coercive power becomes a political issue. When the United States government in 1973 imposed a temporary embargo on grain exports to the Soviet Union to negotiate Soviet acceptance of certain rules that were to govern future purchases, American farmers naturally objected.

Skill in statecraft is a third base of coercive economic power. It is obviously a factor in making decisions to exert such power, and in implementing them. The factors we have identified as determining the outcome and costs of coercion attempts in particular national and international contexts require estimates that are difficult to undertake. A decision to coerce would not be rational unless the expected probability of success multiplied by the value of achieving compliance exceeded the expected costs. And even when a decision to attempt coercion has been made, further decisions are needed in the form and timing of implementation. To give an example, it was reported in January 1976[5] that Secretary of State Kissinger had initiated a policy of selecting those nations that had sided against the United States in United Nations voting for cutbacks in American economic aid. State Department officials singled out Tanzania and Guyana as possible targets, because they had voted in the U.N. General Assembly to condemn Zionism and to oppose the American position in Korea. If the intent was coercive, and there is every indication that it was, one would suppose that this step was not taken before a careful estimate of the susceptibility of aid-receiving countries to such pressure. In the event of economic retaliation by the United States, are these countries able to obtain more aid elsewhere, e.g., from the Soviet Union or China? How dependent are they on American aid and, above all, how do the costs of compliance compare for these countries with the costs of defiance? The costs to another actor are not easily estimated, for they ultimately depend on subjective values. Given the present temper of many less developed countries that have become increasingly critical of the United States, the targets of this American attempt at coercion might well be outraged and find strong sympathizers elsewhere. This action contemplated by the United States could, in the end, make opposition in the United Nations more solid than before. Clearly, such coercive measures require careful consideration before they are taken, and skill in evaluating the range of consequences is critical. We need hardly emphasize that all these tasks of statecraft involved in wielding coercive economic pressure can be performed well or badly and that the level of relevant government skills can be an important determinant of outcomes.

So far, we have assumed that coercive economic power arises out of a structure of economic interdependence that is highly asymmetrical—that is to say, a relationship that makes one actor one-sidedly dependent on the other. At this stage, we must introduce a further complication. Interdependence is mutual dependence, and this limits the independence of both actors, making each vulnerable to the other, though usually not equally. In the real world, the actor who is the target of a coercive power play may be able to react by attempting counter-coercion. In principle, the two actors might even be equally vulnerable to one another's control over the supply of different things. This would be similar to the case of bilateral monopoly in which a process of attrition would either permit the side with greater staying power to win or lead eventually to a compromise settlement. Because the opportunity costs are greater, it is less likely that a state will attempt economic coercion when it is vulnerable to a significant counter-attempt. If it does, its power to coerce—a net phenomenon—is correspondingly reduced. But the more economically vulnerable state might also be able to bring non-economic counter-influence to play. It might use diplomacy and appeal to third countries for support. If it is strong enough, it might even threaten military reprisals. Thus, when the Arab countries imposed their oil embargo in 1973, American government officials announced

112

repeatedly that the United States would consider resort to military measures in the event the embargo would have a strangulating effect. While this was not a formal threat, the possibility was hinted at. This is not to suggest that a militarily weak country will not attempt the economic coercion of a militarily stronger one. To make a military counter-threat and, if unheeded, to execute it is fraught with risks and consequences that are likely to be acceptable only when the issues at stake are correspondingly high. Nevertheless, when the difference in military strength is great, the inferior country will take the risk of a military riposte into account when the conflictual issue involved is more than minor.

The Costs of Attempting Economic Coercion: A state that attempts to coerce another by economic pressure is apt to incur considerable costs. The most immediate is that an economic threat may be defied. If that happens and the threatening state fails to initiate the sanction, defiance has been successful, and the reputation of the threatening country, having been caught in a bluff, suffers accordingly. On the other hand, in the event the threat is executed, other costs will be incurred. The target state may succeed in defiance, find help elsewhere, and form a coalition of countries that are international rivals of the state attempting coercion. As already mentioned, it may be able to retaliate economically. Mutual vulnerability is likely to increase as international economic interdependence is deepened. Other states may take measures to reduce their economic dependence on the pressuring state. Many disadvantageous things can happen, and to accept the risks is an appreciable cost. For example, there are weighty considerations that tend to restrain the Saudi government from reimposing a future oil embargo. Its leaders are not interested in seriously disrupting the capitalist economies that are an immensely profitable market or in weakening the United States whose power balances that of the Soviet Union in the Middle East.[6] Similarly, the fact that the Soviet Union has been selling oil for some years to eastern European communist states appreciably below world-market prices gives considerable leverage to the Soviet government. But, in order to maintain smooth hegemony in the region, Soviet leaders are also interested in avoiding political troubles with their clients and having them prosper economically. These considerations tend to inhibit Soviet resort to coercive means. Costs in terms of adverse international repercussions may be generated, even if the target state eventually yields. On the other hand, a successful coercion attempt may have benefits beyond the compliance of the target state in that a resolute power display deters third states from adopting certain courses of action likely to cross important interests of the successful country. It is for this reason that states sometimes decide to attempt coercion for exemplary purposes as well as for the immediate object of making the target state comply.

There are apt to be domestic as well as international costs when economic coercion is attempted. No direct economic costs are entailed if a state attempts coercion by suspending aid or some other unrequited benefit previously extended to the target state (e.g., tariff preferences). Economic costs do result, however, when trade is forced out of the most economic channels and when the target state is able to resort to economic reprisals. Thus, if a country denies exports to another, it may find alternative markets only at lower export prices. In addition, there are likely to be domestic political costs if the burden of executing economic sanctions falls on interest groups that must be compensated for their losses or whose political opposition may have to be absorbed by the government, or if sections of the influential public are opposed to the policy on other grounds. For example, when President Ford imposed, in 1975, a three-month embargo on wheat sales to the Soviet Union in order to muster bargaining power for the negotiation of a grain purchase agreement with that country, American farmers were naturally irate because the embargo caused wheat prices to fall.[7]

The potential costs of exercising economic coercion are apt to reduce its attractiveness. Economic sanctions that are implemented and fail to coerce impose a clear-cut loss. A successful threat tends to be more cost-effective than a threat that must be executed or is revealed to have been a bluff. Economic leverage, like all power, works best when it works without being invoked.

Active Versus Passive Economic Power: So far, our explicit discussion has been about coercive economic power. We may call this *active* economic power. It is putative power that can be used against others. It is useful to distinguish active from *passive* economic power which gives invulnerability to the economic power of others. The less vulnerable a state is to economic pressure by others, the greater its passive economic power. Great overall economic power is composed of the sum of great active and great passive economic power. But states can possess great passive economic power while having little or no putative active power. The Soviet Union and China, for example, are not dependent on external economic supplies essential to their viability. They would be hurt economically if the outside world would refuse to meet their demand for certain things, but the deprivation involved would afford little or no coercive power. Even if they experienced a bad crop year and needed grain imports to sustain domestic consumption, their populations could be fed, though on a poorer diet. On the other hand, the countries in the European Community possess appreciable assets for exerting economic power—not to wield coercive power in dramatic conflicts of high diplomacy but in matters where routine and lower-order applications of economic leverage count—but all of them (except Britain and Norway) are vulnerable to any interruption of foreign energy supplies. Markedly underdeveloped countries with largely traditional economies capable of producing the essentials of life, such as Paraguay and Burma, have great passive economic power while enjoying no active economic power whatever. Some of these countries would be disadvantaged if their receipts of foreign aid and imports of capital goods and food were cut; they would experience some unemployment and a halt in economic development. But the resulting economic distress would be far from paralyzing and, in many cases, tolerable for a considerable period of time. Wealth tends to breed vulnerabilities. It should be noted, however, that any degree of passive economic power is not only a function of the structure and scope of international economic dependence but also of the strength of government. It is probably easier for the Soviet Government to cope with a substantial shortfall of meat and other high-grade food than for the United States government to remain strong in the face of a stoppage of oil imports.

All countries can foster passive and some can deliberately develop active economic power, although usually not without costs. They can obviously promote passive economic power by minimizing economic interdependence with the outside world and especially by avoiding dependence on essential supplies. Until recently, the Soviet Union avoided such dependence on the capitalist countries. But the maintenance of a high degree of self-sufficiency is costly, since its pursuit means foregoing the gains that can be reaped by participation in the international division of labor. Following the Arab oil embargo of 1973, Presidents Nixon and Ford advocated measures to prevent the United States from becoming unduly dependent on oil imports. However, they met strong Congressional resistance motivated by considerations of the immediate domestic costs involved. When substantial participation in international economic interdependence is unavoidable or held desirable, states can still, usually at a cost, minimize dependence on external supplies of particularly vital things. Many countries have therefore protected key industries (e.g., basic food and steel), while otherwise engaging in a great deal of foreign trade. Beyond this, states can minimize inroads on their passive economic power by diversifying the composition of exports and imports, by trading with more rather than fewer countries, and by foregoing any special trade and aid relationships with particular patron states. Japan, for example, which is extremely dependent on fuel and raw material imports, has taken great care to buy from as many exporting countries as is feasible. In order to reduce vulnerability, states can, furthermore, establish emergency stockpiles of vital goods. The United States has been doing so for strategic materials since World War II, the Soviet Union maintains reserve stocks of grains, and the industrial oil-importing countries increased fuel stocks after the Arab oil embargo. Finally, states can enter international agreements to share supplies at a time of scarcity. Thus, in 1974, the major oil-importing countries concluded the Brussels agreement which set up the International Energy Agency. One of its programs envisages international sharing of oil in a future emergency engineered by oil-exporting countries. But all actions designed to promote passive economic power face opportunity costs that raise problems of internal distribution and are thus apt to be resisted politically by one interest group or another.

On the other hand, states can also promote their active economic power but, again, usually not without costs. For instance, they may be able to expand production of items on which foreign countries vitally depend and cultivate trade with and aid to countries through especially attractive offers that will make these states vulnerable to interruptions. Often, the purpose is to establish and maintain a patron-client relationship. Nazi Germany was remarkably successful in doing this in the 1930s with some East European countries which she hoped to have as allies in the event of war, and following World War II, the Soviet Union became oil and natural gas supplier to the East European communist states. But the possibility of developing active economic power by such means is open to relatively few countries, because these means are circumscribed by the distribution of natural resources, by degree of economic development, and by the size of national economy and foreign trade. However, active economic power can also be assembled by international agreement. Such collaboration was essential to the coercive economic power of the Arab oil-exporting states in 1973. Yet, such ways of bolstering active economic power also entail costs of an economic or political nature.

Economic Versus Military Power: The coercive employment of economic leverage is an option most likely to appeal to conflicting governments in issue areas in which military threats are inapplicable because their use would be regarded as illegitimate or otherwise disproportionately costly. Indeed, it is in matters of low policy that economic coercion is most likely to be effective. Recourse to economic coercion is then seen not as a substitute for resorting to military force but as an instrument for protecting national interests not vital enough to bring military options into play, yet too valuable to be easily abandoned.

However, as already mentioned, recent speculations about changes in international relations have posed the question whether there has been a diminution of the utility of military power for purposes of conflict resolution and an accompanying increase in the utility of economic power. It has been suggested that economic power is becoming, to a degree, a substitute for military power.

In the past, national economic power has been of no avail against a state that resorted to military power when vital interests were at stake. Military power clearly has been the ultimate form of power that trumps all others. This is still true. Of course, economic warfare has been frequently employed along with military warfare, as was the case in World Wars I and II. The primary intention in doing so has usually been to weaken the opponent.

116

But, using economic coercion to force termination of hostilities has sometimes been a secondary purpose.

In recent decades, there has been perhaps some decline in the utility of military power for certain purposes. New normative standards have somewhat circumscribed the purposes for which military power can be used. There has also been a spreading recognition that there are far superior alternatives to military force in terms of cost-effectiveness for assuring national economic welfare and growth. The opportunities for using cheap military power, as many industrial powers did in the underdeveloped parts of the world not so long ago, have disappeared. These and other reasons have made the aggressive resort to military power less attractive. But, such a diminution in the utility of military power does not necessarily mean that the coercive employment of other forms of power has increased. There is no natural law that makes the amount of international coercion constant. It is possible that nations, or certainly a large number of nations, have become less coercible than they used to be.

It is also possible, indeed likely, that the economic goals of organized societies are receiving higher priority relative to other state objectives. This has increased the incidence of international economic conflicts where an appeal to force is regarded as inappropriate, ineffective, or too costly. The trend has certainly been observable in most of the advanced industrial states and also in the Third World in general. This development should have increased the incidence of low-level attempts at economic coercion, but whether this has actually happened, or the degree to which it has, is hard to estimate. Certainly, at a time in which the less developed countries have become exceedingly sensitive to economic coercion by the richer states and incessantly accuse them of practicing neo-colonialist exploitation, the usability and utility of coercive economic power may also have decreased. However, it is difficult to generalize on these matters, especially because there has been little empirical study. It may well be that the suggested effects apply more to some international actors than to others. Thus at the present time, it may be easier politically for less developed countries to apply economic pressure against ex-colonial powers, provided they can muster the means, than the other way round. This would mean that political and moral restraints, whose effectiveness is itself a variable, are rather unevenly distributed.

It is also in order to ask whether the cumulative increase in international economic interdependence has not augmented national vulnerabilities that can be exploited for the purposes of economic coercion. One would expect so. But, here too, rash generalizations are inappropriate. Vulnerability to economic leverage is not just a result of interdependence as measured in aggregative terms (e.g., by the ratio of foreign trade to national income), but also of structural factors that make denial costly to the target state. Increased economic interdependence will increase vulnerabilities only to the extent that they augment the costs of denial and do so asymmetrically among nations.

Furthermore, the growth of economic interdependence is likely to be unevenly spread in the future, as it has been in the past. Until now, it has increased most among the European countries engaged in the process of forming an economic union and among all the highly industrialized states as a group. But the countries of the European Community are naturally restrained from exercising economic pressure against one another except in circumscribed areas (e.g., West Germany may withhold increases in funds for the development of backward areas in the Community unless it gets satisfaction on the level of agricultural subsidies). Within the larger set of capitalist states, the coercive use of economic leverage is more permissible but only in issue areas in which the application of economic pressure has been customary (e.g., on matters of trade and monetary policy). Since many of these wealthy countries are also allies for security purposes, recourse to economic coercion on high policy issues is much less probable. However, these states have also developed huge needs for imported fuel and raw materials that must be met, if their high level of economic activity is to be sustained. As the case of the Arab oil embargo demonstrated, this development has engendered new and important vulnerabilities. Yet, it is unlikely that the exporters of material goods other than oil will be able to assemble cooperatively the degree of monopolist power that would facilitate effective attempts at economic coercion. Nor does there seem to be anything as urgent as the demand for oil.

We have seen that states have rarely succeeded in the past in achieving a sufficiently high degree of control over the supply of valuables to make economic coercion effective in matters of high policy. It is doubtful that this will happen more often in the future than it has in the past. There are now, as there were before, too many nations that offer markets, export supplies, give aid, and invest abroad. And, as happened before, few have enough aggregate leverage or political unity to attempt a coercive play when the stakes of conflict are high.

Coping: We have already identified the means by which countries can strengthen their passive economic power in order to reduce the chances of being subjected to economic coercion, especially successful coercion. These are essentially measures of economic deterrence and defense. We have likewise explained that in issue areas in which some exertion of economic power is fairly routine, the stakes are usually not high enough to justify serious concern. Moreover, it is extremely difficult and rare for a single state or even a group of states to muster enough control over supply to attempt economic coercion in matters of high policy, when the conflictual issues at stake are more important. Coping with the problem, in general, is therefore not high on government agendas.

Nevertheless, governments are not indifferent to economic vulnerabilities. Even if an attempt at economic coercion in matters of high policy fails, the defying target state suffers economic losses, because it takes time to tap and adjust to alternative supply or market sources. Nor are countries indifferent to economic vulnerabilities that can be exploited by other states in conflicts involving minor stakes. Bargaining losses can accumulate over time and touch on sensitive economic issues in terms of domestic politics. Moreover, as the consequences of the Arab oil embargo indicated, any spectacular attempt will remind countries of their vulnerabilities and will induce governments to consider precautionary measures to curtail particular risks. Indeed, the awareness resulting from a spectacular economic power play is apt to put a new light on the desirability of letting international economic interdependence increase without forethought. The governments of the industrial oil-importing countries certainly have become alert to their international economic insecurity. However, as we have also pointed out, such insecurity can be remedied or curbed only at considerable costs in terms of finance and policies that affect domestic prices and incomes. Nothing much can be done without sufficient domestic political support. Various private individuals and groups will react differently to available trade-offs between immediate sacrifice and more future economic security. If considerations of short-term personal and group advantage prevail, political resistance is apt to limit sharply the means of coping with particular problems of national economic security. Governments' domestic strength is therefore a crucial factor (assuming that the governments themselves are united on the issue). If prudence is neglected because governments are too weak to pursue policies that impose immediate costs on the public, the national vulnerability to economic coercion is a joint result of economic factors and political short-sightedness or weakness.

Monopolist Market Power

Having examined coercive economic power from several dimensions and in great detail, we can discuss more briefly the other purposes to which economic leverage may be put, because there is a great deal of analytical overlap. The use of monopoly power for exacting high economic profits in international markets is familiar because of its universal practice in national economies and in the international economy. It has also received extensive treatment in economics textbooks. The custom of seeking monopolist or oligopolist profit whenever market power encourages it has a long history and has encountered little normative objection internationally. We may expect it to continue as a matter of routine.

119

In recent years, however, the economically less developed countries, who depend on the export of raw materials and basic foodstuffs as a mainstay of economic life, have raised the monopoly issue in the United Nations and other forums. They have also made it a major item in their confrontation with the wealthy capitalist states and the international economic order they have fashioned. The actions of OPEC have lent the issue a special acuity. The "Third World" countries maintain that pervasive monopolist practices in the capitalist states—both on the part of producers and labor unions—have made the prices of their export goods, particularly manufactures, rise in relation to the prices that the less developed countries, without similar monopoly power, receive for their raw materials and foodstuffs. The resulting terms of trade are thus regarded as exploitative. These states do not demand that monopolist structures in the capitalist world be dismantled but that their right to establish counter-monopolies be recognized, and, indeed, that the capitalist states assist them in setting up and policing international commodity agreements.[8] They insist that only effective intergovernmental control can achieve the degree of monopolist market power that emerges without formal agreement from the dispersed monopoly power of many actors in the capitalist economies.

However, it is far from easy for less developed countries to create effective counter-monopolies, in particular because together they do not account for a sufficient proportion of world supplies or because they find it hard to agree, and remain agreed, on a common price policy. Counter-monopolies would be far more feasible if the industrial importing countries were to participate in their establishment and implementation by agreeing on export prices, financing buffer stocks, or in some other way, as has happened in the cases of the international tin and coffee agreements. The capitalist states naturally resist these demands which are, after all, designed to raise prices against them. The present question is how far they are willing to make concessions either as a matter of equity or one of coping with the political pressure that the Third World, backed by the communist states, is able to bring to bear in their demands for a more just international economic order. Further, OPEC's support of these demands also permits the introduction of some degree of economic pressure. The outcome of this attempt not to curb monopolist market power but to spread and distribute it more evenly over the world remains to be seen.

Supporting and Weakening Other Economies

The third distinct purpose to which international economic leverage can be put by governments is that of weakening or strengthening other national economies without any intent to influence their governments or public (although in practice both purposes may be combined). The intent is to shape international situations and to affect the capabilities of other countries; but there is no specific demand on behalf of which the action is initiated.

We have already noted that to weaken the national economy that sustains an opponent's military strength has often been a form of economic warfare practiced in wartime. But this is a policy that has appeal only when hostilities are protracted, and their outcome is determined by mutual attrition. Beginning in 1947, the United States imposed a peacetime export embargo on strategic goods against the USSR, subsequently extended it to China, and induced its allies with varying and, over time, diminishing success to participate in this policy. One problem with such a use of economic power is the difficulty of drawing a line between strategic and non-strategic goods. The case of prohibiting the export of weapons to a potential opponent is clear-cut. But how far should one go in extending the embargo to capital goods (e.g., computers, machine tools) that can be used to produce arms or civilian products? In the final analysis, all exports that increase the economic productivity of another country can be said to support its military output eventually, and the denial of exports has therefore some weakening effect.

Yet neither the Soviet Union nor China has been prevented from generating an impressive capability for military production in relation to its overall level of development. Soviet leaders have been determined not to depend on the outside world for arms and to accord a top priority to its domestic armament industry in the allocation of scarce resources. In the end, the American embargo has probably harmed the Soviet civilian economy more than the military sector. Thus, while a rigorous export embargo on strategic goods can hurt the overall economy of a large and fairly developed country, and perhaps slow down somewhat the growth of its armaments industry, an embargo on more than weapons and components, which is not without costs, is unlikely to prove effective over the longer run and is, of course, doomed to failure if there are alternative exporting countries that do not take part in the embargo.[9] Moreover, whatever effect the practice may have in creating difficulties for the target country, the policy may also sustain that country's hostility and tend to increase the likelihood of a military conflict.

The non-proliferation treaty of 1968 provides for a collective prohibition of the export of nuclear arms binding on all parties, and the International Atomic Energy Agency administers some safeguards to prevent the diversion of nuclear materials to military use. These arrangements do not constitute the exercise of economic leverage, since they rest on the agreement of all parties. Since the early 1970s, however, there has been mounting concern lest the expanding export of nuclear civilian technology will, despite existing safeguards, permit more and more importing countries to develop a potential for developing nuclear weapons. The United States has

121

been negotiating recently with other main exporters of nuclear reactors and related technologies to tighten the conditions under which future exports will be undertaken. Should these countries come to an agreement along these lines and execute it without consent of the importing states, an application of economic leverage toward restricting the armaments industry of the countries will be involved.

To identify cases in which one country restricts or suspends trade with or aid to another in order to weaken its economy is not easy because such intentions are usually unstated and may be additional to doing these things for coercive purposes. One might suspect that the very sharp contractions of trade between the Soviet Union and China, since these two powers split on political and ideological grounds, and also the suspension of Soviet aid and technological assistance to China, had as one Soviet purpose, the objective of keeping China economically and militarily weak. The sharp cut in American aid to Chile after Señor Allende established a left-wing government presumably had the purpose of weakening the Chilean economy and thus putting pressure on the government's hold on power. The boycott administered by Arab countries against foreign firms doing business with Israel was clearly intended to harm the Israeli economy. Finally, economic leverage has often been practiced clandestinely to weaken a foreign government by giving financial support to opposition parties.

Conversely, states use economic leverage to strengthen foreign national economies and governments, because they are interested in their viability or in their capacity to resist external threats or enemies in international or internal war. We need not detail these practices, for the historical record is replete with cases. The United States alone has, during and since World War II, supported numerous allies and client states around the globe. The Soviet Union and China have widely engaged in this practice—massive Soviet aid to Cuba being a prime example. Ex-colonial powers—such as France—have supported former colonies; Arab oil-producing countries, especially Saudi Arabia, have supported Egypt and Syria, etc. In 1974, the Federal Republic of Germany lent Italy five billion marks in order to help the Italian government, which faced the prospect of electoral losses to the Communist party, to weather a serious balance-of-payments crisis. In 1976, the struggling democratic regime in Portugal received aid from West Germany and France, and the United States announced similar plans. In some of these cases, to be sure, to establish a general position of influence—a purpose discussed in the next section—has been an objective associated with the aim of strengthening a friendly state or government. Finally, countries that are better off economically give aid to those that are worse off through international organizations, especially the specialized agencies of the United Nations, such as the World Bank and the International

Monetary Fund. Although motivations of self-interest in terms of cultivating an international reputation for doing good may not be entirely absent, the official intention is to give diffuse support to the welfare and economic development of poorer societies.

The success or failure of all of these operations obviously depends on a host of situational factors, including the indigenous capabilities of countries that are being harmed or supported, and the actions of third states. Nor is it easy to identify success or failure. For example, one might take the view that American support operations were successful in the cases of South Korea and Taiwan but failed in South Vietnam (prior to military intervention), Laos, and Cambodia. United States support of Israel may be considered a successful case. But a conclusive evaluation of outcomes is restricted by the fact that many conditions were involved in bringing them about, and we cannot know what would have happened in the absence of the operations. Yet the use of economic leverage in order to support or weaken a country or government may not aim at spectacular results. Even moderate costs imposed or support given can be effective in terms of modest objectives, especially if such economic leverage is employed along with other means.[10] And, unlike the case of using economic leverage for purposes of coercion, there is no high control threshold over the supply of valued things below which effectiveness is improbable. On the other hand, the strengthening or weakening of the target country can be reduced or offset entirely by the intervention of a rival power, as happened, for example, when the Soviet Union increased its economic aid to Chile after the United States withheld credits from Allende's government.[11]

The economic bases of the leverage involved depend, as in the case of coercive economic power, on the precise method employed. If it is privileged access to a market, the size of that market is a key factor; if it is the closing of a market, the trade volume that is cut off is critical. If it is the food supply, arms, or oil, the country must have a corresponding supply capacity; if it is economic aid, including credits, the donor country must have an exportable surplus capital, etc. And, when coercive economic power is being applied, the operating state must have a government authoritative and strong enough to receive public support despite incurred costs. Finally, the element of statecraft enters into the equation in terms of making and implementing all the relevant decisions.

Achievement of General Influence

The final purpose for which international economic leverage has been used is achieving a general position of influence in another country or the reduction and elimination of such influence by a rival state. The purpose is not to exert economic coercion or to set up a basis for coercive operations later on (although, in practice, both purposes may be pursued simultaneously), but to evoke in the other country diffuse sympathy and identification with the donor state in the sense that the former will voluntarily pursue policies that are desirable to the latter. In the event of success, relations between the two societies will hopefully become friendly. When the object is to erode a rival state's general influence in another country, that country's shift to non-alignment or neutrality may be the relevant success measure.

The economic means employed for this purpose are exactly the same as those that are used when the purpose is simply to support another state or government, and naturally so are the bases of leverage. Historical examples are difficult to identify with confidence, because the operations that are intended to foster general influence and those that aim merely at support are the same and because general influence is easily adulterated by the infusion of attempts at economic coercion. As a matter of debatable judgment, one might cite large-scale American economic support of India during the 1950s and 1960s as a probable case, though not a pure one. United States support of some Latin American countries, such as Brazil and Mexico, may also have belonged to this category during the past, as probably did past Soviet support of Egypt and recent Soviet support of India, and as do Chinese aid operations in Africa.

If one accepts these and similar cases as good examples, it becomes immediately clear that the general influence that may be achieved by economic operations tends to be precarious. After the war of 1967 and the death of President Nasser, the Soviet Union lost the position of influence it had established in Egypt when, beginning in 1955, it generously provided that country with arms and economic aid. The United States established little overall influence in India, where its position was replaced under Indira Gandhi by that of the Soviet Union and lost its influence in such countries as Greece and Turkey. Its influence in Mexico also declined sharply under President Echeverria. The history of Indonesia is an example of how quickly the influence of one great power can be replaced by that of a rival. Of course, the temporary establishment of overall influence may be regarded as successful enough.

But the historical record does pose the question whether the employment of economic leverage is a good means, at least by itself, for achieving durable relations of sympathy, let alone friendship. There are two reasons that tend to limit effectiveness. First, the purpose of fostering general influence is easily adulterated by the occasional attempt at effecting coercion. Like all power, economic power is susceptible to corruption even when the original intent was merely to establish friendly relations. And in any case, even if this does not happen at once, the recipient of economic values, being the weaker party, may well suspect that, sooner or later, it will. The very position of being the one-sided recipient of economic values forecloses true equality, and this fact tends to militate against the emergence and maintenance of a genuinely friendly relationship. Friendly relationships tend to prosper when influence is mutual, and it is as difficult to be a good patron as it is to be a good client. Second, bilateral aid relationships easily generate frictions when the donor country chooses—and it is apparently a choice hard to resist—to specify conditions for the use of arms or economic aid. Third, the chances are that two countries of unequal power and wealth, positioned in different stages of economic and political development, and often located in different parts of the world, naturally generate divergent and frequently conflicting goals and preferences. This tends to obstruct or corrode the identity or complementarity of purposes on which a position of general influence depends. And, even if there is enough identity and complementarity of interest between the two countries at one time, the recipient society may be politically unstable, and a revolution or coup d'état or less dramatic political change may sharply alter public interests and government policy and thus jeopardize the donor country's position of influence or bring it to a quick end. Changes in the policies of the donor state can also undermine a relationship that has previously been equable and harmonious.

Finally, in view of the frictions that easily emerge in dealings between a patron and a client, the durability of a friendly relationship depends on whether or not alternative sources of aid are available to the recipient country. When President Sadat turned increasingly against the Soviet Union after 1973, substantial aid from Saudi Arabia and Kuwait, and perhaps hopes for American support, were probably a factor. On the other hand, unrelenting United States hostility forced Cuba to turn to Soviet aid.

Summary

The phenomenon of international economic power is very complex. Such power derives from the use of economic leverage. Leverage arises from national control over things of great economic value to other countries. Economic power is *not* a simple consequence of national wealth but rests on a particular configuration in the international distribution of valued things. Leverage can be used for several distinct purposes: the extraction of monopolist prices, the weakening or strengthening of other countries, the cultivation of general influence, and the establishment of coercive influence over other states. All these applications involve costs of one kind or another, and their effectiveness depends on a variety of contextual conditions. Power, in the narrow sense of coercive influence over the behavior of other states, develops only in specific situations. Whether or not the employment of appropriate means, i.e., economic leverage, yields such results depends on several variables. The uses of international economic leverage and their consequences cannot be understood unless the complex interaction of these factors is fully appreciated.

Footnotes

1. For a more extensive analysis of international economic power and for bibliographic references on the subject, see Klaus Knorr, *The Power of Nations* (New York: Basic Books, 1975), Chaps. I, IV, VI–VII.
2. However, if a monopolist charges higher prices to one set of countries and lower prices to another, he may pursue other objectives than monopoly profit, e.g., he may want to support or strengthen those that can buy at relatively lower prices.
3. *New York Times*, 1 December 1976, p. 1.
4. For a definition of political will see Chap. I.
5. *New York Times*, 9 January 1976, pp. 1, 5.
6. For a discussion of these restraints, see Hanns Maull, "Oil and Influence, The Oil Weapon Examined," Chapter 10 of this volume.
7. *New York Times*, 26 December 1975, p. 1.
8. This case is complicated by the fact that the international market prices of raw materials and foodstuffs tend to fluctuate much more widely in response to changes in demand and supply than do prices of industrial products, and the less developed exporting countries also want international commodity agreements for the purpose of stabilizing—not raising—prices and, thereby, export earnings.
9. Cf. Knorr, *The Power of Nations*, pp. 142–146; Gunnar Adler-Karlsson, *Western Economic Warfare: 1947–1967* (Stockholm: Almquist and Wiksel, 1968).
10. William Schneider, *Food, Foreign Policy, and Raw Material Cartels* (New York: Crane, Russak, 1976), p. 12.
11. Ibid.

CHAPTER 5

Structural Power and National Security

Cheryl Christensen

The bulk of national security analysis has assumed that threats to a nation's survival, or its core values, come primarily from the actions of other states and must be coped with at that level. Hence, heavy emphasis has been placed on developing capabilities (defense) to thwart such actions or to prevent them from being attempted in the first place. Of course, it has been recognized that "structures" are important both in creating capabilities and in determining the likelihood of threatening actions. Such structures may be defined as the formal or informal "rules of the game," institutions, and regularized behavior patterns. However, less attention has been focused on structures as sources of generalized threats or on the possibility of changing structures to escape from threatening situations. This has occurred largely because accepted structures are taken for granted, and in practical terms, it is difficult for a state to alter them.

Changes in international economic relations have sparked a new interest in the relationship between international structures and national security. One of the most striking features of the contemporary international economic milieu is that previously accepted (or tolerated) "rules of the game" are increasingly being questioned. Because the United States has been heavily involved in establishing and maintaining international economic structures, it is directly affected by processes which raise "questions of who will exercise political control and how."[1] The issue at stake is not just which actors can affect the immediate behavior of others, but which (if any) can create new rules and relationships to facilitate economic activity.

Attention is now focused on an aspect of power which has previously been easy for American scholars to overlook. Almost everyone has recognized that in attempting to enhance or preserve their perceived security, states (as well as other international actors) have tried to exercise power over the behavior of others. This "behavioral power" is the ability of an actor to get others to modify their immediate behavior in compliance with, or in anticipation of, its demands, wishes, or proposals.[2] Yet, while control over the behavior of others has been an important aim of international political actors, it is only part of their power activities. An historically important dimension of state action, especially for great powers with multiple resource bases and large repertoires of means, has been the attempt to structure or restructure the international environment. The idea is not just to control actors in specific situations, but to gain some control over the flow of events, over overall relationships, or over situations.[3]

Realizing this makes it important to distinguish between two levels of analysis:

> . . . a process level, dealing with short-term behavior within a constant set of institutions, fundamental assumptions, and expectations; and a structure level, having to do with long-term political and economic determinants of the systemic incentives and constraints within which actors operate.[4]

In pursuing objectives, actors have structural power when they can change relations which act as "long-term political and economic determinants" and which serve as a context for future action. More precisely, an actor or group of actors (A_s) has structural power with respect to a collection of actors (A) if A_s can generate, maintain, or transform relations among members of A or the rules for regulating those relations to affect orientations, action opportunities, or the distribution of costs, risks, and benefits.[5]

Of course, gaining control over situations is not divorced from being able to affect the immediate behavior of others. However, for affecting behavior, other, more subtle mechanisms exist. Bachrach and Baratz recognize a "second face" of power—the ability of an actor to control the agenda of interaction. They argue that:

> To the extent that A succeeds in doing this, B is prevented for all practical purposes, from bringing to the fore any issues that might in their resolution be seriously detrimental to A's set of preferences.[6]

Even more subtle control over situations may be achieved by an actor who can affect the range of *possible* outcomes by affecting the opportunities or resultant payoffs available to other actors. When one actor can limit outcomes at the process level because it can affect the costs or efficacy of action at the structural level, the actor need not intervene at the process level to try to change another's behavior. A_s may still prefer one outcome to another at the process level, but all possible outcomes lie within the range of A_s's ability to adapt to them.

The concept of structural power helps make more clear the potential links between arenas of "low politics" and national security. It has been almost automatically assumed that national security is achieved or lost through the outcome of "high politics" confrontations. Yet "taken-for-granted" rules and structures can contribute significantly to maintaining or eroding national security. Structures which are inadequate for coping with new threats endanger security. Rules which generate or exacerbate conflicts that undermine fundamental political and military capabilities may similarly erode security. Modifying underlying relationships or the regimes which manage them frequently requires that some actor or group of actors be capable of exercising structural power.

This chapter will try to show that recent changes in the international political economy both reflect and imply changes in the structural power of different groups of actors. Although there may be many consequences, two are directly related to national security concerns. First, changes in international economic structures may affect the schedule of resources, means, costs, risks, and benefits underlying actors' abilities to exercise (or resist) behavioral power attempts as well as the scope within which such attempts are feasible. One actor's structural power may change (or be used to change) other actors' behavioral power potential both within and outside economic arenas. The "oil weapon" is an example. Second, international economic structures may be direct or indirect sources of threats to or guarantees of some actors' perceived security. "National security," then, becomes associated (correctly or incorrectly) with particular international structures. Changing international economic relations (e.g., increasing interdependence) and shifts in some actors' capabilities for controlling them, may alter the national security agenda and precipitate new controversy (or uncertainty) about the definition of "national security" itself. This is presently the case regarding American "leadership" in international economic affairs.

In judging how significant particular features of the international economy may be for particular nations, such as interdependence, it is important to distinguish between an actor's being sensitive to external forces and being vulnerable to them.[7] Sensitivity means that an actor is liable to experience costly effects from outside actors in a given situation. These effects may pose serious threats and may make it costly to resist others' behavioral power. As Clark Murdock pointed out in Chapter 3, vulnerability means continued liability, even after efforts have been made to escape the situation.

Structural power provides an important link between sensitivity and vulnerability. How vulnerable a nation is depends on the range of available options or, in other words, what are the alternatives to the situation in which sensitivity occurs? Vulnerability also depends on the cost of alternative actions. Both the range of alternatives and the associated distribution of costs, risks, and benefits often depend on an actor's position in wider structures. The capability to change structures or to generate or destroy particular relations which affect the range of choices for action can permit a nation "vulnerable" in one area to be merely "sensitive" or to escape undesirable interdependence altogether. Similarly, a nation which can maintain a structure of power over vulnerable actors may perpetuate its advantages. Judgments about sensitivity and vulnerability are static assessments of future options when they are made only in terms of a given structure; they are elements of a dynamic strategy when the broader capacity for structural power is considered.

Examining the structural power of different actors, then, can add depth to analyses of how vulnerable they are to others' action or to new types of threats. This paper will examine the structural power of different configurations of actors in two arenas salient to American national security: international oil production and energy supplies, and the proposed New International Economic Order (NIEO). Before doing so, however, it seems appropriate to discuss the concept of structural power in general.

A Preliminary Discussion of Structural Power

A truly general discussion of structural power would examine the ability of actors to change relations in the international environment and within domestic environments. This chapter, however, will focus primarily on international structural power and examine domestic structuring only as it is affected by international economic relations. A consideration of domestic structures may be found in Chapter 3 and 6 of this volume.

In attempting to assess an actor's structural power, we need to consider three questions:

1. Can A_s *directly* modify an international structure (regime or underlying relations) for its perceived benefit? In particular,

    a. Can A_s create or reorganize international economic relations to generate new resources or new means for employing them? Examples could include OPEC's ability to change relationships among producing governments, multinational oil companies, and oil importers to gain control of new resources and new means of using them (embargo, oligopolistic price setting). Another example is the ability of banks and businesses to create new international networks to provide means for using their financial resources.

    b. Can A_s modify international economic relations to change the magnitude and distribution of costs, risks, and benefits of action? An example is the United States' ability to institute a new international monetary regime after World War II to remove or reduce the risk of competitive devaluation by decreasing government cost and risk relative to temporary balance of payments deficits.

2. Can A_s create, maintain, or transform international economic relations which affect the ability of other nations to carry out internal restructuring? In particular,

    a. Can A_s shape international economic relations to affect the resources or means available to other governments for internal structuring? For example, international lending relationships and the ability to specify what constituted "credit-worthiness" affected the resources LDCs could obtain for structuring their economies.

    b. Can A_s shape international economic relations to make the costs, risks, or benefits of some forms of domestic structuring more, or less, prohibitive? For example, multinational corporations may arrange their production networks to increase the costs of nationalization or deny governments tangible economic benefits from nationalization.

    c. Can A_s shape international economic relations so that costs or benefits become particularly attached to some groups within another actor's domestic arena, inhibiting or facilitating attempts to handle conflicting domestic interests? For example, rules for adjusting balance of payments deficits may increase domestic inflation with uneven effects on domestic groups, which may, in turn, alter a government's ability to maintain or create a sense of "common interest" among diverse groups.

    d. Can A_s shape transnational relations among subnational actors to affect the structuring latitude of other governments in their own domestic arenas? For example, establishing new international institutions which permit coordination and communication among subnational groups may enable them to block internal restructuring which does not serve their perceived interests.

3. Can A_s generate, maintain, or transform international economic relations to enable it to affect the domestic structure of other actors directly? In particular,

    a. Can A_s reproduce elements of its own structure in the domestic structure of others? Examples include the attempts of colonial powers to implant their legal and commercial codes in newly independent states and the ability of multinational corporations to structure production in some host countries.

    b. Can A_s generate international economic relations which forge connections between it and elements of another country's domestic structure? For example, the organization of international commerce around "market principles" may establish the need for training or educating elites in less advanced countries—and in the process shaping their orientations.

Many of the illustrations of structural power are not things which actors can accomplish immediately by a specific exercise of behavioral power. In most instances, time and coordinated activity are required. In particular, the successful exercise of structural power may depend on an ability to initiate

131

self-reinforcing patterns. Wallerstein argues that if one actor in a particular situation

> ... has a *slight* edge over another in terms of one key factor *and* there is a *conjuncture* of events which make this *slight* edge of central importance in terms of determining social action, then this slight edge is converted into a large disparity, and the advantage holds even after the conjuncture has passed.[8]

Timing and the ability to promote cumulative effects are critical to exercising structural power. Behavioral power successfully exercised in one situation may thus be part of a process of exercising structural power.

Bearing this in mind, it is important not to overemphasize the capacity actors have for shaping relations and "establishing" structures. The "conjuncture of events" may be beyond the control of any actors, as was the *coincidence* of climate change and internal weakness in feudal structures which preceded the emergence of capitalism.[9] Similarly, the "slight edge" may be the result of relatively non-manipulable factors, such as geography or geology. In addition, most relations, and certainly patterns of relations, give rise to changes which were not anticipated, or desired, by actors that may have initiated or changed them. This fact makes both maintaining and transforming relations much more problematic than a manipulative approach to structuring would suggest.

The importance of time and unforeseen consequences, in turn, makes it difficult to interpret both general structuring processes and the exercise of structural power. For example, authors discussing behavioral power have distinguished between relatively coercive and non-coercive behavior modifications. Coercive behavioral power produces action (or inaction) through threats or sanctions of some kind.[10] The coercive exercise of behavioral power, rationally reconstructed, uses threats to impose higher costs and risks—making some options in a specific situation prohibitively expensive. Such coercive behavioral power has been the primary focus of national security-oriented discussions of power. However, it is also possible to change behavior through non-coercive means in accordance with pre-established desires. An actor may offer incentives or rewards without attached threats. The actor may shape another's behavior by making an action clearly preferable to other alternatives in terms of the other actor's own choice criteria. At a later time or under changed conditions, however, what was initially accepted as non-coercive may be seen as coercive. For example, the recipient actor may come to expect the rewards or options provided and see their termination for any reason as a "threat" designed to coerce.

A related distinction applies to structural power. An actor capable of affecting international structures may do so in a way which makes it more difficult for others to realize their goals or defend their perceived interests.

On the other hand, to further its own interests a state may also enhance the resources or means available to others—as occurs when one actor provides a "collective good." As with behavioral power, the interpretation may change. Actors who initially provide a collective good for reasons tied to their own interests may find that their interests at some later point are not served by the arrangement—and that attempts to change the situation will be interpreted (correctly or incorrectly) as an option-restricting exercise of structural power. Thus, it becomes conceptually difficult to distinguish between attempts to abandon old structures in favor of new ones and past efforts to create and maintain the original structure. Both represent the exercise of structural power, but each may affect other countries differently. This ambiguity, inherent in the process of change, makes it intellectually (and politically) difficult to assess causality and purpose.[11]

As with behavioral power, it is necessary in discussing an actor's structural power to identify the resources which provide a *base* for it, the *means* available for using those resources, the *scope* (what kinds of relations can be affected), and the costs, risks, and benefits which attempting structural power entails.[12] While it is difficult to describe the capacity for structural power by creating static lists, an attempt will be made initially to present several hypotheses about the resource bases needed to generate, maintain, or transform relations. More dynamic treatments will emerge from the later discussions of international oil production and the NIEO.

It is obvious that generating, maintaining, or transforming relational patterns requires resources. The real question is how much and what kinds of resources. Baumgartner et al., focusing primarily on hierarchical control relations, hypothesize that generating such relations requires A_s to control a disproportionate quantity of desired resources vis-à-vis other actors.[13] One key to generating new relations is the ability to provide something others want or need but cannot easily obtain elsewhere. In essence, A_s acts as a monopolist, oligopolist, or monopsonist in a key resource arena.

There are several examples of structural power which are at least consistent with this hypothesis. Both the United States by the end of World War II and Britain in the early nineteenth century had disproportionate shares of key economic resources. Gilpin associates the decline of their "monopoly" with decreasing structural power in noting that:

As happened with Britain in the latter part of the 19th century, the United States no longer holds the monopoly position in advanced technologies. . . . As was also the case with Britain, the United States has lost the technological rents associated with its previous industrial superiority. This loss of industrial supremacy on the part of the dominant industrial power threatens to give rise to economic conflict between the rising and declining centers of industrial power.[14]

133

To take another example, OPEC's ability to affect international economic relations is based on its oligopolistic control of petroleum resources. (See Chapter 10 for a discussion of oil as a weapon.)

It is also possible, however, for structural power to be based upon the range of resources available to A_s. Baumgartner and Burns hypothesize that the ability to generate new economic relations sometimes rests on A_s' ability to control a wider range of resources than other actors.[15] A_s may be able to create new relations among actors because it has significant (but not necessarily overwhelming) control over a range of resources. A_s could thus create "packages" of relations, using resources in one arena to support structuring activities in another, or it could create more significant "barriers to entry," as can a vertically integrated firm. The case of A_s is undoubtedly stronger if it has control over a disproportionate share of several key resources.

Both the United States and Britain, during the period in which their broad structuring efforts were made, had a wide range of resources. Britain's pre-World War I military forces were substantial, and its naval forces particularly so. The United States, after World War II, held the bulk of the Western world's productive capacity, monetary reserves, and military forces. In both cases, the ability to create and for a time sustain wide-ranging economic regimes depended both on the quantity of resources and the range over which these resources extended.

A combination of military and economic resources was also the basis for the initial expansion of European countries and the creation of what Wallerstein has termed the "world economy."[16] Speaking of the initial expansion of capitalism in the sixteenth century, Wallerstein argued:

> In a capitalist world economy, political energy is used to secure monopoly rights (or as near to it as can be achieved). The state becomes less the central economic enterprise than the means of assuring certain terms of trade in other economic transactions. In this way, the operation of the market (not the *free* operation but nonetheless its operation) creates incentives to increased productivity and all the consequent accompaniment of modern economic development.[17]

Whether a quantitative preponderance of resources, a broad range, or some combination of both provides the base for structural power is in large part an empirical question. However, it is possible to speculate about appropriate bases by considering the *scope* over which structural power is attempted, the strategies available for engaging in structural power, and the limits of the structure established. For example, A_s, with a wider range of resources than other actors, could follow a *supportive* strategy trying to make relations in different arenas mutually supportive. Relations might be generated in one arena so as to make a positive contribution to the functioning of

134

relations in another. Such a structuring strategy has a large scope. Such structuring would seem *a priori* to require as a base at least a disproportionate range of resources and possibly a disproportionate quantity of resources in some arena. On the other hand, A_s might follow an *insulating* strategy, attempting to generate relations in one arena which would function without explicit connections to other arenas. Such structuring could *logically* be based on disproportionate control of a single resource, as long as events within that area occur more or less independently of events outside of it. Given OPEC's limited *range* of resources, it tends to follow this second strategy, as will be seen below.

Of course, resources alone cannot be equated with structural power. It matters greatly what actors do with their resources; hence the *means* available for utilizing resources becomes an important consideration. The Spanish experience in the sixteenth century provides an example which may help illuminate present issues. Spain possessed a disproportionate quantity of a key economic resource (bullion) and a range of resources (military and political). Yet, while Spain established an empire in the New World as well as in Europe, she did not successfully exercise structural power in the world economy of the time. For:

> the metals which enriched Spain parasitically . . . flowed out into those countries where its purchasing power was greatest. . . . Genoese bankers monopolized the profits from the exploitation of American mines; Genoese outfitters controlled the provisioning of the fleets. Meanwhile Italian, Flemish, and French merchants seized control of the colonial trade by means of the fairs at Medina del Campo and the embarkations from Seville and Cadiz. Far from reacting, the monarchy became more and more involved in dangerous financial disorders that tied it to the capitalist machinery on the far side of the Pyrenees; at first the tie was indispensible, then ruinous, and finally sterile.[18]

As Wallerstein puts it, the bullion "may not have done too much more for Spain than pass through its ledgers."[19]

While structuring resources were available, the *means* for using them to generate and control economic relations were not. Spanish people did not develop banking skills and hence lost an important means for controlling the flow of capital. They did not develop productive investment policies, and indeed, sterilized potential investment funds by using gold ornamentally and ploughing money into political and military attempts to obtain more bullion from its colonies.[20] An inability to control international economic relations ultimately contributed to the failure of Spanish attempts to achieve military and political domination of Europe.

Several categories of means may be used for international economic structuring. First, new formal institutions may be created, facilitating (or

135

inhibiting) certain relations. The establishment of the IMF and World Bank provides one example; a comprehensive institution to oversee multinational corporations would be another. Second, innovative practices which facilitate existing interaction or open new interaction possibilities may be used to change international economic relations. Britain's innovations in banking systems (including deposit accounts) in the nineteenth century provides an example. So does the present ability of larger multinational banks to facilitate short-term capital flows—hence, the Eurocurrency market which handled much of the initial flow of petrodollars. Third, behavioral power used in a cumulative way may then be used for international economic structuring. OPEC, as an instance of transformed relations, provides an example. The details are presented later, but in essence OPEC made a series of (successful) attempts to change companies' price positions. Price increases and later participation agreements gave genuinely new options to producing countries.

Thus far the focus has been primarily on establishing relations. It is equally important, however, to consider the resources required to maintain or transform structures. A_s' ability to maintain relations depends only *indirectly* on its resources vis-à-vis other actors. It depends *directly* on the resources it can (or will) make available for structuring *relative to* the resources required to meet the structure's maintenance costs.[21] It makes little difference if others' resources increase relative to A_s' if resource growth does not increase the structure's maintenance costs. On the other hand, a decline in A_s' resources (even if it were matched by a decline in others' resources) would be troublesome if the costs of maintaining relations remained constant or rose. In a world where everyone suddenly became uniformly poorer, maintaining previous relations could be much more difficult.

It could also be more difficult for A_s to maintain a structure if resources did not decline (either absolutely or relatively), but the demands on those resources from other sources increased. A_s might then find it more difficult, or even less desirable, to devote resources to maintaining an international structure.

Difficulty in maintaining international economic structures may also occur because a structure's maintenance costs are rising relative to A_s' available resources. Rising maintenance costs may signal fundamental flaws in a regime A_s is trying to maintain. The flaws may be inadequacies in the regime per se or contradictions between a regime and the structure of another international arena. Both these problems have been associated with the Bretton Woods regime.[22] Maintenance costs may also rise because other actors' resources have increased and are directly contributing to rising maintenance costs. This can happen because the structure becomes more complex, or because other actors become capable of challenging or circumventing previously accepted (or tolerated) relations in ways which A_s must

136

counter by expending more resources. It is frequently suggested that contemporary international economic relations between the United States and other OECD countries have become more difficult to maintain on past terms, because Europe and Japan now have strengthened economies capable of competing with the United States.[23]

The means for maintaining a structure, then, must include ways of absorbing, distributing, or deflecting costs. If A_s has resources over and above its requirements, it may simply allocate them to maintaining the structure—with some cost—unless *no* better alternatives existed. Frequently, however, this is not desirable. One of the problems oil companies found in trying to maintain their oligopoly before World War II was that some companies were unwilling to purchase concessions they thought unlikely to be profitable simply to keep other companies out. As a result, questions of the distribution of costs may be significant. Throughout the period of oligopolistic company control of oil, for example, ways were found to shift maintenance costs to others. Sometimes costs were shifted to parties willing to bear them (e.g., U.S. government via tax provisions); sometimes to third parties unaware of their role as bearer of costs, or unrepresented in negotiations (e.g., consumers); and sometimes to unwilling parties (e.g., lower revenue to producer governments). Clearly, however, the actor onto whom costs are shifted must be capable of bearing them. Finally, there are ways of deflecting costs—for example, persuading actors who could impose costs not to do so or using behavioral power in another arena linked to the cost issue. Hence, the U.S. government urges the adoption of "voluntary import quotas" to reduce the costs of trade arrangements with the threat that mandatory quotas will be enacted, or the promise that "rewards" in other areas will be granted for compliance.

The fact that A_s *can* maintain an international structure does not imply that it should. Indeed, Gilpin suggests that one of the risks involved in maintaining a structure is that A_s may adapt to structural requirements too completely.[24] Being able to maintain privileged access to markets could blunt the incentive to make future-oriented production changes. Determining *whether* a structure should be maintained may be much more difficult than ascertaining *how* it is to be maintained. Crises focus attention on rising costs or shrinking resources. The processes of international interaction may not focus as dramatically on declining (or questionable) benefits associated with relatively constant maintenance costs.

Up to this point, structural power has been examined as an abstract concept. In the following section we shall examine two substantive issues. The first case will focus on the events leading up to the use of oil as a weapon. The aim will be to demonstrate the kinds of changes—in resources, opportunities, coalitions—which led to a new capability for behavioral power on foreign policy issues. This is an example of structural

137

transformation which is partly due to company maintenance failures, partly due to OPEC strategies for structural change, and partly due to exogenous forces (e.g., growing demand for oil imports). Second, we shall examine the demands for a New International Economic Order as an illustration of the politicization of structural power. Whether such a politicization can do more than focus attention on issues, however, remains to be seen.

American Structural Power and International Oil Production

The United States government has never attempted a comprehensive restructuring of international oil production. Choices about structuring were made, but as we shall argue, they reflected the weakness of the American government, not its strength. This is clear with respect to three important issues: oligopolistic control of production, responsibility for maintaining the international production structure, and the dependence of Western Europe.

Oligopolistic Control of Production

International oil production has never taken place under "free market" conditions. Oligopolistic control has been the rule, not the exception. Before World War I, U.S. oil companies had little interest in attempting to produce abroad. U.S. domestic production was substantial (indeed, the U.S. was the world's largest producer for many years) and its production easily met domestic needs. International oil production was primarily in the hands of the oil companies of leading colonial powers, and governments were frequently instrumental both in negotiating concessions and in maintaining the oligopolistic structure. After World War I, however, concern arose within the U.S. that the depletion of oil during the war, combined with rapidly increasing domestic consumption, could leave the United States short of oil. In addition, concern was growing that the British domination of key oil rich areas, especially the Middle East, could eventually leave the U.S. open to either income or denial threats. Indeed, at the time the London *Daily News* boasted:

> Britain will soon be able to do to America what Standard Oil once did to the rest of the world—hold it up to ransom.[25]

During the 1920s, both the U.S. government and the major U.S. oil companies became interested in obtaining concessions abroad. One clear intention was to guard against the possibility of U.S. oil shortages which might arise in the future. Another was to permit U.S. industry to expand into what was at the time a lucrative business.

The U.S. government actively pushed the idea of an "open-door" policy regarding American access to international oil areas. It claimed that the concept of non-discriminatory access to commercial opportunities should be guaranteed. In seeking to expand commercial access, the State Department attempted to employ diplomatic leverage to help American oil companies enter previously restricted areas. For example, it intervened to help Standard Oil of New Jersey (Exxon) to purchase part of an Iraqui concession held by the Turkish Petroleum Company (later Iraq Petroleum).[26] Company shareholders included British, Dutch, and French companies. In order to avoid having the U.S. government intervene on behalf of a single company, a group of major American oil companies was established, with Exxon representing all of them in negotiations with the Iraq Petroleum Company (IPC). But arguments were directed toward incorporating the U.S. companies in the system, rather than changing the system. Hence, the diplomatic claim that the U.S. had "contributed to the common victory and has a *right* therefore to insist that American nationals shall not be excluded from a *reasonable share* in developing the resources of territories under the mandate."[27] In 1928, IPC shareholders permitted the American companies 23.75% participation. But this was conditional on U.S. companies accepting the rules of the oligopoly. In particular, they were required to agree to sign the 1928 Red Line Agreement, which updated a 1914 agreement among IPC members providing that shareholders would not compete with each other for future concessions within areas covered by the agreement (roughly, the old Ottoman Empire). While this was clearly inconsistent with the open-door policy, the State Department permitted the companies to sign.

The U.S. government also exercised behavioral power to open investment areas. An example involved Indonesian concessions. Before 1918 Shell had directly controlled oil production in the Dutch colony. In 1918 the law was changed formally permitting other companies to enter, but in practice the Dutch government continued to give new concessions solely to Shell. The U.S. government threatened to use provisions of the Mineral Leasing Act (which permitted the denial of leases on U.S. public lands to companies of any nation that discriminated against U.S. companies) against the Dutch.[28] The threat that Shell might lose access to future production in the U.S. appeared persuasive, and the Dutch government gave assurances that future leases would be granted on a non-discriminatory basis. However, shortly thereafter a new concession was granted to Shell, and the U.S. government denied Shell leases on several pieces of federally owned land, and threatened to withhold all future leases unless discriminatory concession granting in Indonesia ceased. The Dutch government capitulated, and in 1928 Exxon was officially awarded an Indonesian concession.[29]

In neither case, however, was an attempt made to do more than gain access to the established structure. In addition, U.S. companies entered production by simply playing by the rules. Exxon and Gulf entered Venezuela by buying up the concessions awarded to minor U.S. independent oil companies (e.g., Maracaibo Oil Exploration Company). Because Gulf and

Exxon had capital and technology, they were able to expand Venezuela's production rapidly. Within six years (1922 to 1928), Venezuela moved from being an insignificant producer to being the second largest oil exporter (after the United States).[30] Greater production from Gulf and Exxon concessions led to their controlling the bulk of Venezuelan production (54.8% by 1929) and for their increasing importance as international producers.[31]

By the 1930s, American oil companies were significantly involved in international oil production. There was also a "surplus" of oil, implying declining prices unless companies coordinated. Major oil companies (including American) then attempted to establish a structure which gave them both the ability to make decisions about the level of oil production and made it possible to coordinate these decisions to achieve a common goal—higher revenues.

They attempted to negotiate agreements which would maintain world market prices *and* established market shares. In 1928, for example, the "As Is" agreement was made to restrict competition. It provided that participating companies (including Exxon, Shell, and BP) would avoid overproduction and not engage in "destructive competition" in established markets. Major companies also made "preemptive" purchases of concessions to prevent new companies, not parties to the "As Is" agreement, from entering international oil production or to upset the balance among existing major producers. In some cases, however, preemptive purchasing failed—expanding the number of companies. For example, Socal (Standard Oil of California) tried to obtain a concession in Bahrain which Gulf had received on option before its participation in IPC came into effect. Under the Red Line agreement, Gulf could not hold the concession itself and had to offer it to IPC. British investors, members of IPC through BP and 40% ownership of Shell, were unwilling to spend the money to obtain the concession. Since Gulf could not retain it unilaterally, it sold it to Socal, bringing a new company not bound by competition agreements into Middle Eastern oil production. Shortly thereafter, Socal struck oil in Bahrain, exacerbating the oversupply problem. The same thing happened when Socal attempted to expand into Saudi Arabia. IPC initially intervened in an attempt to get the concession for itself in the interest of "keeping out all competitors."[32] But, IPC, not realizing the implications of another large-scale production center in the Mideast, failed to make a strong offer to King Ibn Saud in 1933 and thus allowed the Saudi concession to pass to Socal. Internal rivalries within IPC had prevented unified and defensive action.

The oil companies' success in structuring the international environment was mixed. In some cases, they apparently did limit production and competition which would have been destructive to prices. But they could not expand the scope of their structuring to limit domestic production in the largest production region (the U.S.), and hence could not effectively control prices. Attempts to structure the international environment were costly. Costs involved spending money in a weak market period to buy up concessions which might not be worth the price—simply to insure that they did not fall into the hands of companies that could use them to destroy existing market conditions. In several key instances, actors simply were unwilling to pay the costs of implementing, or maintaining, the structure.

Responsibility for Maintenance

Throughout the interwar period, then, major oil companies undertook to strengthen and maintain an oligopolistic structure which incorporated new American companies. U.S. government involvement was negligible. During World War II, however, pressure was put on some companies to ask for government assistance. The war brought financial problems for the King of Saudi Arabia, and he tried to pressure oil companies operating in the country to provide additional revenue to the Saudi government. Socal and Texaco initially advanced $6.8 million against future royalties, but when more was needed, sought U.S. government assistance for Saudi Arabia. While such assistance was impossible to provide directly, the American government suggested that the British advance a portion of their Lend Lease loan to Saudi Arabia. From 1941–43, the U.K. sent $40 million to Saudi Arabia. Fearful that the British would gain greater influence, the oil companies advanced an additional $5 million and lobbied for direct U.S. financial aid to Saudi Arabia.

The American government, however, was becoming concerned about meeting the fuel requirements of the war. Some domestic officials began to argue that the government should take control of the Saudi concession for security reasons. A Petroleum Reserve Corporation was organized to begin negotiations for the government's purchase of the concession. This was the first in a series of attempts to provide direct governmental control over oil production abroad. All were strongly opposed by private oil companies, and all failed.

When negotiations with the Petroleum Reserve Corporation commenced in 1943, CASOC (the Socal subsidiary formed to develop the Saudi concession) rejected the U.S. bid to purchase the entire concession. The offer was then made for controlling interest, but this was rejected. A third offer was made for the purchase of one-third interest, but when one of the companies increased the asking price, negotiations were broken off. As the Secretary of the Interior and Petroleum Administrator for the war later stated:

They (Texaco and Socal) came up here to the Hill and built a fire under us on the theory that this was an attempt on the part of the government

141

to take over a private-business enterprise, which of course, was against the American tradition, as they put it, and perhaps it was. But this was more than a business enterprise, this involved the defense and safety of the country.[33]

Subsequently, the Petroleum Reserves Corporation attempted to institute a project to build a government-financed pipeline from the Persian Gulf to the Eastern Mediterranean. This also was severely opposed by the oil industry and could not gain Congressional support. It, too, was abandoned.

The U.S. government then attempted to restructure international arrangements to provide more direct control over the important production in the Persian Gulf states. Britain controlled 81% of production in 1943, with 14% in the hands of American companies. The U.S. government obtained a draft Anglo-American Oil Agreement in 1944. The agreement provided for the creation of an International Petroleum Commission to oversee international petroleum affairs and recommend methods by which supply and demand could be matched "so as to further the efficient and orderly conduct of the international petroleum trade." Again, the oil industry opposed the measures, and the Senate did not ratify the agreement.

This set of experiences indicates the problems the American government faced in generating a domestic consensus to restructure international oil production and trade—even in the middle of war, when oil was clearly a strategic resource and other Western governments owned part of their major oil companies. The failure was significant for the post-war structure of international petroleum production and trade, for as Krueger states, after the failure:

> . . .the [U.S.] government now, for the most part, divorced itself from the international petroleum industry. These events signified as well a virtual cessation of the Government's efforts to obtain an information base independent of the companies, which might help it to form petroleum policy and take independent action.[34]

The consequences of the failure of the U.S. government to gain direct control of oil production—and the subsequent decision to leave oil to the companies' management—left most of the maintenance of the structure in private hands.

Oil Dependence in Western Europe

At the end of World War II, the Middle East was considered a secure source of Western oil—in part because of traditional British influence in the area, sustained later by the Seven Sisters cartel of oil companies. Indeed, the current European and Japanese dependence on Middle Eastern oil re-

142

flects basic policy decisions by the United States and Europe following that war. American evaluations of European prospects for economic recovery after the war unanimously agreed that adequate supplies of petroleum "would be the limiting factor" in European recovery.[35] Severe restrictions on the export of American oil made it impossible for the U.S. to supply petroleum to Western Europe. Three separate American reports thus recommended that (a) the Middle East serve as the source of European oil, (b) that tanker production in Europe be increased to assure a continuous supply of needed crude, and (c) that refinery capacity be developed in Europe, permitting it to meet its petroleum needs without exacerbating balance of payments problems.[36] The Marshall Plan was instrumental in providing funds to accomplish these goals.

Early on, it became apparent that European dependence on Middle Eastern oil made it potentially vulnerable to politically motivated supply disruptions. Indeed, in three separate instances, "oil crises" arose. In 1951–53 Europe's supply of Iranian oil (16% of OEEC's consumption) was cut off by international oil companies' boycott of Iranian oil in retaliation against the nationalization of the industry. The Suez crisis of 1956 brought about a severe disruption of Europe's oil supply. In 1967 the closing of the Suez Canal again affected the flow of oil to Europe. Yet, in each instance, despite the clear dependence Europe had on Middle Eastern oil, the oil-producing countries were unable to gain any significant leverage vis-à-vis the consuming nations.

When Iranian oil became unavailable, Europe was supplied from other regions of the world, primarily Central and South America. Acting under the provisions of the 1950 Defense Production Act, the U.S. government reached a *voluntary agreement* with the petroleum industry. U.S. oil companies operating abroad and other cooperating companies expanded their production in order to meet the requirements established under the agreed-upon rationing system. Later, other Middle Eastern producers (primarily in Saudi Arabia and Kuwait) increased their production and took over the Iranian share of the European market. The crisis was, from the European perspective, successfully met. Its outcome established a principle which governed relations among producing countries, consuming countries, and oil companies until the early 1970s.

> Commercially the companies proved very quickly that they were in a strong position to boycott the Iranian oil industry and that no producing nation could boycott the companies as successfully. The basic truth of the oil imbalance in the world thus became clear during the Iranian oil crisis: Iran depended on Europe for marketing of its oil. Without Europe the Iranian oil trade died. But without Iran, the European entrepreneur turned to alternate sources. Therefore, the foundation

was thus laid for the then current oil policy axiom that, during oil boycotts, it is the producing nation, rather than the consuming nation, that is bound to be the chief loser.[37]

When the Suez Canal was closed in 1956–57, coincident with the sabotaging of Iraq Petroleum Company pipelines, nearly two-thirds of Europe's oil supply was interrupted.[38] In order to prevent the industrial collapse of Europe, it was necessary to keep a constant flow of 3,250,000 barrels per day going to Europe. The U.S. assumed responsibility for meeting this need, arguing that it was essential both to the industrial survival of Europe and to the maintenance of military forces there.[39] Additional oil became available from three sources: increased U.S. production and exporting U.S. stockpiles; oil from the Caribbean; and Middle Eastern oil diverted from its normal course in the Western Hemisphere.[40]

The European response to the Suez crisis, in the context of the increased economic strength Europe achieved in the 1960s, was to assume more economic control over its oil imports. Western European-owned oil concerns moved into areas formerly controlled by the Seven Sisters. European countries built the world's largest tanker fleet, one which was far less dependent on the Suez Canal. The success of these policies is indicated by the fact that when the Suez Canal was closed in 1967, there was no oil emergency, and U.S. assistance was not required. In addition, attempts were made to diversify suppliers, although a heavy dependence on Middle Eastern nations remained. The consequence was a judgment (*circa* 1967) that Europe's oil situation was secure enough to make it insignificant in shaping Middle Eastern policy.[41]

By the late 1960s, the United States itself was becoming more dependent on imported oil and lost the capacity to provide the kind of support which had been available in 1957. Hence, supply security depended even more heavily on the ability of oil companies (private and state-owned) to maintain control of supplies. Yet their ability to do so was declining.

Maintenance Failure and the Rise of OPEC

The formation of OPEC significantly changed the range of options open to multinational corporations in resisting attempts at behavioral power by producer governments. A series of particular concessions added up to a structural change. Many examples could be chosen, but one will be focused on for purposes of illustration. The coordination and information-sharing capabilities of OPEC meant that it was at least *possible* for oil-producing states to play off some international oil companies against others in a relatively effective and systematic way. The process, called "leapfrogging" depended on the ability to isolate companies, so that the costs and risks they faced in non-compliance would be overwhelming. After a concession, other

144

companies could then become the targets of behavioral power, since producer governments could "reward" compliant companies with the resources non-compliant companies stood to lose. Such strategies became *attractive* in the late 1960s, when the demand for oil increased sufficiently to make the market favorable to sellers, thus reducing the costs that anything less than a unified front of corporations could impose on producer governments.

In 1969, Libya attempted to raise its revenues by forcing increases in both the posted price of oil and the tax rate. Libya focused pressure on Occidental, an independent which did virtually all its business in Libya. The risks of non-compliance were high, since Libya continued to cut back Occidental's production quotas, threatening its existence since it could not continue to absorb the costs from internal funds nor did it have other production facilities to make up for lost Libyan production. Occidental tried to negotiate a "safety net" with Exxon, which would have given it guarantees of replacement oil in the event of continued cutbacks. Exxon was unwilling to agree, and Occidental agreed to both price increases and tax increases.[42] Most other independents in Libya then yielded, and when the U.S. government advised companies it could be of little assistance to them, the major oil companies conceded as well.[43]

Other producer governments quickly demanded, and received, smaller tax increases. The fact that more moderate states joined in coalition with more radical states (such as Libya) in the following OPEC meeting raised the stakes to the point where oil companies faced serious risks unless they coordinated action. Hence, they established an agreement, the Libyan Producer's Agreement, which provided a means of sharing any production cuts companies in Libya might encounter. The companies attempted to force negotiation to take place between a group of oil company representatives (the London Policy Group) and OPEC as a whole.[44] The aim was to prevent "leapfrogging" based on the particular weaknesses of companies in radical Libya. In addition, government involvement supporting the companies' strategy was expected. It was decided that a U.S. government mission should be sent to Iran, Saudi Arabia, and Kuwait to: (a) prevent an impasse in discussions which could result in interrupted oil supplies; (b) indicate why the U.S. government had taken steps under anti-trust laws to permit companies to negotiate jointly; and (c) to gain assurances that producers would continue to supply oil at reasonable prices.[45] The attempt backfired, however, from the perspective of the companies, when the State Department indicated to the Shah that it did not intend to become involved in the details of negotiations. It further responded to the Shah's statement that OPEC resented the condition of an OPEC-wide negotiation, and accepted assurances that the Gulf countries would accept conditions negotiated with oil companies and adhere to them even if more favorable terms were obtained by other countries. The companies were then advised to work out open negotiations with Gulf producers and deal separately with Libya.

The companies accepted the recommendation of the State Department and negotiated the Teheran agreement with the Gulf states, which provided an increase in government revenues of about $0.30/barrel. In 1971 the Tripoli agreement provided Libya with increases of about $0.65. OPEC continued to press for more concessions, this time revenue increases through "participation agreements." With companies unable to reorganize relations to control the sequence of challenges, leapfrogging continued until the 1973 embargo and unilateral price increase.

The above account cannot pretend to be a full account of the structuring of international oil transactions. Nor does it mean to imply that multinational corporations became structurally powerless, for as the embargo demonstrated, they continued to have the capability to *direct* flows of oil even though it was difficult to control the volume of supplies. What it does attempt to suggest is that multinational corporations gradually lost structural power, in the sense that they could no longer set the terms of access to resources, to limit the policy alternatives of producer governments, impose an effective definition of what were "legitimate" transactions, or keep the distribution of risks and costs from shifting against them. A variety of changes in the international milieu which international oil companies could not control (including the simultaneous "boom" of major industrial countries and the increasing number of independent oil companies entering the international market) made it far more difficult for oil companies to shape international transactions, even *among* companies. The crucial factor—the change from a buyers' to a sellers' oil market—leading to OPEC power is an example of a "windfall" factor in changing the distribution of structural power. The internal reorganization attempted was simply insufficient to meet the increased challenges, and without the ability to persuade other actors (e.g., the U.S. government) to absorb some of the risks of resisting further attempts at behavioral power, they conceded. Because U.S. governmental policy had relied so heavily (albeit tacitly) on the ability of international oil companies to provide needed oil imports on stable terms, their loss of structural power eventually had implications for the U.S. and its allies, as well.

Structual Power as a Political Issue:
The New International Political Order

The next case is different, for international institutions are the forum for an explicit attempt to generate international structural change—including a redistribution of tangible resources (e.g., 1% of GNP as an income transfer) and a change in the distribution of economic opportunities and risks (e.g., providing advantages and guarantees which are claimed to be just compensation for what was in the past a distribution skewed in favor of the presently rich nations). Virtually all the major issues addressed in the Seventh Special Session of the General Assembly involve the relative distribution of access to resources, economic opportunities, and costs and risks of international economic transactions. In seeking to alter such distributions in favor of the developing world, the Group of 77 is, in reality, attempting to exercise direct structural power.

A quick review of major issues will make clear the nature of the challenge to the present international economic order.[46] The Group of 77[47] has pushed for changes which would improve trade terms for developing countries and ensure market access for their products. The traditional argument (formulated before OPEC's actions to raise oil prices) is that many LDCs were "locked into" a world division of labor which made them primarily producers of raw materials and tropical products needed by colonizing nations. Colonial policy in many cases not only introduced the crops to be grown and controlled the extraction of raw materials, but explicitly limited the growth of local manufacturing. As a result of these patterns, newly independent countries faced a series of risks and costs associated with development which the first industrial nations had not incurred. In particular, because their economies were heavily (and artificially) dependent on a few exports, they simultaneously faced the problem of generating capital for development through international transactions *and* diversifying their exports so as to make their earnings less subject to price fluctuations. Diversification had high costs, however, and many states simply were unable to pay them. In addition, it was risky. Introducing new primary product exports entailed the risk of flooding the market with goods (whose production and sale could not be coordinated by LDCs) and decreasing earnings. Attempting to diversify into industrial products, or semi-processed raw materials, entailed the risk that efforts to market products abroad would be thwarted by more powerful producers in developed countries. Hence, the present demands for *guarantees* that markets will not be closed to LDC producers if they become capable of producing lower cost products which might displace domestically produced goods in industrialized nations.

LDCs have also sought to push for changes in the distribution of risks and costs associated with primary product production. They have advocated international commodity agreements to stabilize prices within certain ranges (generally at levels high enough to increase LDC earnings) and that the costs of stabilization and the risks of mismatched supply and demand be internationalized through formal international stockpiling funded by a Special International Fund. In addition, there have been proposals to internationalize the risk of inflation-induced changes of purchasing power by indexing the price of raw materials to those of key industrial products. The effects of internationally transmitted inflation, then, would be borne not by

LDCs (as balance of payments problems or reduced international purchases) but by nations engaging in international commerce generally.

In demanding non-reciprocal economic changes, LDCs are also attempting to redistribute costs and risks, while seeking to increase the range of economic options available to LDCs and developed countries. Essentially, their argument is that "reciprocal" concessions among very unequal parties imply "non-reciprocal" costs and risks. An LDC which removes trade barriers protecting an "infant industry" to match a reduction by a developed country is risking its ability to develop an industrial capacity. The developed country generally incurs only the risk of increased competition (marginal producers will be pressured) and the costs of adaptation (seeking greater efficiency, decreasing profit margins). In addition, LDCs argue, the products which they *can* export to developed countries are usually not vital to their economy, while the industries for LDCs may be much more nationally significant. As Gilpin showed in Chapter 2, history is filled with examples of "developing countries" acting to reduce the burden of inequality.

Most LDC demands have not only stressed changing distributions of risk, cost, and opportunity, but formalizing or institutionalizing the changes. Hence, they have sought integrated commodity agreements, formal and binding agreements on stabilizing export earnings and technology transfer, and *general* procedures for coping with increasing debt burdens. Here their stance differs sharply from the U.S. position, which seeks to recognize specific problems (some countries, some commodities, some debts) and handle them on a case-by-case basis—leaving transaction patterns relatively unchanged and opening the way for "concessions" at some point, "denials" at others. It is in seeking relatively general, relatively enduring changes in economic relations that LDC demands become attempts at exercising structural power.

While it is relatively easy to recognize the push for a New International Economic Order (NIEO) as an attempt at structural power, it is more difficult to understand how the nations in question can make the attempt or achieve their goal. What resources can they bring to bear? How can they employ their resources? Can they achieve some measure of effectiveness in an arena as large as the "international economic order"?

A starting point for addressing these questions is offered by Gosovic and Ruggie when they observe that demands for a new order

> . . . are coming to be expressed within a policy context whose parameters are expanding; the issue of contention at the Seventh Special Session was not so much *whether* but *what kinds* of collective arrangements to construct in order to deal with Third World demands, particularly in the commodity and raw materials fields. This represents an important shift in the posture of the major industrial countries. What produced

this shift was the confluence of forces and events that preceded the Session: essentially the fact that new international economic order negotiations became progressively entangled with oil diplomacy.[48]

The impact of the OPEC price increases, and the Organization of Arab Petroleum Exporting Countries (OAPEC) embargo, was significant in ways which will be explored shortly. Yet, a variety of other factors have been important, including the past history of dialogue among less developed countries, the rising influence of LDCs in selected international institutions, relations among Western industrialized countries, and domestic conditions within key industrial societies. By exploring these factors, in addition to the significance of the OPEC experience, some evaluations of the attempt at exercising "structural power" inherent in the NIEO can be offered.

It is important to remember that while the phrase "new international economic order" was coined in 1974, dissatisfaction with key elements of the existing order began much earlier and was rooted primarily in the obstacles LDC leaders encountered in formulating and implementing effective *independent* national economic programs. By the early 1970s, a series of conferences and institutional dialogues had resulted in a relatively well-defined set of complaints with the existing international economic structure.[49] The primary focus of the Group of 77 has been on development-related issues, almost none of which were *inherently* salient to developed countries. By and large, however, LDCs lacked the ability to get wealthier nations to recognize development issues per se as worthy of major international attention. Neither were Third World countries able to exert much influence on economic conditions (deteriorating terms of trade, unstable export earnings) which affected them, nor on new international actors (multinational corporations, international lending institutions) which became more important to their national economic activity. While industrial development, "economic independence," and increased national wealth were key elements of national security for many Third World countries, they found themselves threatened by outside involvement in their economies, primarily in response to other actors' perceptions of *their* security and interests. This awareness was important, for it linked the struggle for "economic independence" with previous struggles for political independence against colonial (now neo-colonial) countries.

In this context, the OPEC price increases and the OAPEC embargo became particularly important. From the position of non-OPEC LDCs, linking the issues of the NIEO to oil diplomacy provided a means, previously unavailable, of raising the salience of their demands. From the position of OPEC countries, linking questions of oil diplomacy to the NIEO provided a way of expanding the scope of their economic power, while helping to legitimize their actions in the eyes of poorer countries immediately disadvantaged by higher oil prices. The concept of "collective self-reliance" had been given a concrete referent and had been shown effective in bringing about major international economic changes. In addition, the aftermath of the embargo and price increases demonstrated that changing international economic relations could produce more wealth and draw in technology and expertise which recipient nations *could autonomously direct*. OPEC became an exemplar for the Group of 77, indicating that coordinated action (even with internal conflicts on many issues) could produce much-desired goals.

The OPEC experience helped solidify the Group of 77 in another way. Third World countries are by no means homogeneous—in their political orientations or in their economic characteristics. Moderate and radical impressions of international economic reality are different. Some radical leaders saw actions to achieve "economic independence" as leading to a final destruction of the capitalist international economic structure. More moderate leaders had no desire to destroy the system but simply wanted to change it. The fact that there was no catastrophic collapse of international commerce (as some predicted) after OPEC's actions helped mediate the differences between radicals and moderates. Moderates saw that major wealth redistributions were *economically* possible; radicals could hardly deny that substantial gains had been made with less-than-total destruction of the capitalist system.

The "link" between oil and other international economic issues was, for the developing countries, made relatively early. In 1974 Algeria requested a U.N. Special Session on the subject of *raw materials and development*, a forum where discussing oil prices would be embedded in other issues salient to less developed countries. This became the Sixth Special Session. American attempts to keep consumer-producer talks limited to oil (part of an attempt to restructure the negotiating environment by presenting a "united front" of consumers) did not succeed, and the Paris Conference of 1975 saw representatives of the "developing" countries present proposals to "look at the whole structure," while American and European delegations came primarily prepared to discuss energy. The meeting ended with developing countries maintaining the link between energy and wider international issues, while the U.S. was still unwilling to link them. The head of the American delegation stated: "We recognize the need for imaginative new initiatives in this area, and are indeed prepared to discuss these other issues *elsewhere in appropriate forums*."[50] An unofficial reaction among some Europeans, however, accepted a link, and within a month Kissinger stated that the failure of the Paris meetings indicated that "the dialogue between the producers and consumers will not progress unless it is broadened to include the general issue of the relationship between developing and developed countries."[51]

The inability of Western industrial nations either to present a "united front" (which *might* have limited discussions to oil) or to reduce their dependence to the point where discussions would be less valued meant that the United States and other industrialized nations not previously inclined to treat demands for a NIEO seriously had to do so now—at least on the diplomatic level. There was now risk involved for the industrialized nations: the risk that discussions with oil producers might not materialize. The political importance of the Special Session was indicated at an OECD meeting during the summer of 1975. Gosovic and Ruggie report that:

> The recurrent themes of these discussions were that confrontation was to be avoided at all cost, the Special Session must be a success, and the structure of international economic relations as it affects developing countries could and must be improved. With the exception of Japan and the Federal Republic of Germany, expressions of commitment to the last of these themes varied only in intensity.[52]

The negotiated agenda eliminated some of the clearly unacceptable themes for industrialized nations (e.g., permanent sovereignty over natural resources, control over multinational corporations). Hence, it was possible for the U.S. and other industrialized nations to negotiate in a forum where conflict was not inevitable, while it was possible for the Group of 77 to "test the seriousness" of industrialized countries.

Because the Group of 77 is not homogeneous, it has been argued that it is possible to find member states for whom proposed changes would be economically undesirable, at least in terms of immediate effects.[53] Thus, a major U.S. aim was, and has remained, breaking up the Group of 77 into more manageable pieces. Yet, during the Special Session, and subsequently UNCTAD IV, the Group of 77 negotiated through a single spokesperson, while the industrialized nations had multiple negotiators. This unity has given the Group of 77 a decided diplomatic advantage over the major industrialized nations. Indeed, in both the Special Session and UNCTAD IV, the coherence and organization of the Group of 77 has allowed them to exercise more direction over the course of negotiations than most observers from the West had expected.

While some of the seriousness with which diplomats now discuss the NIEO is the result of the OPEC experience, it is necessary to probe a bit deeper. One might argue that conceding major structural changes as an adjunct to oil diplomacy is irrational, if the only "threat from the Third World" lies in Western dependence on imported oil.[54] There are at least two other issues to consider. The first issue is the extent to which countries within the Group of 77 have the ability to disrupt or destabilize commercial transactions. Whether this is a national security threat, or simply a nuisance, depends upon how sensitive economic prosperity in industrialized countries

151

is to instability, and how important continued prosperity (or minimally, economic recovery) is to their conceptions of national security.

A second, and more fundamental, issue is whether or not the "threat from the Third World" is different under changed structural conditions. The key condition has to do with the ability of the Group of 77 to act as a single unit in economic, as well as diplomatic, settings. The proposals for commodity stabilization advanced by the Group of 77 have stressed the need for a common stabilization fund used to stabilize prices for some 10–18 commodities. Contributions to the fund would come from both producers and consumers of the range of products and would be used to accumulate stockpiles of products. These stockpiles, in turn, could be held or sold to stabilize commodity prices within established ranges. Such a proposal, it is claimed, would make it easier to get commodity agreements to work, since they could deal simultaneously with potentially substitutable products. Furthermore, it is argued, fluctuations in one commodity could offset fluctuations in others, making the cost of stabilization less than it would be if each commodity were handled separately. American objections to the program are essentially dual: that such a wide-reaching program would be economically and administratively unwieldy. It would introduce major inefficiences while perhaps not giving LDC producers substantial gains. Second, the administration of the program could be used for political purposes or become subject to political control. The latter, clearly, is a major concern of industrialized countries who undoubtedly fear that their political role would not be decisive.

During UNCTAD IV, however, members of the Group of 77 began to suggest that, if industrialized nations' support were not forthcoming, they themselves would provide the capital to begin such a commodity stabilization program.[55] Although systematic estimates have not been made, a Third World delegate estimated that, at the very best, $3–6 billion would be necessary to capitalize a stabilization fund for the program.[56] Furthermore, the poorer nations argue that if they could raise $1 billion, they could borrow commercially to raise the $2 billion necessary to meet minimum capitalization requirements.[57] Clearly, such a "stabilization fund" would support more than integrated commodity agreements. It would, in essence, capitalize a producer's agreement.

If such an agreement could be organized and funded, it would require a substantial revision of the present evaluation of the "Third World threat." There are many reasons. First, analyses of the potential for cartel formation have proceeded on the assumption that they would be formed by major producers of the product in question, and the producers would bear the costs and risks associated with its implementation. Formation might be more likely if costs and risks were more widely distributed. Second, arguments about the substitutability of mineral resources again have assumed

152

that their production was independent. With coordinated agreements involving potential substitutes, the situation might be different. Third, it has been assumed that the economic staying power of producers forming a cartel would be limited: either because the cartel would not transfer revenues massive enough to provide the kinds of wealth OPEC received, or because the economies in question were so dependent on sales relative to the consumers' dependence on purchases from them that they would become unable to bear the costs which could be imposed. Neither of these arguments would necessarily hold if the revenue base were a larger, more diversified, group of countries. Fourth, it has been assumed that cartels would disintegrate, for well-known economic reasons. Such analyses exclude the political benefits accruing to previously weak nations who acquire collective resource bases. The ability to be more autonomous and to exercise behavioral power over formerly dominant nations is itself a significant benefit. This is especially true if one of the aims of organization is to change the political reality as well as to gain wealth.

It is not at all clear that the Group of 77 has the resources necessary to carry out such a program. To this point, the ability to restructure has appeared to rest on essentially diplomatic bargaining resources: the ability to link oil diplomacy to NIEO demands, the numerical importance of LDCs in key international forums (especially in the U.N. system), the lack of unity among industrial nations, and the fact that industrial nations perceive themselves vulnerable to damage from oil-producing states in concert. Restructuring through the diplomatic process is undoubtedly less costly (if it can be achieved) than is restructuring through an OPEC model writ large. Furthermore, the latter course requires different resources, including capital, economic expertise, and coordination, which have traditionally been lacking in many less developed countries.

Some of the conditions contributing to the diplomatic gains of the Group of 77 have less to do with the developing nations and more to do with changes within and among industrialized countries. Several of these are worth noting, although they cannot be fully explored here. First, the debate about a NIEO does not occur only in political and economic terms. There is also an ethical-moral dimension. The poverty, sickness, and hunger prevalent in many less developed countries is well known, as is the growing gap between the poor in less developed countries and people in industrialized societies. Within many Western societies, there is a moral-ethical commitment to eliminate radical inequality. Some of them (particularly Scandinavia and the Netherlands) have engaged in domestic policies which emphasize the elimination of inequalities which deny basic human needs, such as education, medical care, food, shelter. Arguments for a "more just" international economic order often rest both on the facts of poverty in much of the Third World and upon the judgment that present economic

153

arrangements deny many LDCs the tools they need to handle their own problems. The latter position, in turn, rests on fundamental critiques of the capitalist system and market failures, which have been important in shaping domestic policies designed to eliminate poverty and radical inequality. There is thus in some parts of the industrialized world the commitment to change present conditions, even if the conditions are advantageous, because they produce (or preserve) unacceptable conditions. The Swedish and Dutch identification with NIEO demands in large part reflects such moral-ethical commitments.

Second, there are great differences among industrialized nations in the extent to which relatively unregulated "market forces" are weighted in domestic and regional economies. Most industrialized countries have greater overt government involvement in economic affairs than does the United States. It is simply difficult, then, to argue that increased political involvement in the economy is per se unacceptable. It is similarly difficult to argue, given the history of multinational corporate oligopolies and wide-spread acceptance of the idea that economic relationships are not political, that the present international structure is either a "free market" or the reflection of transpolitical economic realities.

Finally, there is the significance of the changing role of the United States in international economic affairs. It could be argued that after World War II, the structural power exercised by the United States *opened alternatives and opportunities* for the major nations considered (primarily Europe and Japan). Recent exercises of structural power (for instance, changes in the monetary structure, as examined in Chapter 9) are more akin to adjusting the distribution of costs, risks, and opportunity costs to advantage (or limit damage to) the nation exercising it. While the United States, and in addition Germany and Japan, appear to have benefited from the new "market forces," other nations have not experienced clear benefits. Indeed, it can be argued that sustaining Western industrial nations' participation in the monetary system, including Italy and Britain, will involve considerably greater costs for stronger industrial nations. At present, the U.S. is not willing, and is perhaps unable, to shoulder these costs unilaterally; nor are other nations such as Germany or Japan. In this environment, where economic sensitivity still implies important economic effects for domestic economies, it is illusory to expect a "unified front" among industrialized nations. Divergent views do not reflect simply a "lack of will" but the inability to find a *way to consider* the sharing of costs and risks in the international economic interactions which are still vitally important to industrialized nations. From this perspective, one might consider the difficulty the U.S. has encountered in forging a common position even on oil diplomacy— complicated by new costs emerging from its reluctance (or inability) to pay the increasing costs associated with maintaining the security of European petroleum supplies.

The combination of these factors suggests several points about the NIEO as an attempt at structural power. First, as innumerable writers have suggested in other contexts, the strength of the Third World lies in its ability to organize and maintain solidarity. Without collective action, individual less developed countries have virtually no ability to exert structural power. Indeed, this has been their condition for the last 30 years. Whether organizing to change international structures will prove to be easier than organizing "common markets" in the Third World remains to be seen. Second, with collective organization, new resources become available to LDCs in theory, and new means for gaining and employing those resources likewise become usable. Third, maintaining the solidarity of any Third World collective will remain, for the foreseeable future, primarily a political task, which will quickly come to be the problem of finding acceptable ways of assuming and sharing costs and risks. This is, in part, the same task facing industrialized nations.

The Implications of Structural Power

The kind of international structuring which occurred during and immediately after World War II cannot be repeated in the present context. The United States had such a significant share of both the economic and military resources of the Western world that it was able to undertake broad, complementary structuring activities. In addition, it had a disproportionate share of the skills necessary to undertake structuring activities. Finally, it was clearly recognized that the old structure had collapsed. The costs of collapse (especially for Britain) were associated with the war, not with concerted restructuring attempts on the part of Western nations. Most Western nations had lost a great deal by the end of the war, and promises of restoring some of those losses could be coupled with conditions on the nature of future actions. No nation or group of nations, be it OPEC or the Group of 77, holds a comparable base of structural power today.

The OPEC countries, even considered collectively, do not have the resources or skills to structure economic arenas beyond oil production, and possibly the oil industry. It matters greatly what OPEC countries do with their resources, and thus far it appears that attempts to develop internally, establish military forces, and increase domestic consumption will use the bulk of the oil revenue. Even in these areas—industrialization and military forces—success depends on importing equipment and expertise. The ability to alter fundamentally the *way* in which expertise is transferred (presence of foreign nationals or exposure of nationals to the educational systems of other countries) is still lacking. Similarly, structuring the terms on which industrial imports are supplied has been difficult. Indexation seems an unlikely prospect, and OPEC has found it difficult to raise oil prices enough to offset the rise in industrial import costs since 1974. The Saudi refusal to agree to another price increase in early 1977 clearly signals the limitations of pricing strategies as a way of protecting against deteriorating trade terms.

Similarly, while OPEC price increases certainly affect the Western industrial economies, OPEC countries can neither control the effects nor exploit them for their own benefit over and above their revenue gains. For example, one of the effects of higher oil prices (and corresponding increases in the price of other energy sources) is that consumption patterns are changing in many Western economies. More consumer income must be spent on energy, which implies weakening demand for other consumer goods unless real income grows. Yet OPEC countries can do little to exploit this change, and indeed, indirectly bear some of its costs in their investments in Western countries. A weakness of investment and technical skill as well as political restraint keeps them from being able to enter Western economies and control production (as opposed to purchasing real estate or making portfolio investments).

This suggests that, at best, OPEC nations collectively will follow an insulative structuring strategy, attempting to gain more control over the oil industry by moving into processing and marketing while trying to *insulate* this structure from disruptions in other economic arenas. At worst, from the OPEC perspective, additional resources will simply "pass through the ledgers" of oil-producing countries. This is a prospect some states already recognize and hope to avoid.

If this analysis is correct, it has profound implications for the ability to achieve a NIEO. Establishing an order based on a generalized commodity stabilization program without the cooperation of industrialized countries would imply not only initial costs, but prolonged maintenance costs. Some of these, of course, could be met from the additional revenue such a program might extract from industrialized countries. But some group of nations would have to provide "collective benefits" to make the structure work, as Saudi Arabia does for OPEC itself. Clearly, given the uniquely important role oil plays in industrial economies, OPEC is a likely candidate for paying maintenance costs. Whether it has the resources vis-à-vis its own economic requirements to do so is problematic—especially in light of the ability of most OPEC nations to overspend their oil earnings.

There are also implications for the Western industrial nations. Despite rhetoric about achieving greater "energy independence," reliance on imported oil is likely to continue. As long as it does, and the ability to set prices lies outside the industrial nations' capabilities, they will be sensitive to the economic changes higher oil prices bring. The pre-OPEC structure of international oil production, as well as current difficulties in distributing the costs and risks of economic change among OECD countries, suggest that it will be difficult to reorganize relations satisfactorily to handle this sensitivity.

The conclusion is that the present international economic milieu poses significant threats for most major groups of nations. Certainly, non-oil-producing LDCs face the most severe economic threats from present international economic patterns. Yet, the economic consequences for OECD countries are not negligible, and neither are those to most OPEC countries. OECD countries, considered collectively, have the resources to *attempt* to structure their economic relations to *insulate* them from disturbances originating in the international oil sector. OPEC nations, considered collectively, can *attempt* to structure international oil production to insulate it from disturbances in other economic arenas. Given the close link between oil and industrial production, however, it may be that these seemingly disjointed structuring efforts will produce a satisfactory international economic structure. The issues raised in discussions of the NIEO are likely to persist in attempts to negotiate a broader international economic structure, primarily because they are a political reflection of the fact that structural power is the issue at stake. Whether, as much as how, these competing claims for structural power can be resolved will affect the national security of many countries in the years to come, and it is clear that at this point in time, structural power will be *pluralist*.

Footnotes

1. Robert Keohane and Joseph Nye, "World Politics and the International System," in *The Future International Economic Order: An Agenda for Research*, ed. C. Fred Bergsten (Lexington, Mass.: Lexington Books, D. C. Heath and Company, 1973), p. 118.
2. The definition follows Klaus Knorr, *The Power of Nations* (New York: Basic Books, 1975), p. 4.
3. Jeff Hart, "Three Approaches to the Measurement of Power in International Relations," *International Organization* 30, 3 (Spring 1976): 296–303 comes close to the conception of power as control over situations.
4. Keohane and Nye, "World Politics," p. 117.
5. The definition builds on the attempt to define metapower or relational power in Tom Baumgartner and Tom Burns, "The Structuring of International Economic Relations," *International Studies Quarterly*, 19 (June 1975): 128–30; and Tom Baumgartner, Walter Buckley, Tom Burns, and Peter Schuster, "Metapower and the Structuring of Social Hierarchies," in *Power and Control: Social Structures and Their Transformation*, ed. Tom Burns and Walter Buckley (Beverly Hills, California: Sage Publications, 1976), pp. 224–26.
6. Peter Bachrach and Morton S. Baratz, *Power and Poverty: Theory and Practice* (New York: Oxford University Press, 1970), p. 7.
7. The discussion follows Keohane and Nye, "World Politics," p. 124.
8. Immanuel Wallerstein, *The Modern World System* (New York: Academic Press, 1974), p. 98.
9. Ibid., pp. 30–36.

10. Knorr, *Power of Nations*, p. 4, and Chapter 4 of this volume.

11. This is not unique to structural power. The general problem for power is discussed in Hayward Alker, "On Political Capabilities in a Schedule Sense: Measuring Power, Integration and Development," in *Mathematical Approaches to Politics*, ed. Haywood Alker, Karl Deutsch, and John Stoetzel (New York: Elsevier, 1973).

12. See Knorr, *Power of Nations*, pp. 10–14 and Chapter 4 of this volume for a summary of these points.

13. Baumgartner et al., "Metapower," p. 241.

14. Robert Gilpin, "Three Models of the Future," in *World Politics and International Economics*, ed. C. Fred Bergsten and Lawrence Krause (Washington, D.C.: Brookings Institution), p. 46.

15. Baumgartner and Burns, "Structuring," pp. 132–34.

16. By a world economy Wallerstein means a system where economic arrangements are the basic linkages among actors over a domain larger than that of any political system. Wallerstein, *Modern World System*, p. 15.

17. Ibid., p. 16.

18. Jaime Vicen Vives, *Approaches to the History of Spain* (Berkeley: University of California Press, 1970), pp. 97–98.

19. Wallerstein, *Modern World System*, p. 200.

20. Ibid., pp. 193–200.

21. The terminology of maintenance costs comes from Benjamin Cohen, *The Question of Imperialism* (New York: Basic Books, 1975).

22. Cf. for example A. L. K. Acheson, J. F. Chant, and M. F. J. Prachowny, eds., *Bretton Woods Revisited* (Toronto: University of Toronto Press, 1972). Also see Chapter 9 of this volume.

23. This is the thesis advanced by Keohane and Nye, "World Politics," pp. 126–40.

24. This is a general theme of Gilpin, *U.S. Power and the Multinational Corporation* (New York: Basic Books, 1975).

25. Leonard Mosley, *Power Play: The Tumultuous World of Middle East Oil, 1890–1973* (London: Weidenfeld and Nicolson, 1973), p. 26.

26. The discussion which follows draws heavily on Robert B. Krueger, *The United States and International Oil, A Report for the Federal Energy Administration on U.S. Firms and Government Policy* (New York: Praeger, 1975), pp. 40–42.

27. U.S., Congress, Senate, Subcommittee on Multinational Corporations, *Multinational Oil Corporations and U.S. Foreign Policy*, 94th Congress, 1st sess., 1975, p. 317. (Henceforth cited as *Multinational Hearings*).

28. Ibid., pp. 34–35.

29. For a more complete account of the penetration of U.S. firms, see Anderson G. Bartlett et al., *Pertamina, Indonesia National Oil* (Tulsa: Amerasian Ltd., 1972).

30. For a general history, see Edwin Lieuwen, *Petroleum in Venezuela* (New York: Russell and Russell, 1967).

31. *Multinational Hearings*, p. 337.

32. H. St. J. B. Philby, *Arabian Oil Ventures* (Washington, D.C.: Middle East Institute, 1964), p. 106.

33. U.S., Congress, Senate, Special Committee Investigating the National Defense Program, *Petroleum Arrangements with Saudi Arabia*, 80th Congress, 1st sess., 1948, p. 25237.

34. Krueger, *International Oil*, p. 52.

35. The three reports which provided evaluations of European needs in this area were: U.S. Department of the Interior, *National Resources and Foreign Aid*, Report of J. A. Krug, Secretary of the Interior, 9 October 1947 (Washington, D.C.: Government Printing Office, 1947); President's Office of Governmental Reports, *European Recovery and American Aid, Report by the President's Committee on Foreign Aid*, 7 November 1947 (Washington,

D.C.: Government Printing Office, 1947); and U.S., Congress, House, Select Committee on Foreign Aid, *Petroleum Requirements and Availabilities*, Preliminary Report Number Five, 80th Congress, 1st sess., 1947.

36. Ibid.
37. Shoshana Klebanoff, *Middle East Oil and U.S. Foreign Policy* (New York: Prager, 1974), p. 98.
38. Ibid., p. 128.
39. U.S., Department of Interior, Office of Oil and Gas, "Report to the Secretary of the Interior from the Director of the Voluntary Agreement, as Amended May 8, 1956, Relating to the Foreign Petroleum Supply," Washington, D.C., 30 June 1957 (mimeographed) as cited in Klebanoff, *Middle East*, p. 129.
40. Klebanoff, *Middle East*, p. 130. Since the 1930s the United States conservation policy sought to maintain underground reserves to supply needs in national emergencies for up to 10–12 years. The reserves were drawn down during the Suez emergency and not replenished.
41. Ibid., p. 219.
42. H. Schuler, "The International Oil 'Debacle' Since 1971," *Petroleum Intelligence Weekly*, 22 April 1974 (Special Supplement), as cited in Kruger, *International*, p. 65.
43. *Multinational Hearings*, p. 125.
44. Ibid., p. 129.
45. Ibid., p. 148.
46. Issue summaries are drawn from Branislav Gosovic and John Ruggie, "On the Creation of a New International Economic Order: Issue Linkage and the Seventh Special Session of the UN," *International Organization*, 21 (Spring 1976): 310–43.
47. The Group of 77, now composed of 113 less developed countries, is the major negotiating organization for LDCs on international economic issues.
48. Gosovic and Ruggie, "Creation," p. 310.
49. The institutional roots of the discussions go back into UNCTAD and its focus on the problems of trade and development facing the Third World. For general discussions, see Branislav Gosovic, *UNCTAD: Conflict and Compromise* (Leiden: Sijthoff, 1972) and Robert Walters, "UNCTAD: Intervener Between Poor and Rich States," *Journal of World Trade Law*, VII, 5 (September 1973): 527–54.
50. *New York Times*, 8 April 1975.
51. *New York Times*, 29 May 1975.
52. Gosovic and Ruggie, "Creation," p. 320.
53. See Roger D. Hansen, "The Political Economy of North-South Relations: How Much Change?" *International Organization*, 29 (Autumn 1975): 921–47 for such arguments.
54. For an analysis of the prospects of cartel formation and stabilization agreements, see David L. McNicol, "Commodity Agreements and the New International Economic Order," California Institute of Technology Working Paper 114, November 1976. (Mimeographed.)
55. *Washington Post*, 28 May 1976.
56. Ibid.
57. Ibid.

CHAPTER 6

Domestic Constraints on International Economic Leverage*

Stephen D. Krasner

Introduction

The Arab oil boycott and the quadrupling of petroleum prices in 1973 and 1974 have brought new interest to an old question: the relationship between national security and economic relations. National security involves a wide variety of goals, with perhaps the clearest being political power—the ability to change the behavior of other actors. In addition to political power, international economic transactions also impinge on a number of other state goals. They have been noted by Klaus Knorr in Chapter 1. State goals include the desire to achieve high and stable income levels for both the society as a whole and specific groups within it and to assure access to supply, markets, capital, and technology sources.

This chapter focuses on the point that the ability of a state to achieve these objectives depends only *in part* on its place in the international system. Small underdeveloped states may find themselves either passive victims or beneficiaries of decisions taken by others; large developed states can defend themselves more actively. However, the ability of central decision-makers to further national security goals also depends on their relations with their own society. Achieving collective good can be stifled by internal as well as external resistance. A nation's leaders must not only look outward toward their international environment, but they must also look inward toward domestic pressure groups. The basic attributes of economic power—size and level of development—establish only the outer boundaries of a state's political capabilities. Central decision-makers cannot utilize resources that they do not have, but at the same time, they may not be able to manipulate resources nominally under their control. If central political decision-makers can easily change the behavior of societal groups, then they can fully utilize all of the nation's resources. If private groups are able to thwart public initiatives or use governmental institutions for private purposes, however, then the ability of even large, developed states to achieve national goals affected by international economic transactions will be limited.

The state's strength in relation to its own society can be envisioned along a continuum ranging from weak to strong.[1] Positioning along this continuum depends on the answer to two questions:

1. Can central decision-makers autonomously formulate policies that are designed to further the collective or general goals of the country?
2. Can central decision-makers implement their policy preferences?

If the answer to the first question is negative, we are inevitably dealing with a weak political system in which central decision-makers do not move to further the collective good. Their inability to do so could be the result of several factors. First, individuals holding the reins of power might be more interested in "feathering their own nests" than in furthering the general aims of their society. In such a situation bribery and extortion would be more potent forms of political currency than conceptions of the national good. Second, the society might be so internally divided that there would be no agreement either among the mass or the elite on what constitutes the general good. Such situations are most common in countries where there are very strong ethnic divisions. It is not clear, for instance, that the Catholics and Protestants of Northern Ireland could come to any agreement on public goals. Third, central decision-makers might be unable to formulate policies designed to further the general good because the political system is dominated by a particular class or group from within the society. This is, of course, the Marxist view of capitalist states. For Marxists, the notion of the national interest is meaningless, because the state is but the servant, in one form or another, of the dominant class in the society.

It is assumed here that central decision-makers are usually able to formulate a coherent set of objectives; that personal cupidity, societal divisions, or the dominance of particular groups does not occur so frequently as to render the very concept of the state meaningless. However, the ability of a state to formulate a set of objectives does not necessarily imply that they can be carried out. As we have noted, a state may be frustrated at the international level because it is small and underdeveloped. Or, a state can be frustrated on the domestic front. Even after having established a set of goals, central decision-makers might be unable to implement them because of resistance from groups within their own society. While the objectives of central decision-makers might benefit the society as a whole, this does not necessarily mean that each group within the country will secure the same returns, or even that some groups in the country will not suffer actual losses. There may, in Knorr's terms, be a failure of national will. This is particularly true with respect to foreign economic policy. For instance, lowering tariffs will raise income for the society as a whole, but it will also hurt import-competing industries. Hence, the ability of a state to carry out its objectives depends on its ability to control its own domestic society. A strong state is one that can formulate collective goals and implement them. A weak state is one in which decision-makers cannot or will not formulate general aims or, having formulated them, are unable to carry them out because of resistance from particular domestic groups.

A state's ability to accomplish its international economic objectives is then a function of three distinct sets of relationships. First, it is necessary to specify the resources that are nominally under state control. The simplest summary measure is probably gross national product. Second, it is necessary to analyze what proportion of these resources can actually be controlled by central decision-makers to accomplish state purposes. As Chapter 4 pointed out, wealth alone does not mean power; it must be mobilized and directed. Third, it is necessary to examine the state's international situation and its ability to use its resources to change the behavior of other actors or to protect itself from undesired consequences of its involvement in the world economy. This chapter is primarily concerned with the second question.

In terms of this conception of domestically weak and strong states, countries in the present international system can be grossly lumped into three groups. Communist regimes are closest to the strong end of the spectrum. Less developed countries are closest to the weak end of the spectrum. The advanced market economy countries that are the principal concern of this essay—the United States, Western Europe and Japan—fall some place in between.

Communist Regimes

Authoritarian communist regimes, such as the Soviet Union, are characterized by a high degree of concentration of power and authority. There is no recognition of the legitimacy of an independent private sphere of activity, even though such private activity may exist. There is great reluctance to leave economic decisions to the workings of the market. Instead, prices, resource allocations, and output are largely determined by central planning agencies. Government institutions decide where factories will be built, how much housing will be constructed, what enterprises will receive capital.

Communist regimes have kept tight control over international intercourse: emigration has been limited, and trade has not been determined by market considerations. Despite the considerable increase in the exchange of goods between the Eastern Bloc and the rest of the world since 1970, there is still a disproportionate amount of trade among members of the Communist Bloc, particularly the Soviet Union and its Eastern European satellites. Furthermore, there was a conscious political decision to increase trade with the West; this development was not dictated in some automatic way by the workings of the market.[2] Foreign direct investment is modest in the Eastern Bloc. The import of foreign technology must be approved by economic planning agencies. In general, command economies are strong states, and their leaders are able to formulate coherent sets of objectives. They are *usually* able to implement them.

This is not to say that communist regimes are omnipotent. Cheating is widespread. The private sector does remain important in some areas: in Poland more than 75% of agricultural production comes from private farms. Popular resistance is possible: in the summer of 1976 the Polish government was forced to rescind food price increases because of street rioting. However, these qualifications should not blind one to the fact that authoritarian regimes are likely to be able to use a greater proportion of their domestic resources to accomplish state objectives than are the governments of advanced market economy countries or of less developed countries.

This does not mean that authoritarian regimes are necessarily better, or even that they will be internationally more powerful. Obviously, there are great costs in terms of individual liberty associated with communist systems. Also, in terms of economics, a command economy may involve rigidities that inhibit economic development. Advanced economies are highly complex, and it is difficult to control them through the use of a central plan. Efforts to decentralize economic decision-making have created strains for communist political systems, because they threaten the role of the Party as the sole repository of political legitimacy.[3] However, such decentralization may be critical if resources are to be efficiently allocated and if new technology is not only to be developed, but also put to use. Indeed, the Soviet Union has a large core of scientific workers and has made some significant advances in non-military as well as military technology. However, the problems of moving technology into the production process have been severe.[4] In sum, communist regimes are strong in the sense that their central decision-makers can utilize a large proportion of the nation's economic resources for state purposes, but the actual level of these resources may be lower than under a freer political system, because a highly centralized planned economy may stifle economic growth.

Less Developed Countries

At the opposite end of the spectrum from communist states are most countries of the Third World. They not only have few resources, but their governments are able to mobilize only a small proportion of what they do have for state purposes. Often their leaders have not been able to formulate a clear set of public goals, and even when objectives are specified, it may be impossible to implement them. This situation is a reflection both of culture and institutional capabilities. There is still a large traditional sector in most Third World countries. Many individuals are not closely bound to the na-

163

tional government—their ties to traditional institutions and groups, such as tribes, are stronger than those to the larger national whole. Further, there is widespread distrust of central political authorities. Because there are few trained individuals, the bureaucratic apparatus in many Third World countries is weak; corruption is encouraged because salary levels are often very low. In general, political institutions in LDCs tend to be more rigid, less complex, and less autonomous than those in more developed countries.[5]

In the area of foreign economic policy, smuggling is a serious problem. For instance, during the 1960s Burma adopted an explicit policy of cutting its ties with the rest of the world. Rather than leading to autonomous development, this created a huge black market. It has recently been estimated that sale of contraband in Burma is greater than legal trade.[6] (In 1976–77 the governing Council announced a reversal of its economic policies in order to re-enter the established patterns of international investment and development.) A substantial proportion of Senegal's peanuts are smuggled into Gambia. During the 1960s a third of Togo's cocoa exports were smuggled in from Ghana.[7] Corruption has also made it difficult to control the movement of goods. Petty bribery of customs officials is common in many Third World countries. This not only may mean a loss of revenue for the government, but may also make it impossible to control the kinds of goods that enter the country. Furthermore, wealthy economic actors, including foreign corporations, can also undermine efforts to control trade. One of the most glaring cases of this kind of activity involved payments of $1.25 million by United Brands to high Honduran officials in order to get a reduction of a newly imposed export tax on bananas. This tax was not only designed to raise the government's revenue, but also to further the creation of an international cartel.[8] Smuggling, bribery, and extortion all lessen the ability of a state to control activities within its own domestic jurisdiction. Even if political leaders are themselves free of venality and can formulate a clear commercial policy in such an environment, they may still be unable to implement their plans. LDCs cannot do much to further their national security, not only because they are vulnerable internationally, but also because their domestic political systems are weak.

Advanced Capitalist States

The advanced market economy countries present the most complex picture of the relationship between the state and its domestic society. They all fall at some intermediate position between communist countries and many LDCs. Their central distinguishing characteristic is the multiplicity of institutional forms, both public and private, that exist in the economy. All of these countries, even those with the most statist traditions, recognize that private activity is legitimate; that the state may attempt to guide, but it does not have the right to eliminate the non-public sphere. This recognition

164

places some limits on the kinds of policy instruments that the state has at its disposal to change the behavior of private actors. Democracy also imposes restraints. Either shifts in ruling coalitions, the need to compromise to hold coalitions together, frequent changes in the dominant party, or divisions between the executive and the legislature may make it difficult to formulate and pursue a coherent set of objectives designed to further the national good.

However, the political systems of advanced capitalist states show considerable variation in their strength—that is, in the ability of the state to formulate and implement collective goals. Japan probably has the strongest state; the U.S. may have the weakest. After the Second World War, Japanese central decision-makers were able to formulate and implement a clear set of objectives. American leaders have been able to establish goals, but their ability to carry them out has often been frustrated or limited by their inability to control various groups within American society.

Japan

From the Second World War until at least the 1970s, there was a clear consensus among the Japanese elite about state economic objectives. The Japanese wanted rapid economic growth, which implied a high level of investment. It also implied a high export level so that Japan could import the raw materials that she needed for her industries. There was general agreement that industrial growth would take place through private corporations. This set of goals can be seen as an extension of the dominant thrust in Japanese policy since the Meiji restoration of 1868; namely, catching up with the West.[9]

Japan's efforts to accomplish its objectives can only be judged a fabulous success. Success has been, at least in part, a reflection of a strong political system—of a state that has been able to exercise strong influence over its own domestic society. This strength is a reflection of attitudes and beliefs, the dominance of a single party for an extended period, the position of the bureaucracy, and the structure of Japanese banking and industry.

Japanese attitudes and beliefs have helped legitimate an activist state. Before 1945, Japanese society was understood in terms of a just hierarchical order under the Emperor. This world view was destroyed by defeat and occupation. However, the importance of the group—whether it be the family, the firm, or the bureaucracy—remains a central feature of Japanese society. This stands in sharp contrast to the American vision in which the individual is at the heart of the legitimating myth. In Japan, individuals strive to honor their group; in America individuals strive to fulfill themselves, or, in the earlier version of liberalism, so that they can choose freely to honor God.[10] Communal attitudes extend into the relationship between Japanese business and the state. In Japan there is a belief in the efficiency of private enterprise, but there is also a belief that the government can and should correct things if they go astray. The government is regarded as a well-intentioned guide for the private sector. The state, for its part, regards large businesses as a national asset and has been unwilling to allow them to fail.[11]

There are two other specific attitudes that make it easier for Japanese central decision-makers to direct business. First, bureaucrats are held in very high esteem in Japan. Such high status existed even during the Tokugawa period that preceded the Meiji restoration.[12] Second, the pursuit of profit has never been held in very high esteem. There is no assumption that the hidden hand will automatically lead to socially desirable outcomes. Furthermore, Japanese businessmen have generally been willing to take a long-term perspective; they have not set their sights on maximizing short-term profits.[13] Both the respect accorded to bureaucrats and the willingness of businessmen to forego immediate returns make it easier for the state to direct the domestic economy. Directives are less likely to be questioned, and they are less likely to conflict with the goals of individual firms, because long-term plans are more flexible than short-term profit-maximizing ones.

The second factor that has facilitated the state's ability to influence the behavior of its domestic economy has been the position of the Liberal Democratic Party (LDP). The LDP has won continuous control of the Japanese Diet since 1955. While the Party has been divided by factions organized around individual leaders, its members have generally voted as a bloc in the Diet. Furthermore, all groups in the LDP have accepted the goals of growth-investment-export.

The third factor that has made effective state action more possible in Japan than in other advanced capitalist countries has been the role of two major executive departments, the Ministry of International Trade and Industry (MITI) and the Ministry of Finance. These bureaucracies can intervene in the economy in a systematic way. They have acted to reshape the structure of particular industries and even to encourage the development of new economic sectors. They have also been able to promote individual firms.

Intervention at the level of the economic sector or the firm (as opposed to the economy as a whole) has been made possible by a wide range of policy instruments possessed by the Japanese bureaucracy, particularly MITI and the Ministry of Finance. MITI has actively coordinated behavior in certain industries by setting goals for output and unit costs. It has been able to grant tax allowances through accelerated depreciation. It has established a system of advisory councils. During the 1950s, MITI purposely moved to develop and rationalize the Japanese steel, petrochemical, heavy machinery, automobile, electronics, synthetic rubber, and airplane industries.[14]

166

In dealing with the international economy, Japan has imposed tighter controls than any other advanced capitalist state. Through the 1950s, the allocation of foreign exchange gave MITI a powerful control lever over the domestic economy. Although the removal of foreign trade quotas began in 1962 and 1963, this had little immediate effect, because Japanese tariffs were still high and there were many non-tariff barriers to trade. Only in the late 1960s, when the Japanese came to realize that they would have very large balance of payments surpluses if they continued their existing policies, did trade liberalization begin in earnest. Direct investment was also tightly controlled for most of the post-war period. In 1973 Japan allowed foreigners to have complete ownership of businesses in Japan for the first time, but even then certain industries were exempt. Furthermore, MITI has had a hand in promoting Japanese exports. International trading companies, which may handle up to 20,000 products, play a much more important role in Japanese commerce than such institutions do in America. Because of distance and cultural barriers, it has been more difficult for individual Japanese firms to secure knowledge of foreign markets. Ten major trading companies dominate this kind of activity in Japan, handling about 50% of exports and 60% of imports. MITI has developed a close relationship with these firms. They provide the Ministry with a convenient point-of-entry to influence the export activities of Japanese companies.[15]

Perhaps the most important source of government influence is its ability to control capital; the Japanese capital market is not highly developed. The Ministry of Finance has pursued a policy of keeping interest rates low, below what is needed to clear the market. It is a disequilibrium system. Allocation has been done through institutional controls rather than the market, and discrimination among borrowers, rationing, and subsidies have been the rule. The Ministry of Finance's decisions about capital allocation have been extremely important in controlling private actors, because Japanese firms rely heavily on outside borrowing. Furthermore, at least before 1972, government policy made it easier for companies to get loans than to issue bonds. Typically, large corporations have had a special relationship with a particular bank. The Ministry of Finance, in turn, has been able to exercise fairly tight control over the banking system. Thus, the Ministry could influence industry through financial institutions. In specific cases, MITI has also had influence because its endorsement has made it easier for a firm to get a loan.[16]

In sum, the Japanese are willing to accept an activist role for the state. The leading party has been—and continues to be—able to hold office for more than two decades. The bureaucracy has been able to affect industrial sectors and even individual firms through its ability to coordinate industrial planning, influence foreign trade and investment, and allocate capital.

The strength of the Japanese state is a product of Japanese history:

167

more precisely, of the level of state intervention needed to begin the industrialization of Japan in the 19th century and to guarantee its autonomy in the face of threats from the more developed countries of the West. Japan, as opposed to Great Britain and the United States, was a late industrializer. Its spurt of industrial growth did not begin until the 1880s. There are certain common features that tend to characterize late industrializers, including France, Germany, Russia, and Japan: the speed of industrialization is more rapid; the scale of industry may be larger; and the role of the state, particularly in mobilizing resources and spending investment funds, is greater.[17]

Japan probably offers the clearest example of this syndrome. In 1868, a new regime came to power in what is known as the Meiji Restoration. It was fundamentally committed to protecting Japan's political and territorial integrity. China was already being nibbled at by the Western powers. Japan faced the same fate. The new leaders moved with astounding speed and decisiveness to modernize the Japanese economy, for such modernization was seen as the key to political security. Feudal practices were abolished. A modern education system was introduced based upon examinations. Japanese were sent overseas to study modern industrial methods. Public officials encouraged private individuals to form modern business organizations such as joint stock companies. The state played a critical role in establishing key industries. It gave assistance in the form of capital, tax exemptions, and direct subsidies. Sometimes the government set up modern factories to demonstrate Western technology.[18] In 1905–06 Japan was able to fight and defeat a major European power, Russia, in a conflict which heralded the First World War in its use of many of the less attractive products of technology, including barbed wire and long-range artillery.

No European country industrialized with the rapidity and depth of Japan. In no European country is there the astounding phenomenon of the major nobility, the daimyo, voluntarily giving up their land to the state. In Japan there was an added dimension to economic modernization—a fierce sense of patriotism.[19] Patriotism was an adhesive which bound the working class and the nobility to the objective of economic modernization. Had Japan failed to transform itself, it would undoubtedly have experienced the same fate as China. The need for strong direction during this period could only be provided by the state: no other institution in the society could have the same command of resources, the same scope of vision, the same claim to the people's loyalty. The pattern of relations that was established during this critical juncture in Japanese history has persisted to the present, although it was substantially modified by the defeat and occupation that followed the Second World War.

The above does not constitute an argument that the Japanese state is an all-powerful institution that can always dominate private actors. Indeed, there have been dramatic examples of failure. Probably the most notable occurred in 1969 and 1970 when Prime Minister Sato was unable to persuade the Japanese textile industry and MITI to accept a secret arrangement for limiting man-made textile exports that had been worked out with the United States. Sato wanted the textile agreement, because Nixon had linked it with the reversion of Okinawa to Japan. While business and government in Japan are close, they are not an organic whole, nor is the ruling Liberal Democratic Party merely the handmaiden of large corporations. MITI has not always been able to fine tune the economy. The Ministry of Finance has not always supported investments in the most economically promising sectors of the economy.[20] The notion of Japan Inc., in which the state and the private sector form an impermeable juggernaut, is exaggerated. Nevertheless, the contrast between the United States and Japan in terms of attitudes, instruments of policy, and political structure is unmistakable. Japanese central decision-makers can intervene and direct their own economy far more easily than can their American counterparts.

The United States

Among the advanced capitalist countries, the U.S. probably has the weakest political system; at least its central decision-makers are less able to control their own domestic economy than are their German, French, and Japanese counterparts. The most striking characteristic of American politics is the extent to which governmental power is fragmented and decentralized. There are key institutions—the White House, the State Department, the Treasury, and the Federal Reserve Board—that are relatively insulated from societal pressures. Central decision-makers within these institutions have been able to formulate coherent policy goals. However, they have often been frustrated in their efforts to carry them out, because power is divided among a wide variety of institutions, both private and governmental.

In the executive branch, it is not clear whether some major departments are controlled by the Congress or by the President. Agriculture, labor, and commerce have explicit ties with private groups; they also may have special relations with Congressional committees.

Within the legislature there is a high degree of power fragmentation. Since the beginning of the century, the ability to make decisions has tended to devolve from the leadership in each house to committee chairman and even to subcommittee chairman. Bills can be blocked at any one of a number of decision-making nodes, including subcommittees, full committees, and conference committees. The jurisdictional authority of individual committees is often indistinct—it is not unusual to find several committees holding hearings on the same issue. Further, there is usually little cooperation between committees with the same formal responsibilities in the two houses.[21]

Most importantly, in terms of analyzing state power, the American political system allows private actors many points of access. Certain regulatory agencies were either set up to protect particular industries or have been captured by them. Certain Congressional committees have been very responsive to particular private groups. The courts have also provided an avenue for private actors to penetrate governmental decisions. Here, challenges have been made not only by specific interest groups, but also by various consumer and environmental organizations that claim to represent the general interest. Even if such litigation ultimately upholds the government's position, it can drag on for so long that state initiatives are effectively frustrated. In sum, the American political system offers many points of access to the decision-making process. While private groups do not determine the objectives sought by central decision-makers, they can often frustrate public initiatives. Indeed, American politics resembles a "black-ball" system: a negative vote by any major actor, public or private, can block policy implementation.[22]

In a formalistic way this situation can be traced to the vision of the Founding Fathers embodied in the Constitution. These men were wary of public power; what they wanted was individual freedom. In establishing their new order they preserved the governments of the individual states; they gave the Congress and the President specific rather than unlimited powers; they established a bicameral legislature; they created an independent judiciary.

In terms of actual behavior, Americans are much more suspicious of an activist state than are Frenchmen or Japanese; direct efforts by the state to control the economy are likely to meet more resistance and to be challenged on ideological as well as pragmatic grounds. American central decision-makers have relatively few policy instruments at their disposal. Some policy-making arenas, particularly at the macro-economic level, are fairly well developed and insulated from societal pressures, but even here state officials can encounter problems. For instance, the Federal Reserve Board in the U.S. has had more difficulty controlling the money supply than the Japanese Ministry of Finance, because the U.S. financial system, with its credit cards, checking accounts, charge accounts, and other forms of quasi-money, makes it more difficult to fine tune policy. Fiscal policy, which depends on taxation and government spending, is further trammelled by societal groups, because new levies must be imposed by Congress, and Congress is exposed and susceptible to private pressures.

Once one goes beyond macro-economic policy, American capabilities become even more limited. The American government has very little institutional capacity to intervene at the economic sector or the firm level. While some taxes, such as the oil depletion allowance, have been applied to particular economic sectors, these have more often resembled bounties for powerful private interests than incentives for following policies deemed to

170

be in the public interest. State credit allocation, which has been a potent instrument of government intervention in other countries, has been virtually non-existent in the United States; American companies finance most of their capital costs through retained earnings, and when they must go outside their own resources, they find a large private capital market in which the state has little control. In terms of intervening with individual firms, American central decision-makers have little leverage. Ties between particular companies and the state are looked upon with great suspicion, because it is assumed that the public interest will be perverted by private powers. In foreign areas, the State Department has studiously avoided promoting the interests of a specific firm as opposed to American industry in general.

The persistence of a weak political system through two centuries is intimately related to the economic, social, and political experience of the United States. In America, it was not necessary to have a strong government, because the society itself was so robust. The country was endowed with abundant natural resources. There was no feudal class which had to be destroyed before modernization could take place. Until recent years, the nation has not faced any serious external threats; indeed, it has not been invaded since 1812. Although America has been involved in two world wars and many other conflicts, its motivation for entering these forays cannot be explained in terms of protecting territorial or even political integrity—the two most unambiguous foreign policy goals. Social conflicts have been mitigated not by public action but by American abundance: people could have more, even if the distribution of wealth and income remained relatively unchanged. America has had a weak state not only because of the Lockian proclivities of the Founding Fathers, but also because it has generally not needed a strong one.[23] However, this weakness has limited the ability of American leaders to utilize economic capabilities for political purposes.

Two recent cases of foreign economic policy, both directly related to national security, illustrate the problems that a weak political system can present for central decision-makers. They are economic ties with the Soviet Union and the response to the energy crisis.

Economic relations with the Soviet Union could give the U.S. a foreign policy instrument for altering the behavior of its great rival, at least in modest ways. However, the potential has not been effectively tapped. The limitations on the exercise of American power have reflected the inability of central decision-makers to control groups within the U.S., not just the external aspects of relations between the U.S. and the Soviet Union.

After the Second World War, the international economy was divided into two blocs. Exchanges between Eastern Europe and the rest of the world were very low until well into the 1960s. In terms of increasing American political leverage, it was not a particularly useful situation. To translate

171

American economic resources into political power, that is, to use the export of goods and technology to modify Soviet behavior, two conditions are necessary. First, American central decision-makers must be able to offer goods and services to the Soviet Union. Second, they must be able to adjust the level of exports to changes in Russian policies; that is, they must be able to reward and punish Soviet political actions by manipulation of economic relationships.

Commercial ties with the West are not trivial for the Soviets. Their grain harvests have been erratic both because of inefficient management and difficult natural conditions: 75% of the grain growing areas in the USSR are at latitudes above the northern border of the continental United States, where there are greater dangers of frost and drought. The Soviets have also been interested in American technology. Their highly centralized system makes technological innovation difficult. Clearly the USSR can carry out some impressive projects, such as the space program, but it has had difficulty extending new technology throughout the economy. The import of new techniques from the West may allow the Soviet leadership to increase living standards without liberalizing their own economy and society.[24] It is foolish to hope that an American Pepsi-Cola plant, or even American wheat, can fundamentally change the nature of Russian behavior. The Soviet state is too strong for that: the effects of a poor harvest can be translated into lower consumption with far fewer political repercussions than in a liberal society. However, skillfully adjusted, American economic power might be used to alter Russian behavior on some issues.

Unfortunately, the experience of the last decade has demonstrated that the structure of the American political system precludes sensitive manipulation of international economic flows. In the early 1960s, Kennedy began considering an easing of commercial restrictions on the Communist Bloc. But a real increase in trade did not begin until around 1970. Soviet imports from the U.S. have risen very quickly since then. But the benefits have been one-sided. American central decision-makers were unable to develop a flexible policy because of constraints imposed by domestic pressure groups.

The most important manifestation of extended trading activities has been an increase in Soviet wheat purchases. In 1972, the Russians imported large amounts of grain from the United States. They were able to do this without the U.S. Government having any clear idea of the extent of their purchases. After the Soviets had completed their procurements, the price of wheat shot up, a loss for both American consumers and American farmers. Other large Soviet purchases were made in later years. Basically, the Soviet Union was able to use the United States as a grain reserve; American stockpiles were used to offset Soviet crop failures.[25]

The United States has moved to ameliorate the disruptive effects of Russian grain imports, but in doing so it has virtually eliminated the possibility of using these transactions to further political objectives. After 1972, economic intelligence was improved. But in 1974 and 1975, temporary export controls were met with howls of indignation from American farmers, who felt that they were being used as tools of the Administration's foreign policy, which indeed they were. Finally in the fall of 1975, an agreement was signed in which the Soviets agreed to purchase between six and eight million tons of grain annually from the United States. This satisfied American farmers, who now had an assured export market.[26] But it precluded any possibility of using grain sales to further political objectives, the initial reason for increasing commercial relations with the Soviet Union. In the fall of 1976, both Presidential candidates made public statements against export controls. For grain to be an effective instrument of political policy, it would be necessary for the United States to regulate sales, to make adjustments which would reward or encourage certain kinds of Soviet political behavior and punish others. The October 1975 Agreement meant an American commitment to sell (unless there was a disastrous harvest), not just a Soviet commitment to buy. In effect, the inability of American central decision-makers to resist demands from the agricultural sector has eliminated grain sales as an instrument of American foreign policy. (For an extended analysis of the limitations on food power, see Chapter 11.)

A second example related to Soviet-American trade also illustrates the fragmentation and weakness of the political structure. In 1974 Senator Jackson and Representative Vanik succeeded in attaching to the Trade Act an amendment which denies most favored nation treatment and export credits to any country which does not allow free emigration. The Jackson-Vanik Amendment was aimed at increasing the number of Jews allowed to leave the Soviet Union. After some hesitancy, it was endorsed by the American Jewish community. It was strongly opposed by the Administration; Nixon and Kissinger saw commerical relations as an instrument which could be used to change foreign rather than domestic Soviet policies. The Jackson-Vanik Amendment made an already complicated set of negotiations with the Russians even more difficult, and they eventually denounced the trade arrangement that had been reached with the Administration. The fragmentation of the political system had allowed the Congress to introduce a whole new range of goals into trade relations with the USSR.

A second Congressional initiative also limited U.S. flexibility. The 1974 Trade Act included an amendment authored by Senator Stevenson which limited Export-Import Bank credit to Russia to $300 million over a four-year period. This was less than had been extended between 1972 and 1974.[27] Placing an absolute ceiling on government loans, like the wheat agreement, precluded the flexibility necessary to translate American economic power into effective political power. Thus, in dealing with the Soviet Union, the United States has appeared capable of only two kinds of policy:

173

breaking commercial ties altogether or surrounding them with rigid restraints. Neither allows American statesmen to transform economic resources into political power. (An exception to this conclusion concerning U.S. weaknesses in structuring economic relationships with the Soviet Union must, however, be cited: the U.S. has been able, to a considerable extent, to determine such policy with respect to the export of "strategic goods.")

The weakness of the American political system is also illustrated by the U.S. reaction to the set of events that took place during the early 1970s, which has become known as the oil crisis. The oil crisis involved the quadrupling of prices, a production cutback by Arab states, an oil embargo against the United States, the Netherlands, Portugal, South Africa, and Rhodesia, and the nationalization of major foreign oil companies by host-country governments.

In dealing with energy-related questions, especially oil, American central decision-makers confront a particularly powerful group of private actors. The American corporations involved in the international movement of oil are very large—five out of the seven companies that have dominated the world petroleum industry are American. Further, the oil industry is important for many areas of the United States; in 1970 petroleum was the largest source of mineral income for 13 states.[28] For a number of states the value of natural gas and oil production amounts to a substantial proportion of total personal income: 45% for Wyoming in the mid 1960s, 39% for Louisiana, 17% for Texas.[29] The oil industry is very well organized, with the American Petroleum Institute, which had a budget of $17 million in 1971, acting as an umbrella organization. There are separate Oil and Gas Associations in Texas and Oklahoma, California, Oregon, Washington, Nevada, and Arizona. There are numerous functional organizations, including the Independent Petroleum Association of America, the Independent Natural Gas Association, the National Stripper Well Association, and the National Petroleum Association (representing East Coast refiners).[30]

In addition to the oil industry, a second set of actors has become increasingly influential for the energy related matters—environmentalists. Since the mid-1960s, concern about the degradation of the environment has been a salient issue in the United States. Many new federal and state laws have been enacted, and support has come from a wide spectrum within the population. Environmentalists are represented by well-organized groups, such as the Sierra Club, which have been active in Congressional campaigns and lobbied for specific legislation.

Aside from the power and diversity of private groups interested in oil and energy matters, a great multiplicity of public institutions have some authority. State bodies, such as the Texas Railroad Commission, set production quotas within their states. The Atomic Energy Commission and its successor, the Nuclear Regulatory Commission, make determinations about the construction of nuclear power plants. The Environmental Protection Agency is involved with virtually any exploration of new supply sources or the construction of new power plants. The Labor Department investigates working conditions in coal mines. The Interior Department exercises control over federal lands, where much mining takes place. The State Department has been concerned with the foreign activities of U.S. companies. The Treasury Department has been involved with tax payments on foreign earnings. All major energy issues are likely to be fought out in Congress. Finally, the courts have been increasingly involved in energy issues, in part because of the more activist role of environmental groups. In sum, energy matters present American policy-makers with particularly acute problems, because there are many active and well-organized private actors, and power is diffused among governmental agencies.

Until the fall of 1973, however, the system worked extremely well. In the two decades after the Second World War, an unprecedented increase in world energy demand was met with no notable shortages and with astounding price stability. The major corporations were able to anticipate demand, develop new supplies, construct refining facilities, and market their product with great efficiency. Unfortunately, in 1969, things began to come unglued. In that year Libya demanded higher oil payments. This set off a chain of events which culminated in the quadrupling of oil prices in 1973 and 1974 and the complete nationalization of the oil industry a few years later. These developments had serious political costs for the United States. They strained the cohesion of the Western alliance. They increased the military, economic, and political dangers emanating from the conflict in the Middle East. They made the international monetary system more unstable by creating a new source of potentially volatile international liquidity, petrodollars (excess reserves held by oil-exporting states in the form of short-term funds). They helped plunge the industrial West into its most severe economic crisis since the Second World War: in 1975 unemployment in developed market economies was at a 40-year high. They imposed a huge additional economic burden on less developed states. Changes in oil policy did not mean the downfall of the West, but nationalization, and especially higher prices, did impinge upon the core objectives of American central decision-makers.[31]

The oil crisis demands an obvious response. The United States must become more independent. It must reduce consumption and increase production. From the perspective of the collective goals of the society, there is no alternative. Yet domestic policy thus far has been extremely ineffectual. Internationally, the U.S. has taken the lead in working out new institutional arrangements among Western industrial states. In September 1974 an emergency oil-sharing arrangement was concluded. Agreement was also

175

reached on an international floor price for oil and on emergency stockpiles. The U.S. is beginning its stockpile program. However, one major aspect of this cooperative effort, the establishment of a $25 billion fund to ease the balance of payments effects of higher oil prices (the so-called safety net) has not come into being because Congress has refused to appropriate the funds.

However, these international measures will have little effect unless the U.S. can act decisively within its own borders. As the largest producer and consumer of energy among the advanced industrial nations, what the U.S. does at home has an international as well as a domestic impact. A reduction of American imports could ease supply problems for Western Europe and Japan. Decisive action, in terms of restricting consumption or increasing output, or both, might be understood by the OPEC countries as a signal of the seriousness of American concerns. This might help to moderate the policies of the oil-exporting states in the short and medium term. In the long term, if the cartel is to be broken and international oil prices are to be held constant or even lowered, it will be necessary to force the OPEC producers to become residual suppliers to a world energy market that is primarily satisfied from other sources. This cannot be done without greater energy independence in the U.S.

However, American policy at home has been a dismal failure. It took more than two years after the oil embargo to pass a new energy bill and this act was a hodge-podge of compromises. It was 250 pages long with some 18 pages alone devoted to the pricing of crude oil. Price controls on oil were extended through the 1976 elections. Although some modest mandatory efficiency levels were imposed on automobiles, voluntary, not mandatory, conservation targets were suggested for industry. It took many months to agree on how a U.S. stockpile should be procured and stored.[32]

Little progress has been made on conservation or the development of new supplies. A study by the International Energy Agency ranked the U.S. 15 out of 18 countries in terms of conservation.[33] Gasoline consumption has risen since 1973 as motorists have increasingly ignored lower speed limits. The sale of large cars increased during 1976. The development of alternative supply sources has been held up by litigation and skyrocketing capital costs. For instance, in 1974 when a consortium of four companies halted their plans to develop what would have been the nation's first commercial shale oil plant, they stated that estimates of production costs per barrel had risen from $7.00 to $11.00 in one year, and that construction cost estimates had risen 40% in six months. Plans to produce synthetic fuel from coal and shale were drastically scaled back. Not only have utilities trying to build nuclear power plants run into increasing difficulties with Federal regulations and environmental lawsuits, but Westinghouse, a major supplier of uranium fuel, publicly announced in late 1976 that it would not be able to meet its contractual obligations.[34] Implicitly, the United States opted for the

OPEC solution to its energy needs. It is yet to be seen whether the Carter administration will diversify U.S. energy sources while seeking Congressional and public support for its conservation, taxation, and tax-rebate proposals. The ineffectuality of American policy has meant higher imports: U.S. dependence on Arab oil supplies doubled from 5.6% of total demand during the first six months of 1975 to 12.4% during the first six of 1976.[35]

The fragmentation and decentralization of power in the American political system has made it difficult if not impossible to formulate a coherent energy policy. Plans put forth by the Executive have been continually modified or rejected by the Congress. Corporations have refused to make large new capital investments without government guarantees; antipathy toward the companies has made the Congress very reluctant to grant such assurances. At the same time, the state has never seriously contemplated nationalizing the industry or compelling it to undertake certain projects. Oil companies are diversifying into other activities, including such remote areas as retailing and land development, rather than investing in the development of new energy supplies, because the government has not been able to provide them with a stable and predictable environment. More public attention has been given to the possibility of forcing a break up in the level of vertical integration of oil companies—hardly a solution to the *energy* problem—than to any other aspect of the structure of the industry. Through administrative hearings and court action, environmentalists have been able to delay the development of new sources of supply and of new coal and nuclear generating plants. Public utilities have become embroiled in struggles with the Environmental Protection Agency that have, at least in one case, led to a halt in the construction of a plant already underway.[36]

It is only fair to note that none of the industrial nations emerged from the oil crisis unscathed. France scampered to work out special deals with producing states at the same time that its existing special arrangements were proving to be of no benefit. Japan initially tried to follow an independent line: a high-ranking cabinet official traveled to the Middle East in the fall of 1973 and promised economic assistance to several oil-exporting states. But this policy was soon reversed, and by early 1974 Japan had returned to its more usual role of following the lead of the United States.[37] However, none of the other major industrial states enjoyed America's level of self-sufficiency. None, with the possible exception of Britain, had substantial reserves that could be developed within their own borders. A successful policy against the oil-exporting states, that is, one which could lower prices and maintain adequate supplies, can only be fashioned by the United States. And this it has failed to do.

Summary

Any analysis of the international coercive leverage of a state must take into consideration domestic as well as international factors. A state with

177

relatively small resources may be able to exercise greater leverage than one with larger resources, if its central decision-makers have greater control over their own domestic society. The most fundamental determinant of that control is the strength of a country's political institutions. If these institutions are rigid rather than adaptive, if they are simple rather than complex, if they are subordinate to particular societal groups rather than autonomous, then it will be difficult for central decision-makers to extract the domestic resources needed to further international goals.[38]

Adaptability, complexity, and autonomy are associated with higher levels of economic development and more modern societies. Hence, in terms of the strength and weakness of domestic political systems, the most salient division is between industrialized and non-industrialized countries. In general, the countries of the Third World have weaker political systems: their leaders are less able to influence their own domestic societies.

Among the industrialized nations a basic distinction can be made between communist and capitalist states; that is, communist countries usually have stronger domestic political systems than capitalist ones. Communist leaders are more able to manipulate their own societies. Communism does not admit the legitimacy of a private sphere of activity. It assigns to one political institution, the Communist Party, a monopoly on legitimate political activity. Communist countries deny the efficacy of the market: resources within the society are allocated largely by state planning authorities. This is not to say that communist regimes are all-powerful. The level of corruption, minor cheating, bribes, and clever deals is substantial. Private property has not been eliminated. Religion is still important. Indeed, the reliability of some armies in Eastern Europe is suspect. Nevertheless, in comparison with industrialized capitalist states, it is far easier for regimes in communist countries to manipulate their own societies than it is for those in capitalist ones.

While political systems in capitalist states may, in general, be weaker than those in communist ones, there are considerable differences among them. Probably Japan and the United States occupy the opposite ends of the spectrum. In Japan, the public is more willing to accept an activist role for the state. Relations between business and government agencies are more intimate than in the U.S., and public institutions have a wider arsenal of policy instruments with which to influence private behavior. These differences are related to the experiences of the U.S. and Japan in the process of industrialization. In America, this process began early in the 19th century and progressed slowly and with little state direction. In Japan, industrialization took place quickly during the last decades of the 19th century with a great deal of state intervention. Patterns established during these critical junctures have persisted to the present day, although in Japan the defeat and occupation following the Second World War constitute another critical

178

experience in the nation's history that has substantially altered earlier modes of behavior.

The above does not mean to imply that strong states are necessarily good ones. In terms of personal freedom, there are many distasteful aspects of authoritarian regimes. Furthermore, it may be that in the long term, more liberal societies are also internationally stronger. John Locke, in arguing for the advantages of liberalism, even for the sovereign, stated that free men were more likely to be productive than serfs, and a more productive society would be better able to defend itself.[39] As economic relations become more complicated, this argument may assume even more force. The development and introduction of new technology, the search for new markets, the training of individuals for new tasks, may now be so complex as to defy central direction. A freer society may be able to perform these functions better and thus grow more rapidly, because decision-making is decentralized. Thus, although capitalist societies may be weaker in the short term because they lack control of existing resources, they may be stronger in the long term than authoritarian regimes, because the resources under their command may increase more quickly.

* I would like to thank Peter J. Katzenstein and the other contributors to this volume for their comments on an earlier draft.

Footnotes

1. The concept of weak and strong states is developed in Peter J. Katzenstein, "International Relations and Domestic Structures: Foreign Economic Policies of Advanced Industrial States," *International Organization, 30* (Winter 1976). The analytic framework of this essay draws heavily on Katzenstein's work.
2. Andrzej Korbonski, "Detente, East-West Trade, and the Future of Economic Integration in Eastern Europe," *World Politics*, XXVIII (July 1976): 575–80.
3. Wolfgang Leonhard, "The Domestic Politics of the New Soviet Foreign Policy, "*Foreign Affairs, 52* (October 1973); and Kenneth Jowitt, "Inclusion and Mobilization in European Leninist Regimes," *World Politics*, XXVIII (October 1975) discuss the economic and political problems of decentralization in Communist regimes.
4. John W. Kiser, III, "Technology: Not a One-Way Street," *Foreign Policy, 23* (Summer 1976).
5. For a discussion of institutionalization, see Samuel P. Huntington, *Political Order in Changing Societies* (New Haven: Yale University Press, 1968), pp. 12–24.
6. *Wall Street Journal*, 3 August 1976, 1:1.
7. Jorge I. Dominquez, "Smuggling," *Foreign Policy, 20* (Fall 1975): 95.
8. *New York Times*, 19 April 1975, 1:1; *Los Angeles Times*, 22 February 1976, VI, 7:1.
9. Gardner Ackley and Hiromitsu Ishi, "Fiscal, Monetary and Related Policies," in *Asia's New Giant: How the Japanese Economy Works*, ed. Hugh Patrick and Henry Rosovsky (Washington: Brookings Institute, 1976), p. 161; Ezra F. Vogel, "Introduction: Toward More Accurate Concepts," in *Modern Japanese Organization and Decision-Making*, ed. Ezra F. Vogel (Berkeley: University of California Press, 1975), p. xv; and Lawrence B. Krause and Sueo Sekiguchi, "Japan and the World Economy," in Patrick and Rosovsky, *Asia's New Giant*, pp. 412–13.
10. Nathan Glazer, "Social and Cultural Factors in Japanese Economic Growth," in Patrick and Rosovsky, *Asia's New Giant*.

11. Eugene J. Kaplan, *Japan: The Government-Business Relationship: A Guide for the American Businessman* (Washington: U.S. Department of Commerce, Bureau of International Commerce, 1972), p.10; Henry Wallich and Mable I. Wallich, "Banking and Finance," in Patrick and Rosovsky, *Asia's New Giant*, p. 274; and Hugh Patrick and Henry Rosovsky, "Japan's Economic Performance: An Overview," in Patrick and Rosovsky, *Asia's New Giant*, p. 53.

12. Albert M. Craig, "Functional and Dysfunctional Aspects of Government Bureaucracy," in Vogel, *Modern Japanese Organization*, pp. 4–5.

13. Richard E. Caves in collaboration with Masu Uekusa, "Industrial Organization," in Patrick and Rosovsky, *Asia's New Giant*, p. 464; and Vogel, "Introduction," p. XXII.

14. Caves with the collaboration of Uekusa, "Industrial Organization," pp. 488 and 493; Krause and Sekiguchi, "Japan and the World Economy," pp. 412–13.

15. Krause and Sekiguchi, "Japan and the World Economy," passim.

16. Wallich and Wallich, "Banking and Finance," passim.

17. Alexander Gerschenkron, *Economic Backwardness in Historical Perspective: A Book of Essays* (Cambridge: Harvard University Press, 1962), pp. 5–30.

18. Yasuzo Horie, "Modern Entrepreneurship in Meiji Japan," and David S. Landes, "Japan and Europe: Contrasts in Industrialization," pp. 100–02 both in *The State and Economic Enterprise in Japan: Essays in the Political Economy of Growth*, ed. William W. Lockwood (Princeton: Princeton University Press, 1965); and Edwin O. Reischauer, *Japan: The Story of a Nation* (New York: Knopf, 1970), Ch. 8.

19. Landes, "Japan and Europe," pp. 111–12.

20. Gerald L. Curtis, "Big Business and Political Influence," in Vogel, *Modern Japanese Organization*; Philip H. Trezise with the collaboration of Yukio Suzuki, "Politics, Government, and Economic Growth in Japan," in Patrick and Rosovsky, *Asia's New Giant*; I.M. Destler, Hideo Sato, Priscilla Clapp, Haruhiro Fukui, *Managing An Alliance: The Politics of US-Japanese Relations* (Washington: Brookings Institute, 1976), p. 39; and Vogel, "Introduction," pp. XVI–XX.

21. Samuel P. Huntington, "Congressional Responses to the Twentieth Century," Richard F. Fenno, Jr., "The Internal Distribution of Influence: The House," and Ralph K. Huitt, "The Internal Distribution of Influence: The Senate," all in *The Congress and America's Future*, ed. David B. Truman (2nd ed.; Englewood Cliffs, N.J.: Prentice-Hall, 1973).

22. This argument draws heavily on Huntington, *Political Order*, Ch. 2; Theodore J. Lowi, *The End of Liberalism* (New York: Norton, 1969); and Grant McConnell, *Private Power and American Democracy* (New York: Knopf, 1966).

23. This argument is developed in Louis Hartz, *The Liberal Tradition in America* (New York: Harcourt, Brace and World, 1955); Huntington, *Political Order*, Ch. 2; and David Potter, *People of Plenty* (Chicago: University of Chicago Press, 1954).

24. Raymond Vernon, "Apparatchiks and Entrepreneurs: U.S.-Soviet Economic Relations," *Foreign Affairs, 52* (January 1974): 253–54; Leonhard, "The Domestic Politics;" and Adam B. Ulam, "Detente Under Soviet Eyes," *Foreign Policy, 24* (Fall 1976): 157–58.

25. Robert L. Paarlberg, "Agripower and Interdependence: Meeting the Soviet Threat to World Food Security," (Paper presented at the 1976 Annual Convention of the American Political Science Association, Chicago, Ill., September 2–5, 1976), p. 4; Marshall Goldman, "The Soviet Economy is Not Immune," *Foreign Policy, 21* (Winter 1975–76): 82–83.

26. Paarlberg, "Agripower," pp. 8–12.

27. Daniel Yergin, "Strategies of Linkage in Soviet-American Relations," (Paper presented at the 1976 Annual Convention of the American Political Science Association, Chicago, Ill., September 2–5, 1976), pp. 16–17.

28. U.S., Bureau of the Census, *Statistical Abstract of the United States*, 1971, p. 650.

29. Derived from figures in U.S., Bureau of Mines, *Mineral Yearbook*, 1967, Vol. III.
30. Robert Engler, *The Politics of Oil* (Chicago: University of Chicago Press, 1961), pp. 382–84.
31. For a particularly grim assessment, see Edward Friedland, Paul Seabury, and Aaron Wildavsky, "Oil and the Decline of Western Power," *Political Science Quarterly, 90* (Fall 1975).
32. *Wall Street Journal*, 28 January 1976, 28:1; 18 March 1976, 4:1; and *New York Times*, 13 November 1975, 1:5; 10 December 1975, 17:1.
33. Robert L. Paarlberg, "Domesticating Global Management," *Foreign Affairs, 54* (April 1976): 570.
34. *Wall Street Journal*, 7 October 1974, 7:1; 22 December 1976, 4:1; and *New York Times*, 7 June 1976, 45:2.
35. *New York Times*, 17 August 1976, 43:8.
36. *Wall Street Journal*, 7 January 1977, 8:1. See also Frank N. Trager, ed., *Oil, Divestiture and National Security* (New York: Crane, Russak and Co., 1977).
37. Kenneth I. Juster, "Japanese Foreign Policy Making During the Oil Crisis" (unpublished B.A. dissertation, Harvard College, 1976).
38. Huntington, *Political Order*, pp. 12–24.
39. Richard H. Cox, *Locke on War and Peace* (Oxford: The Clarendon Press, 1960), pp. 180–82; and John Locke, *The Second Treatise of Government*, parag. 42.

Part II

CHAPTER 7

Military Strength: Economic and Non-Economic Bases

Klaus Knorr

Throughout history governments have been concerned with the material bases of military strength, and in recent centuries this involvement has been the traditional focus for relating economic factors to considerations of national security. Military capability was a major preoccupation of mercantilist thought. Adam Smith, the forefather of modern economic reasoning, held defense to be "of much more importance than opulence,"[1] and he devoted a chapter of *The Wealth of Nations* to the subject. Many of his successors have advocated or tolerated protecting vital defense production as a legitimate reason for deviating from free trade. This concern about military strength remains important today, even though other and more novel considerations of national economic security are being raised on the contemporary scene. Foreign economic behavior can hurt a society in an interdependent world, but inability to provide for adequate deterrence and defense can destroy a society as a sovereign entity.

This chapter will present only a summary discussion of nations' military potential, since more extensive treatments are readily available.[2] It will also relate economic factors to non-economic components, because currently the most interesting problems for modern societies highlight this connection.

The Economic Potential for Military Strength

The development, maintenance, and employment of military forces for a nation's deterrence and defense or for aggressive purposes require men, arms, and other supplies. These are generated from a country's labor force, from its capital, and from its natural resources. They are so drawn directly when nationals are recruited into the armed forces and supporting personnel structures and when weapons and other supplies are produced domestically. They can be drawn indirectly, when national products are exported and exchanged for materiel produced abroad, or when the importation of relevant things is financed by drawing upon a country's net financial claims on foreigners (if any). A proportion of nations' economic capacity

Table 1
GNPs for Selected Countries, 1974[5]
(in 1974 U.S. dollars)

Above $400 billion	U.S.A. (1,400), USSR (797)
$100 to $399 billion	West Germany (385), Japan (367), France (292), China P.R. (223), United Kingdom (192), Italy (158), Canada (136)
$10 to $99 billion	Brazil (94), India (79), Poland (76), Australia (61), Belgium (53), Iran (31), Yugoslavia (27), Indonesia (18), Nigeria (17), Egypt (11), Israel (10)
Under $10 billion	Pakistan (9), Chile (9), Cuba (6), Singapore (5), Zaire (4), Sudan (3), Jamaica (2)

is thus allocated to the military sector. If a country receives military or economic aid or loans from abroad, it is given a commensurate access to the resources of other nations and can use these in order to add to its military strength.

The aggregate of goods and services produced by a nation under conditions of full employment—the Gross National Product (GNP)—affords a rough measurement of its productive capacity. Countries devote varying proportions of GNP to defense—in 1974, it was less than 1% for Austria and more than 19% for Egypt—depending on their external environment and on how they choose to cope with it. Nevertheless, absolute amounts of military spending are, on the whole, closely correlated with GNP. In that year, the United States spent $95.9 billion (6.15% of GNP), an amount that is larger than the GNP of all but nine states in the world. The United States and the Soviet Union together accounted for an estimated 60% of the defense outlays of all countries.[3] This is not surprising, since the magnitude of GNPs is a product of size of population (or labor force) and degree of economic development (or labor productivity).

The use of this measure for international comparison involves several technical difficulties[4] that preclude accuracy, but it indicates rough orders of magnitude. Expressed in 1974 U.S. dollars, Table 1 indicates comparative GNPs for 1974 which suggest classes of countries' economic military potential.

Table 2 indicates GNP estimates and populations for some major countries in 1975.

Changes in the overall economic capacity of countries to produce will naturally affect their military potential, although economic capacity is only one component of military potential. Relative changes in economic capacity therefore suggest international shifts in the distribution of military potential.

184

Table 2
GNP of Major Areas in 1975[6]

	GNP (billion dollars)	Population (millions)
United States	$1,516	214
NATO Allies of the U.S.	1,604	340
Japan	491	111
Soviet Union	787	255
Peoples Republic of China	237	935

In addition to aggregate size, the structure of a nation's economic capacity is important for judging military economic potential. Like the civilian population, the armed forces must be assured of food, clothing, housing, fuel, and other goods and services that are not specific to the needs of the military sector. Many countries can produce all or most of these things; petroleum products, which must be imported by most states, are a notable exception. In addition, however, armed services need weapons systems and must generate the skill required for their efficient maintenance and use. Countries differ in the degree to which their productive capabilities are suited to meeting these requirements. The production of crude steel, motor vehicles, and electric power is a fairly good indicator of national differences in the capacity to produce most of the technologically less demanding things that armed forces need.

Ever since warfare has become industrialized, the level of industrial and technological development has been a major factor determining a country's ability to produce sophisticated arms and, to a lesser extent, its ability to service and employ such arms efficiently. To manufacture complex modern weapon systems (e.g., aircraft, submarines, tanks, antiaircraft artillery, missiles) and associated systems for target acquisition, command and control, and logistical support, demands a level of skills that only the most industrialized countries can achieve.

The enterprises producing this hardware, in turn, draw on numerous other industries, manufacturing computers, optical equipment, engines, machine tools, metals, etc. In the major capitalist countries, there are few specialized firms (mostly in the aerospace area) that produce only or mostly military goods. There are many other firms that make arms or components but produce mostly civilian goods. At a somewhat lower level of technological development, some countries (e.g., India) are able to produce some modern weapons (e.g., artillery and even aircraft), especially if they can import the technology in the form of licenses. Below this level, they must perforce depend on weapons imports.

The ability to develop and produce sophisticated arms is also determined by the factor of scale. Arms production calls for such massive inputs of high-level resources (e.g., in the aerospace industry) that only the United States and the Soviet Union are capable of producing the whole range of weaponry. Such highly developed countries as Britain and France can do so only selectively, for a limited number of systems, although they can expand this range by organizing joint development and production and by cultivating export markets. Indeed, only substantial arms exports have permitted Britain and France to manufacture as many weapons as they have in recent years. Other countries that are highly industrialized (e.g., Canada, Sweden, Israel, and Switzerland) are too small to manufacture more than a few types of modern arms. National potential in this crucial area is extremely limited.

The importance of the technological base has been further elevated by the accelerating rate of weapons obsolescence. The arms producers, especially the United States and the Soviet Union, are engaged in a continuous qualitative arms race. Survival in this competition makes inordinate demands on precious resources available for Research and Development (R&D) that yield a stream of improved designs and inventions and that are, in turn, supported by a rich infrastructure of scientific progress. This has made funds for R&D and the training and recruitment of highly skilled scientists and engineers a key factor in the military potential of societies that make claims to being great military powers. A state that falls appreciably behind in this innovational race courts technological dominance by and technological surprise at the hands of other states.

Until World War II, secure access to raw materials, food, and fuel was regarded as a primary component of a nation's military potential. Yet, assured supplies of these goods have, in general, become less critical as the inputs of technology have increased. This is so partly because complex and expensive weapons are far more effective per unit than were their predecessors, so that they are deployed in relatively small numbers. The main difference, however, is that the use of modern weaponry makes prolonged wars of attrition much less probable than before. The military use of raw materials and fuel in peacetime absorbs only a small fraction of total consumption in the highly developed states. For instance, the military services account for less than 5% of U.S. oil consumption.[7] This is not to say that an assured supply of these goods has become a negligible problem, especially in major weapons-producing states. But to the extent that these goods must be imported, adequate supplies can be safeguarded by stockpiling and rationing to cover all contingencies except prolonged warfare. Neither the United States nor the Soviet Union is seriously handicapped in this matter.[8]

Because complex modern weapon systems are and can be produced only in a small number of states, the military potential of all other countries would be hopelessly outclassed were it not for the international transfer of arms. Countries can, of course, import armaments and to that extent, their

186

ability to manage commensurate export surpluses is a significant economic basis of their military strength. If this asset is lacking or insufficient, and they are unable to obtain credits, they are reduced to receiving arms as gifts from allies or patron states or to do without.

While arms have been traded in significant volume among industrialized states for some time—amounting to about $3.0 billion annually in 1972 and 1973,—there has been a recent vast outpouring of modern weapons to Third World countries, especially to the now highly affluent oil-exporting countries, particularly in the Middle East. In terms of constant (1973) prices, Third World arms imports grew from an annual average of $1.5 billion in 1964–68 to an average of $4.4 billion in 1974–75.[9] Of these, 56% went to the Middle East, 12% to North Africa, 12% to Latin America, and 11% to the Far East. The five largest arms importers, from 1965 to 1975, were Iran, Egypt, Syria, Israel, and India (in that order). These imports have been accompanied by a large influx of technical advisors and training personnel from the industrial exporting countries. For instance, Americans in that capacity are present in the tens of thousands in Iran alone. It is also assumed that a considerable number of less developed countries may be interested, following the example of China and India, in building up a capability for making nuclear arms on the basis of nuclear power installations and technology imported from the industrial states. The requisite capacity grows as nuclear reactors spread over the world.

It is far from clear that the less developed countries importing highly complex weapons systems are capable of properly maintaining and employing them in the immediate future. It takes time and a lot of effort to train local personnel to fly and service supersonic military aircraft. But as North Vietnam, Egypt, and Syria demonstrated, countries that are incapable of producing modern arms can learn to employ them with considerable effectiveness; and some of the new precision-guided weapons, capable of destroying more complex and expensive aircraft, tanks, and ships, are comparatively easy to maintain and operate.

These spreading imports of modern armaments have already affected the balance of power in the Middle East and may before long also reduce the military superiority of the extra-regional great powers. But although the international transfer of sophisticated weapon systems is resulting in a remarkable diffusion of advanced military technology, dependence on imports constitutes a vulnerability, because supplies can be disrupted in various contingencies. Moreover, dependence on supplies from a particular industrial state gives the latter some coercive leverage because it is not easy, for political or obvious technical reasons, to switch to an alternative import source. For example, Egypt's quarrel with the Soviet Union after 1973 caused the latter to limit the delivery of spare parts and new weapons so severely that Egypt's armaments grew quickly obsolete relative to those of

Israel or Syria. At the same time, Israel's dependence on the United States as practically the sole supplier of imported arms gave the latter considerable leverage over Israeli policy. Imports are a far from perfect substitute for domestic arms production.

Of course, the significance of modern technology as a base of national military strength depends of the armament requirements of different types of conflict. The capacity to develop and manufacture nuclear bombs is irrelevant to engagement in conventional warfare; much of sophisticated conventional weapon technology has only limited value in guerrilla war; and the resource base that sustains the projection of military strength far from the homeland is not needed by countries interested solely in defending their boundaries.

Over time, national economic bases of military strength change directly with the rate of economic development and the expansion of industries and services vital to arms production. Britain's military preeminence during the first half of the nineteenth century resulted from her lead in industrialization. By the beginning of the twentieth century, other Western societies, especially Germany and the United States, had caught up enough with British industrial capacity to challenge her military lead. If the United States emerged from World War II as the greatest military power, it was made possible by her enormous economic, industrial, and technological superiority. Although her capacity in these respects has grown greatly since then in absolute terms, that of other nations—for example, West Germany, France, Japan, and the Soviet Union—has increased more rapidly. While her economic base is still the largest, it is less superior than three decades ago. From 1950 to 1974, the American GNP fell from 34.2 to 25.1% of the world total, while the Soviet share expanded from 11.4 to 12.8, West Germany's from 5.2 to 6.5 and Japan's from 2.8 to 7.7%.[10] For the decade from 1965 to 1974 alone, the share of the United States in the total GNP of all developed countries slipped from 35 to 30%.[11] Britain's GNP also declined from 5.5% in 1950 to 3.3% in 1974.[12]

Japan and the Western European countries have also developed technologically to an extent that reduces American superiority, although, being smaller countries, they still suffer from deficiencies of scale. Aggregate American expenditures for Research and Development (R&D) in constant dollars remained at about $22 billion between 1968 and 1974.[13] But the proportion of American GNP spent on R&D declined over the last decade, while it expanded substantially in West Germany, Japan, and the Soviet Union. In 1973, that percentage was 2.4 in the United States, compared with 3.1, 2.4 and 1.9 in the USSR, Germany, and Japan respectively. Similarly, the number of American scientists and engineers engaged in R&D per 10,000 population declined after 1969, whereas it rose in the other three countries.[14] Although these trends are ominous, this country's technological capacity is still very high and, overall, excels that of all other states. Moreover, the productivity of R&D resources in the Soviet Union seems to remain comparatively low. Compared with the United States, the Soviet Union has made less and more uneven progress in high technology and is therefore interested in importing such technology from the West. However, this has evidently not seriously disadvantaged military applications, because her governments have been determined to allocate the best of her technology to the military sector, at the expense of production for the civilian market.

Some of the less developed states—for example, Brazil, India, and China—have made sufficient industrial progress in recent decades to provide an appreciable and increasing basis for national military strength, and the major oil-exporting countries have experienced a spectacular advance in economic capacity since 1973. However, the vast inflow of hard currencies has so far augmented the latters' economic basis for military strength only through the ability to import modern armaments and military know-how. The development of an indigenous industrial foundation for arms production requires present plans for economic development to bear fruit and is limited in any case by the factor of scale, because most of the countries involved have small populations.

It is crucial to appreciate that there is no one-to-one relationship between the economic-technological capacity and the military strength of nations. To some extent, countries can offset an inferiority in sophisticated arms by using more men, by training them more rigorously, and by infusing them with superior morale. North Vietnam was able to do so during the war against South Vietnam and the United States. China furnishes an interesting contemporary example of a state that capitalizes on numbers, training, and high morale in order to compensate for its still low level of industrialization and technological capability. Its military doctrine emphasizes "people's war" against any aggressor.[15] Moreover, economic and technological resources constitute only one basis of military strength. There are two others that are no less important. First, the extent to which national resources will be transformed into effective military strength depends upon the level and quality of military statecraft that directs the process of transformation. Second, the level of military strength generated depends on the proportion of national resources that are allocated to this purpose and, in the final analysis, on the will to devote precious assets to it.

The Impact of Military Statecraft

The amount and quality of military forces derived from manpower and other resources depend crucially on the skill with which these resources are employed. It is critical to designing military capabilities appropriate to meet-

189

ing present tasks and future contingencies, and to producing, maintaining, and using military force efficiently.

As many historical examples indicate, merely spending money on defense does not assure in the future high-quality military performance against an opponent with equal or lesser economic potential. At the beginning of World War II, Great Britain and France together possessed an economic and technological potential greatly exceeding Germany's; yet the latter country had little trouble in achieving military occupation of much of the European continent because it used its resources with superior skill.

Among the many tasks that can be executed well or badly by civilian and military authorities, the following are the most critical: (1) The design of a force structure that is oriented toward future, not past, needs; (2) the recruitment and training of officers and men; (3) the formulation of strategy and tactics; (4) the development and production of weapons systems; (5) the supply of logistical support; and (6) the maintenance of an effective system for military intelligence, communications, and control.

Guidelines for performing these administrative tasks can, of course, be derived from the evolving capabilities of other states, including allies and possible enemies. Much military planning is in this sense reactive. Yet, it is far from easy to estimate the military effectiveness of any military forces prior to engagement, especially because qualitative factors are hard to evaluate. Certain things—such as military manpower and number of armored divisions, war ships, and ICBMs—are readily counted. But comparing entire weapons systems involves difficulties resulting from qualitative differences in hardware. Soviet surface navy ships, for example, surpass American counterparts in firepower but are inferior to them in staying power at sea. Which is the best design? In addition to these differences in weapons design, there also are differences in training, morale, military leadership, and tactics that are hard to evalute. The greatest difficulty of military statecraft, however, is that decisions must deal with future, uncertain contingencies. What opponents may have to be faced with, what allies, under what circumstances? What sorts of conflicts are most likely to arise?

The difficulty is particularly severe in the development of major weapons systems—such as bomber aircraft, strategic submarines, and major surface ships—because they have a lead time stretching many years into the future.[16] Thus, R&D on major new naval equipment in the United States has, in each case, taken several years to bear fruit. Another several years are required for the decision on which technological choice to adopt, and several more years are needed for building the ships. In recent decades, the whole process has taken from 12 to 16 years. By the time the ship joins the fleet, it may be obsolete if the navies of possible opponents have been developed with superior skill or luck. The fundamental problem of military statecraft is that decisions must be made under appalling conditions of uncertainty. While new administrative tools—such as systems analysis,[17] including cost-effectiveness analysis, are helpful—they are only helpful for solving problems of sub-optimization. If applied properly, systems analysis can be extremely instructive in how to trade off increases in speed, range, and payload, and even monetary costs, in the design of military aircraft, and similarly in making many other decisions on this level. Yet, no such techniques can assure the overall maximization of future military value derived from given resource inputs. The absence of suitable analytical techniques[18] and refractory conditions of uncertainty preclude this with reference to the top decisions. The rational method of coping with uncertainty, of course, is to hedge one's bets, to take out plenty of insurance against the contingency that one's favorite forecasts may turn out to be wrong. Yet overall resource constraints forbid adequate insurance, even in the case of the wealthiest states and of those most determined not to stint on provisions for military deterrence and defense. Technological advances spurred by arms races have raised equipment costs for many military operations by an enormous factor above the levels of World War II (e.g., the costs of bombers, air defense, and of landing tanks on defended beaches). As a result, decisions on selecting and distributing investments to various weapons systems have become extremely critical, and they have to be made on the basis of judgment. Tough choices are unavoidable. The choices to be identified, evaluated, and exercised by decision-makers are clearly as hard as they are crucial to national military strength. The level of relevant administrative competence and its actual employment without being seriously hindered by political constraints, especially administrative politics, are thus vital determinants of national military strength.

The Will to Achieve Military Strength

A nation's manpower, other resources, and high military statecraft yield military forces only to the extent that resources are authoritatively committed to this purpose. Economic and administrative capacity count for nothing without such commitment through a political process that is structured principally by the country's form of government. Making this commitment is a political problem because the resources set aside for the military effort are diverted from civilian consumption and investment (both private and public). Resource diversion constitutes the opportunity costs in each society for creating and using military forces. As Stephen Krasner demonstrates in the last chapter, countries differ greatly in their ability to extract sacrifices and to make their societies assume those costs.

With the exception of the mechanism mentioned below, the release of resources for producing, maintaining, and employing military forces requires payments. This is the financial aspect. Normally, national governments acquire these means through taxation. The distribution of the finan-

191

cial burden depends then on the structure of the tax system. National authorities can also acquire the necessary finance in part by borrowing from the domestic public. If the borrowed amounts are matched by public savings, the burden of the military effort is passed on to future generations. If they are not so matched and the national economy is operating at the level of full employment, the effect is inflationary. The burden of an effort financed in this way is distributed over those members of the public who are disadvantaged by inflation in terms of real income. If borrowing is used while the economy is suffering from unemployment, unemployed resources are apt to be put into production and tax revenues will then rise as the national income expands. To the extent that the national military effort is financed by loans or gifts from abroad, the immediate financial burden falls on the lending or donor country.

National resources required for the military effort can also be commandeered. The most important way in which this happens occurs when military manpower is conscripted rather than bought in the labor market. Conscripts receive usually only a small fraction of the pay given to professional soldiers, and to that extent the real burden of the nation's military effort is placed on them. In modern nations employing professional soldiers, the wage bill constitutes a high proportion of the defense budget—around 50% in the United States and the United Kingdom—and, in terms of financial pressures, nations with conscripted forces have a corresponding advantage.

In the first place, the decision to allocate public funds to the military sector is a governmental one. Even where governments are able to dictate relevant policy without anticipating appreciable costs to their authority, they face hard choices for public expenditures, because public revenues are always a scarce resource in relation to claims on them, and leaders as well as publics will be sensitive to the opportunity costs of allocating resources to the military effort. In the large majority of nations, however, governments need to be more or less sensitive to various public interests. Influential publics may perceive the need for armed forces and national priorities of alternative levels and patterns of public expenditures differently than their governments. They may exert influence to make their preferences count. Governments can, of course, resort to persuasion and bargaining in order to manipulate actual or potential opposition to their chosen policy. Governments also decide which publics will be appeased and which can be neglected.

The question of national priorities raised by military demands turns on the relation between the expected utility of satisfying these demands, on the one hand, and the expected disutility imposed by opportunity costs, on the other. The utility that governments and publics attribute to alternative levels of defense expenditures depends on their perception of actual or potential military threats in the external environment or of the value of making such threats to others. But these calculations can also be affected by other considerations such as international status; the need for military forces for domestic purposes; and the self-interest of special groups in the government bureaucracy, the military services, and the defense industry.

International threat perception is an extremely difficult operation. History abounds with examples of gross misperceptions, whether involving overestimates or underestimates.[19] This holds expecially true of external military threats that are potential rather than acute, that is, perceptions concerned with the risk inherent in the presence of states that, although not presently engaged in hostile behavior, possess the military capabilities to mount serious military threats and cannot be safely expected to remain peaceful.

The fundamental problem of threat perception is posed by the fact that—whether directed toward conjecturing on the intentions or capabilities of other states—its empirical basis consists of incomplete, obsolescent, ambiguous, and sometimes deceptive information. International threat perception is an act of inference from ambiguous data, and no one interpretation can justify confidence or compel unanimity. Every careful case study[20] has shown that it is easy in retrospect to pick the right from the misleading clues—in technical jargon to pick the signals from the noise. However, the selection process prior to the event is guided by preconceptions about the object state's behavior that, even if informed by a rigorous study of the past, are frequently misleading regarding the future. Forecasting is extrapolation from existing trends. But existing trends can be misconstrued or, even if read correctly, can be temporary and soon replaced by others. There is and can be no knowledge about the future. All there can be is speculation.

Moreover, the intrinsic difficulty of making reliable forecasts invites various predispositions to intervene in the perceptual act. Ideological and emotional fixations can do so. Historically speaking, though, wishfulness has probably been the most frequent cause of misperception, that is, of either overestimating or underestimating external threats. Because the act of inference from ambiguous information is permissive, it is easy to predict what one would like to see happen. Finally, the dismal record of statecraft in this area is not well known and therefore does not inspire proper caution.

Whatever the true difficulties of statecraft in this matter, they are even greater and more unknown to larger publics that lack proper information and analytical skills. Take the problem of potential threats. Suppose a government makes a correct estimate of such a threat emanating from a particular state, prudently augments its capabilities for deterrence (i.e., for making it less probable that a potential threat will become acute), and nothing happens. No acute threat arises for a number of years. It is easy in this case to conclude that no threat existed or that military deterrence and defense efforts were not needed. Thus, the utility of alternative levels of national military effort is hard to evaluate. On the other hand, the disutility of spending more on defense is readily appreciated, because there is no uncertainty about the opportunity costs. The civilian use of the resources diverted to the military sector have been sacrificed for reasons that involve uncertain future benefits. It is obviously easy for societies to be divided on these issues.

Making proper provision for deterrence and defense is further complicated when a country is interested not only in self-protection but also in protecting friendly countries and allies or, still more ambitiously, in assuming the role of protecting the international status quo from the aggressive use of force by other states (or of altering the status quo by means of military force). Such extended deterrence and defense naturally increases costs. For instance, the United States has in recent decades taxed itself in order to guarantee the security of numerous other countries. The benefits to the United States justifying this additional burden are not as clear as the value of immediate self-protection, and they are easily subject to doubt when foreign beneficiaries tax themselves less in contributing to their security than does the United States (e.g., some NATO allies), or when foreign beneficiaries are states whose political system and domestic behavior are unappealing if not repulsive (e.g., South Korea).

Societies do not, of course, act as perfectly rational actors in dealing with these matters. Decisions on national military efforts are affected by attitudes endemic to the political culture of societies. These attitudes are the precipitates of previous historical experience and the product of political socialization. Their strength in various segments of society differs, and they are naturally subject to change over time in the light of new collective experiences and changes in political socialization.

Historically speaking, societies differ in their perception of the outside world as actually or potentially hostile; in their predisposition to regard war as natural, legitimate, and inevitable; and in the value they place on national autonomy and security, or on goals requiring the aggressive use of force. National military efforts have tended to be the larger, the stronger these perceptions and attitudes were and the more they were shared by governments, elites, and other publics.

Furthermore, national military efforts have also tended to be large where the sense of national solidarity was strong in the face of external danger. A powerful constraint favoring national solidarity in the face of international crisis encourages collective effort at the expense of divisive preferences and demands.

National military efforts have tended to be large where governments and important elites were keenly sensitive to external dangers or to the opportunities of using military power aggressively. Military effort is also large where publics let leaders make the relevant decisions either out of obedience to an authoritarian government or by their ready support to legitimate government in democratic societies. The strength of government and its "autonomy" from particularistic interests are thus important factors. They facilitate the output of collective as against private goods either by fiat or ready consent. And provision for deterrence and defense is a collective good that may be less appreciated than competing collective goods, such as public transportation, health, and education.

A final factor that, historically speaking, has made for relatively large military efforts is the influence of people who directly benefit in terms of career expectations, prestige, and income (i.e., the "military-industrial complex" in contemporary parlance).

Conversely, defense efforts tend to be relatively small in societies in which cultural predispositions are indifferent or hostile to military values; where the sense of national solidarity is feeble; where governments are weak; and where the influence of the beneficiaries of defense programs is exceeded by that of groups benefiting from a low level of military spending and from the expanded production of other public goods and services. Such orientations tend to become especially effective in the absence of immediate military threats to national security, whether realistic or not, and in the presence of a time discount that stresses immediate and concrete benefits over uncertain future benefits, such as the prevention of military threats and defense against them at some future time.

It has been widely observed that the democratic capitalist nations as a group have recently become more reluctant to spend resources on defense and that this trend is generally not noticeable in the rest of the world. In the former set of countries, real defense outlays (measured in non-inflated monies or as a proportion of GNP) have tended to contract. In the United States, expenditures (expressed in Fiscal Year 1977 dollars) have decreased from $110 billion to $100 billion between FY 1964 and FY 1977 and as a proportion of GNP have fallen to 5.4%, the lowest in decades.[21] Soviet military spending, on the other hand, seems to have risen substantially.[22] These societies have also experienced growing difficulties in recruiting manpower for their armed services. Where conscription still prevails, the length of military service has been shortened, and the United States and Great Britain have shifted to all-volunteer forces with a consequent increase in personnel costs.

It is, of course, difficult to generalize about these societies, and it is far from clear whether, or to what extent, these changes result from transient conditions. Particularly in the United States, they may have largely resulted from a post-Vietnam mood that has already shown signs of evaporating. Several analysts, however, have suggested that these changes have deep-seated causes[23] and, though there is no reliable knowledge about these things and any hypotheses must be taken with appropriate caution, it may be worthwhile to reproduce the main points briefly. As we shall see, they fit rather well into the conceptual framework presented above.

According to these suggestions, the political culture of the democratic capitalist societies is showing a growing distaste for war and the military virtues, and an increasing reluctance to spend scarce resources on defense. The traditional concepts of war as national, legitimate, and inevitable have become weakened for reasons that are not clear but probably have something to do with the traumatic experience of mass destruction in recent wars, especially World Wars I and II; the emergence of nuclear technology threatening still greater, almost unimaginable, destruction; and the vast expansion of higher education and the associated ability and eagerness to question received beliefs and values.

The same set of societies has also experienced some weakening of attitudes supporting national solidarity in general as well as in responses to external security threats. Two conditions have been suggested as important in accounting for this change. First, previously underprivileged segments of these societies (religious and ethnic minorities, unskilled workers, women, and youths) have gained increasing influence as a result of a progressive democratization of political life. The process has augmented tensions within these societies and caused a diffusion and reordering of loyalties, with particularist identifications and demands conflicting with claims that emphasize national priorities and unity. Second, there has been a tendency, in particular among the young and highly educated, to approach the solution of political problems with more ideological commitment and less pragmatic willingness to compromise. This has made political division more rigid and the issues at stake less easily subordinated to claimed national interests.

The process of democratization in the capitalist democracies and the aforementioned developments associated with it have also engendered a weakening of government and government authority. As more groups with newly gained influence press sectional welfare demands, attitudes toward government and acceptance of government policy have become more suspicious and calculating. The rise of ideologized "issue politics" has led to a decay of identification with political parties, and they have become less able than previously to mobilize popular support for national causes cutting across group interests. Expanding demands for welfare, which governments have been less able to resist, have been pressing hard on non-welfare expenditures, notably for defense, and tended to produce public deficits.

The shift in national priorities resulting from these political and social changes evidently reflects the growing influence of interest groups, including bureaucratic ones, that have a strong stake in the expansion of welfare outlays. And these groups are now influential enough to contest and check

196

the influence of groups with contrary interests, especially those with a self-interest in the maintenance of a strong defense posture. The "military-industrial complex" has lost in relative power.

Finally, these transformations have been accompanied by a spreading disinclination to perceive threats to military security as serious. This shift has been assisted by a vigorous reaction, perhaps overreaction, to previous beliefs that had exaggerated the threat to the West from the USSR and a monolithic communist front, by the assumption that mutual nuclear deterrence had rendered war obsolete as an instrument of foreign policy, and by hopes that détente had ushered in an era of enduringly stable relations with the Soviet Union.

The question of whether these developments in the West amount to a dangerous slackening of will to provide adequately for deterrence and defense in a world that is scarcely free from the exercise of violence cannot be answered with any confidence one way or the other. To the extent that these developments express changes of mood, they may prove evanescent. And even if the underlying political and cultural changes persist, the behavior of other states may evoke keen perceptions of insecurity and, as a result, a willingness, however grudging, to do what is necessary for enhanced security. The British experience from the 1860s to 1939 is interesting from this point of view.[24] During this period, the United Kingdom exhibited some of the very symptoms we have observed in contemporary democratic societies. The rise of new ideals about how international relations should be structured peaceably increasingly rivalled traditional concepts that regarded prompt resort to military force as the inevitable sanction in settling major international conflicts. International economic interdependence—Britain's high dependence on foreign commerce and investment after the adoption of free trade—was seen as making any disruption caused by major warfare a profound threat to national welfare. Her global commitments in defense of overseas empire were seen to be excessive, as other countries and potential enemies became industrialized. Most importantly, progressive democratization, beginning with the extension of the franchise in 1867, induced a cumulative shift of national priorities in favor of domestic welfare programs. As a result, Great Britain began in the late 1860s to follow a foreign policy of appeasement, based on a disposition to settle international quarrels by negotiated compromise and to avoid resort to major armed conflict. The ill consequences of this disposition in helping to bring about World War II are well known. But it is also worth emphasizing that, when the United Kingdom was compelled to fight in World Wars I and II, the British did so with superb dedication. Of course, although this historical example should give pause to any observers who decry the weaknesses of contemporary democratic nations in providing for their security, it can give no assurance of a reversal in the event critical challenges should occur.

In any case, as already stated, the recent developments in the capitalist democratic societies are not shared by non-Western societies. In the communist one-party states, government may suffer at times from internal factionalism, but government authority is solid, especially in the Soviet Union and China, in the sense that leaders have no difficulty in allocating massive resources to the military sector or in conscripting manpower for the armed forces. Patriotic attitudes are sedulously fostered in these countries; the military are in uncontested charge of cultivating respect for the martial virtues, and the mass media express incessant sensitivity to external security threats.

If the political and cultural trends we have discussed persist in the capitalist democratic countries while remaining absent elsewhere, they will justify doubts about the ability of these countries—still by far the richest in material resources, as a group and per capita—to provide adequately for deterrence and defense and hence for their survival as independent societies in a world that otherwise shows no signs of losing its dangerousness. As Samuel Huntington put it with reference to the United States, the vulnerability of contemporary democratic government ". . . comes not primarily from external threats . . . but rather from the internal dynamics of democracy itself in a highly educated, mobilized, and participant society."[25]

We have presented this extensive, even if tentative, analysis, because it is so easy to assume that national wealth readily yields military strength and security. Nothing could be further from the truth. While national riches are a vital basis for national military strength, they are only one such basis. Without the will to employ them in sufficient part for purposes of international security, that security is apt to be in jeopardy. National will, in this as in any other matter, is an aggregation of individual wills. It is a matter of political energy that can be collected and focused on a purpose backed by substantial agreement among those who exert influence. The magnitude of national will, however, depends on how widely shared the intensity of interest is.

Footnotes

1. Adam Smith, *The Wealth of Nations* (New York: Modern Library, 1973), p. 431.
2. See Klaus Knorr, *The Power of Nations* (New York: Basic Books, 1975); Klaus Knorr, *Military Power and Potential* (Lexington, Mass.: D.C. Heath and Company, 1970). See also, Charles J. Hitch and Roland McKean, *The Economics of Defense in the Nuclear Age* (Cambridge, Mass.: Harvard University Press, 1960); and Gavin Kennedy, *The Economics of Defense* (Totowa, New Jersey: Rowman and Littlefield, 1975).
3. U.S., Arms Control and Disarmament Agency, *World Military Expenditures and Arms Transfers, 1965–1974* (Washington, D.C.: 1976).
4. The problems are discussed in Kennedy, *The Economics of Defense*, Chap. III.
5. The list for the first two classes is complete. All figures are from *World Military Expenditures and Arms Transfers, 1965–1974*.

6. U.S., Department of State, *Indicators of Comparative East-West Economic Strength, 1975* (Washington, D.C.: November 1976).

7. For other examples, see *SIPRI Yearbook 1976; World Armaments and Disarmament* (Stockholm: Almquist and Wiksell, 1976), p. 97.

8. On the U.S. position, see William Schneider, *Food, Foreign Policy, and Raw Materials Cartels* (New York: Crane, Russak, 1976), Chap. IV.

9. *SIPRI Yearbook 1976*, pp. 140–41.

10. U.S., Department of State, *The Planetary Product in 1974* (Washington, D.C.: 1975), p. 14.

11. In terms of constant dollars, see Arms Control and Disarmament Agency, *World Military Expenditures and Arms Transfers, 1965–1974*, pp. 14, 50.

12. U.S. Department of State, *The Planetary Product in 1974*, p. 14.

13. National Science Board, *Science Indicators 1974* (Washington, D.C.: Government Printing Office, n.d.), pp. 2ff, 30ff.

14. These data must be interpreted with caution. What really counts is the *productivity* of R&D resources. However, because R&D outputs are hard or impossible to measure—how can we evaluate the output of basic research?—we are necessarily reduced to comparing inputs.

15. See the interesting report of Drew Middleton in *New York Times*, 1 December 1976, pp. 1, 16.

16. For an interesting discussion of these problems, see Kennedy, *Economics*, Chaps. V–VII.

17. For a good but optimistic examination of these management tools, see Alain C. Enthoven and K. Wayne Smith, *How Much is Enough? Shaping the Defense Program, 1961–1969* (New York: Harper and Row, 1971), especially Chaps. I–II.

18. Military statecraft at this level has received little systematic study. As a result, decisions are made primarily on the basis of crude rules of thumb, the often obsolete "lessons of the past," intuitive judgment, and the bias of men in high positions of leadership.

19. For a detailed examination of the problem, see Klaus Knorr, "Threat Perception," *Historical Dimensions of National Security Problems*, ed. Klaus Knorr (Lawrence, Kansas: University Press of Kansas, 1976), pp. 78–119.

20. See ibid. For three revealing detailed case studies, see Roberta Wohlsteller, *Pearl Harbor: Warning and Decision* (Stanford, California: Stanford University Press, 1962); Barton Whaley, *Codeword Barbarossa* (Cambridge, Mass.: MIT Press, 1973); Avi Shlaim, "Failures in National Intelligence Estimates: The Case of the Yom Kippur War," *World Politics*, XXVIII (1976): 348–80.

21. William Schneider, Jr. and Francis P. Hoeber, *Arms, Men, and Military Budgets* (New York: Crane, Russak, 1976), pp. 12–14.

22. Ibid., p. 14. Note, however, that comparative estimates of Soviet military expenditures are extremely difficult to make. For the best discussion of these problems, see Andrew W. Marshall, "Estimating Soviet Defence Spending," *Survival* (March/April 1976): 73–79. See also Kennedy, *Economics*, Chap. III.

23. See Richard Erb, *National Security and Economic Policies*, American Enterprise Institute, Reprint No. 14, May 1976; Samuel P. Huntington, "The Democratic Distemper," *The Public Interest*, 41 (Fall 1975): 9–38; Morris Janowitz, "Toward a Redefinition of Military History," *World Politics*, XXVI (July 1974): 473–508; Bruce Russett, "The Americans' Retreat from World Power," *Political Science Quarterly*, 90 (Spring 1975): 1–21; Knorr, *The Power of Nations*, pp. 69–74. See also Chapter 6 above.

24. See Paul M. Kennedy, "The Tradition of Appeasement in British Foreign Policy, 1865–1939," *British Journal of International Studies*, II (October 1976): 195–215.

25. Huntington, *Democratic Distemper*, p. 37.

CHAPTER 8

Contemporary Security Dimensions of International Trade Relations

Ronald I. Meltzer

The conduct of international trade produces a complex array of linkages between national security and international relations. Trade flows reflect the pursuit of domestic interests and goals interacting in a global environment characterized by different levels of power capabilities and interdependence. In this chapter, international trade relations will be explored from a perspective that has become increasingly compelling in contemporary world politics: how international trade relates to national and collective security concerns. First, an overview of the changing character of trade relations since World War II will be presented. Second, two sets of issues confronting current multilateral trade negotiations will be examined in light of broadened security conceptions relevant to national governments in an economically interdependent world. They are international safeguarding and adjustment assistance and export controls and access to supplies.

Security Concepts and International Trade Relations

Historically, international trade relations have reflected governmental security concerns—even if such considerations are narrowly defined in military terms. Robert Gilpin provides many examples in Chapter 2. For instance, strongly associated with the Bretton Woods plans for liberalized trade patterns was the desire to prevent beggar-thy-neighbor policies that were seen to breed conflicts contributing to World War II. For several decades, U.S. support of European integration and its willingness to withstand trade discrimination vis-à-vis Europe and Japan derived in large part from security concerns pursued within a cold war context.[1] Indeed, as détente with the Soviet Union began to develop, the waning of traditional security considerations in the late 1960s and early 1970s became an important factor behind emerging trade conflicts among Western countries.[2]

Overt linkages between international trade and narrowly defined security concerns could also be seen in a variety of national programs aimed at preserving increased control over and access to materials perceived to be vital for defense-related goals.[3] Similarly, trade policies have frequently

200

been used as strategic instruments of coercion and denial, particularly when the actual use of force has been perceived as inappropriate.[4]

A more recent dimension of the relationship between security concerns and international trade stems from increased patterns of economic interdependence. As national economic trends, pay-offs, and policies become more entwined with those of other societies, there is greater national susceptibility to disruptive and injurious impacts from abroad. In these circumstances, it becomes an increasingly realistic policy perspective to identify international trade matters with security concerns.

As Krause and Nye point out, security can be conceptualized as a negative goal, involving the absence of acute threats to minimally acceptable levels of basic values deemed essential by society (or groups of societies).[5] In this respect, trade policies affect security concerns to the extent that they act as both instruments and objectives towards achieving and protecting basic values, such as desired levels of economic growth, welfare, and independence.

For developing countries, a broader conception of security has always been important, since trade relations, particularly as they relate to economic development, have traditionally constituted the stuff of "high politics." In a world of penetrated and mutually sensitive societies, an expanded security notion has become increasingly relevant to developed countries. The exact measure of salience that international trade may have on security concerns varies with particular contingencies. It can range from critical importance in a specific situation, e.g., dealing with the maintenance of vital access to markets to preserve national economic viability (Ghana's need to export cocoa), to longer-term considerations, e.g., involving the future structure of relations among trading nations (U.S. concern about evolving discriminatory trade blocs deriving from regional groupings).

In a basic sense, gaining and preserving security hinges upon national power capabilities to achieve essential values. Yet, with increased global interdependence, one country's relative capabilities often depend on external actors and events.[6] For example, policy goals relating to acceptable levels of employment and inflation are shaped by and tied to trade flows molded not only by home governments, but also by foreign governments. Involved here are not only policy interconnections across national societies but also across issue areas. In such an environment, international policy discontinuities can distort or defeat national efforts to achieve basic objectives—or even produce new difficulties for policy-makers.[7]

But if policy linkages and mutual dependencies have broadened, the same has not been true for the utility and fungibility of power across varied policy areas. This does not mean that there is no longer a hierarchy of national capacities to achieve basic values or to provide insulation from disruptive external impacts to those values. It does indicate, however, a greater international diffusion and decentralization of capabilities and re-sponsibilities required to secure desired outcomes relating to those basic values. As Stanley Hoffmann has noted,

> Today interdependence breaks all national eggs (power capabilities) into a vast omelet . . . I don't know where my power ends and yours begins, since my power is partly your hostage and vice versa, and the more I try to force you to depend on me, the more I depend on you.[8]

This condition even attends relations among states that are unequally en-dowed in overall power capabilities. Thus, the perceptibly increased im-portance of developing countries in contemporary international trade rela-tions is predicted not only on their much publicized possession of key commodities, but also on the need for their effective participation in inter-national negotiations, if broadly based multilateral trade accords are to be reached and made lasting.[9]

Such interconnectedness—shared pay-offs regarding the achievement of basic values and mutual capacities to shape those outcomes—has given rise to the notion of *collective economic security*. Krause and Nye define this term as "governments' acceptance of international surveillance of their domestic and foreign economic policies, of criticism of the effects of their policies on the economic security of other countries, and of various forms of international presence in the operations of markets."[10] Strongly behind the functioning of collective economic security is accep-tance of the principle of collective cognizance—that there is legitimate international interest in national security concerns involving the willingness of national governments to submit such concerns to multilateral dialogue, study, and policy formulation.[11] A significant example of such multilateral surveillance to maintain collective economic security can be seen in recent OECD agreements pledging members to avoid trade-restricting measures in periods of economic difficulty. Such an OECD presence has gone far to militate against national trade policies that would shift economic burdens onto others.[12]

Increased interdependence provides an important impetus towards ac-cepting such collective mechanisms. As Joseph Nye points out, "Insofar as nations become entwined in each other's welfare, they have a positive in-centive to co-operate and to avoid destructive actions."[13] To promote col-lective economic security measures among interdependent nations, it is important to find acceptable ways to sort out and order the complicated trade-offs that are involved when different governments pursue various policies of national economic welfare. The objective is to foster generalized positive-sum outcomes or joint gains, rather than have unilateral efforts to seek individual gains prevail, since they are often met with retaliation and eventual joint loss.[14]

Several important tasks critical to the functioning of collective economic security have been identified.[15] First, there is the need for *assessment*—the collection and evaluation of information about current and future economic developments and problems. Such data are critical to joint planning efforts aimed at preventing, or more ably dealing with, perceived threats to collective economic security. Such a task can play a vital role in mitigating crisis conditions and in instituting "early warning systems" designed to activate multilateral remedies. For example, one suggested area for pursuing collective assessment and forewarning activities involves monitoring trade-affecting financial trends. Recent monetary disturbances have highlighted the need for such a mechanism to fill the institutional gap between GATT and the IMF.[16]

Second, *regulation* is an important task in promoting collective economic security. The establishment of internationally accepted rules governing behavior is especially critical in contemporary international trade relations. Many new issues, such as scarcity of supply and export control concerns, have arisen, and GATT codes provide little regulatory guidance in these matters. In addition, developments regarding more traditional trade issues, such as access to markets in agricultural trade, have likewise pointed to the need for reforming present GATT provisions, if collective economic security is to be fostered.

Third, the provision of *equity* is an important aspect of activities designed to achieve collective economic security. This task relates to the insurance of joint gains and fair distributive effects among member states and within respective societies. The problem of accommodating economic welfare values among nations in different competitive positions is particularly relevant here, because equity in international trade relations has both international and intranational dimensions which often present conflicting policy impulses. Nonetheless, equity remains a key element of any approach to trade problems that seeks collective economic security, since domestic pressures for unilateral remedies to trade-associated economic difficulties often cannot be stemmed—even if they would lead to longer-term costs—unless participating governments can offer equitable benefits from multilateral agreements which alleviate losses at home.

Finally, providing *emergency relief* is an important task in achieving collective economic security. The will and capacity to extend multilateral relief for short-term, severe difficulties are essential to avoid responses to trade problems that would lead to injuries for others or joint losses. For instance, in commodity trade, price and supply conditions are subject to both man-made and natural disruptions that can lead to potentially acute crises. Emergency relief provisions would alleviate deprivations threatening to collective economic security. Examples of multilateral efforts in this respect are emergency oil-sharing and financing programs worked out by industrial

203

nations at the International Energy Agency and at the OECD, as well as measures being considered at the ongoing Conference on International Economic Cooperation (CIEC) to provide short-term protection for developing countries' purchasing power from export earnings that have been severely eroded by inflation and recession.[17] In trade relations, such relief is often the mirror interest to providing equity, since both elements are often entwined as related faces of trade problems between competitors and between producers and consumers. Domestically, emergency relief provisions are also vital to accommodate those groups whose specific interests would be injured, despite aggregate national gains from multilateral approaches to trade issues.

The attainment of collective economic security is by no means a phenomenon arising naturally out of conditions of international economic interdependence. In a significant sense, collective economic security can be considered as an international public good which requires certain levels of cooperation and constraints to become effective. In general, the propensity of states to engage in such collective efforts hinges on the interplay between the need to become dependent on others to perform vital tasks and the desire to keep such dependency at a minimal level.[18] In this context, effective collaborative arrangements require an accommodation of different national incentives, costs, and pay-offs regarding participation.

The difficulties of achieving a viable "production" of an international public good such as collective economic security in trade relations can be broadly categorized into three areas: (1) national unwillingness to submit short-term interests and direction to more long-term international concerns and formulations; (2) conflicting perceptions of priorities among potential members; and (3) institutional problems in administering vital tasks necessary for the attainment of collaborative arrangements.

A fundamental basis for national unwillingness to engage in cooperative commitments derives from "interdependence costs" posed by such involvements. Broadly, these costs entail the acceptance of circumscribed options or loss of autonomy by national governments, often leading to increased exposure to risks of disruptions caused by external economic and political actions.[19] In addition, there are often significant costs that stem from agreements to participate in collaborative arrangements, e.g., accepting smaller market shares for exports or devoting specified resources for the maintenance of supplies of potentially scarce materials. It is frequently the case that the distributive effects of such arrangements between and within national societies are uneven. Whereas the trade-offs involved may produce long-term benefits for society as a whole, e.g., more stable trade flows or more secure access to supplies, there are likely to be domestic groups whose interests will suffer from participation in such arrangements. Political mobilization by these groups can forestall national involvement in such

204

collective economic security efforts, forcing a government to forego the benefits of an international public good because of an unwillingness or inability to inflict deprivation on particular domestic interests. Such uneven impacts of adaption costs are even more difficult for governments to accept, if the timing is such that benefits accrue well after the costs occur.[20]

Another basis for national reluctance to engage in such international collaboration may be a desire to maintain a preferred short-term position within a problematic international policy area. For example, despite the apparent problems and breakdowns in international monetary relations in the late 1960s and early 1970s, the achievement of broad-based reforms was made difficult by the continued short-term competitive edge enjoyed by certain countries within this failing monetary regime, e.g., Japan.

Conflicting priorities among possible members of a collaborative arrangement can also pose difficulties in achieving collective economic security. For the most part, economic interdependence results in mutual sensitivities and interconnected vulnerabilities such that joint efforts are needed to cope effectively. But, despite shared fates, national divergences regarding specific economic goals and choices of policy instruments to deal with problems can still persist. These differences are heightened among countries of varied levels of economic development. But even among similarly situated countries, there are significant disparities regarding related priorities. For example, within the European Community, some members regard inflation as the principal problem (Germany), while others see correcting payments deficits as the preeminent concern (France). Similarly, disparities in the choice of policy tools to be emphasized can obstruct the achievement of needed policy harmonization, as has been evidenced by the different approaches pursued by the French and German governments in dealing with recent economic troubles. Involved are not only the selection of various fiscal and monetary instruments, but also the desired level of governmental intervention into private sectors.[21] These disparities—and others related to the possible unreliability of collective solutions—are not only obstacles for initiating collective economic security efforts, but they can become sources of difficulty for preserving the continued "production" of such international public goods. Differentials in evolving national capacities and priorities are central to governmental willingness to incur prevailing "interdependence costs" of maintaining collective arrangements.[22]

Finally, problems of administering key tasks necessary for collective economic security represent additional stumbling blocks to its achievement. How to organize the most suitable mechanisms for coordinating national economic policies along cooperative lines is a formidable institutional problem. This concern entails decisions about the most appropriate level and scope of participation and of policy jurisdiction. It has been argued, for example, that the most effective pursuits in this regard may well be among small, homogeneous groups of countries dealing with defined functional areas. But increasingly, problems in international trade relations have involved intersectoral matters requiring policy coordination among countries of disparate backgrounds.[23] One analyst has suggested that perhaps the most efficacious means of collaboration is a transgovernmental "wisemen" procedure that maximizes flexibility and pragmatism in approaching related problems, e.g., the Group of Twenty within the IMF.[24] This institutional path would help to avoid intergovernmental posturing and unwieldy organizational processes that often characterize international forums and negotiations. However, an important liability associated with this approach is its potential for reinforcing the organizational sprawl and decentralization that now trouble many international economic institutions.

A critical variable in organizing collective economic security efforts— and indeed the "production" of any international public good—is the assertion of leadership by a country or group of countries toward that end. Such a leadership role is needed in creating the material wherewithal and political will to forge collaborative arrangements and in ". . . cajoling, persuading, arm-twisting other countries to take their appropriate shares of the cost."[25] As Robert Gilpin notes, in periods of weak leadership, international economic relations often become marked by intense economic competition and growing international economic fragmentation—both anathema to the "production" of an international public good.[26] The post-war leadership exercised by the United States occurred in a era of special circumstances, whereby U.S. economic and military dominance and harmonious policy goals among trading nations recovering from World War II provided conducive conditions for such a role. Present uncertainties about the assertion of leadership—its prerogatives and costs—act to cloud prospects for achieving collective economic security in key areas of trade relations.[27]

The Character of Contemporary International Trade Relations

Since World War II, international trade relations have been characterized by unparalleled growth. From 1950 to 1970, world exports increased over five-fold in value to roughly $300 billion, with annual rates of growth consistently approaching 10%. Among those countries which have dominated international trade and have been most dynamic in their sustained expansion—Western industrial societies—annual increases in exports have even outstripped remarkable yearly growth rates in gross national product.[28]

Accompanying this process of rapid expansion in international trade have been concomitant increases in interdependence among national economies and important structural changes in production and exchange

206

patterns. Ratios of exports to gross national products; growth rates of direct foreign investments and international capital movements; shortened time-lags in cyclical trends among trading nations; and high levels of tourism, technology transfers, and the use of foreign workers all indicate active economic interpenetrations and mutual sensitivity among national societies.[29] Trade-influenced structural changes have occurred not only among different national economies—whereby per capita income gaps between developed and developing countries have widened, reflecting in large part the former's predominance in the production and trade of manufactures—but also within national economies. For both economically advanced and developing countries, serious domestic adjustment problems and structural inequalities have been created in the wake of contemporary international trade relations.[30]

Underlying these patterns and effects has been a fundamental dilemma that faces virtually every national government; on the one hand, demands are placed upon governments to achieve increasingly wide-ranging economic goals for their societies, yet more and more, unilateral governmental capacities to control factors shaping national economic conditions have become diminished. Such a dilemma, and the prospect of painful trade-offs between enjoying gains from active involvement in international economic relations and preserving national autonomy and self-direction without disruptive external impacts have made the formulation of trade policies increasingly politicized.[31]

Throughout most of the post-war period, the conduct of international trade relations has largely been carried out within the basic framework prescribed by the General Agreement on Tariffs and Trade (GATT). As Richard N. Cooper has indicated, the result has been that international trade policies have been rather successfully suspended on their own non-politicized "track."[32] However, this system of interaction no longer prevails as it did in the past, advancing the politicization of international trade relations. Indeed, the essential tenets of the GATT framework—non-discrimination, minimum governmental interference with trade flows, periodic multilateral efforts of trade liberalization focusing on tariff reductions among principal suppliers, and reciprocity—are no longer preeminent policy guidelines followed by the major trading nations. In addition, deep-rooted dissatisfaction with extant priorities and pay-offs within GATT negotiations has led less developed nations to orient their attentions and loyalties towards trade and development platforms organized under the United Nations Conference for Trade and Development (UNCTAD). This international organization has emerged as a rival, although beleaguered, locus for policy formulation and negotiation that further threatens the jurisdiction and legitimacy of the GATT framework. Moreover, increasing levels of East-West trade have produced additional concern about the inadequacies of the present GATT order, particularly relating to transactions among disparate economies and politically divergent nations.[33]

The prevailing GATT system derived from attempts by Western governments to avoid a recurrence of the 1930s beggar-thy-neighbor experience and to restore orderly and liberalized conditions of international commerce.[34] In significant ways, impressive progress has been made towards achieving expressed goals under this system. Evolving from a period of bilateralism, trade and monetary restrictions, and economic disruption and stagnation, the post-war era of trade relations reached new heights in gaining multilateral cooperation, liberalized transactions, and economic expansion.[35] But despite these successes, trends in international trade relations since the Kennedy Round of 1967 now seem to strain the capacity of existing arrangements to meet current goals and needs. This situation has aroused resurgent protectionist impulses throughout many societies and an underlying sense of crisis associated with present international trade relations. As Gilpin argued in Chapter 2, the supports of the liberal interdependent world economy have weakened.

Several major factors have contributed to such current difficulties. First, monetary relations have been an unsettling force in shaping international trade patterns. Despite short-term agreements reached since the breakdown of the Bretton Woods system in 1971, monetary relations are still in a state of flux, and the future development of trade policies hinges upon building an efficient and stable basis for exchanging goods and services.[36]

Second, lowering trade barriers has become a much more problematic activity, since dramatic tariff reductions achieved through successive multilateral rounds of negotiations have, in effect, left a bedrock of unresolved and newly formed difficulties. The principle of non-discrimination and the proportion of international trade conducted under most-favored-nation (MFN) treatment have been substantially eroded over the past twenty years, stemming from the establishment of regional groupings and their associated preferential trade agreements and, more recently, from the granting of generalized preferences to developing countries. Thus, vested interests have been created against reducing trade barriers that would diminish margins of preference enjoyed by respective member-states and by recipients of hard-earned special treatment policies.

In addition, emerging trade patterns and consequent structural changes reflecting a shifting international division of labor have presented critical problems of resistance and adjustment to trade liberalization in many traditional industrial sectors. In these primarily labor-intensive areas, evolving industries and trade interests of the developing world have become pitted against those in economically declining regions of developed countries, where competitive advantage, or indeed survival, has often been maintained by protection against such liberalization. Negotiating mutual accommodation on trade problems in this context, given the domestic social and political implications, has proved to be painstakingly difficult. In a similar sense, reducing trade barriers in the agricultural field has entailed a complex array of problems, as the striking failures of past GATT negotiations to reach accords on agricultural trade liberalization have proved. A major factor behind the negotiating impasses has been the maintenance of national agricultural support systems aimed at aiding farm communities. These programs reflect domestic political and social sensitivities that often supercede international goals of efficiency, stable supplies at moderate prices, and liberalized market access.[37]

Third, new trade problems have emerged which have exacerbated present conditions in international trade relations. While not novel in their character, non-tariff restrictions have taken on heightened importance in international trade.[38] In addition to overtly discriminatory practices, such as import quotas, export subsidies, and government procurement programs, public policies relating to health standards, consumer and environmental protection, and industrial development can create significant distortions in international trade.[39] In an era of reduced tariff barriers, these restrictions pose great difficulties for multilateral efforts at trade liberalization, since their forms, effects, and purposes vary so widely, making them less susceptible to traditional bargaining principles developed under GATT.[40]

Another emerging problem in international trade relations involves the operation of multinational corporations (MNC). Global MNC activities offer fundamental challenges to the conduct of international trade. Their operations affect local conditions of production, employment, and competition within both host and parent countries, and these enterprises can heavily shape international trade flows—often in a manner that circumvents the regulatory capacities of national governments and international organizations.[41] As a result, MNC operations have generated domestic political pressures aimed at limiting these firms' activities. Such a response can easily take on trade-restricting dimensions, as exemplified by the Foreign Trade and Investment Act (Burke-Hartke bill) introduced into the U.S. Congress in 1972.[42]

Security of foreign supplies and potential scarcities in critical raw materials represent additional new trade issues troubling contemporary international trade relations. Export controls and concerns about access to foreign supplies have taken on new prominence, with GATT rules and practices offering little guidance on how to proceed towards handling these problems.[43] Furthermore, commodity trade in general has opened up a host of complex and contentious issues concerning efforts by developing countries to create "a new international economic order."

These overlapping and protracted difficulties have caused policy-

209

making and negotiations in international trade to be at once highly politicized and conflictual, yet more and more compelling lest a more antagonistic situation develop. Since the end of the Kennedy Round, protectionist and trade-disruptive measures have become more prominent, as seen, for example, in the litany of post-1967 trade bills introduced into the U.S. Congress and in the frequent unilateral actions taken by major trading nations which have impeded a liberalized flow of international trade.[44]

These developments, coupled with increased instability in international monetary relations, created new impetus for holding a seventh set of multilateral trade negotiations under GATT. Toward that end, more than one hundred nations gathered in Tokyo on September 14, 1973, declaring their intention to initiate a new round of negotiations to

> . . . achieve the expansion and even greater liberalization of world trade . . . through progressive dismantling of obstacles to trade and the improvement of the international framework for the conduct of world trade; and . . . secure additional benefits for the international trade of developing countries.[45]

Since that time, conditions affecting international trade relations have heightened the need for multilateral agreements in order to avoid what C. Fred Bergsten sees as furthering trends towards "an outbreak of international trade wars."[46] The decline of inflation, which during its height in 1974–75 led to the reduction of import control measures for counter-inflationary purposes, has resulted in the renewal of pressure for trade restrictions to protect "sensitive" industries and to deal with undiminished unemployment. In addition, conflicts have arisen over alleged self-benefiting interferences with trade flows, e.g., export subsidies and dumping, as governments have sought through trade policies to quicken the pace of their recovery from deep recessionary conditions. Fluctuating exchange rates and monetary disturbances have further complicated trade relations, creating possibilities of selective trade advantages that violate GATT principles, e.g., "dirty floats" and competitive devaluations. Finally, many developing countries' positions in international trade have been further weakened by large trade imbalances and heavy debt burdens associated with energy and food requirements and with the impact of world recession. This situation has made for more disgruntled relations with industrial countries and for further impatience with potential remedies pursued through traditional trade negotiations.[47] Thus, the current GATT round stands at a critical juncture in international trade relations, as it is widely perceived that significant new accords and ground rules are required for the conduct of international trade to proceed on an orderly and progressive basis in the future.

The Current Multilateral Trade Negotiations:
An Examination of Two Sets of Trade Issues and
Their Security Dimensions

Throughout the post-war period, multilateral trade negotiations have been held under GATT to promote trade liberalization and to achieve economic welfare goals shaped by attendant trade flows. These negotiations have usually been convened at critical junctures in international trade relations, representing concerted efforts to overcome difficulties threatening the progressive course of liberalized international trade relations. The present Tokyo Round is no exception. Indeed, the current state of trade conditions, in the words of a former U.S. official, ". . . makes past trade talks look simple by comparison."[48] As another observer has noted, "Probably never before has GATT negotiated long-term decisions in such crisis circumstances."[49] In order to examine key elements of contemporary trade relations and their security dimensions more fully, two important sets of trade issues confronting the Tokyo Round negotiations will be assessed: international safeguarding and adjustment measures, and export controls and access to supply.

International Safeguarding and Adjustment Measures

Safeguard actions against import disruptions involve cross-cutting interests and dynamics reflecting critical trends in international trade relations. These trends include increased global mobility of production factors and economic interdependence; changing patterns of international competitiveness and consequent structural impacts; and governmental efforts to enhance and protect different, often conflicting economic welfare concerns.

In order to promote trade liberalization and an international division of labor that efficiently utilizes resources, it has been widely recognized that mechanisms are needed to protect domestic industries from undue harm stemming from increased import competition. Short-term safeguards act to ease longer-term adjustments and to "prevent one country's salvation from becoming other countries' burdens . . . ." Some safeguards are essential to facilitate changing production and trade patterns.[50] In this vein, the Tokyo Declaration of 1973 specifically called for negotiations toward establishing a multilateral safeguard system that would accommodate importing countries' needs without jeopardizing others' export opportunities.[51]

An increasingly important element behind the issue of safeguards is the role that developing countries have played in exporting manufactures to industrial markets, especially in labor-intensive lines of production. From 1962 to 1972, for example, world trade in manufactures grew some 13% annually, but manufactured exports from the developing world expanded by 20% per year over this period.[52] Indeed, in some industries, average

211

import rate increases from less developed nations have exceeded 30%.[53] However, the overall level of developing countries' export volume is rather low, as they represent only marginal suppliers in most industrial items.

Gaining expanded export opportunities in this realm has long been a prized economic development goal of developing countries.[54] Their strong adherence to this objective of achieving further industrialization and trade in manufactures was reflected in the 1975 Lima Declaration, which proclaimed the developing countries' goal of producing 25% of the world's industrial goods by the year 2000.[55] Thus, a major focus for less developed nations in the current trade negotiations is aimed at securing expanded access to industrial markets and at calling upon industrial countries "to desist from hindering structural change in their economies brought about by the progressing industrialization in the developing world."[56]

Concern about import flows and safeguards also remains a highly significant and contentious trade issue among industrialized countries. Provisions for relief from import competition have long been included in U.S. trade legislation, and GATT Article 19 directly deals with such circumstances.[57] Indeed, much of the problem that now confronts negotiations at the Tokyo Round relates to the inadequacies of present provisions to handle safeguarding needs in the contemporary international economic environment.

The present safeguard system prescribed under Article 19 authorizes governments to take emergency measures to restrict imports, if it can be shown that there is actual or threatened "serious injury" from imports to domestic industries. The use of safeguards is subject to prior notification in most cases and to non-discriminatory application. The Article also provides that exporting countries affected by such measures may withdraw trade concessions or, as further interpreted, may receive compensation in other concessions that the restricting country may grant. If no compensation is forthcoming, affected governments can take retaliatory action in kind, such as imposing import restrictions of their own.[58]

As with other areas of trade relations, the principles of non-discrimination and reciprocity are built into the present safeguarding guidelines. But both principles have been troublesome to governments in their use of such GATT provisions. The basic difficulty with non-discrimination derives from the fact that usually only selected exporters are the sources of injury, not all suppliers. Thus, as a mechanism designed to halt disruptive import flows, this Article lacks precision in implementation. This condition is exacerbated by the rule of reciprocity, since compensation in kind can be too costly and imbalanced in effect. Reciprocity also imposes political difficulties for the import-restricting government, requiring officials facing domestic pressures for rectifying perceived foreign injuries "to explain . . . why compensation should be given for what cannot but appear (as) . . . a rightful action."[59] A further problem with the Article's provisions

212

is that there is no clause for periodic review of injury claims. These shortcomings have prompted one observer to note that "the article is too exacting in that the country invoking it risks retaliation (or risks paying too much) for taking emergency action, and, at the same time, it is too lenient in allowing emergency protection to become permanent."[60]

In practice, such problems have led governments to avoid invoking Article 19 when faced with threatening import competition. Instead, other means and approaches for protection have been preferred, such as negotiating "voluntary" export restraints or simply imposing import quotas.[61] The possibilities for abuse, inequitable consequences, and joint losses are heightened in such circumstances where extant multilateral mechanisms are perceived as inoperative. The result is a further politicization of international trade relations in this critical area.

Safeguard mechanisms have been the focus of keen domestic political interest, particularly in the post-Kennedy Round period. Business and labor leaders have felt that under existing legislation and international rules "temporary relief from injurious import competition was virtually inaccessible. . . ." Reflecting this sentiment, the U.S. Trade Act of 1974 has buttressed provisions for unilateral steps to deal with harmful disruptions. Government officials clearly acknowledged that such legislation was vital, since "the functioning of this mechanism will not only help restore domestic support for our liberal trade policy but will also encourage our trading partners to be more responsive to proposals for establishing new guidelines (on safeguards) for international trade during the negotiations."[62]

Foreign governments have expressed great concern about this legislation's protectionist tendencies, especially given a relaxation in its eligibility criteria for import relief to threatened industries.[63] Such alarm was heightened when many petitions for relief were filed quickly after the passage of the new trade bill. These claims involved over $1.5 billion in imports to the United States in 1974.[64] While the actual governmental response to such petitioned relief has thus far been quite restrained, the possibility of enacting extensive import restrictions makes for a destabilizing condition in which retaliation and an overall reduction in trade could likely result.[65] This prospect has produced strong impetus for forging an acceptable multilateral safeguard system at the current GATT round.

In viewing safeguarding policies in international trade relations, security considerations—both on a national and collective basis—arise. As noted, national security interests become salient when core values are perceived to be threatened by external factors and events, and for governments, both on the export and import sides of this issue, such threat recognition is a highly sensitive element of the policy-making environment.

From the export side, gaining security of access to markets is of fundamental importance. This is especially true for developing countries. As noted, they have become increasingly engaged in trade flows affected by safeguarding measures. Given their need for economic development, trade liberalization in areas in which they possess an increasing competitive advantage becomes a key to export expansion and to broadened benefits from international trade relations. Thus, as one observer has noted, "In the long run there is probably no single issue of greater importance to LDC interests than international safeguards."[66]

Despite such high salience for developing countries, their capabilities to deal with potentially adverse impacts in this area are limited. This is a result of their narrow export range, their high dependency on export earnings, and their lack of alternate sales outlets. Such a situation provides for less national leverage in working out acceptable safeguard mechanisms than is available to industrial countries with similar export interests. Industrial countries can more effectively deter others' trade restrictions, since their retaliatory measures can be more costly. Reflecting the limited coping mechanisms that developing countries can draw upon in the face of import relief measures imposed by industrial nations, less developed countries have pressed for Western adoption of the principle of "compensation for market disruption," since remedial power clearly remains in the hands of the industrial countries.[67]

For developing countries, a central concern in approaching safeguard policies revolves around the inclusion of adjustment assistance in any mechanism used by countries threatened by import competition. Such assistance is vital, since it provides the means by which the focus of trade policy will be converted from short-term protection from threatened injury to longer-term liberalized market access, permitting the importing country to facilitate a diversion of resources away from affected industries to lines of production that would not necessitate trade barriers. As Gerhard Fels has stated, adjustment assistance "involves a shift from the provision of security by actual or potential trade limitations to security by assisting restructuring."[68] Reflecting this perspective on safeguarding, UNCTAD resolutions have stressed the importance of industrial conversion within developed countries to promote adaption to changing economic conditions favorable to developing countries. Indeed, it has been suggested that economically advanced countries devote a certain proportion of their gross national product to finance such trade-liberalizing conversions.[69]

Western governments have recognized the strong attachment that less developed nations have given to favorable safeguarding and adjustment assistance policies as steps toward realizing economic development goals. For example, in acting upon a 1976 finding of import injury sustained by the U.S. footwear industry, the Ford Administration chose to implement adjustment assistance rather than import restrictions.[70] Provisions for such restructuring aids were bolstered within the Trade Act of 1974.[71] In addition, the U.S. Government has announced that it will seek to include in a safeguarding code negotiated at the Tokyo Round provisions that will "grant special treatment to developing countries that are minor suppliers or new entrants in a developed-country market during the period that safeguards are in effect."[72]

But such recognition of developing countries' perspectives on these issues does not fundamentally alter difficulties faced by importing countries in this area of trade relations. In addition, the domestic impact of import competition remains a central trade issue among industrial countries, since these nations dominate trade in manufactures. The key national security focus for import-receiving countries involves the extent to which flows of foreign supplies threaten the viability of local industries and the economic well-being of associated communities. National coping mechanisms have traditionally depended upon trade-restricting measures, despite any longer-term costs, such as distorted price levels and less efficient utilization of resources. Political mobilization related to these latter problems has been far more muted and diffused than is the case for claims for import relief.

In industrial societies, organized labor has been a highly visible and politically powerful force on this issue, since there has been a considerable erosion of jobs in many key industries affected by import competition. Trade unions have strongly urged the use of import restrictions to protect "sensitive" industries, focusing on such measures as a means to maintain employment levels. In addition, they have looked upon proposals for adjustment assistance with great mistrust, a position largely shaped by unmet expectations and severe inadequacies associated with past legislation.[73] From their standpoint, proposed restructuring efforts should be aimed at the modernization and rehabilitation of productive facilities, rather than at the reallocation of resources into new pursuits—a much more security-threatening path for local firms and workers.[74]

Given the strong domestic interests in safeguarding and adjustment assistance policies and the high salience that these measures have for economic welfare and security concerns, it is not surprising that there is serious reluctance by governments to have such key trade issues handled in a manner that reduces the "prerogatives" of national policy-makers.[75] But such a perspective can pose problems for policy harmonization in this area. For example, there is a need for substantial policy coordination among import-receiving countries, since differentials in access conditions and restructuring efforts can result in maldistributed import flows that can cause havoc among national systems and can provoke eventual joint losses. This problem is reflected in American complaints that significant amounts of Japanese imports to the United States include supplies diverted from obstructed European markets.[76]

A potentially viable framework for approaching international

215

safeguarding in a manner that maximizes collective economic security has emerged in analyses directed towards the Tokyo Round negotiations.[77] First, a safeguard system should specify the temporary nature of protective measures, setting a pre-established time-limit for the imposition of import-relief actions. Second, new restrictive measures should allow for reasonable import growth during the application period. Third, short-term relief action should be accompanied by substantial domestic adjustment assistance efforts to insure the temporary nature of safeguards and the longer-term momentum towards trade liberalization. Fourth, the implementation and handling of such measures should be subject to multilateral surveillance and mediation.[78]

Within such a framework, the tasks critical to the achievement of collective economic security can be fulfilled. The need for regulation would be satisfied in a multilateral safeguard code that would specify conditions for resorting to such mechanisms, governing behavior and responsibilities associated with such actions. Assessment functions so vital to insuring cooperation and to preventing further difficulties would be handled by a proposed international panel for mediation and surveillance. Finally, the provision of equity and of emergency relief would be fulfilled in allowing effective temporary "breathing space" for affected industries, while, at the same time, permitting a reasonable expansion of access during the safeguard's application and promoting efforts to realize eventual liberalized market access.

A key factor behind the effectiveness of any collective economic security approach to trade problems is the tension between short-term policy exigencies and longer-term policy objectives. Given the nature of domestic political mobilization, policy formulation focusing on future trends often gives way to actions designed to ameliorate immediate problems, even if longer-term consequences of such actions may be severe.

This dynamic can be seen in policy-making regarding safeguards and adjustment assistance, especially involving transactions between developed and developing countries. Short-term protection of inefficient industries in developed countries and generally blocked access to industrial markets for developing countries can result in devastating effects to producers in poor nations vulnerable to such adverse external actions. In the long run, such responses to domestic pressures for protection can pave the way for a collision course with significantly undesirable outcomes for developed countries. Christensen suggested, for example, that present attempts at collusion by raw material producers represent an extended outgrowth of the failure of developing countries participating in the GATT system to obtain adequate export earnings for sustaining economic development programs. In a similar sense, the growing prospect of large-scale bankruptcy among major developing countries and the financial strains that can follow in its wake for industrial nations result "because the creditors did not allow the debtors to pay off their debt, and not because the debtors were unwilling to pay."[79]

Reconciling the incompatibility of protectionist reactions to import competition with long-run aims of liberalized, stable international trade relations remains a difficult order for industrial nations. In the past, vibrant economic expansion tended to mitigate such conflicts, since domestic injuries from import competition were less prominent amidst impressive overall economic growth rates and trade gains. In such a "fair-weather" environment, favorable economic conditions also engendered more governmental willingness to negotiate accommodating arrangements in critical cases, e.g., "voluntary" export restraints in textiles. Furthermore, the prevailing GATT framework represented highly respected norms for governing trade behavior, acting to defuse and deflect domestic pressures for trade restrictions. Thus, the "whole"—overall trading relations—became a more decisive policy focus than particular impacts on local industries.

But, as the prosperity of the post-war recovery period and the gains from increased trade have leveled off, economic difficulties such as high unemployment have reappeared as more central concerns of foreign economic policy-making. Claims of import injuries become much more compelling vis-à-vis the maintenance of liberalized trading standards. Such shifting priorities have been expressed by labor and business leaders in many industrial sectors affected by significant trade flows. For example, in response to a large Japanese import presence in the American electronics market, one leading U.S. manufacturer has stated:

> We really believe in free trade because it's the right way of doing business. The thing we are fighting for here is the protection of our own employees. . . We've got to tell them (Japanese producers) that, on a temporary basis, you can only have a certain share of our market.[80]

As indicated, a major focus of current trade negotiations in this area involves forging a balance between short-term protection against import injuries and long-term maintenance of liberalized trade relations. Whereas the latter goal is oriented to increased economic growth and efficiency on an aggregate basis, creating expanded economic opportunities in many societies, these beneficial effects are often not transferable to those sectors facing heavy losses from import competition. Thus, the relative political force of liberalized trade objectives becomes weakened, if their pursuit does not compensate those domestic groups experiencing short-term deprivations in economic welfare. Any multilateral trade agreement in this area will need to be sensitive to the exigencies of this dynamic, if there is to be a restoration of confidence and legitimacy in such collaborative efforts.

Export Controls and Access to Supply

Another major set of issues at the Tokyo Round involves export controls and access to supplies. These matters burst into highly politicized prominence whereby ". . .the industrial world was gripped by something close to hysteria over developments in international commodity markets."[81] Since the traditional focus of GATT centered on liberalizing access to markets, and since concerns about supply denial and export restrictions were so sudden and unfamiliar, there was no mention of the need to deal with these problems in the Tokyo Declaration that inaugurated the current multilateral trade negotiations.[82]

The key events that propelled export control and supply access issues into heightened consideration were the July 1973 restrictions placed on U.S. sales of soybeans and other feeding stuffs and the selective Arab oil embargoes imposed during the 1973 Yom Kippur War. Beyond such shocks, increased alarm was raised by fears that OPEC successes would spark a rash of cartels in other raw materials; by unstable conditions in international commodity trade with export prices at unprecedented levels; by severe shortfalls in major cereal crops; and by spiraling inflation coupled with an evolving psychology of doom.[83] Such conditions have moderated, but left as a significant political residue has been the widespread recognition that export controls and access to supplies represent compelling issues in the conduct of international trade relations which require national and international policy accommodation. For despite conflicting evidence about long-term trends of global scarcities in vital resources, short-term difficulties associated with these issues affect basic economic welfare goals among interdependent societies, and they evoke very real security concerns to the extent that core societal values can become threatened.[84]

Governments have resorted to the use of export controls in recent times for several basic purposes. First, as Knorr illustrated in Chapter 4, such trade-distorting actions have been used as instruments of political leverage, seizing upon others' potential or real vulnerabilities to flows of resources in order to shape desired political outcomes. This type of trade lever was most clearly seen in the witholding of oil shipments by Arab producers. Second, export controls have also been applied as strategies to develop and implement cartel actions. OPEC activities have stood as a model to other raw material producers, who view collusive behavior among suppliers as an important step towards creating "a new international economic order."[85] Third, countries have used export controls to deal with domestic inflationary pressures, in effect transferring such pressures to foreign consumers by diverting intended foreign shipments back to the domestic market. Controls on exports of scrap steel and cereals implemented by many countries fit within this category.[86]

218

For consuming nations, export controls and access to supply issues raise the prospect of considerable threats to the core values of economic well-being, since disruptions in the flows of supplies can resonate throughout national economic life. Such effects evoke national security considerations even beyond the more traditional concerns about dependence on foreign supplies for resources deemed essential for economic sustenance and defense. Curtailment of access to key materials can significantly affect prevailing market forces within societies, exacting high costs and instabilities regarding levels of domestic production, employment, and inflation. In addition, resources may be diverted from normal economic activities into programs designed to cope with threats to supplies. For example, as a result of perceived vulnerability to adverse events in commodity trade, large Japanese expenditures were devoted to building up stockpiles in key industrial materials during 1974. These stocks were quickly liquidated via exports in succeeding periods as the commodity scare receded. Not only did such responses exacerbate inflation, monetary instability, and recession in Japan, but they also contributed to greater uncertainties and strains for other nations' policies regarding these materials.[87]

Instabilities and threats associated with export controls and supply access have also fueled a sense of generalized insecurity in foreign economic policy-making. Such a policy milieu can lead governments toward self-protecting measures which have disturbing effects in other trading realms. For example, in response to U.S. export restrictions and generally unstable conditions in commodity trade, France has evidenced increased resistence to American arguments for liberalizing EEC agricultural policies.[88] These various types of impacts regarding access to supply, taken both individually and aggregately, give rise to an identification of trade problems in this area as issues which evoke national security considerations.

From the perspective of export-controlling countries, national security concerns are also reflected in their actions. For commodity producers, controlling levels of available supplies represents an instrument to enhance, at least in the short-run, trade benefits deemed vital to domestic economic viability, since these raw materials comprise the basic national economic resource in many instances. For developing countries operating in an environment of longer-run worsening terms of trade vis-à-vis industrial imports, actions to upgrade export earnings—even if through collusive practices—represent efforts to compensate for past perceived deficiencies and inequities in the prevailing GATT system. In a more immediate sense, many developing countries' desires to emulate OPEC activities in relation to their own commodity trade stand as rather desperate responses to maintain their purchasing power in the midst of greatly increased external demands on national expenditures, not the least of which are oil-related. As noted, even for more economically advanced countries, resorting to export controls has become a means to ease domestic burdens of supply shortages and bottlenecks that can threaten key areas of national economic life, such as employment and price levels in affected industries.

Export controls and access to supply issues have emerged in an international economic order quite unprepared for this development. The most relevant GATT prescriptions for dealing with such matters are, in the words of a former U.S. trade official, "virtually worthless."[89] Article 11 does preclude quotas and other restrictions on exports as well as on imports, but it exempts "export prohibitions or restrictions temporarily applied to prevent critical shortages of foodstuffs or other products essential to the exporting contracting party." The range of export controls presently used remains outside the regulatory grasp of GATT, as such provisions were clearly intended to deal with specific post-war circumstances.[90]

Seeking guidelines and mechanisms by which nations can deal with threats of supply disruption is a major concern at the current multilateral trade negotiations. Indeed, providing mandates to negotiate suitable international regulatory instruments has been an important element of national approaches to cope with this problem. For example, the U.S. Trade Act of 1974 gave prominence to authorizations to negotiate a new set of rules concerning export controls and access to supplies. In addition, however, the U.S. trade bill empowered the executive to retaliate against nations which imposed "illegal or unreasonable" export restraints against the United States. Such retaliation would be in the form of witheld trade concessions that would otherwise allow freer access to U.S. markets.[91]

The problems of restricted supplies and national means to cope with such threats were also explored during the 1974 Congressional extension of the 1969 Export Administration Act. This legislation was amended to provide executive authority to invoke export controls in retaliation to foreign export restraints injurious to the United States, in effect reinforcing the provisions of the trade bill. But attempts at broadening the capacity to respond to future adverse foreign actions were resisted.

Reflected in this moderate position was the recognition that retaliatory measures could lead to further deterioration in this area of trade relations and to eventual injuries to U.S. export opportunities. For example, agricultural export interests were mobilized during Congressional deliberations on these matters, and their presence was an important factor behind the bill's recommendation that resolution of problems associated with access to supplies should be managed through international negotiations, relegating retaliatory measures to a more secondary role.[92] This posture portrays political sensitivity to an underlying dynamic shaping national policies on export controls: in the long-run, there is a significant relationship between the disposition of access to supply problems and the accommodation of access to market concerns.

Multilateral negotiations dealing with security of supply issues must, in effect, start from scratch, given the paucity of guidelines relevant to current practices. Indeed, one of the first tasks facing negotiators is sorting out various types of policies that can result in restricted access to supplies, e.g., differentiating short supply controls from restrictions that are based on other considerations. A major objective will be the pursuit of regulations to achieve non-discriminatory export sales and equitable access to foreign supplies. Thus, any workable code must entail provisions relating to conditions governing the justification, use, and duration of controls; to disciplinary measures to insure compliance; and to compensation for injured parties. Also important to the operation of such a code will be international mechanisms for monitoring national actions in this area and for providing consultations and mediation.[93]

In such a multilateral code, then, one can identify important elements of a framework that can lead towards the achievement of collective economic security in this area. As seen, regulatory and assessment functions are central to negotiations on these issues. In addition, emergency relief and equity provisions critical to realizing joint gains for both producers and consumers are needed. In this regard, there is the need for mechanisms through which short supplies would be fairly shared in order to minimize disruptions and injuries among participants, as well as for compensatory measures available to producers during periods of shortages, since many countries rely on such exports for vital national economic goals.

A basic problem affecting the negotiations on these issues—and as a consequence, the possibilities for achieving collective economic security in this area—involves deciding upon the appropriate scope of potential agreements to be reached. This concern entails decisions regarding not only the number and type of countries participating in such accords, but also the extent of linkages to other trading issues and goals. Strongly reflected in such uncertainties is the close connection between access to supply issues and more general problems associated with international commodity trade. In addition, future trends concerning possible scarcities of key natural resources remain unclear. Thus, there is a reluctance by many governments to engage in long-term international commitments, lest they find themselves bound unnecessarily to costly programs aimed at securing desired supply levels.

Deciding upon the scope of negotiations to secure stable access to supplies goes to the core of a highly contentious issue in trade relations between industrial and developing countries—the establishment of systematic international commodity agreements. It has been argued, for example, that gaining security of supplies requires policy measures that go beyond short-term rules for export controls and that the most effective focus should be directed towards enhancing domestic production and securing export markets for commodity trade which would upgrade and stabilize earnings for producers.[94] At the 1976 UNCTAD IV conference, developing countries proposed the adoption of an "integrated program for commodities," which would set up international stockpiles for key commodities financed through a common fund, as well as provide for expanded compensatory financing and processing opportunities for producers of raw materials.[95] Resistence by industrial nations to such comprehensive approaches for dealing with supply problems was evident in their response to this proposed program. Western governments prefer instead to approach commodity problems on a case-by-case basis and to minimize interferences with market forces as much as possible.[96]

Given the experience of the recent past, when in an atmosphere of rather overblown reactions to the events of 1972–74, many governments rushed to cope with new-found "commodity power" by pursuing costly bilateral and unilateral arrangements, it seems unlikely that large-scale commitments will be made by developed countries in negotiating multilateral agreements on supply problems at the Tokyo Round.[97] A more minimal posture will probably be assumed in attempts to regulate export control practices within a fairly narrow scope. For example, it has been suggested that negotiations should initially focus on steps that industrial nations can pursue among themselves "to restore order" in this area of trade relations.[98] Such an approach would call for policy coordination among OECD members, in effect, insulating Western governments from potential conditions that would make demands by developing countries more compelling.

A corollary aspect of this posture would likely be continued efforts to decouple the policy treatment of supply access issues from consideration of programs to establish systematic international commodity agreements. Western resolve to resist cross-issue linkages could be seen in the December 1976 CIEC deliberations. Despite presumptions that granting further resource transfers to developing countries at the Paris meeting might result in a moderation of OPEC price increases, Western governments remained steadfast in separating the consideration of these two policy areas.[99]

Continuing such an approach would significantly curtail the scope of collective economic security efforts in this area, reflecting Western attempts to minimize concessions to developing countries in overall commodity trade, while at the same time seeking to reduce economic threats arising out of access to supply problems. How well this can be carried out depends in large part on whether such a posture can satisfy Western governments' needs for adequate and stable commodity supplies. Recent studies indicate that the United States faces little vulnerability to serious injuries from foreign supply interruptions.[100] However, other Western societies, such as Japan, remain more open to very costly external supply impacts. Nonetheless, at this point, developing countries have not been able to forge a strong lever—either on their own or with the aid of OPEC nations—to force Western governments to grant the types of concessions that developing countries see as vital to their own economic security goals.

Summary

As Klaus Knorr has indicated, national security concerns arise when basic societal values are perceived to be threatened by adverse foreign economic actions and events. In a world of heightened interdependence, such threat perceptions can occur with added frequency and intensity, given the level of interpenetration and mutual sensitivity experienced among national economies. In this context, international trade relations can evoke strong security concerns, particularly since the prevailing GATT order has evidenced significant shortcomings in dealing with contemporary trading conditions.

In examining the relationship between international trade and security concerns, some important considerations emerge which bear upon the future handling of trade issues and upon the possibilities for satisfying security interests in this field. An important element involves the extent to which governmental responses to trade problems are primarily national or multilateral in their scope. Adverse domestic impacts of international trade can create forceful political pressures for governmental remedies. How these problems are approached by governments can significantly affect overall trade patterns. If remedial measures remain predominately unilateral, they can often evoke similar or retaliatory responses by other governments and eventual situations of joint loss. Thus, over time there are important limits to national capabilities for sustained management of trade-related problems—despite their short-term effectiveness.

Since World War II, this basic fact has been widely recognized, as international institutions and mechanisms have been formulated to overcome such national limitations. Indeed, the very existence of such cooperative structures operating in international trade relations has acted in the past to restrain national actions that would lead to disruptions and hardships for others.[101] But in a trading environment in which key domestic groups experience significant deprivations in economic welfare and in which GATT remedies stand as inadequate or repudiated, the balance between dealing with short-term exigencies and maintaining longer-term objectives regarding a liberalization of international trade can be heavily skewed in the direction of reshaping trade flows in a manner that is perceived to avoid threats to basic domestic goals—this despite repercussions that might result in deteriorated overall trade relations.

As noted, with unresolved issues and newly formed problems producing an evolving crisis in international trade relations, a basic objective for holding the present Tokyo Round has been the restoration of an acceptable multilateral trading framework. Towards that end, the notion of collective economic security represents a potentially viable standard for approaching the conduct of international trade. It is predicated upon the recognition that there are shared fates and mutual capabilities regarding the achievement of basic societal values and that these conditions require multilateral policy accommodation directed towards outcomes of joint gain. As indicated, the performance of key tasks relating to regulation, assessment, equity, and emergency relief are needed within such mechanisms to cope with trade difficulties.

Fundamental to the effectiveness of any collective economic security approach is how well its measures can satisfy domestic claims and demands made upon governments participating within its intended scope. As seen in the cases of international safeguarding and adjustment assistance and of export controls and access to supplies, realizing this requirement in a manner sufficient to achieve necessary agreements can be very difficult, given the heterogeneity of interests, levels of development and competitiveness, and domestic political complexions among major trading nations.

The major difficulties in achieving collective economic security outcomes can be broadly categorized into three basic areas: (1) national unwillingness to submit short-term interests and direction to long-term international formulations and concerns; (2) conflicting perceptions of priorities among potential members; and (3) institutional problems of administering tasks necessary for such collaborative efforts. Thus, serious obstacles must be confronted to negotiate collective economic security arrangements in trade relations.

In such a context, it has been suggested that the scope of international negotiations needs to be broadened. To accommodate trading nations with highly varied interests and problems, it is thought that negotiations should focus on intersectoral trade-offs reached through collective bargaining.[102] For example, in international trade relations, problems relating to supply access eventually become inexorably tied to concerns over access to markets. But to expand the scope of international negotiations in such a way would also require a heightened political will in order to forge needed compromises and to strengthen multilateral approaches to trade problems. As seen, "interdependence costs" and other liabilities associated with such pursuits may indeed be high—particularly as the gains from such involvements may be undramatic, unevenly distributed, or slowly achieved.

In recent times, governments have begun to concentrate efforts towards protecting short-range national interests and independence, especially as the benefits from liberalized international trade and economic interdependence become less obvious or more diffused. In many cases, a basic thrust of foreign economic policy has been to insulate the local economy from international economic impacts using government controls of

224

various sorts. Indeed, as Gregory Schmid has noted, for the first time in the post-war era, nations have been placing more new restrictions on international economic relations than they are removing or modifying.[103] Economic nationalism, once the *bête noire* of international economic relations, has become a much less offensive perspective to contemporary national policy-makers. This is particularly true when maintaining uncontrolled exposure to international transactions results in serious deprivations to important domestic interests and in risks of national economic disruptions. In the face of such conditions, the policy demands of strengthening the management of interdependence have a very narrow range of domestic support. Perhaps this will mean the most viable focus for collective economic security efforts will be limited to multilateral codes and supervision regarding the application of national trade controls.[104] If this is the case, its achievement will remain arduous but nonetheless significant.

Footnotes

1. For further discussion along these lines, see Eric Wyndham-White, "Negotiations in Prospect," in *Toward a New World Trade Policy: The Maidenhead Papers*, ed. C. Fred Bergsten (Lexington, Mass.: D. C. Heath and Company, 1975), p. 323.

2. For reference to American sentiment regarding the need to orient trade policies more toward domestic economic considerations and less toward foreign political relations, see *United States International Economic Policy in an Interdependent World*, Report to the President submitted by the Commission on International Trade and Investment Policy, Vol. 1 (Washington, D.C.: General Printing Office, 1971), p. 2. See also C. Fred Bergsten, Robert O. Keohane, and Joseph S. Nye, "International Economics and International Politics: A Framework for Analysis," *International Organization*, 29 (Winter 1975):20, for similar sentiment reflected in former Secretary of Treasury Schultz's comment that "Santa Claus was dead."

3. For further discussion, see Wilbur F. Monroe, *International Trade Policy in Transition* (Lexington, Mass.: D. C. Heath and Company, 1975), p. 17, and Leland B. Yeager and David G. Tuerck, *Foreign Trade and U.S. Policy* (New York: Praeger Publishers, 1976), p. 148–57.

4. See Chapters 4 and 11 in this book; also see Monroe, *International Trade Policy in Transition*, p. 37ff for discussion of East-West trade in this context. See Bergsten, Keohane, and Nye, "International Economics," p. 8–9 for further comments regarding the changing environment for the use of force and its meaning for trade measures.

5. Lawrence B. Krause and Joseph S. Nye, "Reflections on the Economics and Politics of International Economic Organization," *International Organization*, 29 (Winter 1975):330.

6. For further discussion of such linkages, see Joseph S. Nye and Robert O. Keohane, "World Politics and the International Economic System," in *The Future of the International Economic Order: An Agenda for Research*, ed. C. Fred Bergsten (Lexington, Mass.: D. C. Heath and Company, 1973), pp. 131–32.

7. A clear example of this phenomenon can be seen in France's "Plan Barre," an attempt to curb French inflation, economic stagnation, and unemployment by relying upon the stimulus of a strong German growth rate. For further discussion of this Plan and the difficulties that France would experience upon a reduced German growth rate, see Lawrence A. Veit, "Troubled World Economy," *Foreign Affairs*, 55 (January 1977):270.

8. Stanley Hoffmann, "Groping Toward A New World Order," *New York Times*, 11 Janu-

ary 1976, Section 4, p. 1. See also Per Magnus Wijkman, "GATT and the New Economic Order," *Intereconomics, 8* (1975):243–44, for further reference to a decentralization of power regarding international economic relations.

9. See Bergsten, Keohane, and Nye, "International Economics," p. 11.
10. Krause and Nye, "Reflections," p. 331.
11. See Joseph S. Nye, "Collective Economic Security," *International Affairs* (Fall 1974): 584–85.
12. This OECD agreement was made on May 30, 1974 and renewed in 1975, 1976, and 1977. For reference to its importance, see "Cohesion of Industrial Democracies: Precondition for Global Progress," Speech by Secretary Henry A. Kissinger before the Organization for Economic Cooperation and Development, June 21, 1976, *Speech, The Secretary of State,* Office of Media Services, Bureau of Public Affairs, U.S. Department of State, p. 3. See *New York Times,* 18 December 1975, p. 71, for report on the impact of such an OECD agreement on British formulation of economic policies at this time.
13. Nye, "Collective Economic Security," p. 587.
14. See ibid., p. 590 and Krause and Nye, "Reflections," p. 332.
15. The following discussion draws upon Nye, "Collective Economic Security," pp. 592– 94.
16. See Wyndham-White, "Negotiations in Prospect," pp. 339–40 for proposals in this area of international economic relations.
17. For comments on emergency oil-sharing and financing programs, see Kissinger, "Cohesion of Industrial Democracies," pp. 4–5. See also *New York Times,* 17 May 1976, p. 14, for reference to difficulties faced by commodity producers from the developing world stemming from lost purchasing power by export earnings.
18. John G. Ruggie, "Collective Goods and Future International Collaboration," *American Political Science Review,* 66 (September 1972):881.
19. Ibid.
20. See Bayless Manning, "The Congress, The Executive and Intermestic Affairs: Three Proposals," *Foreign Affairs, 55* (January 1977):309, for discussion of how economic interdependence involved differential "intermestic" reactions and impacts. See also Gregory Schmid, "Interdependence Has Its Limits," *Foreign Policy, 21* (Winter 1975–76):190.
21. See Veit, "Troubled World Economy," p. 221.
22. See Ruggie, "Collective Goods," p. 881.
23. See ibid., p. 889. See Stephen N. Brown, David Price, and Satish Raichur, "Public-Good Theory and Bargaining Between Large and Small Countries," *International Studies Quarterly, 20* (September 1976), for discussion arguing that the "production" of international public goods may be best maximized by enlarging and mixing the scope of participation and policy areas.
24. See Veit, "Troubled World Economy," p. 278. For discussion of the importance of such a "wisemen" procedure in coordinating Western agreement on granting trade preferences to developing countries, see Ronald I. Meltzer, "The Politics of Policy Reversal: The American Response to Granting Trade Preferences to Developing Countries and Linkages Between International Organization and National Policy-Making," *International Organization, 30* (Autumn 1976).
25. Charles Kindleberger, "US Foreign Economic Policy, 1776–1976," *Foreign Affairs, 55* (January 1977):415.
26. See Robert Gilpin, "Economic Interdependence in Historical Perspective," Chapter 2 of this volume p. 59.
27. See Kindleberger, "US Foreign Economic Policy, 1776–1976," pp. 415ff and C. Fred Bergsten, Georges Berthoin, and Kinhide Mushakoji, *The Reform of International Institutions* (New York: The Trilateral Commission, 1976), pp. 10–14, 26–28, for further

comments regarding present difficulties and options for such a leadership role. See also Schmid, "Interdependence Has Its Limits," pp. 191–92, for discussion of special circumstances of the post-war era.

28. See *Policy Perspectives for International Trade and Economic Relations*, Report by the High Level Group on Trade and Related Problems to the Secretary-General of OECD (Paris: Organization for Economic Cooperation and Development, 1972), pp. 16–17.

29. See ibid., pp. 17–18, and Schmid, "Interdependence Has Its Limits," p. 189.

30. See *Policy Perspectives*, p. 20. Within the West, as well, structural changes have witnessed increased competitiveness of European and Japanese producers vis-à-vis those in the United States. See Monroe, *International Trade Policy in Transition*, p. 131.

31. See Klaus Knorr's Chapter 1 of this volume for further discussion on these points. See also C. Fred Bergsten's discussion of interdependence and national autonomy in his "Interdependence and the Reform of International Institutions," *International Organization*, 30 (Spring 1976):363.

32. See Richard N. Cooper, "Trade Policy is Foreign Policy," *Foreign Policy*, 9 (Winter 1972–73), for further comments relating to this phenomenon. The "tracking" of trade policies separate from more politicized realms was also very much a product of an earlier cold war period.

33. The Tokyo Declaration of 1973, which issued the call for a new set of multilateral trade negotiations under GATT, specifically made reference to the need to find better ways to handle trade relations between East and West. See also *Policy Perspectives*, pp. 97–100, for further discussion of trade relations with planned economy countries.

34. See Hugh Corbet, "Commercial Diplomacy in an Era of Confrontation," in *In Search of A New World Economic Order*, ed. Hugh Corbet and Robert Jackson (New York: Halsted Press, 1974), p. 19.

35. See *Policy Perspectives*, p. 23.

36. For discussion on the importance of links between trade and monetary policy-making and problem-solving, see ibid., p. 32; Gerard Curzon, "Crisis in the International Trading System," in Corbet and Jackson, *New World Economic Order*, pp. 33–34; Charles L. Schultze, "The Economic Content of National Security Policy," *Foreign Affairs* (April 1973):537; and C. Fred Bergsten, "Future Directions for U.S. Trade Policy," in Bergsten, *Toward A New World Trade Policy*, p. 343. See also Janet Kelly's chapter in this volume.

37. See *Policy Perspectives*, pp. 34–35 and D. Gale Johnson, "The Impact of Farm-support Policies on International Trade," in Corbet and Jackson, *New World Economic Order*.

38. For an excellent general work in the area of non-tariff restrictions, see Robert E. Baldwin, *Nontariff Distortions of International Trade* (Washington, D.C.: The Brookings Institution, 1970). For discussion on how fluctuating exchange rates have increased the importance of non-tariff barriers in world trade, see Bahram Nowzad, "Fluctuating Exchange Rates and World Trade," *Finance and Development*, 13 (December 1976).

39. See *Policy Perspectives*, p. 36.

40. See Monroe, *International Trade Policy in Transition*, p. 79–80.

41. For further discussion on regulatory efforts in this respect, see Robert O. Keohane and Van Doorn Ooms, "The Multinational Firm and International Regulation," *International Organization*, 29 (Winter 1975), and Paul A. Tharp, Jr., "Transnational Enterprises and International Regulation: A Survey of Various Approaches in International Organizations," *International Organization*, 30 (Winter 1976).

42. For a brief discussion of the bill's provisions, see Monroe, *International Trade Policy in Transition*, p. 99.

43. Difficulties in this area of trade relations will be discussed in a later section of this chapter.

44. For further discussion of these measures, see C. Fred Bergsten, "Crisis in US Trade Policy," *Foreign Affairs* (April 1971) and Monroe, *International Trade Policy in Transition*, pp. 98–99.

45. This excerpt from the text of the Tokyo Declaration is quoted in Monroe, *International Trade Policy in Transition*, p. 102.

46. C. Fred Bergsten, "Let's Avoid a Trade War," *Foreign Policy, 23* (Summer 1976):24.

47. See ibid., pp. 27–31, for further development of these points. For a discussion of major Third World objectives regarding the Tokyo Round negotiations, see Peter Hermes, "Preparations for the Nixon Round," *Intereconomics, 6* (1973):174.

48. See Peter Peterson, "New Dimensions for Trade Talks," *New York Times*, 9 September 1973, Section 3, p. 1.

49. Wijkman, "GATT and the New Economic Order," p. 243.

50. Monroe, *International Trade Policy in Transition*, p. 7.

51. See ibid., p. 80.

52. See Jan Tumlir, "Emergency Protection Against Sharp Increases in Imports," in Corbet and Jackson, *New World Economic Order*, p. 264.

53. See Frank Wolter, "A Sound Case for Relocation," *Intereconomics, 12* (1975):366.

54. See Gerhard Fels, "Adjustment Assistance to Import Competition," in Corbet and Jackson, *New World Economic Order*, pp. 245–50 for further discussion of this goal and of the reasons behind the increasing competitiveness of manufactured exports from the developing world.

55. For further discussion of this declaration, which was produced as a result of the Second General Conference of the United Nations Industrial Development Organization (UN-IDO) held in Lima, Peru during March 1975, see Branislav Gosovic and John G. Ruggie, "On the Creation of a New International Economic Order," *International Organization, 30* (Spring 1976):315.

56. See Wolter, "A Sound Case for Relocation," pp. 366–67.

57. The actual implementation of "escape clauses" for import relief has been relatively rare within the United States. From World War II to the Trade Act of 1974, there have been 169 petitions for relief under "escape clause" provisions, and only 21 decisions were made to grant such relief during this period. See William B. Eberle, "U.S. Trade Policy—Appearance and Reality," *New York Times*, 7 December 1975, Section 3, p. 14.

58. See Guido Colonna di Paliano, Philip H. Trezise, and Nobhiko Ushiba, *Directions for World Trade in the Nineteen-Seventies* (New York: The Trilateral Commission, 1974), p. 24.

59. Tumlir, "Emergency Protection," p. 265.

60. Ibid., p. 262.

61. See S. J. Anjaria, "Nontariff Issues in the MTN," *Finance and Development, 13* (June 1976):22.

62. Eberle, "U.S. Trade Policy," p. 14.

63. For discussion of the Trade Act's provisions in this respect, see Karel Holbik, "The U.S. Trade Reform Act of 1974," *Intereconomics, 4* (1975):123 and Monroe, *International Trade Policy in Transition*, p. 106–7.

64. These imports included shoes, bolts, nuts, and screws, and specialty steel. For discussion of the specialty steel case and the EEC reaction to a finding of injury regarding this item, see *New York Times*, 18 March 1976, p. 59 and 6 April 1976, p. 49. See also Edwin L. Dale, "How the New Trade Law May Backfire," *New York Times*, 26 October 1975, Section 3, p. 2, for more general comments regarding these claims and foreign responses.

65. See *New York Times*, 1 May 1976, p. 29, for a report on the modest use of the Trade Act provisions by the Ford Administration.

66. Monroe, *International Trade Policy in Transition*, p. 70.
67. See "Supplement: UNCTAD IV," *Development Forum*, IV (April 1976):1.
68. Fels, "Adjustment Assistance to Import Competition," p. 251.
69. See Nobuyoshi Namiki, "Internal Adjustment Problems of Japan," in Corbet and Jackson, *New World Economic Order*, p. 102.
70. See "Hemispheric Cooperation for Development," Speech by Secretary Henry A. Kissinger before the Sixth Regular General Assembly of the Organization of American States, July 9, 1976, *Speech, The Secretary of State*, Office of Media Services, Bureau of Public Affairs, U.S. Department of State, p. 4.
71. See Monroe, *International Trade Policy in Transition*, pp. 106–7, for such provisions.
72. See Kissinger, "Hemispheric Cooperation for Development," p. 4. See *New York Times*, 21 July 1976, p. 43, for report of complaints by developing countries regarding U.S. proposals in the safeguarding negotiations.
73. See Guy F. Erb and Charles R. Frank, Jr., "U.S. Trade Reform and the Third World," *Challenge*, 17 (May/June 1974):62–63, for figures indicating that the overall net impact of imports on employment has been slight. However, aggregate statistics often conceal very real difficulties for particular industries, e.g., textiles, steel, automobiles.
74. See Monroe, *International Trade Policy in Transition*, p. 70.
75. See Anjaria, "Nontariff Issues in the MTN," p. 24.
76. See Fels, "Adjustment Assistance to Import Competition," pp. 256–57.
77. For discussion of various positions and proposals regarding safeguarding and adjustment measures at the current multilateral trade negotiations, see Anjaria, "Nontariff Issues in the MTN," pp. 22–24.
78. The elements of this basic framework were discussed and suggested in different writings covering this area of trade relations and throughout emerged rather uniform expression of the need to include such provisions in any operative system negotiated at the Tokyo Round. See Tumlir, "Emergency Protection," p. 269; *Policy Perspectives*, p. 84; and Colonna, Trezise, and Ushiba, *Directions for World Trade*, pp. 25–26.
79. See Wijkman, "GATT and the New Economic Order," p. 245.
80. This quote is from Amory Houghton, Jr., Chairman of Corning Glass; See *New York Times*, 4 January 1977, p. 15.
81. Edward R. Fried, "International Trade in Raw Materials: Myths and Realities," *Science*, 191 (20 February 1976):641.
82. See Hajo Hasenpflug and Deitrich Kebschull, "Obstacles to Transatlantic Trade," *Intereconomics, 5* (1976):134.
83. See Fried, "International Trade in Raw Materials," p. 641.
84. See Monroe, *International Trade Policy in Transition*, pp. 74–75, 117–19, and 139–40, for discussion of various viewpoints regarding long-term trends for natural resources.
85. For a discussion that stresses the threat of proliferating cartels, see C. Fred Bergsten, "The New Era in World Commodity Markets," *Challenge*, 17 (September/October 1974).
86. See Colonna, Trezise, and Ushiba, *Directions for World Trade*, p. 22 and Monroe, *International Trade Policy in Transition*, pp. 75–76 for further discussion of these three types of motivations for export controls.
87. See Fried, "International Trade in Raw Materials," p. 642.
88. Hubertus Adebahr, "The New US Foreign Trade Concept," *Intereconomics, 10* (1973):305.
89. For a report on this characterization by William B. Eberle, see *New York Times*, 23 July 1974, p. 57.
90. Colonna, Trezise, and Ushiba, *Directions for World Trade*, p. 22.

91. See Monroe, *International Trade in Transition*, p. 110. Sweeping retaliatory powers, which would give the President authority to cut off assistance, suspend credits, and curtail U.S. foreign investments, were not included in the final provisions of the bill.
92. See Guy F. Erb, "Controlling Export Controls," *Foreign Policy*, *17* (Winter 1974– 75):81–82 and Monroe, *International Trade Policy in Transition*, p. 111.
93. Erb, "Controlling Export Controls," p. 83.
94. See Monroe, *International Trade Policy in Transition*, pp. 117–18.
95. See "Supplement: UNCTAD IV," p. 1.
96. For a discussion of Western reactions, see *New York Times*, 17 May 1976, p. 14 and 30 June 1976, pp. 49, 62. For reference to Secretary Kissinger's proposals in this area, which included plans for an international resources bank, see *New York Times*, 12 May 1976, pp. 57, 61. For discussion of the UNCTAD IV resolutions and outcomes on these matters, see *New York Times*, 31 May 1976, pp. 1, 3.
97. For thoughts along these lines, see Fried, "International Trade in Raw Materials," pp. 643–46, and Monroe, *International Trade Policy in Transition*, pp. 118–19.
98. See Colonna, Trezise, and Ushiba, *Directions for World Trade*, p. 23.
99. See *New York Times*, 14 December 1976, pp. 55, 59.
100. See *New York Times*, 30 December 1976, p. 31. Also, Clark Murdock's review of American trade vulnerabilities in Chapter 3.
101. Bergsten, "Interdependence and the Reform of International Institutions," pp. 361–62.
102. See Gosovic and Ruggie, "New International Economic Order," p. 314.
103. See Schmid, "Interdependence Has Its Limits," pp. 193–95.
104. See letter by Adam Yarmolinsky in *Foreign Policy*, *22* (Summer 1976):221, for discussion on the need for "international bargains" involving government controls, and a response by Gregory Schmid, pp. 222–23.

230

CHAPTER 9

International Monetary Systems and National Security

Janet Kelly

Introduction

It has been observed, most often by the impecunious, that money is power. Although oversimplified, this observation applies as much to the affairs of nations as it does to the affairs of men. The authors of this book have stressed that international economic links create both state capabilities and state vulnerabilities. Here we shall see that ties established in the international monetary system also imply international power relationships— some states gain security from the monetary system while others lose.

Two basic statements can be made at the outset about the connection between international money and international power and security. First, the kind of system in operation affects the distribution of power, wealth, and hence security among states. Secondly, the distribution of power and wealth also affects the kind of monetary system in use. Thus, changes in an overall power distribution will tend to cause changes in relative monetary power or perhaps even changes in the design of the international monetary system itself. These simple statements belie the difficulties of predicting the exact nature of any particular monetary system or any particular power hierarchy; other factors ranging from ideology to earthquakes will also enter into the equation. And as both Knorr and Krasner have emphasized, wealth does not automatically translate to power or security. Over the longer run, however, there does tend to be a congruence between monetary power and power in general. The evolution of the post-war international monetary system illustrates this axiom.

The events of the past decade provide an ample number of cases in which money and state power interacted. In that period the international monetary system underwent several fundamental changes. To the extent that money and national security are related, it can be assumed that these fundamental changes reflected alterations in the international balance of power. In the first period, from the Second World War until 1968, the *Bretton Woods* system governed the world monetary system, that is to say, both gold and the dollar served as international currency. In 1968, gold was

231

virtually abolished from the Bretton Woods system, and the dollar was the unofficial international money—the Bretton Woods system was now really a pure *key currency* system. In 1970, the members of the International Monetary Fund acted to superimpose on the old system an *artificial currency*, the SDR (Special Drawing Right), which would also serve as a money to be used among states. Finally, in the period 1971 to 1973, the Bretton Woods system (as it was still called) was gradually abandoned in favor of a system of *floating* currencies, a system almost without rules.

These changes make the recent past a laboratory for the study of monetary systems and their relationship to international politics. Scholars and politicians alike saw that the monetary changes accompanied real changes in the international structure of power, but the actual content of the relationships was often misunderstood. Some suggested that since the old system of Bretton Woods had crumbled away, the world should devise a new monetary plan which would allocate costs and benefits equally to all nations. What these reformers failed to consider was that:

——no system will be able to spread costs evenly

——the most powerful countries *prefer* costs to be spread unevenly

——the most powerful countries (or country) hold as least a veto over the shape of the monetary system.

Thus, while Bretton Woods had reflected the distribution of power and created an asymmetrical distribution of benefits, it was unlikely that another system would differ significantly in this respect.

Others saw in recent monetary turbulence large alterations in the world balance of power—the relative decline of American power would inevitably bring monetary chaos as the system adjusted to the power shift and as the U.S. dollar also fell from its position of dominance. They were correct in associating the deterioration of the Bretton Woods system, dominated as it was by the United States, with a change in world power relationships, but they were too quick to write off either the dollar or American dominance in the monetary system.[1]

Changes in the nature of the international monetary system reveal important facets of the international struggle for power and security. The particular system in operation determines which countries and which groups within countries get special advantages. A country with gold mines will consider the gold standard to be an admirable system. In a sense, that country owns a "printing press" for the world currency. On the other hand, countries without resources might prefer an artificial currency system in which all countries are dealt a certain number of "poker chips" without paying anything at the start. Once a particular system is operating, countries and interest groups will also try to maneuver at the process level to win maximum benefits for themselves. One country might try to devalue its own currency in order to increase its exports. Since important things are at stake, let us examine how competition among states operates in the international monetary arena.

Monetary Systems in Theory

Money International

What is an international money? A common definition of money says that it is anything people think it is—anything commonly accepted in payment, be it shells for Indians, cigarettes for prisoners of war, or francs for the French.[2] Similarly, international money is anything commonly accepted among states in exchange for their goods and services. There need not be a formal agreement among states as to what is money, but there will usually be an informal one. Where no money of any kind exists, only barter can bring about an exchange of goods. Gold and silver have been the most durable international monies, but in the nineteenth century, gold gradually came to be accepted as the ultimate international money (even though in practical terms, gold itself was not exchanged). No formal system or set of rules had to be drawn up, because it was generally accepted by all states that gold was the final value against which all else could be measured.

Once there is an international money, it follows that each national currency will have a value in terms of it. For many years, $35 equalled one ounce of gold. Internationally, once a trader knew the cost of an object in terms of the national currency, he could easily calculate its cost in terms of the international currency and then in terms of every other currency. Trading from country to country would be simple if these rates of exchange never moved. But more often the rates move around considerably. Since there are markets for national currencies, their values are affected by government intervention and by supply and demand for the currency generally. These supply and demand factors are affected, in turn, by the world demand and supply for that country's goods and services. If, for instance, the Germans managed to keep the prices of their goods low and made popular products, the demand for German marks would be relatively high. This pressure might force up the exchange rate for marks unless the government intervened and offered marks in the free market in order to meet the traders' demand.

A system may be one of fixed rates or of floating. With fixed rates, governments intervene whenever it is necessary to keep their exchange rates constant in relation to the international money. Under floating rates, values are allowed to fluctuate with market forces and no specific international money is (theoretically) needed. The system may be anywhere between absolutely fixed and freely floating; governments may intervene a little bit or a lot. Floating originally implied that governments would not intervene at all, but in practice most have at one time or another. To distinguish between these two approaches, a float without government intervention is a *clean* float and one with government intervention is a *dirty* float.

A monetary system may be a universal one or a bloc system. The universal system is one in which all states agree to the same rules, while in a bloc system, separate systems coexist, with each governed by different rules. It is a matter of great importance to a country what kind of rules it must follow in its international monetary relations and what kind of exchange rate it maintains. For some countries fixed rates impose a high burden. This is true whenever a country's prices tend to rise at a different rate than the prices in the rest of the world. Fast-rising prices under a system of fixed rates will produce falling exports and, perhaps, unemployment. On the other hand, floating rates could be a hazard for countries heavily dependent on trade with others, if floating meant frequent large swings in exchange values. Some economists have speculated on a perfect system and what countries should be within the same bloc to produce the most gains and least problems. This is what they call the "optimal currency area."[3] But monetary blocs are created from tradition, geography, and politics, not from economists' pens.

Since the nineteenth century, countries have shown a tendency to accept the national currency of one country as international money. The British pound was widely considered "as good as gold" for most of the nineteenth century, and the dollar came to be used increasingly in the twentieth. The two actually coexisted as international currencies in the years between the wars. Those were years of instability, when the world acknowledged no clear leader in either the economic or political spheres. When national currencies are used as international money in this way, they are called *key currencies*.[4] Both sterling and later the dollar assumed their predominant positions in spite of the general principle that gold remained the ultimate international money. A key currency becomes, in effect, international money because states accept it in payment, and because it is considered a store of value and a standard unit by which other currencies are valued, now and for the future. A state accumulates reserves in the key currency by running a balance of payments surplus, that is, by selling more abroad than it buys. The key currency country is expected, in turn, to maintain the value of its currency. Like the man with money in the bank, a state with large reserves is considered a rich state. Saudi Arabia may look like a desert, but its international reserves convince us that the Saudis are indeed rich. The case of the Saudis should also remind us that monetary power derives from other advantages: Saudi Arabia needed both oil and the

234

power to keep its oil profits in order to achieve its powerful monetary position.

A currency comes to be "key" because people in countries see it as being as valuable (or more valuable) as the underlying reserve, say, gold. When does a key currency develop? Several conditions must exist. First, the particular national currency must be valued as a worthwhile asset, valuable in terms of real purchasing power and valuable as an investment. Dollars produce interest for their holders, while the holder of gold must actually pay in order to store bullion. Second, the key currency must represent a claim on the widest range of goods. It will tend to be the currency of that state which produces the greatest variety and volume of goods. Thus, if all states were equal in size and wealth, there would probably be no key currency. Third, the key currency must be available: the key currency state will have to run a balance of payments deficit about as large as the demand for holding the key currency abroad. This third condition imposes a certain burden on the key currency country if it resists running such a deficit. Other countries may have important currencies—the Swiss franc, the Japanese yen, the German mark—but these are simply valuable to hold. That is mainly because these countries refuse to run balance of payments deficits. Only the dollar currently fulfills (more or less) these three conditions for key currency status.

Sterling was the key currency of the nineteenth century. Rather than ask for gold in payment for goods, countries began to accept pounds instead, and they kept these pounds in London banks, using them like bank accounts to pay other countries they traded with. It was assumed that gold could ultimately be bought for pounds. Sterling declined as a key currency, because England lost its premier position as a supplier of goods. In Chapter 2, Gilpin argues that the spread of industrialization made England's relative decline inevitable. She also began to run such large deficits in her balance of payments that the supply of pounds abroad became greater than the desires of individuals and states to hold them. Confidence in sterling eroded as England began to restrict its use, and holders tried to sell it for other assets. It was finally devalued in 1931, an event which confirmed the loss of faith in sterling which had developed with Britain's faltering world position.[5] During the 1960s, the United States made a mistake similar to Britain's: she ran a deficit too large to maintain the dollar's value. It was America's inability or unwillingness to cure this deficit which produced the transformations of the monetary system of the late 1960s and now of the 1970s. But Britain's decline accompanied a visible loss of place in the world power league and even then, the pound continued as an international currency for perhaps fifty years beyond the point where Britain fell behind the United States and Germany. It is yet to be seen whether the dollar will follow the pound into relative obscurity, particularly since the United States dollar still fulfills the conditions necessary for a key currency. Before these issues are discussed, however, it would be well to establish what is at stake in international monetary questions: security and power for states.

International Money and National Security

National security is more than a well-trained army and nuclear submarines. A nation is secure in the widest meaning of the term when it feels no threat to its own values. To be secure from threats generated from the outside, a country needs assurance of its physical integrity, but it also needs to be able to carry out its internal goals in the economic and social spheres. A nation needs to be wealthy enough to defend itself and its borders, and it needs to be independent enough to pursue its internal goals. The international monetary regime to which a state belongs affects its ability to be secure in this sense.

The ownership of international money reserves means a state has *buying power*, power which may be important in time of war. That power may make possible claims on goods, and it can go further as a claim on loyalty, on arms, or on support in a crisis. An important product of the Arabs' accumulation of "petrodollars" is their new-found military prowess, a prowess which comes from buying new weapons virtually "off the shelf" and then buying foreign trainers to teach their own armies how to fire them. (It could be argued that everyone, including the Arabs, would be more secure if they did *not* have these weapons, but that is a problem with weapons in general.)

More subtly, international money can give a state *influence* over others, without any actual purchases being made. Lending international reserves to other countries creates a dependency bond which allows the lender to make demands. Equally, the threat of withdrawing credits or investments may also give a country influence opportunities. Such methods must be employed with some discretion and tend not to be publicized. But there was little doubt in 1976 that credits from the United States and the European Community to Italy were contingent on the Italians keeping the Communist Party out of the cabinet.[6]

The other side of the influence coin is a country's *independence* of action. Security can involve the extent to which a comfortable monetary position can protect one state from the influence of others. A debtor nation like Britain today undoubtedly looks with yearning to the days of a century ago when she was mistress of the seas and international creditor without peer. If there were threats to her security, they came from within. By 1956, a hobbled Britain had to withdraw from a military invasion of Suez in large part because of selling pressure against her currency and the refusal of the United States to help defend the pound under the circumstances.[7]

In these three areas of buying power, influence, and independence, it will be noted that the key currency country holds a peculiar advantage. Its currency is itself a reserve currency, freely available for use in international dealings. Other countries must run a balance of payments surplus or borrow in order to hold reserves, while for the key currency country no such exchange is necessary. It may hold reserves such as gold, but it is generally assumed that others will not ask for reserves. As long as a country does not spend too lavishly abroad (which would create an oversupply of the key currency in relation to foreigners' desire to hold that currency), the key currency country can buy more, influence more, and be more independent, on the whole, than its trading partners. The situation of the key currency country supports Rousseau's claim that "money is the seed of money."

National security goes beyond physical security: internal security requires certain levels of welfare and stability to retain support for the state as constituted. Here, the connection with international monetary strength is less clear, but there is a connection. Various schools of economic thought have been sensitive to the link between a nation's place in the international monetary system and its wealth and stability. The two most important schools are the mercantilists and the liberals (the nineteenth-century advocates of laissez-faire). Both concerned themselves with increasing wealth and social harmony, but they had different ideas about how to meet those ends.

The mercantilists, who were important until around 1800, believed that the accumulation of international monetary resources, at that time gold and other precious substances, would accrue to the power and wealth of the state.[8] While gold accumulation may seem to benefit no one, in a sense the mercantilists were right. The accumulation of reserves did make sense in the mercantilist period in that it could increase employment, ease the difficulties of government finance, and thus potentially facilitate the conduct of war. Mercantilist theory held that the sovereign should intervene in the domestic economy to promote exports as well as to ensure the smooth development of the internal system. Such a mercantilist policy was potentially beneficial—if the king pursued it with wisdom. As time went on, however, government intervention started to hinder economic growth. Any policy associated with mercantilism came to be associated with government imbecility and kingly short-sightedness.

Two men dealt serious blows to mercantilist theory. In Britain, David Hume had reasoned as early as 1752 that efforts to increase wealth by restricting the free flow of trade and money would tend to defeat themselves. He said of countries trying to amass reserves by smothering imports, "I answer, if they lose their trade, industry and people, they cannot expect to keep their gold and silver . . . ."[9] Hume's good friend, Adam Smith, extended the argument for government non-intervention to virtually all areas of economic activity. In 1776, Smith published his book *The Wealth of*

Nations and liberal economics became a full-blown system. It was founded on the belief that the economy runs more smoothly and will grow more quickly if the government refrains from intervening. This view is still held by most Western economists.

Laissez-faire economists like Smith and his many followers no longer approved of the policy of accumulating reserves, since, according to them, things would work out best if the government followed no policy at all. These traditional liberals basically accepted the same international monetary system as the mercantilists did (the gold standard) but demonstrated that the gold standard would run itself—that equilibrium would come naturally if left to itself. A free market system does in theory tend to produce maximum world production: the problem is that governments often pursue other goals than maximum world production. Sometimes they seek higher domestic employment or production, and sometimes they seek economic independence or autarky. Thus, opting for non-intervention does not always serve an individual state's needs. Despite the arguments of the liberal economists, states may continue to interfere in the economic system and try to build up their monetary reserves.

Even in a liberal system, the growth of reserves would reflect a balance of payments surplus. This surplus could be viewed as an *indicator* of relative autonomy or autarky to the extent that dependence on imports is low. This independence serves as a strong support in time of war—and a source of protection from the influence of powerful states. If an excess of exports brought the surplus, then domestic employment has probably benefited as well. Reserves which grow because of capital inflows also indicate success in reaching the welfare goals of the state: investors seek out those countries where economic growth is most likely and where political stability is more probable. Whatever the cause and effect, it remains that states with growing international reserves are envied for their good fortune. While mercantilists are now said to have been short-sighted, they did recognize the identity between international reserves and national wealth which the liberals tended to downplay.

While economists continue to berate them for it, most states continue to follow mercantilist theory when they can, and for the instinctively felt reasons set out here. Every student of international monetary relations should keep this fact in mind, for it explains many of the events of the last years—events which otherwise appear elusive and mysterious. States will try to assure that the current monetary system is one which grants them the most reserves; and within any system, the states will work to win reserves even while using liberal rhetoric to declaim the virtues of free markets and non-interference. All hope that *other* states refrain from intervening, since it is generally accepted that the benefits of intervention in international markets come only if no other state does the same.[10]

There is one exception to this tendency to accumulate reserves: the key currency country. It was seen above that the key currency country does not need to amass extra reserves, in fact, it must generally run a balance of payments deficit in order to supply the system with a growing international money supply to match growth in the world economy. It prefers that no other country try to accumulate its currency, since this would create an imbalance and concentrate an excess supply of the key currency in that surplus country. At that point, the surplus country gains a certain amount of power and might threaten the key currency country by dumping the key money and causing a crisis. It will be to the advantage of the key currency country to encourage the development of system-wide rules which would prevent mercantilistic policies on the part of the other system members. In fact, both Britain and the United States have followed a policy of discouraging both accumulation of surpluses and state intervention by other countries to bring about growth in international reserve assets. Such a policy on the part of the key currency country may in the end promote the collective good, since, aside from its own desire for an open and non-interventionist monetary system, there is no other state sufficiently interested in independently putting aside mercantilistic policies for what may be only a small gain.

Peculiarities of Monetary Power

It has been asserted here that a country's national security is affected by its position in the world monetary system, because international money promotes power. The possession of monetary resources confers purchasing power, influence, and independence on the possessor. If states must act to establish monetary structures which favor their own interests, however, their monetary power must also depend on other sources of power, for instance, the power to impose a given set of rules on one's trading partners. The most powerful state within a system will attempt to write the rules of the monetary system so that the rules promote the state's own goals. It will, in other words, excercise *structural power* in the monetary sphere. Such structural power, however, depends upon a whole range of resources, well beyond monetary resources in the form of gold or foreign currencies. (For a full discussion of structural power, see Chapter 5.) Monetary power depends in part on a country's overall power potential. Only in a system where no state has a preponderance of power will the monetary system result from bargaining among equals with benefits flowing equally to all. In this way, an asymmetrical world balance of power tends to produce asymmetries, or inequalities, in the world monetary system. Such imbalances have always characterized the relations among states, and monetary power is no different.

Monetary power is, however, distinct and unique in a number of ways. The main peculiarity of monetary power comes from its *derivative* nature. A state, like an individual, has monetary resources because it has something else that others want. It develops monetary resources because it has oil or high technology goods or fertile land. Money only represents these other things and is not anything in particular except in relation to them.

Money also plays a unique role as the "conveyor belt of interdependence." It is principally through the mechanism of the international money markets that the effects of economic events in one country are transmitted to other countries. The conveyor belt tends to run in only one direction to the extent that the relative effects of external events on a country are greater when that country is (1) economically less powerful and (2) relatively dependent on foreign business dealings. This "asymmetry" especially irritates those countries which are affected most by external economic events.

Even though the monetary system is intimately connected to the existence of interdependence, the politics of monetary interdependence are also of a special kind. Trade policy, energy policy, agricultural policy—all of these instantly call to mind specific constituencies within countries which will react quickly to foreign events affecting their welfare. These are highly charged questions which in today's democratic societies soon become politicized. Domestic constraints act to limit the autonomous exercise of state power. Yet the monetary system does not bring to mind any particular groups whose vital interests are at stake. Exporters may want a depreciated currency, but at the same time importers will want the opposite. Bankers may prefer fixed exchange rates as a result of their conservative impulses, but they still make money under floating rates. Most citizens do not understand the monetary system at all, while they may understand very well the effects of textile quotas on their jobs in North Carolina, or the effects of the decision to go to Mars on their jobs at the Jet Propulsion Lab in California. Like money itself, monetary interdependence is derivative. Money links together those countries joined through trade, investment, travel, or any other economic dealings.

All of these considerations make the nature of international monetary relations a rarified area of politics. The international monetary system remains largely in the sphere of elite politics, although with some important exceptions. Central bankers and finance ministers still meet secretly over weekends, priding themselves on their ability to avoid leaks to the public. Yet, even if the average man continues to be only vaguely aware of the impact of the international monetary system on his interests, it is apparent that governments are fully aware. As will be seen below, they all pursue their interests as vigorously as possible when it comes to matters of international money.

Before the Dollar

The course of history has seen many monetary systems, but the classic monetary system which grew gradually over centuries was the gold standard. Key currencies played no role, because separate national currencies did not exist in the sense they do today. National monies took the form of minted coins, usually gold or silver stamped with the seal of the king or sovereign. Every money historian will recount anecdotes of this or that king who chipped his coins or substituted a cheaper metal for gold. In the end, even counterfeiters at the princely level would tend to get discovered, and the smart trader would raise the price to those offering notoriously cheapened coins. But the gold standard in its pure form failed to survive intact into the modern era.

Before the dollar had become the key currency of the world monetary system, the world lived under what has been variously described as a gold standard, a gold exchange standard, a sterling exchange standard, and both a new and an old gold standard. Whatever the names applied, between about 1800 and the First World War, the world relied on the use of both gold and holdings of pounds sterling in dealings among states and among the individuals of different states. Contrary to popular belief, the nineteenth century seems to have suffered repeated currency crises which in retrospect bear a striking resemblence to those seen more recently.

Many things may be said about the period before the dollar, but for our purposes, it is enough to notice that countries came naturally to do business in sterling at a time when British trade dominated world markets. Was this because Britain was more powerful than other states, or did the use of sterling contribute to Britain's power? Britain herself believed that the advantage of controlling a key currency was worth defending—most of Britain's monetary history in this century is testament of her fight to preserve that position. But once Britain had lost her position of hegemony in arms as well as in trade, there was no way in which the pound could be preserved as a global currency. The benefits of being a monetary power seem only to go to countries with power in other spheres. The First World War marked Britain's underlying military weakness and also sapped her economic strength. It was only a matter of time until another country and another currency would take over.

Bretton Woods

The dollar became the natural heir. Between the wars, however, the United States did not fully realize either the advantages of being a key currency country or even how to act like one. At a time when the United States should have been allowing the dollar to flow abroad, authorities allowed inflows instead during the great stock market boom of the late 1920s. The 1930s brought even greater chaos and, in the end, a desire to devise an orderly system. The result was the Bretton Woods agreement of 1944. It set up a system of fixed exchange rates, reserves kept in both gold and dollars, and an organization to run things in the International Monetary Fund (IMF). The United States kept its main reserves in gold.[11]

Judging from the political origins of exchange regimes, it could be expected that the United States would be the chief beneficiary of the Bretton Woods system. It was American in design and virtually unopposed by the prostrate powers of Europe. The U.S. held a large proportion of the world's gold and, of course, practically all the dollars. America received veto power in the IMF and saw to it that countries in arrears would have to submit to that organization's demands. The system's rules included prohibitions against restrictions on the movement of money generally. (Long-term movements of investment funds were not included under this stricture, but the profits on foreign investment were.)

It must be said that the dollar did not become a reserve currency simply by the fiat of the most powerful. There was a genuine desire by other countries to hold dollars to buy U.S. goods, to defend the home currency's value, and to hold reserves in a currency whose value was guaranteed in terms of gold. In fact, with U.S. willingness to run payments deficits (like a good key currency country), other countries benefited on the whole.

This position of the dollar gave the U.S. a special bonus. Since everyone wanted dollars abroad, Americans could buy foreign goods, or even foreign companies, pay with dollars, and be assured that foreigners would keep the dollars rather than exchange them for U.S. gold holdings. It was as if a person bought a book, paid by check, and the bookshop failed to cash it. He would get the book for free. But it might be that every month when his bank statement came in, he would worry that the shopkeeper would cash the check. What if all shopkeepers kept his checks? The temptation to spend beyond his means would surely be great. But someday the outstanding checks might exceed the bank balance—and all of those shopkeepers might ask their due. In fact, the United States had gotten into this position by the late 1960s. There were far more dollars held abroad by individuals and governments than there were U.S. gold reserves—and the holders started to get nervous. The fear that they would all attempt a run on U.S. reserves also made America nervous and led to new systemic measures in 1968.

A look at Table 1 below will show how American reserves appeared to get smaller and smaller in relation to all of the dollars held abroad. In Column 1, we see that between 1958 and 1971, foreigners increased their liquid dollar holdings from $16.8 billion to almost $60 billion. Meanwhile, Column 2 shows that American reserves (which include gold and some other assets) decreased from $22.5 billion to about $12 billion. Thus, by

Table 1
U.S. Reserve Asset Position
($ billion)

Year	U.S. Liquid Liabilities to Foreigners	U.S. Reserve Assets
Dec:		
1958	16.8	22.5
1959	19.4	21.5
1960	21.0	19.4
1961	22.9	18.8
1962	24.1	17.2
1963	26.3	16.8
1964	29.0	16.7
1965	29.1	15.5
1966	29.8	14.9
1967	33.1	14.8
1968	33.6	15.7
1969	41.9	17.0
1970	43.2	14.5
Aug:		
1971	59.9	12.1

Source: U.S. Board of Governors of the Federal Reserve System, *Bulletin* 57 (December 1971):12.

1971, there were five times as many dollars held by foreigners as there was gold. This was what was meant by the "dollar glut" or the oversupply of the key currency.

Until the time when people started to get nervous about the dollar, the system had worked well, and it had worked particularly well for the United States. America built up a tremendous stock of assets abroad, while the need for dollar credit gave the United States a great deal of real and potential world influence. Most American investment was not government directed, but other countries felt threatened by the presence of so much foreign ownership concentrated in one power. Credits to foreign countries were, on the other hand, often from the government itself, and the United States did use this "credit weapon" to elicit political quid pro quo's. Left-wing governments could be fairly sure that American money would not be forthcoming—this kind of pressure might make the use of physical threats completely unnecessary. But within these constraints, developed countries prospered under the Bretton Woods system, which provided stability for economic dealings, sufficient liquidity for growth, and open exchanges for the free flow of capital into productive investment.

243

Bretton Woods' exchange rate system depended on fixed rates and harmonization among participating countries' economic policies in order to keep the rates fixed. If the dollar was fixed vis-à-vis gold, then countries were expected to remain fixed vis-à-vis the dollar. This required that they try to keep their price levels in line with price levels in the United States, at least over the long term. For developing countries, which tended to have high inflation, there was the constant worry about balance of payments deficits, IMF pressures to cut government spending or wages, and perhaps frequent currency crises. For low inflation countries, like Germany, there was pressure to revalue the currency when all else failed. Sometimes it seemed that America was like the mother who said, "Everyone's out of step but my son John." But for many years, the United States was able to get all the other countries to go along and put up with the impact of interdependence among the Bretton Woods countries.

If so much harmonization was necessary, why did other countries go along? For the most part, they had no choice, as Bretton Woods was the only system available. More importantly for the longer term, the United States saw to it that the others derived important benefits. The system worked to the overall advantage of the United States, but in fact, exchange rate relationships within the system tended to work to the advantage of America's trading partners' trade. Their economies' growth benefited from their exports and from global trade growth. Had the United States tried to keep all of the benefits for itself, surely Bretton Woods would not have lasted as long as it did. This "reward" to important members of the system constituted America's chief *means* of maintaining it.

Bretton Woods also demanded something of the key currency country. It had to be able to force other countries to devalue or revalue their currencies against the dollar if their balance of payments went into a large surplus or deficit. It was relatively easy to force a country to devalue, because the country would already tend to be in a weakened position. But forcing revaluation on a country was another matter, since that country would, in effect, be asked to reduce its exports, increase imports, and write down the value of its foreign exchange reserves—all unpleasant things to ask of a country whose only fault seemed to be success.

Of course, if the key currency country were to keep its inflation rate low relative to the rest of the world, the necessity of forcing others to revalue would not come about very often. Unfortunately, in the 1960s, the Americans found it more and more difficult to restrain inflation, mainly because of budget deficits, excessive domestic money creation, and a number of other factors. With the Great Society and the Vietnam War, the United States wanted both guns and butter. The dollar tended to become overvalued in relation to currencies like the mark and the yen. The system's disadvantages to the U.S. were:

244

1) The U.S. could only force others to revalue with great difficulty. This could be taken as a sign of declining power held by the United States generally.

2) It could not devalue unilaterally for both technical and political reasons, or at least, this is what the politicians thought.

3) Overvaluation of the dollar began to have an adverse effect on American exports and by the late 1960s produced complaints from domestic labor.

4) Periodic exchange crises occurred for the dollar and other currencies, increasing in intensity by the late 1960s.

In the first half of the sixties, the advantages of Bretton Woods still seemed to outweigh the disadvantages. It was thought by many that the weakness of the dollar would prove temporary: piecemeal policies were installed to buy time until the dollar recovered. The Johnson administration particularly tried to stop dollar outflows by controlling the drain of investment and bank credits from the United States. These controls had perhaps their most significant effect in moving much of the world's international dollar business to London, creating what has come to be called the Eurodollar market. By 1968, these measures had accomplished little—and spending for the war in Vietnam tended to make the dollar's problems look more permanent.

1968: A Pure Key Currency

By 1968, the dollars held by foreign governments had really become a threat to the U.S. reserve stock of gold. France's President de Gaulle often articulated the threat and sometimes asked for gold to remind the U.S. of its vulnerability. Lyndon Johnson, who was the American President during the dollar's decline of the mid-sixties, said later in his memoirs:

> France had been building its gold reserves and was doing everything possible to force an increase in the official gold price. This was one of several times when I was tempted to abandon my policy of polite restraint toward De Gaulle, but I forced myself to be patient once again.[12]

It was odd that the world's most powerful country had become so weak in the monetary sphere. The potential for influence now seemed to run against the key currency country and in favor of those holding the key currency abroad. De Gaulle played his monetary cards adroitly and doubtless gained prestige (for a time) from his ability to cow his nervous ally.

The United States, however, was not without its weapons: monetary, political, and military. It had managed to use Germany's military dependency to elicit support in monetary affairs. Britain, too, could be depended

245

upon for different reasons. Most countries, in fact, had developed a vested interest in the continuance of the dollar standard, since they all held dollars as reserves themselves and since a limping standard seemed preferable to the possible chaos of change. For the United States, the obvious solution was a new exercise of structural power: a change in the rules to prevent other countries from trading in their dollars for American gold. It was a tribute to continued American dominance that in 1968 this was exactly what the U.S. accomplished.

In March 1968, dollar holders began to buy gold in great volume. Rather than continue to sell gold, the United States called for an end of government activity in gold markets while letting private operators continue to buy and sell among themselves. This created the so-called two-tier gold market. It abolished the gold market among governments who agreed not to trade in gold, but allowed a free market among private holders in which the gold price could rise. While governments promised not to dump dollars on the U.S., private citizens could still dump dollars on foreign exchange markets. But a tough series of measures in the United States tended to defuse attacks on the dollar for the next two years or so. Reversing a long-standing policy, President Johnson imposed mandatory limits on capital outflows by corporations and set stringent standards restricting international lending by domestic banks. Combined with a tougher monetary and fiscal policy, such actions allowed the President to buy time and to succeed in avoiding a monetary collapse.

What does this episode say about security? In 1968, the United States still held a preponderance of influence over its major trading partners. It managed to get a fair approximation of the structural change it wanted at the time. Yet, its position of monetary weakness caused the United States to be subjected to the influence of others. In order to procure the agreement of other countries in 1968, the U.S. was expected to take some of the burden: it had instituted capital controls and made them even stricter in early 1968—higher taxes were also imposed domestically later that year. As the U.S. declined in influence as a result of its embarrassing monetary position, other countries gained. Without tanks or guns, both Germany and Japan had become monetary giants and could thereby occasionally ignore American demands, at least in the monetary sphere. While the United States continued to be a strong power, its loss of monetary power began to be associated with the end of an era of American hegemony. Monetary relations seemed to affect the way in which people viewed the underlying international system taken as a whole.

Second Interim Solution: SDRs

Back in the 1950s, when most countries desired more dollars or other reserves, it was suggested that the Bretton Woods system was miscon-

246

ceived. Why should the level of world reserves be determined by (1) gold, which grows erratically and too slowly, and (2) U.S. balance of payments deficits, which irregularly supply foreign central banks with extra reserves? Neither of these seems to have anything to do with the rate of growth of the demand for global liquidity. A better solution would be a special reserve asset called "Special Drawing Right" (SDR) created rationally to supply the right amount of reserves for all. The dollar could then be done away with as a key currency.[13]

How would such an "SDR system" work? It was thought that the world should try to create an international money to supplement gold and dollar reserves just as individual governments create money for spending within one country. Experts thought that if there were an international currency made specially for use among countries, then the need to use "key currencies" for trade and other international payments would decline. This new international currency could be issued by the International Monetary Fund which represented all of the important non-communist states. These IMF members would agree on how much the world money supply should increase in a year and then would divide that among the members. Since this is basically what domestic central banks do, why not carry this into the world sphere?

During the height of Bretton Woods, the U.S. (as the most powerful country) saw little merit in such a suggestion. The United States liked the way the system worked and did not want an artificial asset to replace dollars in foreign central banks. As politics would predict, nothing was done. By the mid-1960s, however, when American reserves began to be threatened, such a plan had new virtues. Because of the existence of so many dollars abroad (the Eurodollar market was now growing by billions), there was no longer any real need for extra liquidity—so from a rational point of view, the world no longer needed *more* reserves, artificial or real. But by instituting a new reserve, now called SDRs, the U.S. could get certain benefits and no particular drawbacks. It made the U.S. appear serious about international monetary reform by adopting the position of respected and disinterested economists. It also would give the U.S. (and other countries) a free supply of extra reserves. Negotiations were finally completed by 1969, and in 1970 the first round of SDR distributions took place. SDRs were handed out according to IMF quotas—a method which gave the United States a generous proportion.[14]

The SDRs did not really change the system. They did theoretically act as a first step to a "reformed" monetary system in which the dollar would be replaced as the world's reserve currency. But political reality dictates that as long as the U.S. retains its overall world position of strength, it will be unlikely to accept a monetary system as neutral to its interests as a true SDR system would be. The institution of SDRs in the late 1960s shows the continued ability of the United States to impose its own solutions on its neighbors in that period. Yet the U.S. at that time apparently had lost the power to bring about the change it wanted most: revaluations by surplus countries sufficient to reverse its dollar outflows.

1971: Toward the Float

By the late 1960s, it was obvious that the Bretton Woods system had a serious flaw. There was no authority strong enough to get the United States to control its deficits. Meanwhile, the resurgence of Europe and other countries like Japan meant that the U.S. no longer had the power to dictate to others at the process level, that is to say, about the carrying out of the system's rules. Since America could no longer direct the system to her liking, she naturally began to have less interest in preserving it.

Other countries also showed disillusion. While surplus countries did have vested interests in their undervalued position within the dollar system, they also grew dissatisfied. Their complaints took a variety of forms. For some, it was jealousy of the presumed preeminent and advantageous monetary position of the United States, a position which no longer seemed suitable in an increasingly multipolar world. For others, the Bretton Woods system of the late sixties was simply unmanageable. It demanded more economic policy coordination than countries found themselves willing to undertake. Interdependence, which had formerly connoted friendly and mutually beneficial relationships, began to take on a negative meaning. Eurodollars, which had been hailed as the ultimate in capital market efficiency, now came to be a symbol of instability as these liquid deposits abroad tended to be used as vehicles for currency speculation. The growth of multinational corporations contributed to the number of actors switching in and out of currencies—and creating havoc at regular intervals.

Dissatisfaction with these aspects of the monetary system was in fact dissatisfaction with the high levels of interdependence it required. Germany, a country where inflation brought memories of the great inflation of 1923 and the political chaos which accompanied it, was forced into inflationary capital inflows. Britain, a country where economic growth was increasingly falling behind that of its trading partners, was asked to deflate. Monetary disruptions affected domestic interests more in those countries than in the U.S. Developing countries, most of which found price stability extremely difficult, were required to keep up with the world's pace, or face the IMF's conditions for aid. Even the United States was asked to control its own rate of spending abroad and at home while other political exigencies sometimes seemed to demand the opposite.

America tried at first to use bravado to correct the situation. By what was called a policy of "benign neglect," the U.S. attempted again to force surplus countries to revalue. The technique was simple: do nothing to protect the dollar's international value. That would create such reactions, such as capital flows into marks or yen, that the Germans and Japanese would have no choice but to revalue. Their alternative would be to buy tens of billions of dollars and to undergo inflationary pressures from the capital inflows. There were, in fact, crises in response to this tactic between 1969 and 1971, and some revaluations did take place but not enough to make a long-term difference.

As is well known and often recorded, President Nixon forced everyone's hands in 1971 by a fairly blunt power play. To make the surplus countries revalue, he now ended the fiction that dollars could be turned in for gold (which had really been a fiction since 1968). He refused to support the dollar against other currencies, forcing it to float freely in value, and he added a piece of blackmail by applying tariff surcharges to limit American imports of foreign goods. The negotiations which followed indicated that at that time the U.S. wanted to return to something like the Bretton Woods format with some exceptions: (1) a new exchange rate structure which would effectively devalue the dollar and produce a turnaround in the U.S. balance of payments; (2) de-emphasis on gold as an international reserve; (3) a new system of adjustment which would permit more flexibility in the fixed rates and which would also force countries to revalue or devalue more readily.

No longer a power without serious opposition, the United States could not get everything it wanted anymore. Following their mercantilist instincts, other countries, particularly the Europeans, resisted too large an increase in American exports, since that would have meant a decline in *their* exports. Gold might decline in importance, but it was found that all of the important long-term questions would be the subject of long and hard negotiations. There would be no *faits accomplis* as there had been at Bretton Woods in 1944. But the United States did get a moderate devaluation of the dollar in December 1971 at the Smithsonian negotiations, and the outcome was generally felt to be an American victory. The U.S. was still no doubt the leading power in monetary questions but no longer held the hegemonial position it once enjoyed.

Unfortunately for the U.S., and despite Nixon's pronouncement that the Smithsonian Agreement was the most significant monetary agreement in history, the rates agreed to in late 1971 did not hold. Speculative attacks on various currencies continued, and meanwhile underlying problems of the interdependence of the system had not been addressed.

The United States made reform proposals in the fall of 1972 at the annual IMF conference. These called for more SDRs to be created, without, however, eliminating the role of the dollar. Such a system would have likely meant a dollar-SDR system, much like the Bretton Woods dollar-gold system. Treasury Secretary Schultz also called for new rules to require devaluations and revaluations.[15] These were couched in such a way that had they been in effect during the 1960s, Bretton Woods would not have foundered: surplus countries would have been forced to revalue when their reserves grew. Schultz' plan therefore would have corrected the flaws of Bretton Woods (from the U.S. perspective), while maintaining the advantages accruing to the United States from it.

Events soon overtook the Schultz Plan. In February 1973, rates were no sooner negotiated following a new crisis than the rate structure once again broke down. Finance ministers collectively agreed that things had gone beyond their control and that the only possible alternative was to give up trying to fix rates, at least for the time being. This outcome had not been a preferred policy of the United States and signalled the fact that the U.S. was no longer in control. That was not to say that the U.S. was without power, however, and it quickly assessed the situation to see how advantages could be culled from the debacle. Seven months later, the oil crisis provided just such an opportunity as other consumers of oil scrambled for dollars to pay their foreign bills. Such confusion hit the money markets with OPEC's new-found fortunes that it was generally held that if rates had not been floating in October 1973, floating would have been the outcome in any case. In fact, U.S. policy-makers came to the conclusion that floating rates should be continued. The "liberal" theory that states should not intervene in markets was extended by those who approved of floating to mean that states should even stop intervening in currency markets.

Return to Bretton Woods?

Questions still remain about the distribution of gains and losses under the system of "floating" rates. Does it provide more security for some than for others? Does the United States gain or lose its influence over other countries?

America seemed at least to be able to prevent any other country from exercising control. The French wanted to encourage central bank intervention to stabilize exchange rates but finally agreed in November 1975 to a compromise in favor of only limited intervention to smooth out exchange rate movements. But when it came to real intervention, the U.S., for instance, let it be known to Britain that its usual allowance in the so-called swap network (borrowings among central banks) would be reduced by one half. America also managed to promote some of its pet projects, like getting gold out of the monetary system. In 1975, IMF members agreed to sell off $1/6$ of IMF gold reserves ostensibly for the benefit of poor countries. The dollar continued as the chief world currency for both individuals and governments: the Eurodollar market thrived, and countries continued to use the dollar as an intervention and reserve currency. Dollars met demands for borrowed funds to pay for imports in hard-pressed countries, and American influence over debtors seemed to continue undiminished. And if the United States appeared to bend to the desires of the French when they agreed to control "erratic fluctuations" in currency markets, this was as much a bow to her own international companies who were finding business difficult in a shifting monetary environment. While America seems no longer able to get everything she wants, she has still done well surviving recent upheavals. Under the circumstances, a reformed monetary system probably will remain in the future, unless the United States can be assured that this time it can force revaluation or devaluation on other countries. That outcome will be resisted by other countries, probably successfully, because they no longer want to put up with the subservience such a system requires. In the meantime, the floating system gives the United States a relatively good position from which to influence others. It may even make it more difficult for surplus countries to avoid revaluation.

A few notes may be made on the managed floating system of the 1970s. European countries, recognizing the crucial role of monetary relations in forging economic and political unity, have tried since 1971 to maintain their own bloc within the dollar bloc. Since the 1973 float, they have tried to maintain fixed rates among themselves while floating jointly against the dollar and other currencies. With Britain, Italy, Ireland, and sometimes France and Denmark unable to maintain parity, it has been difficult. Part of the rationale behind such a union derives logically from the political implications of a dollar-centered monetary system. By making diverse European currencies essentially one currency, a monetary power equal to that of the U.S. might be created. But just as it was difficult to bring about harmonization of economic policies among many countries under Bretton Woods, so it is difficult to ask countries as diverse as Ireland and West Germany to grow and inflate at the same pace. The flaws of Bretton Woods seem only to have been transferred to a smaller group.

Some businessmen, though by no means all, find the float uncomfortable and risky. Some exert political pressure, even across national boundaries, to get governments to keep exchange values stable. Most importantly, many countries have found that the economists' promises about floating rates were pipe dreams. Independent economic policy seems no closer to realization under floating rates than under fixed rates.[16] Under fixed rates, independent policies could set off undesirable capital flows, but under floating rates, a country's independent policy produces instead undesirable exchange rate changes—changes larger than optimistic economists had predicted. Such exchange rate fluctuations mean frequent changes in import and export values, and under unfavorable conditions, they can bring inflationary pressures with higher import prices. Britain, for instance, has experienced a constantly falling rate and high inflation. The monetary system will continue to force countries into interdependence as long as they remain economically "open" toward one another, allowing the unfettered movement of goods, services, and money across borders. Since floating rates do not make openness much more palatable than fixed rates did, it is possible that an emergent system, as Knorr predicted at the outset, will be less open than was Bretton Woods. Capital controls may become more important, along with controls in other economic areas.

It was also thought that with floating rates, the role of the dollar would diminish, since exchange rate intervention would occur less frequently. Again, however, mercantilist instincts move countries to intervene in currency markets anyway—the newspapers report daily on the motivations of various central banks when they nudge their rates up or try to press them down. In addition, the dollar has proved to continue as a good investment, and individuals seem to share this opinion judging from the vitality of the Eurodollar market. What were called unwanted dollars abroad (forming the "dollar overhang") now look very much wanted.

The history of monetary transformations seems to mirror concurrent transformations in the balance of power. The United States, still the most powerful Western power, continues to play the dominant role in the monetary system. No longer unchallenged, however, the U.S. cannot dictate the shape the monetary system will take. Similar links between monetary questions and matters of state power and security will be seen when we examine other countries and systems: the Eastern bloc, the oil nations, and the poor.

The Second, Third, and Fourth Worlds

Thus far, we have spoken mainly as if the international monetary system consisted of the OECD countries only, that is, the most industrialized non-communist countries of the world. What of the rest of the world? The communist world, in effect, forms an almost completely separate international system. Soviet planners have historically conducted only as much trade with the outside as they have found absolutely necessary, since trade with the West must be conducted in "hard" currencies like dollars.[17] This separation means that the bipolarity of the military structure parallels the existence of a bifurcated international monetary structure. (China actually belongs to no formal monetary system, having developed a high degree of autarky, or economic independence.) Between the Soviet Union and her allies, a system analogous to Bretton Woods exists where the Russian ruble plays the role of the dollar and where the Soviet Union tends to dominate the economic development of all the states in the bloc. But the ruble differs importantly from the dollar.

Since free markets among ruble bloc countries do not exist, trades between countries often take the form of bargaining over exchange rates which, in turn, means bargaining over what the goods will cost. This kind of exchange rate bargaining also takes place in deals between East and West.[18] The ruble is not considered valuable in the West, just as Russian goods are in relatively low demand. This fact illustrates the way in which the demand for a currency derives from the demand for the goods that currency will buy.

The existence of a dual international monetary system raises questions about the relationship between monetary "power" and the overall power and security position of a state. It is interesting to note that the two monetary systems correspond closely to the perimeters of the two world nuclear and ideological umbrellas. Yugoslavia, for instance, expresses its ideological independence from Moscow most strikingly by its membership in the International Monetary Fund. The deference due to the state with military superiority seems to translate into monetary deference as well. Just as there is, in effect, no dominant global power, neither is there a formal world monetary system. Within a Western monetary structure, the economically less powerful USSR would be subject to monetary pressures, not to speak of the political problems the Soviets see in the free movement of trade. By staying economically and monetarily insulated, the Soviet Union probably increases its stature with respect to the United States.

Within the processes of a monetary bloc, the "satellites" often receive monetary benefits and concessions, seemingly at the expense of the larger power seeking to secure their support. This process has been noted in the East as well as the West.[19] Some observers claim to see in these concessions indications that the superpowers have weakened. That may be so, but it should be remembered that absolute control of one state by another is unusual, and support is always paid for by sharing the system's gains. What can be expected is that the dominant powers will try to maximize their *total* gains from the system, often giving up economic benefits in favor of political control.

The OPEC nations teach another lesson in international monetary relations. With some freedom of action in the shade of the military standoff between the superpowers, they managed a coup in increasing oil prices in 1973 and after. It meant, of course, a monetary windfall—billions of dollars added to their reserves. Early predictions of the World Bank gave the OPEC countries external assets of $650 billion by 1980. While these figures have been reduced considerably, a country like Saudi Arabia today holds reserves of about $45 billion alone. Several results followed.

OPEC's monetary reserves gave them power. The "oil weapon" turned into the "money weapon," that is to say, buying power and influence. Iran and Saudi Arabia bought arms. Arabs supported Egypt and threatened Israel. Even Venezuela's voice sounded louder in Latin America. Certainly, the world power configuration had changed on the strength of shifts in international monetary reserves. The consequences of money power had never been so obvious.

253

OPEC's monetary strength also extends beyond the purely martial realm. When some OPEC countries like Abu Dhabi decided to switch from holding reserves in sterling (a hangover from British colonial days in the Mideast), the rumors set off widespread speculation against the pound which left the British government embarrassed and impotent. OPEC money reserves may enable oil countries to buy into large Western companies, although in this eventuality, political power seems sufficient to counter undesirable purchases within developed countries. The German government, for instance, reportedly headed off an Iranian bid for Daimler-Benz shares by instructing private German banks to buy up the shares offered.

A final way in which OPEC reserves grant power to their holders is in their effect on exchange rate values. Switches from one currency to another by large money market actors can, as in the case of Britain's currency, result in rate changes. If some country sought to sell its dollars, for instance, the dollar's value could fall significantly. To the extent that the dollar's rate becomes subject to OPEC's valuation of it, it follows that the U.S. capability to control the monetary system erodes even further. Luckily for the United States, the OPEC countries do not envisage the demise of the dollar to be in their interest: like most rich people, they develop a certain conservatism, wishing to preserve the value of their assets. But the United States will now have to see to it that it remains in OPEC's interest to keep reserves in dollars. It has been claimed, for instance, that the U.S. decided to intervene in the float in order to maintain the dollar's exchange rate and assuage oil country fears that their dollar assets would shrink. This alteration in the monetary balance signals a change in the balance of influence: the monetary game involves high stakes.

As for the other Third and Fourth World countries, the contingencies of power give them little protection from outside influence and even less power over the international monetary regime itself. Domestic inflations, the most common monetary problems in LDCs, put them at the mercy of their creditors, be it the IMF, national governments, or private banks. The standard IMF-central banker position asserts that inflation is a form of governmental immorality which unhinges the system.[20] But, as E. H. Carr noted, the privileged always tend to "throw moral discredit on the underprivileged by depicting them as disturbers of the peace . . . ."[21] LDCs have complained that the fixed rate system forced them into permanent indigence, since monetary stability required austerity programs which worked against their growth. But floating rates may be no better, with the problems they create.

The LDCs, lacking any kind of power and influence, have little to say about monetary reform. They have virtually no control over the nature of a system which affects their well-being and independence so powerfully. The IMF gold sale agreed to in August 1975 means some extra money for the poorest countries, but the sale is also a politically advantageous policy of the United States in its campaign to diminish the role of gold.

Because of their utter lack of power in other areas, the LDCs also lack monetary power. Mónetary power, it should be remembered, is derivative. And because of their lack of monetary power, they must submit to the various forms of domination implicit in such a position. LDCs do not take the same point of view on these questions, but they generally share a weak monetary position and vulnerability to outside pressure when in need of monetary support.

The debtor countries of the Third World do hold one stick over their creditors—the threat of default. This becomes increasingly important at a time when private bank credits have grown more important. The world thereby increases its interdependence—and it becomes more difficult to decide who is more dependent on whom. But the power of the debtor to threaten the creditor with non-payment is a sorry one. It grants only negative advantages and will fail in the end to produce any real monetary independence.

One Step Forward, or Two Steps Backward?

A well-known international economist, Charles Kindleberger, admitted that, "In the international economy, it has long been recognized that the world of the benign invisible hand does not obtain." Another respected economist, Gunnar Myrdal, concurred in saying, "politics is sovereign."[22] What these economists realize, and what is obvious from this account, is that monetary relations cannot be understood outside of the context of international politics—nor is an understanding of international politics complete without consideration of monetary aspects. Some students see the development of monetary disorders in the 1960s as a sign that somehow the nature of international politics had changed. It is closer to the truth to say that monetary questions naturally intrude on politics (and vice versa) and that the relative monetary peace of the post-war period, short-lived as it was, marked only a brief period of equilibrium in the political system among states.

This is not to say that all monetary systems are the same. Within a given structure of states, some systems work better than others. The disquiet of recent years marks a low point for monetary harmony. While there are those who view the current stalemate of a mixed floating system as a boon, most would only approve if it leads to a reformed monetary system in the West. Some believe with former U.S. Treasury Secretary Simon that floating without intervention constitutes reform; others agree with the French that improvement can only come with relatively fixed rates and decreased importance for the dollar. Many economists, often American, believe that a monetary system functions best when one currency holds special status;

255

others, more often not Americans, hold that no country should be given a special position.

Whatever details would best serve the world, the preceding account should chasten those who call for an international monetary system which would be immune from political influence. As long as there is an international money, states will use it to enhance their interests and security. The United States can still prevent the working of a monetary system of which it disapproves. And as long as domestic economic systems differ, the impact of the international monetary system will continue to be asymmetrical. The system will reflect the power structure in which it exists. Yet some monetary systems do distribute benefits and costs more evenly than others. Richard Cooper points out that formal international arrangements tend to exhibit more symmetry than informal ones,[23] perhaps because of the formal equality of state sovereignty in international law. In an informal system such as the post-1973 float, more powerful countries can maneuver subtly to their own advantage. We have seen how the United States has made the most of its role in recent years.

In the last analysis, however, even a formal system operating in a world of independent nations will not escape the realities of power politics, and its monetary and political benefits will likely accrue to the rich and powerful. As Hobbes, in one of his bleaker passages, said,

> For where there is no Common-wealth, there is (as hath been already shewn) a perpetuall warre of every man against his neighbour; And therefore every thing is his that getteth it, and keepeth it by force; which is neither *Propriety*, nor *Community*; but *Uncertainty*.[24]

Footnotes

1. For various views on the meaning of recent monetary events, see C. Fred Bergsten, "New Urgency for Monetary Reform," *Foreign Policy* (Summer 1975): 79–98; Tom de Vries, "Jamaica, or the Non-Reform of the International Monetary System," *Foreign Affairs*, 54 (April 1976): 577–605. For a complete history of post-war monetary affairs, see Susan Strange, *International Monetary Relations*, Vol. II of *International Economic Relations of the Western World*, ed. Andrew Shonfield, 2 vols. (London: Oxford University Press, 1976).
2. The most complete treatment of the international monetary system can be found in Leland B. Yeager, *International Monetary Relations: Theory, History and Policy* (New York: Harper and Row, 1976).
3. Robert A. Mundell, "A Theory of Optimum Currency Areas," *American Economic Review*, 51 (September 1961); R. I. McKinnon, "Optimum Currency Areas," *American Economic Review*, 53 (September 1963).
4. Key currency originally meant any currency around which other currencies were to be stabilized after the Second World War according to one plan proposed by Professor John H. Williams, *Postwar Monetary Plans and Other Essays* (3rd ed.; New York: Alfred A. Knopf, 1947), pp. 42–60. Key currency has gradually come to refer to a single currency around which all others in a system are stabilized.
5. Susan Strange, *Sterling and British Policy* (New York: Oxford University Press, 1971);

Benjamin J. Cohen, *The Future of Sterling as an International Currency* (London: Macmillan and Co., 1971).

6. West German Chancellor Helmut Schmidt told the press of an understanding reached among the Germans, French, Americans and British on the terms of any loans to Italy. See *New York Times*, 8, 20, 28 July 1976.

7. Hugh Thomas, *Suez* (New York: Harper and Row, 1967), pp. 146–47; Townsend Hoopes, *The Devil and John Foster Dulles* (Boston: Little, Brown and Co., 1973), pp. 384–85.

8. For accounts of the mercantilists, see Chapter 2 of this book, as well as Jacob Viner, "Power Versus Plenty as Objectives of Foreign Policy in the Seventeenth and Eighteenth Centuries," *World Politics*, I (October 1948). For an account of the liberal point of view, as well as a revealing study of the nineteenth-century gold standard, see Marcello de Cecco, *Money and Empire: The International Gold Standard, 1890–1914* (Oxford: Basil Blackwell, 1974).

9. David Hume, "On the Balance of Trade," in *Philosophical Works*, ed. T. H. Green and T. H. Grose, III (Darmstadt: Scientia Verlag Aalen, 1964), p. 347.

10. The economics of trade and money flows can be found in Charles P. Kindleberger, *International Economics* (Homewood: Richard D. Irwin, 1968). The theory of public goods may explain why there is a tendency for countries to pursue protectionist policies in conflict with economic theory. See for instance, Mancur Olsen, *The Logic of Collective Action* (Cambridge: Harvard University Press, 1971).

11. For a history of the Bretton Woods system, Alfred E. Eckes, Jr., *A Search for Solvency: Bretton Woods and the International Monetary System, 1941–1971* (Austin: University of Texas Press, 1975); Margaret G. de Vries, *The International Monetary Fund*, 5 vols. (Washington: I.M.F., 1969 and 1977).

12. Lyndon B. Johnson, *The Vantage Point* (New York: Holt, Rinehart, 1971), pp. 316–17.

13. The best-known plan for a new reserve asset was that of Robert Triffin in his *Gold and the Dollar Crisis* (New Haven: Yale University Press, 1960). For a summary of similar plans see Fritz Machlup, *Plans for Reform of the International Monetary System* (Princeton: Princeton University Press, International Finance Section, 1962). J. M. Keynes had, of course, suggested one of the first of these plans as early as 1943.

14. For a documentary history of the development of SDRs and the questions surrounding them, see Gerald M. Meier, *Problems of a World Monetary Order* (New York: Oxford University Press, 1974), pp. 121–235.

15. Schultz' statement to the International Monetary Fund, 26 September 1972, "Needed: A New Balance in International Economic Affairs," printed in U.S., Congress, Senate, Committee on Finance, Subcommittee on International Finance and Resources, *Hearings*, 93d Cong., 1st sess., 1973, Appendix C.

16. For this, and opposing views of floating, see U.S., Congress, Joint Economic Committee, and House Committee on Banking, Currency and Housing, Subcommittee on International Trade, Investment and Monetary Policy and the Subcommittee on International Economics, *Hearings*, 94th Cong., 1st sess., 1975; also, U.S., Congress, Joint Economic Committee, Subcommittee on International Economics, *How Well are Fluctuating Exchange Rates Working?*, *Hearings*, 93d Cong., 1st sess., 1973. For a range of academic views on exchange rate flexibility, C. Fred Bergsten, *et al.*, *Approaches to Greater Flexibility of Exchange Rates: the Burgenstock Papers*, ed. G. N. Halm (Princeton: Princeton University Press, 1970).

17. Robert W. Campbell, *The Soviet-Type Economies: Performance and Evolution* (Boston: Houghton Mifflin Co., 1974), p. 127.

18. "East Bloc Money Mystifies Many," *New York Times*, 17 August 1976.

19. Zbigniew Brzezinski, *The Soviet Bloc* (Cambridge: Harvard University Press, 1967), p.

468; for a recent confirmation, see Tad Szulc, "'Fire-Brigade Duty' for Brezhnev," *New York Times*, 17 December 1976. There is, of course, a counter-claim that the Soviet Union trades with Eastern Europe at the expense of its satellites. See, for instance, Marshall I. Goldman, *Detente and Dollars: Doing Business with the Soviets* (New York: Basic Books, 1975), pp. 23–26.

20. For a critical view of the treatment of LDCs, Cheryl Payer, *The Debt Trap* (New York: Monthly Review Press, 1975).

21. Edward Hallett Carr, *The Twenty Years' Crisis, 1919–1939* (New York: Harper and Row, 1964), p. 83.

22. Charles P. Kindleberger, "Systems of International Economic Organization," in *Money and the Coming World Order*, ed. David P. Calleo (New York: New York University Press, 1976), p. 16; Gunnar Myrdal, *Against the Stream: Critical Essays on Economics* (New York: Random House, 1975), p. 168.

23. R. N. Cooper, "Prolegomena to the Choice of an International Monetary System," in *World Politics and International Economics*, ed. Lawrence B. Krause and C. Fred Bergsten (Washington, D.C.: The Brookings Institution, 1975), pp. 95–96.

24. Thomas Hobbes, *Leviathan* (New York: Washington Square Press, 1964), p. 175.

CHAPTER 10

Oil and Influence: The Oil Weapon Examined*

Hanns Maull

Introduction

Oil weapon, as used in this chapter, signifies any manipulation of the price or supply of oil by exporting nations, done with the intention of changing the political behavior of the consumer nations. The political potential of the oil price is fairly restricted, so that in effect we are mainly concerned with supply interruptions.

Oil power is the power which stems from the dependence of the consumer nations on oil. This forms the basis of any successful application of the oil weapon and includes all factors which allow the producers to influence and control the political behavior of the consumers. The oil weapon, therefore, is one specific way of using oil power: other ways would be the threat to use the oil weapon, or simply the diplomatic exploitation of consumer dependence.

* * * * * * * * * * *

Two years after the hectic reactions to the first successful application of the oil weapon, the sense of emergency of the "energy crisis" has been widely replaced by complacency. Little as this complacency can be justified in terms of any careful analysis, two rationalizations were conveniently at hand for those unable or unwilling to take drastic actions: first, a world-wide recession plus two mild winters in the industrialized world brought down oil consumption, led to a contraction of OPEC export markets, and forced some producers to adjust prices or export volumes downward. (The wretched winter of 1976–77 and the new Administration in Washington have somewhat lessened the sense of complacency, but the change is still insufficient to affect the argument of this chapter.) This general relaxation of the previously tense supply-demand balance and the reluctance of Saudi Arabia to support fur-

---

* This chapter is a revised version of the first part of Adelphi Paper No. 117 (London: International Institute for Strategic Studies, 1975).

ther price increases led to an effective reduction of oil prices in real terms. The various pricing decisions taken by OPEC, which resulted in the erosion of the purchasing power of oil exports since 1974, created an illusion of market power swinging back towards the consumers. However, it was, in fact, mainly the oil price policy of Saudi Arabia which produced OPEC moderation. Secondly, in one area the doomsday prophecies of 1974 proved unfounded: the shock of massive balance of payments problems for the industrialized countries as a consequence of the quadrupling of oil prices has been absorbed relatively easily thus far by the international financial system. Some industrialized countries managed to return to a positive balance of payments with amazing speed. This effectively shifted the burden of adjustment to the weaker economies and ultimately to the non-oil-exporting developing world.

Yet, the international oil market's seeming return to equilibrium is deceptive. OPEC proved its cohesiveness under pressure and revealed itself as an organization of remarkable strength. This is not surprising, given the stakes at risk if cooperation of the major oil producers failed and the basic simplicity of OPEC's control mechanism: the fixing of the reference price, which leaves the adjustment details to the oil companies. There is now little prospect in the foreseeable future that a contraction of export markets could lead to serious strains in the organization. On the contrary, every indication points to the possibility that the supply-demand balance will tighten again, increasing the strain on OPEC's reserves. A consistent energy policy by the most important actor in the international oil market, the United States, has been thus far blocked by the struggle between Presidents and the Congress, and this—together with the decline of domestic production—has meant that U.S. dependence on imports from the Middle East has increased. The substance of producer power has, therefore, hardly been diminished, and it might well grow further. What must be even more worrying is the small amount of progress towards a settlement of the Israeli-Arab conflict; for, even though the energy crisis and the Middle East conflict are separate problems, they are strongly linked by the present political configuration in the Middle East. Another oil embargo involving production cutbacks is therefore a distinct possibility should the Israeli-Arab dispute escalate once more into open conflict.

An analysis of oil politics and the potential and limitations of the oil weapon are, therefore, still timely. The widespread belief that the successful application of the oil weapon was a unique event in international politics and that its recurrence is unlikely might well be unfounded. Moreover, oil power, though possibly mobilized in different ways from the 1973–74 supply crisis, will continue to be a force in international relations.

Oil is the raw material most intrinsically interwoven with politics, and oil embargoes and boycotts have repeatedly served as political tools. Even though the political leverage provided by the oil trade has been used by countries other than those in the Middle East, this area has been exposed to oil politics three times within less than twenty years—each time in connection with Israeli-Arab wars. In 1956 the Suez Canal and the Iraq Petroleum Company pipeline from the Iraqi oilfields to the Mediterranean were closed, and about two-thirds of Middle East exports to Europe had to be rerouted or were cut off. The result was a moderate increase in the price of oil over a short period of time. Some European countries faced temporary shortages, and certain industries were affected. Overall production in European countries belonging to the Organization for Economic Cooperation and Development (OECD), however, continued to grow. In 1967, the Suez Canal was again closed—this time for a long period. Kuwait, Libya, Iraq, and Saudi Arabia stopped production after the outbreak of the war. This was partly a result of government decisions (Kuwait, Iraq) and partly a result of strikes by oil workers (Libya, Saudi Arabia). The stoppage was then replaced by selective embargoes against Britain, the United States, and West Germany. Again, the success of the "oil weapon" was virtually nil and "hurt the Arabs more than anyone else," in the words of a Saudi Arabian oil minister.[1]

Oil Power : A Political Reality

To find out why oil power has become a political reality since 1967, we have to look at the basis of this power: the trade relationship between producers and consumers. Around 1970 the international oil market was said to have turned from a buyer's to a seller's market. This was a vague way of saying that a fundamental imbalance had developed in the trade relationship between producers and consumers—an imbalance no longer offset by outside factors such as political dependence or economic counter-weights. This allowed the relationship to be used for political purposes.[2] The leverage inherent in such an imbalance stems from the capability to interrupt trade. The larger the difference between the damage the interruption causes the consumer and that which it causes the supplier, the stronger the leverage.

The damage the target country actually experiences depends on the amount of impoverishment the stoppage or the reduction of supplies inflicts. A good indicator is the previous expansion of oil imports, which demonstrates oil's growing importance to the target. The damage experienced is also reflected in the length and costliness of the adjustment process which the supply interruption makes necessary.

One of the main characteristics of the international oil market in recent years has been its rapid expansion. Caused by the parallel boom in all major Western industrialized economies, demand for oil grew at a continuous and even accelerating pace to the 1973 peak. This unprecedented rise was the

Table 1
Oil Import Dependence—United States, Japan
and Western Europe

	Western Europe			Japan			United States		
	1956	1967	1973	1956	1967	1973	1956	1967	1973
Oil imports (mill. ton.)	121.5	443.6	707.3	12.4	116.8	249.3	57.3	116.5	300.8
Imports as % of energy consumption	20.7	52.7	66.3	22.9	67.2	86.0	5.6	7.7	17.7
Arab crude oil imports as % of energy consumption	13.4	36.0	47.8	12.9	33.4	38.5	1.3	0.6	2.1[a]

[a] If dependence on imports of petroleum products derived from Arab crude is included, this figure becomes 5%. Western Europe and Japan do not import significant quantities of products.

Source: *U.N. Statistical Papers*, Series J, various issues.

result not only of the "natural" growth in demand accompanying expanding economies but also of the switch to oil as the predominant source of energy supply.[3] Nowhere in the Western world (apart from Canada) was indigenous production sufficient to satisfy the growing demand, and oil had to be imported to fill the gap between supply and demand. Table I shows the absolute and relative growth of the significance of imported oil in the energy balance of the Western world. It also shows the strong position of the Arab countries as suppliers; attempts to diversify the import sources proved ineffective due to the unique position of the Arab world in terms of oil production (32.8% of world production in 1973) and reserves. The absolute growth of oil imports shows the increasing damage potential, and the relative growth shows the Arab producers' strong leverage vis-à-vis Europe, Japan and—to a lesser extent—the United States. In the case of the United States, dependence on Arab oil accelerated after indigenous production peaked out in 1970.[4]

Since energy is of overwhelming importance for the functioning of all aspects of industrialized economies and societies, the Arab producers' leverage was considerable—unless the consumer economies could adjust to the supply interruptions in such a way as to prevent major disturbances. While they had achieved adjustments at a fairly low cost in 1956 and 1967, the situation in 1973 had fundamentally changed. The supply crises in 1956 and 1967 proved manageable, because supplies were available from alternative sources, although admittedly at a somewhat higher price: Venezuela, the United States, and Iran could step up their production by using excess capacity and divert some of it to European countries affected by the supply interruptions.[5] In 1973, no substantial stand-by capacity was available—certainly nowhere near enough to make up the reduction the Arab oil producers decided upon. Other producers in the Third World also showed no intention of increasing their production, since they, too, profited from the squeeze through its impact on oil prices. Existing stockpiles were hardly more than a temporary cushion against the impact of the Arab oil weapon, and adjustment had to be achieved by savings in consumption and the limited possibilities of substituting other sources of primary energy for oil.

Thus the European countries, Japan, and even the United States faced a situation in which the Arab oil producers provided them with a scarce and enormously important raw material for which there was no real substitute—an optimum precondition for the exertion of political pressure, provided there was no countervailing dependence by the producers on stable oil supplies and/or imports from the consumer countries. We must ask: was the trade relationship between producers and consumers balanced? And, also, was it based upon mutual benefit?

Examining the structure of trade between producer and consumer countries, in order to establish the degree of balance or imbalance in the relationship, one has to consider two further points. Are oil producers sufficiently dependent on goods supplied by the oil consumers to provide realistic counter-leverage? And, are the producers so dependent on the continuation of oil exports that any interruption or reduction would also inflict heavy damage on them?

The Arab countries are to a certain extent dependent on imports from the Western industrialized countries, especially food. For example, in 1972 they imported cereals and cereal products worth at least $297 million from eight industrialized countries (the United States, Canada, West Germany, France, Britain, Italy, the Netherlands and Switzerland).[6] Since the United States has an especially strong position in the world grain market, there appeared to be a possibility of exerting counter-pressure; and this was hinted at by the then Vice-President Ford (January 8, 1974). But it appears doubtful whether a counter-embargo could have been organized by Western grain producers; and, even if one assumes such an attempt would have succeeded, the Soviet Union might have derived considerable political advantage from stepping in to make up the shortfall (American grain exports to the Arab countries were about 2 million tons in 1972, while Soviet grain production in 1973 was a record-breaking 222.5 million tons). Some oil producers also possessed large foreign exchange holdings which gave them a good chance of weathering any prolonged trade war, and this contributed to their low vulnerability.[7]

As for the other form of dependence mentioned, there can be little doubt that the economies of large-scale oil exporters in the Third World have been largely dependent on oil revenues and the indirect benefits derived from oil production. However, for mutual dependence to exist, there must be roughly similar incentives for both sides to continue the trade relationship at the prevailing—or even higher—level. Some producers (the so-called low absorbers) had, however, already more revenues than they could profitably spend, and world-wide inflation and currency devaluations were eroding the value of their foreign exchange reserves. Hence, they had limited incentives to continue the trade relationship on the prevailing, let alone a higher, level. Paradoxically, this imbalance in the mutual stakes of the trade relationship is one of the main strengths of the oil exporters, allowing them to co-operate effectively as a group. This co-operation, in turn, is the basis of their market control and their influence over prices. Higher prices, however, further reduce the incentive to maintain prevailing production levels.

The Loss of Control

So far we have been dealing with imbalances inherent in the trade structure itself. But, to arrive at a more complete picture of the problem, we must consider other aspects of the producer-consumer relationship as well. Though the imbalance of the trade structure was considerably aggravated after about 1970, it can be argued that it existed long before. In the past, the asymmetries in the consumer-producer relationship enabled the consumer countries to control the behavior of the producer states. This control had rested on two pillars: the major international oil companies and Western (first British, then predominantly American) influence in the Middle East oil-producing countries. These allowed the consumers to bring the producers into a world economy working in favor of the industrialized countries (and their oil companies). However, control was gradually eroded by political factors inside and outside the area—most importantly the ascendancy of Arab nationalism and a growing Soviet influence challenging the West. Further, in Arab eyes, the West was compromised by its imperialist heritage and its support for Israel. While oil producers asserted their independence and sovereignty and displayed greater confidence in voicing their grievances and demands, not only were the Western consumers simultaneously becoming increasingly dependent on these countries, they also continued to be politically involved in the Middle East area (e.g., through American support for Israel).

The situation made them vulnerable and exposed them to political demands by the oil producers. By 1970 the erosion of consumer bargaining power and the increase in the strength of the producers were well advanced, and the producers needed only to be aware of the full range of their new power. This constitutes another fundamental difference between 1967 and

264

1973; in 1973 the Arab producers were not only fully aware of their dramatically increased strength but were willing and able to use it.

The catalyst was the revolutionary élan of a new regime in Libya, which wanted to establish its nationalist and progressive credentials by taking the lead in the struggle against Western imperialist influence in the Middle East. In 1970 it put pressure on the oil companies and, in doing so, clearly demonstrated the fundamental shift in bargaining power from the oil companies (which acted for the consumers as well as in their own interests) to the producers. By 1970 Libyan production had been raised to 3.3 million b/d to compensate for the closure of the Suez Canal in 1967, for the production lost as a result of the Nigerian civil war of 1967–70, and for the prolonged interruption of the supply of Saudi oil along the Trans-Arabian pipeline (sabotaged by guerillas in Syria in May 1970). Europe's increased dependence on Libyan oil (25%) was skillfully exploited: one after the other, companies were forced to accept a large price increase and a revised tax structure. This demonstration of oil power led to a series of negotiations for improved terms for producer countries in the Mediterranean and the Gulf, which came to a short-lived standstill with agreements between the oil companies and the producers reached in Teheran and Tripoli in early 1971.

Higher prices suited the oil companies, which wanted to diversify their supply sources by developing reserves in Alaska and the North Sea and unconventional sources of oil, such as tar sands. All these alternatives implied high investment outlays (which had to be financed partly through profits) and higher production costs. But, since higher prices further reduced the incentive for the oil-rich low absorbers to sustain and increase prevailing production levels, the position of the producers was strengthed even more. However, securing higher prices was not the producers' only strategy. Efforts to gain increased producer participation in, and ultimately total control over, oil production in their own countries dominated the year 1972. This, together with concern about conservation led to the introduction of production ceilings in Kuwait and Libya and may have met certain long- and short-term producer interests. But, they certainly also worked as power-increasing strategies which strengthened producer control, increased the squeeze on the international oil market, and made any threat involving supply interruptions much more credible than before.

Application of the Oil Weapon

The *intention* to apply the oil weapon in the Israeli-Arab context had long figured prominently in Arab thinking, and President Nasser had proclaimed oil as one of the three components of Arab power.[9] The closer the linkage between the Arab-Israeli conflict and Persian Gulf politics became (and the alignment between Saudi Arabia and Egypt had finally established such a close connection), the greater the temptation to trade stable and sufficient oil supplies against a change in the United States' Middle East policy. The general mood in the Arab world was definitely moving in this direction, and a clear sign of how far it had progressed came when the Saudi oil minister, Sheikh Yamani, declared on a visit to the United States that his country was prepared to supply the quantity of crude oil needed only if the United States created the right political atmosphere.[10] This clear warning, and subsequent confirmations by King Faisal himself, showed that a growing willingness to use economic pressure to force a change in the American attitude to the Israeli-Arab conflict had pervaded the decision-making level of a country considered one of America's staunchest allies, and whose king, less than a year earlier, had still advocated a policy of "oil and politics don't mix." On October 17, 1973 the OAPEC conference in Kuwait (with the exception of Iraq which followed its own policy) decided to cut production by a minimum of 5% of the September production levels, and each month thereafter 5% of the previous month's output.

The agreement was followed by immediate cuts of 10% by Saudi Arabia and Qatar and 5% by Libya, together with an embargo on oil exports to the United States by Libya and Abu Dhabi. Then, on October 19, President Nixon asked Congress to agree to a $2.2 billion military aid program for Israel. Saudi Arabia reacted by placing an embargo on all exports to the United States. This was eventually applied by all other Arab producers and was extended to cover other countries, primarily the Netherlands (a move which, whether intentionally or not, aimed at the heart of the European oil distribution system: the port of Rotterdam). Egypt, Syria, and Tunisia did not announce any cuts, while Iraq embargoed supplies to the United States and the Netherlands but otherwise tried to restore her output, which had been affected by war damage at the Mediterranean oil terminals in Syria. Iraq dissociated herself from the oil weapon as designed by Saudi Arabia and followed her own line, nationalizing American and Dutch oil interests and urging other producers to break diplomatic and economic relations with the United States and withdraw funds invested there.

On November 4 the Arab oil ministers (again with the exception of Iraq) decided to standardize the level of production; on December 24 production was increased to 85% of the September figure. The OAPEC embargo on the United States was lifted on March 18, 1974—though Syria and Libya dissociated themselves—and Saudi Arabia subsequently increased her production considerably. The embargo against the Netherlands was finally lifted on July 10, the decision having been delayed by a reluctant Saudi Arabia.

Effectiveness of the Oil Weapon

The objective behind the Arab oil producers' decision of October 17 and subsequent measures was to use economic pressure to change the con-

266

sumer states' political attitude to the Israeli-Arab conflict. The system of measures and rules was carefully designed to provide maximum flexibility by means of a range of sanctions and rewards. The United States was, of course, the main target, and the Arab producers expected her to bring pressure to bear on Israel in order to achieve their objectives (return of all territories occupied in the 1967 war, including Jerusalem, and restoration of the legitimate rights of the Palestinians). In theory, the general cutbacks in production were necessary only to prevent circumvention of the embargo (even if most-favored countries had received supplies on the pre-war level, this still would hardly have been sufficient to meet their growing demands). In other words, solidarity was to be made painful for consumers, who found themselves with, at best, the bare minimum of necessary oil supplies, and who could hardly afford to re-export any of them. In addition, Arab oil ministers threatened further sanctions against any country displaying solidarity with an embargoed country.

This system, reportedly elaborated by a group of Arab oil experts long before the October war, was meant to create a shortage in the United States, leading to inconvenience for the final consumer and consequent political pressure on the administration to change its Middle East policy. Other Western consumer countries affected by the oil weapon were also expected to exert influence on American policy through their governments.

However, even though the Arab oil producers managed to build up economic pressure, they were not totally successful. The embargo did not work properly for two reasons: first, some Arab oil evidently "leaked" to the United States despite the embargo; and, secondly, by diverting Arab oil away from embargoed ports and replacing it with non-Arab oil, oil companies managed the international oil distribution system in such a way as to spread the damage fairly evenly. In the case of the United States, total imports of crude and products fell from about 6.6 million b/d in November (when the embargo was not yet effective, due to the time-lag involved in transporting the oil) to about 5.1 million b/d in January. They then increased to around 5.5 million b/d—as opposed to a projected import figure for the first quarter of 1974 of 7.8 million b/d. The shortfall against a projected total oil demand for the first quarter of 19.7 million b/d was thus somewhere between 11 and 14%, not the 17% predicted by the President.[11] Arab oil still reached the United States, though on a small scale. Saudi Arabian imports of 18 million barrels in November amounted to only 7 million in December, while in January the figure was down to 957,000 barrels and in February to 552,000.[12] Libyan oil also leaked through the embargo.

The case of the Netherlands was somewhat similar; there, the embargo caused a serious problem only for a short period in December. A good indicator for the Netherlands is re-exports from Rotterdam's refining

Table 2

Industrial Sector Requirements as % of Total Oil Requirements (1974)
United States, Japan, and Western Europe

	Industry (incl. non-energy use)	Other
United States	16.3	83.7
Japan	38.2	61.8
OECD Europe	33.4	66.6

Source: OECD.

center, which fell to 39% of their normal level in the first half of December but recovered to 90% in January—the embargo had become "almost irrelevant," as the *Petroleum Economist* said, due to the flexibility of the international distribution system. Comparison of the Dutch oil deficit during the last quarter of 1973 with that of other EEC countries and the United States shows that the shortfall was indeed spread fairly evenly, and definitely not in accordance with Arab categorizations of friendly, neutral, and hostile. Deficits ranged from 9% (Netherlands) to 25% (Denmark), with the United States, Germany, France, and Italy in the 11–14% range.[13]

Approximately equal import deficits do not, however, imply equal damage to the economies concerned. Not only was the shortfall for the embargoed United States no higher than those of other, neutral or even friendly, countries, the United States also was in a favorable position because of her consumption patterns.

First of all, her high per capita energy consumption indicates a large saving potential. Secondly, the proportionate dependence of the various consumption sectors differed markedly from that of the other industrialized consumers in Europe and Japan. Since there is considerable flexibility in overall energy consumption (with the possibility of one form of energy being substituted for another), energy savings can normally be translated into oil savings, most conveniently and least harmfully in the transport and the commercial/residential sectors. Tables 2 and 3 show the United States' favorable position in this respect and hence in respect to interruptions in oil supply.

Let us now attempt to assess how the economic pressure exerted on Western consumer countries (despite the apparent partial failure of the embargoes) was translated into political influence. Clearly, the attitudes of Western Europe, Japan, and the United States towards the Israeli-Arab conflict have changed significantly since October 1973. However, it seems misleading to attribute these changes solely to the impact of the oil weapon. The most important of them was, of course, the shift in the United States'

Table 3
Consumers' Energy Saving Capacity and Energy Consumption
as % of Indigenous Production (1971)

Vulner-ability	Countries	Saving capacity indicator[A]	Indigenous oil production as % of consumption	Indigenous energy production as % of consumption
High	Japan, Italy, Belgium, France	0.6–0.8	0–6.0	11.0–22.0
Medium	Britain, Netherlands, West Germany	0.9–1.1	2.0–7.0	51.0–64.0
Low	USA, Canada	1.1–1.4	74.0–98.0	89.0–110.0

[A] The saving capacity indicator calculated by OECD compares the abilities of consumer countries to absorb reductions in oil supplies. These vary according to the different consumption structures.
Source: OECD *Observer*, December 1973, p. 35.

Middle East policy—but Washington had some very good reasons to put pressure on Israel to achieve some progress towards a Middle East settlement, quite apart from the pressure stemming from Arab oil embargoes and cutbacks. First, the Middle East was, and still is, a potential source of superpower conflict (as the events in October 1973 demostrated) and hence a danger to her détente policy. Secondly, American success in bringing Israel to terms with her Arab neighbors' demands and achieving a stable settlement (or even a serious attempt to do so) would no doubt greatly enhance Washington's position in the Middle East, since support for Israel constitutes its most important handicap in the Arab World.[14]

On November 6, the foreign ministers of the EEC agreed on a resolution which also marked a new approach to the Israeli-Arab conflict. The resolution called for Israel to withdraw to the lines she held at the time of the first ceasefire of October 22 (Egypt by that time wanted withdrawal to the same line) and full implementation of U.N. Security Council Resolution 242 in an interpretation which did not differ from the Egyptian one. The inadmissibility of the acquisition of territory by force was set out as one of the principles of the envisaged settlement, and Israel was urged to end the occupation of the areas she had conquered in 1967. The resolution further called for respect for the territorial integrity, sovereignty, and independence of all states in the area and their right to live in peace within secure and recognized boundaries. It also stated that any full and lasting agreement would have to take into account the legitimate rights of the Palestinians.

269

This resolution was widely seen as favorable to the Arabs and provoked bitter criticism in Israel. But, again, it seems an over-simplification to ascribe its content solely to the effectiveness of the oil weapon. Rather, it can be argued that it constituted a new step towards the gradual development of a common Middle East position by the European Community and reflected a slow but clear shift by the British and even West German governments from a pro-Israeli to a more neutral stand. Of course, this shift took into account the Community's high dependence on Arab oil, but the use of the oil weapon speeded up and crystallized the EEC position, rather than fundamentally changing it.[15]

Japan was the most vulnerable of all industrialized consumer countries, and the shortfall in oil supplies seemed to affect economic production fairly directly and seriously. At the beginning of December, the Ministry of International Trade and Industry (MITI) calculated the reduction in oil supplies at 16% and predicted the following consequences: steel production would be down by 8–11% and aluminium by 14%. Furthermore, MITI foresaw a considerable additional push in inflation caused by higher oil prices and shortages.[16] As a result, Japan's modification of her Middle East policy was most marked, even though she finally managed to achieve most-favored nation status without actually breaking diplomatic relations with Israel. All the same, she had to give up her low-profile, business-first foreign policy, which had achieved neutrality towards the Middle East conflict mainly by being vague. As one official put it, "our interpretation of the U.N. resolution 242 has been ambiguous in the past and we are simply modifying it."[17] The modifications included an appeal to Israel to return to the May 1967 borders and negotiate a security agreement with the Arab states. Japan also adopted the principle that no territorial gains by military force should be permitted, and the government further explained that it would interpret Security Council Resolution 242 in accordance with the Arab attitude. The Minister of International Trade and Industry, Mr. Nakasone, explicitly stated that Japan no longer agreed with the principles of the United States' Middle East policy.

An effect of the oil weapon over and above shifting the policies of consumer governments towards the Israeli-Arab conflict was to produce splits and tensions in the Western alliance and within the EEC. These tensions reflected basic interest differences among consumer countries and also, it seems, some mismanagement in dealing with them.

First of all, the differences concerned actual dependence on Arab oil. As pointed out earlier, the United States found herself in a much better position than both Europe and Japan; but even within Western Europe there were marked differences in dependence and vulnerability (see Table 3).

Another fundamental difference involved diverging energy policies. Again, it was France which found herself in a markedly different position from her partners. First, her energy policy had been marked for a long time by the search for stable oil supplies, independent from the "majors." This had led to the creation of government-owned or at least government-influenced French oil companies which sometimes competed strongly with the majors and to a large amount of state intervention in energy and oil policies. Secondly, her energy policy since de Gaulle had developed a strong pro-Arab tendency, since it was to the Arab world that France looked for her stable and independent oil supplies. Great Britain and the Netherlands, on the other hand, were both homes of major international oil companies, and therefore, refused any kind of interventionist government policy—even more so on a Community level. West Germany, Belgium, and Italy fell somewhere between these two poles, the first two leaning towards a liberal policy, the last, through her state company (ENI), following a line similar to France but allowing the international oil companies a greater role.

But the core of the disagreement in the Western alliance and the European Community was the issue of security. During the Israeli-Arab war, the United States pursued a policy which took account of American concern for the global balance vis-à-vis the Soviet Union and aimed to prevent any shift in Moscow's favor. The European countries, however, were primarily concerned about their oil supplies and were not prepared to see their economic security put at risk. Apart from Portugal, which allowed the United States to use an air base in the Azores for her airlift to Israel, European governments preferred to take a neutral attitude and to appease the Arabs. Britain declared an embargo on deliveries of arms and spares to all combatant states; this hurt the Israelis more than the Arabs. West Germany protested (after the war was over) against the use of her ports for the transfer of American war material from Germany to Israel. Secretary of Defense Schlesinger's veiled threat that the United States might reconsider her military presence in Germany demonstrated, however, that Germany faced a dilemma: she did not want to antagonize either the Americans or the Arabs.

Within the European Community a basically nationalistic approach prevailed. The problem here was the embargo against the Netherlands. While the Dutch urged the other member countries to show solidarity and arrive at some form of oil-sharing, France and Britain, anxious not to lose their status as friendly countries in Arab eyes, opposed such a move. (Actually, the EEC had no contingency plans for sharing oil, since this had been left to the OECD; the OECD oil committee, reportedly under French and British influence, decided not to put its oil-sharing system into action.) Though this did little economic damage (since the oil was shared more or less equally by the companies), the political damage to the idea of European solidarity was considerable: the EEC had to face the hard truth that national interests still had priority over European solidarity.

The oil weapon created a situation where the consumer nations had to react; it was no longer possible to gloss over the differences within the Western alliance and the European Community. As problems of oil supply became interwoven with other issues (the essence and character of American-European relations, the size of the Community's Regional Fund), they became increasingly complex and difficult to resolve. This makes it unlikely that the splits and tensions within the West were foreseen and deliberately exploited by the Arab oil producers; it also appears questionable whether they actually served Arab interests. These tensions may have provided an extra incentive for the United States to settle the oil crisis by working for an Israeli-Arab settlement, and the use of the oil weapon did spur the EEC into adopting a united attitude towards the Middle East conflict. Nonetheless, despite any independent and active role which the Arab producers may have expected Europe to play in the process of reaching a settlement, a solution to the conflict still had to be found within the context of super-power bipolarity.

In sum, it is certainly true that the use of the oil weapon caused a change in the Middle East policies of the main consumer countries, but this change did not constitute a total reversal of previous policies and stopped well short of full acceptance of Arab objectives. The fact that the oil weapon was sheathed before any of the stated Arab objectives had been achieved underlines that its success was not unqualified.

Oil Power: Potential and Limitations in the Future

Thus far we have been concerned primarily with the supply crisis of 1973–74. The scope of the analysis will now be expanded to take into account some "guesstimates" about the development of oil power until 1985—a period for which we possess at least some guidelines, derived from the last crisis, the present situation, and factors which will evidently play a significant role over the coming period.

If we want to speculate about the future importance of the oil weapon in international relations, we must first attempt to assess the future development of oil power in terms of the degree of balance or imbalance in the trade relationship between producers and consumers. Have we already reached the peak of oil power, or is it to grow further?

Development of Oil Power

The strength of oil power depends on the development of the oil import gap of major industrialized countries, which in turn depends on assumptions about supply- and demand-price elasticities (i.e., the responsiveness of changes in quantities supplied or demanded to price changes) and any orchestrated measures taken towards consumer self-sufficiency. As to the former, initial assumptions about elasticities appeared to be too optimistic, and although there is at present no clear answer as to the longer-term impact of the higher oil-price level, the economic viability of many alternative sources of energy at present OPEC price levels is still doubtful. Energy policy measures by consumer governments to increase the level of self-sufficiency also have been widely insufficient—most blatantly so in the case of the United States, whose import volumes play a crucial role in determining the future of the international oil market. Recent forecasts, therefore, tend to be pessimistic as to the possibilities of reducing dependence on OPEC oil, as one representative set of estimates presented in Table 4 shows.

On the demand side, these estimates show a total oil import requirement for the OECD area of 27.3 million b/d in 1980, and from 24.1 to 37.8 million b/d in 1985, depending on various assumptions. World import requirements are estimated at 31.3 million b/d in 1980, and 27.7 to 42.9 million b/d in 1985.

Let us now contrast these demand estimates with the production potential of the OPEC countries. In the past, they have shown a desire to maximize their production in order to fuel their ambitious development programs and overcome their state of underdevelopment. Present and future production potential of these producers are listed in Table 5.

A comparison of Tables 4 and 5 shows that the gap to be filled by producers other than those considered as production maximizers will be at least 8 million b/d in 1980, and—assuming a production capacity of 25 million b/d for the high absorbers in 1985—between 2.7 and 17 million b/d for this year. Theoretically, the gap would have to be filled by Libya, Kuwait, Saudi Arabia, the United Arab Emirates, and Qatar.

These figures essentially point towards two different scenarios: one of a relatively tight, contracted market, the other of a further market expansion and substantial additional requirements from OPEC. Conceivably, the first scenario could bring some pressure to bear on OPEC and break the organization apart. Such a development, however, seems unlikely; the producers have a vested interest in high prices and a tight supply/demand balance and are likely to resort to some measure of market control, if the strain on OPEC's production capacity and reserves alone will not lead to such a tight market situation. Furthermore, the assumption that the high absorbers will continue to keep actual output near to the ceiling of production potential neglects the possibility that—given successful industrialization—increased non-oil exports and the replacement of imports by home-produced goods

273

Table 4
Estimated Oil Demand and Import Requirements, 1980 and 1985

	Oil Demand (mill. b/d)				Oil Import Requirements (mill. b/d)				
	1974 actual	1980 (1)	1985 (2)	(3)	(4)	1974 actual	1980 (1)	1985 (2)	(3)	(4)
USA	15.9	18.8	21.4	18.7	23.8	5.9	7.8	8.6	4.3	10.9
EEC	11.1	11.3	12.8	11.8	13.7	11.3	9.0	9.5	8.5	10.4
OECD Pacific (mainly Japan)	5.8	7.9	10.2	9.6	12.1	5.5	7.5	9.8	9.0	11.7
Other non-socialist	37.2	43.7	51.6	46.6	57.3	25.1	27.3	32.1	24.1	37.8
Grand Total	44.2	53.6	63.8	58.8	71.0	28.9	31.3	35.7	27.7	42.9

Assumptions: (1) OECD annual growth rate 4.3% 1974–1980, no extra conservation
(2) OECD annual growth rate 4% 1980–1985, no extra conservation
(3) OECD annual growth rate 4% 1980–1985, conservation program AND accelerated investment in alternative fuels
(4) OECD annual growth rate 4.5% 1980–1985, no extra conservation

Source: IEA.

might reduce reliance on oil for export earnings. Iran, Algeria, Venezuela and, possibly, Iraq might well be capable of achieving such an industrial base in the foreseeable future. The two scenarios both point towards a continued high level of dependence on OPEC supplies, and, therefore, to the perseverance of oil power. Barring the unlikely case of a break-up of OPEC, the difference between the two cases really lies in the relative difference in Saudi Arabia's power. With a fairly tight market and stable or reduced dependence on imports by the industrialized consumers, it will be OPEC, or some key producers in OPEC, as a group which will hold considerable power. In the expanding market scenario Saudi Arabia's position will become of paramount importance, since only this country has sufficient reserves to bridge the gap between demand and supply effectively.

On the consumer side, the developments in the first years after the supply crisis are hardly encouraging. The fall in oil consumption appeared to be almost entirely due to the world-wide recession, and, because of the threat to employment, no energetic and lasting conservation efforts were undertaken. Disillusionment with certain alternative sources of energy (such as nuclear energy and shale oil) for environmental reasons and because of their uncertain profitability prospects, also raised doubts about whether dependence on Middle East oil could be significantly reduced within the next ten years. Certainly, it will be some years before efforts by

Table 5
High Absorbers—Present and Potential Output (mill. b/d)

	1975 (actual)	1980 (estimated)
Venezuela	2.4	3.4
Indonesia	1.3	2.0
Algeria	1.0	1.1
Nigeria	1.8	2.8
Iraq	2.2	4.0
Iran	2.2	4.0
Others	1.5	2.0
Total	15.6	23.3

Sources: BP *Statistical Review of the World Oil Industry*, 1975; OECD, *Energy Prospects to 1985*, Vol. II, Paris, 1975, p. 113.

international oil companies and consumer governments to develop alternative sources of supply so as to change the economic framework of producer power show their impact.

The Problem of Precision: The International Distribution System

The supply crisis of 1973–74 not only revealed the strength of the oil weapon but also exposed some of its weaknesses. Arguably, the most important of these weaknesses is the lack of precision. The producers' handling of the oil weapon and the rules and regulations that accompanied its use confirm that they aimed at discrimination among the various consumer countries. However, the flexibility of the international oil market (which in terms of distribution, transport, and processing is still by and large controlled by the international oil companies[18]) prevailed over attempts to direct the oil weapon against only certain consumers. The very core of the discriminatory strategy, the embargo, failed—a fact which even the producers themselves admitted—so that the only effective sanction the Arab producers possessed was the general cutback in production.

The flexibility of the international distribution system has two main aspects: the tanker (and pipeline) system and the refineries. The question of whether the flexibility of the international oil market can be upheld in these two areas is of paramount importance for the future of the oil weapon in international relations. If the producers succeeded in destroying this flexibility, they would be able to discriminate against a single consumer and therefore apply considerably stronger pressure. The oil weapon would gain

275

immensely in applicability and could be used for a much wider range of objectives.

The Threat of Precision: Bilateral Arrangements and Power-increasing Strategies

In the aftermath of the October 1973 to March 1974 supply crisis there was a rush by consumer governments to conclude bilateral deals with producers so as to secure oil supplies. For some time this posed the real threat of a fundamental change in the international oil market towards strong dependence by single consumers on particular producers. This possibility now appears remote, not least because of a certain reluctance on the part of producers such as Saudi Arabia to enter into agreements of this kind. To be sure, there were quite a number of bilateral deals, but they concentrated on assistance by industrialized countries with producer countries' economic development problems, which opened up possibilities for the consumers to offset part of their balance of payments deficits by increased exports. There is no evidence of the widespread inclusion of supply guarantees in such deals, even though the hope of achieving security of supplies was clearly among the consumers' motives for concluding them.

This (limited) form of bilateralism, however, soon was found to be insufficient to cope with key problems resulting from the developments in 1973 and 1974. It was argued repeatedly and convincingly that a strictly nationalistic economic approach to solving consumer countries' problems would have led to a scramble for markets and competition for the oil producers' revenue surplus. The result would have been increased conflict between consumer countries; the strongest powers would prevail, while the weakest would have found their problems exacerbated. Although to some extent the burden was passed on to the weaker consumers, and in particular, to the non-oil exporting developing countries (which could not increase their exports to pay the higher oil bills, could not hope to attract a large capital inflow from oil producers—except in some special cases—and on top of this had to face inflationary price increases on their other imports, as well), international measures of cooperation did prevent serious damage. The international financial markets, which overall managed to cope quite well with the additional huge quantities of capital, were assisted by specific measures providing for the recycling of oil revenues towards the hardest hit countries (OPEC loans and grants, IMF oil facility, World Bank loans), and by other arrangements such as the $25 billion "safety net" to underpin the orderly flow of oil revenues towards the industrialized consumers with large balance of payment deficits (the safety net fund has, however, not yet been ratified by all OECD members), and bilateral government-to-government loans.

Another area of international cooperation became the security aspect

276

of oil supplies exposed by the 1973–74 embargoes and cutbacks. Here, sixteen industrialized countries agreed on an elaborate emergency supply-sharing scheme enacted within the framework of the International Energy Agency—a scheme essentially providing some degree of deterrence against a further application of the oil weapon by obliging the member countries of the IEA to come to the support of any embargoed member. Finally, international cooperation managed to move beyond a bare producer-consumer confrontation towards some first discussions between the two groups within the framework of the Conference on International Economic Cooperation in Paris.

Bilateralism is, therefore, already a danger avoided. The adoption of a deliberate power-increasing producer strategy for purely political considerations, however, could still pose a serious threat. Such a strategy could be followed in three ways: the producers could try to increase the dependence of consumer countries on energy under their control; they could attempt to destroy the flexibility of the distribution system by building up a large share in it; or they could simply strengthen their hold on the international oil companies (e.g., by building up large shareholdings).

At this writing, there are few signs of such developments, but if they did come about they would clearly lead to a dangerous level of permanent confrontation between producer and consumer countries and/or detrimental economic implications for the producers themselves. For instance, to achieve higher dependence on oil the price would have to be lowered considerably, and even then memories of the last supply crisis would prevent consumers from again relying heavily on imported oil. The producers could also expand their control over energy sources by investing in coal, nuclear energy, and conventional and unconventional oil sources outside their area, thereby gaining a substantial foothold in the world energy industries. This might be desirable for economic reasons, but it would hardly contribute to the producers' political power (which stems from the ability to interrupt supplies), since these investments would be outside their effective control and, because the threat of nationalization works both ways, might even serve as hostages in a future supply crisis. Economically, both producers and consumers could gain from such investments, but a necessary precondition would be to develop safeguards against their political use in any form (though most investments made initially for economic reasons would probably take a different form from those made for purely political, power-increasing purposes).

The same holds true for downstream investment by the producers. Expansion of their activities into the tanker and refinery business, and ultimately also into the consumer distribution networks, can be expected for sound economic reasons—indeed, for the same reasons which turned the international oil companies into integrated enterprises. However, investments aiming at increased political power, so as to enable the oil weapon to be used in a discriminatory manner, would again take a different form. In essence, the problem appears to be one of thresholds: controlling 5% of the world tanker fleet might not be politically dangerous but controlling 20% would be.

The oil producers certainly have the potential to acquire a politically dangerous share in the world tanker fleet. Several producers already possess tankers[19] and have ordered a considerable number of new carriers.[20] After the delivery of present orders (which will take until 1979), Kuwait and Iraq, with approximately 2 million and 1.5 million deadweight tons (dwt) respectively, will own the largest fleets among the Arab countries, while Iran has stated her intention to build up a fleet totalling 1 million dwt.[21] With the foundation of the Arab Maritime Petroleum Transport Company (a suborganization of OAPEC) and its plan to spend $2,000 million over the next five years on tankers, product carriers, and liquefied natural gas (LNG) carriers, and with the further expansion by other producers which can be expected, the combined Arab fleet might amount to some 20 million dwt in the early 1980s. For the journey from the Persian Gulf via the Cape route, the amount of oil which by then could be transported annually in producer-owned tankers would be about 100 million tons. However, compared with a world tanker fleet of 246 million dwt (including combined carriers) in 1974 and 221 million dwt on order,[22] these figures for new-built Arab tanker capacity are not important enough to pose a real threat to the flexibility of the international distribution system.

The tanker market is a purely competitive business, and although limited shipbuilding capacity may prevent the oil producers from gaining sufficient control by ordering new tankers, the present large tanker surplus could enable them to buy a large second-hand fleet. In a time of tanker surplus, private owners might not be assured of full employment of their tankers and could in any case only expect a low return, but producer governments could probably force employment of their fleets to transport their oil.[23] Costs would be no serious obstacle: if tanker capacity costs $150 per dwt, a fleet of, say, 50 million tons (about one-fifth of the present world tanker fleet) would cost $7.5 billion—a sum definitely within the reach of the oil producers.[24] Another possibility is that they could charter a substantial tanker capacity. This could hardly be done at very short notice, since the capacity available within days is minute, but every year about 14% of the world tanker fleet enters the charter market.[25] In either case, however, the consumer governments would receive clear warning signals well in advance.

Another way for the oil producers to increase their power would be to attempt to gain control over the international oil companies. They could try to acquire large shareholdings or, in any future application of the oil weapon, simply attempt to force the companies to stop *all* deliveries to an embargoed country—not only deliveries of the producers' own oil. The first possibility poses the same kind of problems for the producers as all investments outside their direct territorial control; the second depends on the leverage they possess vis-à-vis the companies. This leverage rests on the investments and assets of the companies in the producer countries (they pay lower oil prices than customers without production facilities there). Leverage on both counts has been gradually weakened through participation or nationalization, and, since the producers started to assert themselves and free themselves from the hegemony the companies had long exerted over these countries and their oil industry, the relationship between producers and companies has been moving towards coexistence based on mutual interests: the companies fulfill certain important functions for the producers, which for the time being, they cannot do without.

However, there must be doubts whether in any future supply crisis the oil companies will be as well placed as they were in 1973 to manage the international distribution system efficiently and share out available supplies. Apart from the possibility of stronger producer interference, there also is the question of consumer government involvement: the companies have been heavily criticized for their management in the last crisis.

The emergency program of the International Energy Agency[26] might help the companies to destroy the flexibility of the oil weapon by once more allocating available oil supplies fairly, since it provides them with the necessary governmental approval. Moreover, it would (if effective) provide another barrier to discriminatory application of the oil weapon, since the scheme obliges every member to maintain an emergency oil reserve of 60 (later 90) days consumption and to have contingency plans for reducing oil consumption. If one or more member countries suffer a reduction in supplies of 7% or more, or can be expected to experience such a shortfall, the affected countries will have to activate measures to save 7% of oil consumption. If the shortfall exceeds 12% of demand, a 10% saving will be required—the rest being made up by other members. If this cannot be done, the available oil will be shared among member countries.

The scheme therefore provides an institutionalized device to prevent discriminatory application of the oil weapon against a single member of the IEA. Whether it stands the test of application or could be circumvented or invalidated by the producers remains to be seen. It is certainly true that the scheme depends on the oil companies' control over the international distribution system, since the companies will be in charge of allocation management. Sufficient producer control over the international tanker fleet would therefore most likely invalidate the scheme, or at least require additional measures.

The Ceiling of the Oil Weapon: World Economic Crisis and Fundamental Political Change

If we assume that the future international oil market will retain its present flexibility and that discrimination will be impossible, the damage caused by supply interruptions will be distributed more or less evenly, and it will be the most vulnerable consumers which suffer most.

In the last supply crisis, the most vulnerable consumers were Japan and those developing countries with either little or no indigenous energy resources and heavy dependence on imported oil; next in vulnerability came some of the European consumers. The producers faced a choice of either taking into consideration the impact of the oil weapon on the weaker consumers or else pressing ahead in order to exert pressure on the main target, i.e., the United States. If in the future the producers take into account the situation of the weaker consumers, this sets a fairly low ceiling for overall cutbacks, and it looks as if the oil weapon's lack of discriminatory capability actually gives any target a whole group of hostages—consumer countries weaker than itself. In applying the oil weapon, therefore, the producers not only risk political alienation of non-target countries but also turmoil and unpredictable developments in and around those countries. Once a major industrialized country was caught in a serious economic crisis triggered by shortage of oil supplies, a chain reaction throughout the world economy would probably be inevitable, the consequences of which would be unpredictable, uncontrollable, and might backfire on the producers themselves. Economic crises in the consumer countries would lead to social tensions and political unrest, and dramatic changes could not be ruled out. New radical governments, in the face of tremendous domestic pressure, might decide to try solving the supply crisis by military force—desperate and irrational as such a move might be.

But the producers operate not only within the context of a rather sensitive world economy but also in an international political system, and they have to consider the impact of the oil weapon on this—and especially on the super-power balance. The conservative Arab oil producers cannot be interested in weakening the Western alliance and more precisely the position of the United States, either on a global or a regional level. In the last crisis the United States was clearly given carrot and stick treatment; not only was she subjected to an embargo, she was also invited to play a more prominent role in the Middle East. In future, if a producer thinks an alignment with the United States desirable, the producer will probably not press too hard and will rely on rewards as well as sanctions, since in the long run, an alignment has to be based on mutuality of interest and predictable behavior by both sides. If the United States were antagonized, she would try to reduce her dependence on the producers as quickly as possible and would

280

look for other allies to pursue her interests; these allies might be found within the producer society (perhaps an opposition group which could be helped to power) or in the area. So long as rational behavior prevails among producer governments, consideration for the regional and global political context, as well as for the functioning of the world economic system, sets a limit to the pressure which could be exerted through the oil weapon.

However, even within the limits of this pressure, the built-in time-lag of the oil weapon appears to constitute another problem for the producers. There is a lag in the transport system which means that tankers loaded before the decision to interrupt supplies will still be arriving in the consumer countries for some weeks afterwards—the exact time depending on the distance to the destination. This lag might be increased by the consumer countries' use of stocks and stand-by capacity, possibly within the framework of the IEA. All this means that the oil weapon is a somewhat awkward instrument of political coercion, with a tendency to draw out a crisis situation. On the one hand, this gives decision-makers time, reducing the psychological pressures of an acute crisis and consequently also some of the dangers of irrational behavior. On the other hand, the time-lag inherent in supply interruptions might devalue the oil weapon in certain crises and could be used by consumers to decide on counter-measures or to try to respond in other areas: e.g., by threatening the producer's allies or shifting support to regional rivals.

It appears, then, that the political and economic effects of using the oil weapon cannot be separated; indeed, its power is derived from the economic damage it can inflict. But the economic consequences of a serious supply interruption stretched over years are hardly controllable by the producers. Oil supply shortages cause fertilizer shortages, which, in turn, affect the grain harvests months after the oil weapon has been sheathed. Higher oil prices speed up inflation and trigger a wage-price spiral. Insofar as the oil weapon aims at the basic functions of a society, the decision to apply it resembles the decision to go to war: once it is made, the exact course of events and their consequences might get out of control. This does not exclude the possibility of a further application of the oil weapon, but it does mean that it is not going to be an instrument frequently used for exerting political pressure. The implication also might be that the producers will look for new ways and means to use their oil power.

The Impact of Applying the Oil Weapon

What has been the impact of the first successful application of the oil weapon? Will it enhance or reduce its power? There is some contradiction in the answers to these questions. Certainly, the future application of the oil weapon has now become more credible, since the Arab producers have actually shown the will to use it. On the other hand, it is to be hoped that the consumers will have learned from the 1973–74 crisis; the political risks of relying heavily on energy imported from producers who have little economic incentive to continue the prevailing level of production and who could easily afford to reduce it or even halt it for some time has now become obvious. This awareness should trigger a whole series of processes aimed at reducing this insecurity. As far as increasing self-sufficiency goes, little seems to have happened in that respect so far. Equally, no cohesive attempt has yet been made to explore the willingness of the producers to stabilize production levels in exchange for certain other concessions, say, within the framework of a commodity agreement, or some other producer-consumer compact. But, sooner or later the consumers will be forced to address this long-term imbalance of supply and demand—an imbalance ultimately stemming from the imposition of insatiable consumer demand for oil on the finite oil reserves of a few developing countries with small populations.

While it is far from clear that the consumers have already learned to address the underlying cause of the 1973–74 crisis, some lessons should have been derived as to how to reduce the impact of the oil weapon in the shorter run. The 1973–74 crisis demonstrated that the shortfall of oil which can be absorbed without serious consequences is higher than expected, and that, as long as industrial production and vital transport functions can be upheld, the immediate effect of the oil weapon is limited. By preparing emergency allocation plans, increasing the flexibility of the internal distribution and refining systems, and by coordinating consumer policies, the impact of any future oil shortage could be reduced. Such preparation might, however, be offset by the producers during the period between now and any future use of the oil weapon, due to attempts to reduce the impact of higher oil prices. Reductions in non-essential oil use and deliberate measures and contingency plans to improve the capacity to absorb shortages might have a roughly balancing effect. But, even so, the psychological climate has changed: consumer governments should now be less inclined to panic and resort to *sauve qui peut* policies. While in 1973 no government seemed to know exactly what the oil embargoes and cutbacks really meant for them, the oil weapon and its impact should now be a known quantity. Moreover, the IEA emergency allocation scheme should now provide some measure of economic security for its members. The details of the scheme indicate that quite substantial supply reductions for the group could be absorbed without dangerous shortfalls in oil supplies to any member. The problematical aspect of the IEA scheme might not be its technicalities, and not even its feasibility, but the political tensions within the group in a prolonged crisis. Since the role of oil in the national energy balances of the members varies greatly, even a fair sharing of available oil supplies would imply substantially different impacts on the total energy supply situation of the IEA members. This differential impact of oil supply shortfalls could eventually induce some IEA members to desert the organization.

The net effect ,is that the producers' freedom to maneuver will become more restricted. In order to bring substantial pressure to bear on consumers, they may have to resort to much higher initial pressure, bringing them dangerously near to the limits at which the oil weapon becomes counter-productive.

Producer Solidarity

The solidarity of Arab oil producers proved their greatest strength in 1973–74, but at the same time the crisis revealed the fragility of this solidarity. Differences of interest, mistrust, and concern about the future balance within the Arab world soon created cracks. Producer solidarity will continue to be an important factor in the success of any future application of the oil weapon—and, indeed, might be the decisive factor.

Arab solidarity must be examined in terms of economics. Some oil producers urgently need every penny of their oil revenue to meet their expenditures and might suffer heavily from a substantial loss of revenues over a long period (though in 1973–74 the producers more than made up for the reduction in output by the increase in prices). This possibility did concern OAPEC states—witness the introduction into the important resolutions of October 17 and November 28 of damage-limiting clauses which set a floor to production cutbacks. Indeed one country—Iraq—refrained from *any* general cutbacks, most likely for fear of just such losses of vital revenue. As a consequence of the prolonged struggle with the Iraq Petroleum Company, Iraq had never experienced the same degree of production expansion as the Gulf States. The leadership—already set on a course of rapid economic growth and fundamental social and economic change—therefore decided to adopt a different policy against the United States and the Netherlands. Nationalizing their oil interests and declaring embargoes against them, Iraq did not have to reduce overall production. Algeria and some of the small Gulf sheikdoms also needed all the oil revenues they could get, and the Algerian Head of State, Houari Boumedienne, actually stressed in an interview with a Lebanese newspaper that his country suffered from the general production restrictions, since it did not possess large foreign exchange reserves.[27] Algeria's position also reveals another difference of economic interest: as Boumedienne pointed out in his interview, the Algerian economy is closely linked with the European area and is bound to suffer from adverse developments there.

The first difference could be overcome by designing a production cutback scheme according to each producer's degree of vulnerability to revenue losses, rather than according to a general margin of production cutbacks for all producers (countries like Saudi Arabia, Kuwait, Abu Dhabi, and

283

Libya would then bear the main burden of reductions). For the second difference, which depends on the amount of integration into and sensitivity to the industrialized economies, there is no simple solution.

Producer solidarity would always have to face the problem of a common political objective. Even Arab hostility to Israel in the last crisis did not produce a really unified position, for a rift within the Arab world and within the producer action group soon became evident. Egypt pressed for a political solution based on compromises and cooperation with the United States, while Libya and Iraq refused any kind of negotiated settlement in advance and protested against the conclusion of a cease-fire. Syria's leadership had decided to fight the war along Egyptian lines but faced constant pressure from more radical groups inside the power elite, especially the army, and the tactical moves necessary for President Assad to retain his position resulted in a Syrian course wavering between negotiation and obstruction. This rift between conservatives and progressives and between moderate and radical attitudes towards the Israeli-Arab conflict was bound to reappear over the question of how and when the oil restrictions were to be eased, if at all.

Political moves also indicated the growing dissension in the Arab oil producer group. Libya tried to bridge the rift between herself and Egypt and press for closer cooperation between the two countries, and it seems likely that this was meant as a move to counter-balance Saudi Arabian influence. The decision to lift the embargo against the United States was repeatedly postponed—allegedly because of opposing views about its desirability among the Arab producers. When the lifting was finally declared on March 17, Libya and Syria did not join the Saudi-Egyptian leadership. Arab disunity was probably fostered by the Soviet Union, whose past success in the Middle East was largely due to the conservative-progressive confrontation and the conflict with Israel, and in a direct attack on Egypt, Moscow warned of any premature relaxation in the economic pressure on the United States. Similarly, the decision to lift the embargo against the Netherlands led to a split in OAPEC with Saudi Arabia, delaying the lifting, and Algeria strongly advocating—and then unilaterally declaring—an end to the embargo.

Summary

So far, our analysis of the oil weapon has been concerned with capabilities. Oil power essentially stems from a fundamental and substantial imbalance in the trade relationship between producers and industrialized consumers. This imbalance is the result of an historical development. The structure of the international oil market in the past was set by the major industrialized countries, and in particular the United States, and their instruments, the major oil companies. It is an imbalance resulting from the discrepancies (and in the future, quite possibly from the incompatibility) between the energy needs of the major industrialized countries at the lowest possible cost and the export revenue requirements of a group of thinly populated countries in the Middle East. This imbalance will be eroded only if and when energy prices rise to a level where effective, large-scale substitution of OPEC oil exports becomes feasible, thereby eliminating reliance on OPEC as the main supplier of world energy requirements, or if new technologies could provide the key to energy abundance at low cost.

This implies that oil power will continue to be a factor in international relations for quite some time to come. It might well be that this power will decline somewhat as North Sea and Alaskan oil temporarily provide for the increment in demand. But, this would not imply a fundamental change in the underlying configuration. On the other hand, a continued expansion of energy demand in the 1980s could well lead to new peaks in oil power.

We already pointed out briefly that oil power can be activated in many different ways. Moreover, for a variety of reasons discussed above, the oil weapon will not be its most common manifestation. Threats involving continuation of oil supplies, hints at linkages between production levels, prices, and producer oil policies in general, on the one hand, and other political and economic issues on the other, the use of oil revenues both as a positive and as a negative sanction—these are the most likely forms of oil power in future international relations. The oil weapon, like military power, provides the ultimate threat and deterrent.

The issue of the various forms and types of the manifestation of oil power brings us to the second crucial set of factors determining the future role of the oil weapon: the producers' *intentions*. The most decisive variable for the credibility and effectiveness of oil power, and in particular the oil weapon, is the degree of cohesion among the producers as a group. It was this solidarity which contributed decisively to the success of the oil weapon in 1973–74; but at the same time our analysis also revealed the limits of this solidarity. In the future, then, the application of the oil weapon as an effective instrument in international relations will be linked to the existence or non-existence of acute crises sufficient to motivate a group of producers to develop a common objective and to use their oil power in its pursuit.

The most likely crisis of this type remains the Israeli-Arab conflict should it erupt again into large-scale hostilities. In this case, the pressures and incentives operating on Arab oil producers would be similar to the ones prevailing in 1973–74, although this might not necessarily imply precisely the same kind of action. A different course of events would only appear likely if one or more of the major factors in the present configuration of the Israeli-Arab conflict (e.g., end of U.S. support for Israel, major reorientation in the Arab World, etc.) would change.

A second (though less likely) scenario would be the application of the oil weapon in the case of open conflict among major states in the Persian

Gulf. Again, this would involve a substantial change in the present situation in the Gulf, but given the volatility of this region, fundamental reorientations and realignments cannot be excluded. In any case, large-scale hostilities in the Gulf would inevitably affect oil supplies to the rest of the world (which, by the way, also appears to be a major constraint on the policies of the Gulf states vis-à-vis each other in the sense of a strong disincentive against adventurism in foreign policy).

Finally, we have to consider the whole complex of North-South issues which have become interwoven with the success of the oil producers. Questions of international attempts to restructure the "world economic order" will, in the future, be tackled not without the permanent presence and the occasional assertion of oil power. It is not inconceivable that the oil weapon might even be used in this connection, although a necessary precondition would presumably be that major producers feel themselves deeply frustrated or threatened in the pursuit of their domestic, economic, and social objectives. Insofar as the international oil market can be considered one of the vital parts of the international economic order, the application of the oil weapon in this connection would actually appear most likely in this market itself over questions of export prices and quantities. Possibly the most worrying problem here would be a refusal by oil producers, faced with constantly rising demands made on their reserves, to increase or even maintain production in line with the requirements of the oil-importing nations.

How vulnerable are the major industrialized consumers to another attempt to use the oil weapon? Clearly, all-out economic warfare is unlikely, because of the limitations of this instrument in international affairs spelled out above, as long as both sides avoid total confrontation. Such rational behavior can be assumed, since both consumers and producers would find their freedom of action restrained by the need to act as a group. Limited oil war, on the other hand, would now find a substantially increased capacity of consumer nations to withstand pressure because of unilateral and multilateral emergency schemes, the most important of which is the one administered by the IEA. To overcome this capacity to resist, producer solidarity would have to be very strong—only prolonged cutbacks of substantial amounts might create sufficient disunity in the IEA to break it. This would mean that the oil producers would operate dangerously close to the ceiling beyond which an oil squeeze would have severe world-wide repercussions. On the other hand, even a successful application of consumer emergency schemes would not prevent major discomforts and economic difficulties, thereby creating incentives to find a political solution.

Ultimately, the crucial aspect of the oil weapon appears to be that it is a measure of last resort. Producers will not easily unsheath it; this, however, should give the consumers the opportunity to prevent its application through flexible policies of meeting producers' demands fully or partially where they appear reasonable, making very clear, at the same time, the boundaries of this flexibility set by principles and policy objectives which are not open to compromise. Given the rationality demonstrated by the oil producers so far, this should not be too difficult a task—with the possible exception of an Israeli-Arab conflict. An equally great danger, however, for another oil squeeze might well lie in the inability of the major consumers, in particular the United States, to deal with their energy problems. For, as we have seen, oil power is, in the last analysis, an external reflection of the major industrialized countries' export of their energy problems.

Footnotes

1. Quoted in Walter Z. Laqueur, *The Struggle for the Middle East: The Soviet Union and the Middle East, 1958–1968* (Harmondsworth: Penguin, 1972), p. 153.
2. A. O. Hirschmann, *National Power and the Structure of Foreign Trade* (Berkeley and Los Angeles: University of California Press, 1945).
3. Cf. OECD Oil Committee, *Oil, the Present Situation and Future Prospects* (Paris, 1973), pp. 21–29. The United States was an exception, however, since she had switched (although generally less impressively) from coal to gas, rather than to oil.
4. This is clearly demonstrated by comparing July 1972 and July 1973 supply patterns. During the intervening year indigenous production fell by 2.4%, while crude oil imports increased by 62.5%, residual fuel imports by 5.5% and other oil product imports by 27.2%, bringing the total import share to 6 million b/d out of a total supply of 17.5 million b/d (*Financial Times*, 14 September 1973). Between July and August 1973 alone, crude oil imports from the Arab states more than doubled, from 625,000 b/d to 1,285,000 b/d (*Arab Report and Record*, 16–31 October 1973), p. 484.
5. In 1967 Iran's production increased by 23% while Iraq's fell by 11.5% (Laqueur, p. 153); the United States increased production between May and August 1967 by about 1 million b/d, Sam H. Schurr et al., *Middle Eastern Oil and the Western World: Prospects and Problems* (New York: American Elsevier, 1971), p. 37.
6. *Neue Zurcher Zeitung*, 27 April 1974.
7. A comparison between foreign exchange holdings of Central Banks (which in some cases seriously understates the actual reserves) in late 1973, and of import requirements in the same year (as represented by actual imports) shows that Kuwait could theoretically pay for about six months' imports, Libya for more than two years, Saudi Arabia for two years, and even Iraq for 21 months.
8. In the late 1960s dependence on oil exports for gross foreign exchange earnings was around 75% for Iraq, 85–90% for Kuwait, Libya, and Saudi Arabia, and close to 100% for the sheikdoms in the Persian Gulf. At the same time, the oil sector accounted for just under 26% of GNP in Algeria and 33% in Iraq; Saudi Arabia derived 55%, Libya 60%, and Kuwait and the smaller sheikdoms even higher percentages of GNP from the oil sector.
9. Gamal Abdel Nasser, *The Philosophy of the Revolution* (Cairo; Dar al-Kutub, 1955), pp. 67–69.
10. *Strategic Survey 1973* (London: IISS, 1974), p. 97.
11. European Community, *The European Economy in 1973* (Brussels, 1974), p. 65; *Petroleum Economist* (April 1974): 175; (June 1974): 24; see also, Robert Stobaugh, "The Oil Companies in the Crisis," *Daedalus*, 104 (Fall 1975): 179–202, for a detailed analysis.
12. *The Times*, 10 April 1974.

13. *Petroleum Economist* (March 1974): 98; European Commision, *Energy Balance of the Community* (Brussels: 1974).
14. See Klaus Knorr, "The Limits of Economic and Military Power," *Daedalus, 104* (Fall 1975): 229–43 (230).
15. See Hanns Maull, "The Strategy of Avoidance: Europe's Middle East Policies after the October War," in *Oil, the Arab-Israel Dispute and the Industrial World: Horizons of Crisis*, ed. J. C. Hurewitz (Westview Press, 1976).
16. *The Times*, 4 December 1973.
17. *The Times*, 23 November 1973.
18. The "majors" control more than 60% of the world tanker fleet, by ownership or long-term charter, and a similar proportion of world refinery capacity.
19. Total tonnage in mid-1974 was about 1.5 million dwt in crude, product, and liquified natural gas (LNG) carriers, *Petroleum Economist* (August 1974): 305.
20. Arab orders amount to 4,783,370 dwt. These orders include 714 million m³ of LNG carriers for Kuwait and Algeria. Ibid., 307.
21. *Middle East Economic Digest* (22 March 1974): 335.
22. *Petroleum Economist* (May 1974): 181.
23. Saudi Arabia has already indicated her intention to export 50% of her oil in her own fleet by 1978. Several countries have already introduced legislation giving priority to tankers under their own flag for their oil exports; similar clauses have also been included in agreements on nationalization between governments and oil companies.
24. M.A. Adelmann, *The World Petroleum Market* (Baltimore and London: Johns Hopkins U.P., 1972), p. 126, quotes prices between $100 and $138 per dwt for VLCC (very large crude carriers) from Japanese shipyards in early 1971.
25. Ibid., pp. 104–60.
26. At the time of writing member countries are Belgium, Canada, Denmark, Germany, Ireland, Italy, Japan, Luxembourg, the Netherlands, New Zealand, Spain, Sweden, Switzerland, Turkey, and Britain. Norway has a special associated status with the IEA.
27. *International Herald Tribune*, 2 January 1974.

CHAPTER 11

Food and National Security

Cheryl Christensen

The link between food and national security can be approached from various angles. To a large extent, the relevance of food production and distribution to national security depends on one's perspective about the present world food situation. In other words, one must examine current threats and problems as well as the dynamics which shape the future. For some nations, the contemporary food regime is a source of threat, while for others, it is a guarantee of wealth and perhaps even of power. The magnitude of the threats, as well as the promises of wealth and power, depend upon knowing whether food is (or will be) a scarce resource. In addition, the relationship between national security goals and food depends on understanding *how* food might become scarce and for whom.

The first section of this chapter explores possible links between food and national security implied by different assumptions about scarcity. Then, using the insights developed on scarcity, situations will be defined in which leaders *might* have to operate and take action to preserve or enhance their nations' security. Finally, suggestions will be made about strategies for handling food and national security.

Food, Scarcity, and National Security

One of the most publicized pictures of the contemporary world food situation suggests that food will become much more scarce in the future.[1] The reason is that the quantity of food needed in the future may grow more rapidly than the ability to produce it. The amount of food required for human wants and needs will grow rapidly, partly because population is greatly increasing (primarily in less developed countries) and partly because growing affluence results in diets including more animal protein. In general, meeting protein demands through animal products requires more grain than meeting physical requirements directly from grains, vegetables, and legumes.[2] Furthermore, food production is difficult to accelerate, and many methods for increasing production have economic or ecological constraints. Consequently, food will be increasingly scarce.

Under conditions of increasing scarcity, food-importing countries have several reasons for considering their international food position a matter of national security. First, there is the classic concern about foreign dependence on any essential or strategic resource: supplies may be intentionally or inadvertantly interrupted. Intentional supply disruptions could, in time of war, affect the ability to fight. In peace, there is the fear that supplies might be reduced in an attempt to influence national policy, or that supply conditions might be manipulated to the economic or political disadvantage of the importing state. Inadvertent interruptions could themselves be of national concern—creating potentially serious dislocations within the importing country.

For some nations, however, the concern is even deeper. At least some food-importing countries already find that paying for their imports strains limited foreign exchange or increases indebtedness. The need to import food may, de facto, dictate important national policies as such countries try to compete with wealthier customers for limited food supplies. Failing to obtain imports may create political threats for particular administrations, especially if governments have provided "cheap food" for politically salient groups within the country.

For nations able to export food, steadily growing scarcity implies that food resources will generate increased national income. In addition, food may become a new national security resource, providing a means for exerting leverage over a wide range of countries. If the quantity of food needed can be expected to grow consistently faster than production can increase, there is little reason for exporting nations to fear competition from new rivals.

The prospects for gain by food-exporting nations depend upon the assumption that scarcity will steadily increase. Yet, there is some reason to question this assumption. Much of the population growth in LDCs will generate a physical need for food but not necessarily an economic demand for it. If many people who need more food cannot pay for it, the market demand for food will grow much more slowly than the combined growth in population and affluence-based diets. Indeed, the paying demand for food could grow less than food production, resulting in a "surplus" vis-à-vis the market, yet "scarcity" for the undernourished poor. This situation was, in fact, the reality of the 1950s and 1960s. It was associated with attempts by governments in exporting countries to support farm income through domestic price subsidies, to accumulate large public stocks of "surplus" grain, and to encourage low international market prices. In short, the historical experience of major exporters has not been one of great power stemming from the ability to allocate a scarce resource to eager customers, but one of low prices, market development efforts, and surplus disposal.

Links between food and national security are more complicated when increasing scarcity cannot be assumed. If an exporting nation cannot take its international market for granted, the national security importance of maintaining or expanding it must be considered. For example, the strong international demand for agricultural products since 1972 has resulted in balance of trade gains for the United States—which, in turn, has helped pay for more costly imported oil. Having a paying international market for agricultural products has helped the United States *cope* economically with the impact of OPEC price increases. When continued markets are not assured, there are risks for exporters in imposing undesired political or economic conditions on importers—even in periodically tight market situations. Importers can later turn to other suppliers or cultivate new sources of supply which may compete with traditional exporting countries. This, for example, was Japan's response after the embargo on American soybean exports in 1973.

The links between food and national security for relatively wealthy importers are somewhat different. If there is not steadily increasing scarcity, nations with adequate international purchasing power may find alternative supply sources. The constraints on their ability to do so depend on their wealth, how concentrated the international market is, and the size of their import requirements. They can, alternatively, invest in increasing their domestic food production or invest in increasing the production of nations from which they can more reliably guarantee supplies. Hence, for example, some OPEC nations are investing in increasing the Sudan's agricultural production in hopes of making it the breadbasket for the Middle East.

The links between food and national security for poor importing countries remain unchanged in that imports may still pose an economic hardship or create dependencies which restrict the autonomy of national leaders. However, when food is not physically scarce, there may be relatively little difference between power based upon the ability to supply food directly, and that based on money with which to purchase food.

The fact that hungry people find food "scarce" because they can neither grow enough to feed themselves nor make adequate purchases in the market to meet their physical needs is itself becoming a more significant security concern. Within some less developed countries, there is increasing recognition that agricultural performance can no longer be ignored if any chance for broad-based economic growth is to exist. Instabilities arising from weather-related fluctuations in production affect both industrial growth and overall economic strength. A lack of food becomes a serious constraint on efforts to reduce unemployment and unrest in cities as well as in the countryside.[3] Population growth will put even greater strains on many social structures—especially in countries where the greatest impediments to increased agricultural production lie in the social structure itself. While such instabilities may not immediately topple regimes or generate revolutions, they do make it difficult for many governments to hold out any real hope for progress.[4] Where there exists the need to divert land and resources from export crops (providing the bulk of foreign exchange for many countries) to subsistence production, there may be absolute losses in foreign exchange—something most governments cannot afford when prices for imports of oil, food, and capital goods continue to rise.

Finally, we need to ask *how* food may become scarce—either with respect to demand in the marketplace or with respect to the needs of people unable to enter the market. Either physical constraints or policies can produce scarcity. *Physical factors*, including weather, water supplies, and deteriorating agricultural land may cause declines in production which, in turn, may produce scarcity. Rising population, in the context of limitations on production, implies a per capita fall in production, which may also produce scarcity. *Policies*, such as withholding production from the market or slowing down production, can generate new scarcity. Inadequate reserves, speculation, or panic buying in situations of uncertain or unstable supplies may create scarcity at key times with respect to the market.

How scarcity arises is important in determining the extent of a country's sensitivity or vulnerability. A country is sensitive if it is liable to experience costly effects in a particular situation; it is vulnerable if it continues to bear these costs even after attempts have been made to change, or escape, such situations.[5] Physical problems can, in some instances, be mitigated. While weather remains non-manipulable, reserves will reduce vulnerability to scarcity from fluctuating production. If capital is available, inadequate water and poor land can, to degrees, be modified by technology. Nations able to deal with these physical factors may be able to reduce their vulnerability. If, on the other hand, scarcity arises from the policies of external actors over which states have little or no control, it may be difficult to organize to counter them effectively. For example, speculation occurring within relatively good information networks from which many nations are excluded may be difficult to defend against directly.

Judgments about scarcity and vulnerability, in turn, condition how effective food may be as a national security resource. An exporter, facing a world of sensitive importers who can avoid being vulnerable by taking simple and inexpensive domestic measures, will probably not have much food power over the long run. Furthermore, if the measures taken imply decreasing markets, short-run gains must be weighed against long-run costs. On the other hand, an exporter facing importers with only limited or expensive options for reducing their sensitivity may be in a more secure position for exercising food power.

Finally, it is important to realize that the attempts nations make to adjust to scarcity and each other's behavior can produce both situations of mutual gain and situations of mutual loss. For example, both exporting and importing nations may be disadvantaged by attempts to escape sensitivity through sternly imposed self-sufficiency—those needing food suffer because they cannot obtain it, and those producing it suffer because they cannot sell what they could produce. Similarly, it is possible to envision situations of mutual gain. Eliminating severe market instability and expanding the ability of new groups to enter the market could both reduce hunger and increase producers' sales.

American Food Power

A number of people have recently suggested that American food resources could provide a new kind of food power which could be used to counter actions believed to threaten national security. The simple idea of countering an OAPEC oil embargo with an embargo on food sales to OAPEC countries was easily dismissed.[6] But, the hope that American food power could be used to affect the behavior of food-importing nations remains. A study conducted by the CIA's office of political research suggested that if there were climate changes affecting global production,

> As custodian of the bulk of the world's exportable grain, the U.S. might regain the primacy in world affairs it held in the immediate post-World War II era.[7]

Then Secretary of Agriculture Earl Butz suggested several times that "agripower" is an important lever for future diplomacy.[8]

The idea behind these assertions is that the American government could exercise behavioral power based upon its agricultural resources. Behavioral power is the ability of one actor to get another to modify its behavior in compliance with, or anticipation of, its wishes, demands, or proposals.[9] If we want to know whether America can successfully exercise food power, we need to ask:[10]

1. What are America's agricultural resources—the *base* for its food power?
2. What *means* does it have for employing these resources?
3. What is the *scope* of American food power over other countries—that is, which of their behaviors could be affected by it?
4. What costs, risks, and benefits might America encounter in attempting to exercise its food power?
5. What alternatives do other countries have to complying with the stated American wishes or demands?
6. What is the domain of American food power—which countries could it affect?

The Base for American Food Power

What are America's food resources? Basically, the answer is that the United States produces *grain* far beyond what is needed for domestic consumption and can therefore export it to other countries. The United States

Table 1
U.S. Exports as Percent of World Exports

	Wheat	Grain**
1960/1*	40.9	41.7
1961/2	41.7	43.2
1962/3	37.8	41.6
1963/4	39.6	42.2
1964/5	35.5	42.2
1965/6	38.2	45.3
1966/7	34.9	39.8
1967/8	38.0	41.8
1968/9	29.4	34.7
1969/70	30.0	34.7
1970/1	35.2	35.2
1971/2	30.1	37.1
1972/3	44.0	50.0
1973/4	44.2	47.4
1974/5	41.1	46.4

* Years run July–June.
** Grains included wheat and feedgrains (corn, barley, oats, rye, and sorghum).
Source: USDA, ERS, unpublished computer printout.

accounted for over 40% of world wheat exports and over 46% of total grain exports in 1974–75. While the tight markets of the early 1970's focused people's attention on America's share of world grain exports, this was not the first time America dominated world exports, as Table 1 shows. The concentration, per se, then, is not new. Furthermore, when Soviet imports are taken out of the picture, the situation is essentially the same for recent years as it was before 1972.

America's share of world production has also remained relatively stable over the last fifteen years, as Table 2 shows. The highest concentration occurred in 1972—when there was bad weather in both the USSR and India, two large producers who sometimes import large quantities of grain if domestic crops are poor. Between 1960 and 1975, America on the average accounted for 12.6% of world wheat production and 25.3% of total grain production.

The most significant change was in American grain stocks. Throughout the last twenty years, the United States held stocks which were larger than policy-makers desired. They did so as part of a domestic program to support agricultural prices and farmers' income. Between 1954 and 1962, beginning stocks of wheat averaged 102% of annual utilization—indicating that over a full year's domestic consumption and export commitments could have been met from existing stocks.[11] While U.S. stocks were drawn down in 1963–64

Table 2

U.S. Production as Percent of World Production

	Wheat	Grain
1960/1	15.5	27.2
1961/2	14.8	25.8
1962/3	11.6	23.6
1963/4	13.1	25.8
1964/5	12.7	22.4
1965/6	11.7	25.4
1966/7	11.5	23.1
1967/8	13.9	25.8
1968/9	12.9	23.8
1969/70	12.7	24.2
1970/1	11.7	22.0
1971/2	12.7	25.4
1972/3	12.4	27.4
1973/4	12.6	23.8
1974/5	13.9	20.7

Source: USDA, ERS, unpublished computer printout.

and again in 1967 to meet emergencies abroad, they remained relatively high, as Table 3 shows.

By the late 1960s, policy-makers in the world's major grain-exporting countries (the United States, Canada, Australia, Argentina) began to cut back on grain production—in hopes of reducing record surpluses and raising low grain prices. Between 1968 and 1970, the combined wheat area of the four countries dropped from more than 50 million hectares to 33 million; production fell from over 80 million tons to less than 60 million. A United States Department of Agriculture (USDA) study estimates that if those nations had continued to produce at the 1967 level, they would have grown over 90 million tons more wheat than they actually did between 1968 and 1970.[12]

It was in this context that American sales to the USSR were made in 1972. Although the sales were for more wheat than policy-makers intended, the major aim of the sales was to reduce American stocks. At the time, the sale was considered a "one shot" transaction to help clear away burdensome surpluses while offsetting a Soviet crop failure. What happened, however, was more significant. The political decision by the USSR to buy large quantities of grain and American willingness to sell changed the paying international market substantially. The 1972 Soviet crop was short about 12 million tons, less than the shortfalls of 1963 (20 million tons) or 1965 (16 million tons).[13] Had the U.S. and USSR desired them, substantial sales could have been made in 1963 and 1965. But the Soviet government

295

Table 3
U.S. Stocks as Percent of U.S. and World Annual Utilization

| | U.S. | | World | |
	Wheat	Grain	Wheat	Grain
1960/1	104%	62%	15%	15%
1961/2	107	66	16	17
1962/3	108	60	14	14
1963/4	83	52	13	13
1964/5	66	51	9	12
1965/6	51	36	8	9
1966/7	38	28	5	7
1967/8	30	24	4	6
1968/9	40	31	5	7
1969/70	60	34	7	8
1970/1	59	34	7	8
1971/2	49	23	6	5
1972/3	44	27	7	7
1973/4	23	17	3	4
1974/5	14	13	2	3

Source: USDA, ERS, unpublished computer printout.

chose to cut back domestic consumption rather than make massive imports. In 1972, however, a new Soviet policy aimed at improving the standard of living and presumably furthering détente changed the situation. American stocks fell, and bad harvests, along with additional Soviet purchases, increased the demand for grain exports. Yet, the American government was slow in removing controls on American grain production. The result was that for a time food was scarce, and American stocks remained low until 1976. Weather and policy thus combined to make food scarce.

The effects of these events can be seen in both the quantity and disposition of world stocks. As Tables 4 and 5 indicate, world stocks through 1975 were significantly smaller than they were in 1960 (when world population and grain demand were smaller), and the United States held a smaller share of the reduced level of stocks. With stocks at this level, the United States could not unilaterally stabilize the international grain market with its reserves. In addition, as a result of changed domestic agricultural policy, U.S. stocks are now held almost entirely by the private sector (farmers, cooperatives, grain companies, elevators). This diminishes the government's direct control over them.

An Assessment of National Vulnerabilities: Past and Future

The discussion above leads to the question of the *means* available for using these resources to exercise food power. The American government

Table 4
World Wheat Stocks

	World stocks in 1,000 metric tons	World stocks as percent of world production	U.S. stocks as percent of world stocks
1960/1	74,217	.31	48.2
1961/2	77,346	.34	49.7
1962/3	65,600	.26	55.0
1963/4	70,951	.30	45.8
1964/5	62,655	.23	39.1
1965/6	72,865	.27	30.5
1966/7	54,056	.18	26.9
1967/8	78,894	.27	14.6
1968/9	82,011	.25	17.9
1969/70	107,130	.35	20.7
1970/1	93,771	.30	25.7
1971/2	72,285	.21	27.5
1972/3	73,520	.22	32.0
1973/4	51,586	.14	23.1
1974/5	56,658	.16	11.9

Source: USDA, ERS, unpublished computer printout.

must have some control over agricultural resources if they are to be used as instruments of government policy abroad. In the past, this control was primarily direct control over public stocks, and the means for linking food to diplomacy came from programs to dispose of those stocks. Public Law 480 (later called Food for Peace) permitted the American government to use surplus food in a variety of ways. Politically, the most important means available were Title I sales (first for local currency, then for American dollars on lenient convertibility terms). Title II, which provided for humanitarian aid, was a much smaller part of the P.L. 480 program.

Since 1954, when P.L. 480 began, agricultural commodities have been provided to politically important countries. Between 1954 and 1974, twelve countries each received more than $500 million under P.L. 480[14] (Table 6). Together, these countries accounted for 69% of total P.L. 480 assistance (including humanitarian and relief programs) and 86% of Title I dispersals.[15]

Title I sales provided more than just cheaper food. Because nations often paid for P.L. 480 shipments in local currency, which could not be spent outside the country, they also gained additional financial resources when the payments made for the food exceeded the amount of currency the United States could spend within the country. These accumulations of local currency (called counterpart funds) were loaned or given to the govern-

Table 5
World Grain Stocks

	World stocks in 1,000 metric tons	World stocks as percent of world production	U.S. stocks as percent of world stocks
1960/1	169,416	.26	61.1
1961/2	182,362	.29	63.5
1962/3	155,725	.23	62.3
1963/4	159,005	.24	57.3
1964/5	154,139	.22	56.8
1965/6	157,315	.22	46.0
1966/7	121,561	.16	43.8
1967/8	150,662	.19	30.4
1968/9	163,051	.20	36.2
1969/70	190,034	.23	35.7
1970/1	167,513	.20	41.0
1971/2	129,918	.14	38.9
1972/3	147,496	.24	46.4
1973/4	107,715	.11	39.1
1974/5	110,433	.12	24.5

Source: USDA, ERS, unpublished computer printout.

ments to be used for a variety of projects, including "common defense" expenditures, and loans which increased the government's revenue generally. Table 6 indicates how local funds were allocated between 1954 and 1974. As the table suggests, a large portion of the local currencies went to governments, either as loans or grants, in some cases making it less necessary for them to seek additional tax revenues. A significant amount of money was used for common defense (essentially military expenditures). In Cambodia and Vietnam, the bulk of P.L. 480 local currency was used to support the war effort, until such uses were terminated by an amendment to the Foreign Assistance Act in 1973 (effective July 1974).[16] Title I sales thus provided the American government with a range of means for rewarding, or aiding, politically important countries. Of course, there was also the "threat" (implicit or explicit) that such aid could stop if behavior were not in keeping with American wishes.

At present, American policy-makers seeking to use food to support foreign policy have fewer means for doing so. Sales for local currency were terminated, effective 1972. While there were balance of payments gains to the United States for making this change, a smaller amount of local currency will be available to support foreign government projects or provide financial incentives for projects the United States considers important. In addition, changes in the Foreign Assistance Act now require that at least 75% of

Table 6

P.L. 480 Commodities	Million dollars of P.L. 480 commodities
India	5,016
Pakistan	1,642
South Korea	1,516
South Vietnam	1,437
Yugoslavia	1,202
Indonesia	969
Egypt	912
Brazil	886
Turkey	722
Israel	664
Spain	622
Poland	568

the food distributed under P.L. 480 Title I go to nations with per capita incomes under $300.[17] As a result, the practice of using concessional sales to provide indirect military or political assistance to important allies has been curtailed, or at least, redirected. The direct provision of military assistance, through the use of local currencies for such programs, is also specifically prohibited by legislation. While it is likely that more food may become available to P.L. 480 programs when commercial demand slacks, it is unlikely that quantities will approach the level of the 1960s or that restrictions placed on the food aid program will be removed.

Policy-makers do have a number of means available to direct the flow of commercial exports, which now account for over 95% of U.S. agricultural exports.[18] Under present market conditions, however, they are politically and economically costly. General export embargoes, like the soybean embargo of 1973, can disrupt both political and economic relations with important allies. This is an important consideration, for Europe and Japan remain the largest purchasers of American agricultural exports.[19] The general soybean embargo, for example, had the effect of both creating political tensions between the U.S. and Japan, and encouraging Japan to diversify its import sources by increased investment in Brazil's production and processing facilities.[20]

Selective embargoes, like that imposed on grain exports to the USSR in 1975, are difficult to fine tune. Like oil-producing states, the U.S. Government has trouble controlling the destination of exports without affecting their level. Because the bulk of U.S. grain exports is shipped by multinational grain companies, an embargoed nation may still receive exports.[21] Since grain companies have international sources of supply, they may provide "foreign" exports to the embargoed country. In 1975, Cargill exported soybeans to the Soviet Union from Brazilian, not American, production,

299

Table 7
Import Dependence

Country	:	Wheat % imported (or trade status)	% of calories	:	Rice % imported (or trade status)	% of calories	:	Corn % imported (or trade status)	% of calories
Afghanistan	:	3	54	:	ss	7	:	ss	18
Algeria	:	44	60	:	70		:	80	
Angola	:	85	5	:	uex	2	:	e	21
Argentina	:	e	33	:	3		:	e	
Bangladesh[1]	:	94	14	:	4	32	:		4
Bolivia	:	72	18	:	ss	4	:	mss	25
Brazil	:	66	8	:	e	18	:		18
Burma	:	37	1	:	ss	72	:	e	
Burundi	:	100	1	:			:	ss	14
Cameroon	:	100	2	:			:	ss	15
Cen. African Rep.	:	100	2	:		1	:		8
Chad	:			:	ss	3	:		2
Chile	:	45	47	:	48	3	:	39	
Colombia	:	87	6	:	uex	22	:	uex	20
Costa Rica	:	100	14	:	uex	14	:	46	14
Cuba	:	100	27	:	60	16	:		
Dahomey	:			:		1	:	mss	32
Dominican Rep.	:	100	6	:	mss	15	:	41	3
Ecuador	:	69	8	:	uex	16	:	uex	12
Egypt	:	63	10	:	e	13	:	8	
El Salvador	:	100	6	:	uex	3	:		37
Ethiopia	:	70	10	:			:	mss	13
Gabon	:	100	6	:		2	:		2
Gambia	:	100	2	:	32	36	:		
Ghana	:	100	3	:	48	4	:		22
Guatemala	:	66	1	:	uex		:	5	56
Guinea	:	100	2	:	10	32	:		22
Guyana	:		21	:	mss	35	:		
Haiti	:	100	5	:		3	:	uex	24
Honduras	:	98	5	:	36		:	mss	49
India	:	10	14	:	uex	32	:	3	4
Indonesia	:	100		:	8	46	:	uex	14
Iran	:	17	49	:	19	12	:	65	
Iraq	:	30	39	:	uex	9	:		
Ivory Coast	:	100	5	:	41	20	:	mss	16
Jamaica	:	100	25	:	94	8	:	94	6
Jordan	:	50	49	:	100	5	:		
Kenya	:	uex	3	:			:	uex	46
Khmer Rep.	:			:	uex	73	:		
Korea (S)	:	89	9	:	12	47	:	89	
Laos	:			:	11	85	:		3
Lebanon	:	86	45	:	100	4	:	95	
Liberia	:	100	1	:	28	53	:		

300

Table 7

Continued

Country	Wheat		Rice		Corn	
	% imported (or trade status)	% of calories	% imported (or trade status)	% of calories	% imported (or trade status)	% of calories
Libya	85	44				
Madagascar				64		
Malawi	100	1			mss	84
Malaysia (west)	100	10	16	46	99	
Mali		1	16	9	mss	8
Mauritania		4		5		2
Mexico	24	9	uex	2	uex	43
Morocco	29	40	ss		6	6
Mozambique	91	3	uex	4	uex	20
Nicaragua	100	5	e	9	12	34
Niger				1		
Nigeria			1	2	1	7
Pakistan	14	20	e	47	99	2
Peru	85	16	uex	9	23	9
Philippines	100	6	8	44	5	12
Rwanda						7
Saudi Arabia	67	27	99	13		
Senegal	100	4	72	30	41	5
Sierra Leone	100	3	4	52		2
Singapore	100	11	100	35	100	
Somalia	100	3		7		22
Sri Lanka	100	10	29	48		
Sudan	53	5				
Syria	uex	49	99	3		
Tanzania	44	2	uex	4	uex	23
Thailand			e	72		
Tunisia		54			100	
Turkey	uex	50	mss	2	mss	1
Uganda		2			mss	7
Uruguay	uex	29		3		
Venezuela						
Vietnam (S)	100	3	9	76	60	
Zambia	100	3			uex	60
Zaire	98	7	15	2	25	2

key

ss = self-sufficient (production with neither imports nor exports)

uex = uncertain exporter (exports alternating with imports or no net trade)

e = exporter (steady exporter)

mss = marginally self-sufficient (imports alternating with years of self-sufficiency)

Sources: Trade figures computed from unpublished printout USDA, ERS. Calorie figures computed from the Food and Agriculture Organization, *Food Balance Sheets* (Rome: FAO, 1965).

with a loss of revenue for U.S. farmers.[22] Similarly, because major grain companies have transnational shipping networks, it is possible to substitute grain of "foreign" origin for U.S. grain in contracts, thus adjusting shipping to continue sales.

Both general and selective embargoes have high political costs under present agricultural policies. Embargoes created strong political opposition to Republican leadership, and became a significant political issue in the 1976 presidential campaign.[23] Farmers complained that government officials encouraged maximum production and privately held stocks, then imposed an embargo which triggered a decline in grain prices, decreased farm revenue, and piled up additional stored grain. It was in the context of such domestic political opposition that President Ford in 1976 explicitly rejected attempts to manipulate grain sales to the USSR as a way of modifying Soviet behavior in Angola.

This is not to suggest that it is impossible to make grain sales responsive to political policies, but rather to note that doing so through the relatively crude methods of embargoes (general or specific, temporary or permanent) will involve public controversy, economic disruption, and conflict with other food goals. One of the side-effects of earlier domestic agricultural policies was that large surpluses shielded the domestic economy from international market changes and governmental or private international food transactions. As a result of changed world market conditions and changed domestic policies, the buffer which prior stocks provided no longer exists. Hence, the United States economy is sensitive to both changes abroad and the effects of its own public and private international food transactions. This sensitivity is an example of what Krasner (Chapter 6) portrayed as domestic constraints on a nation's foreign economic policy.

It is, of course, necessary to consider the sensitivity or vulnerability of importing countries to American food power. The cost to the United States and American alliance ties of using relatively coercive means (e.g., curtailed exports) clearly limits the range of states to which such food power might reasonably be applied. It is clear, for example, that two of America's best customers (Europe and Japan) are not likely targets of coercive food power. Indeed, national security may dictate a need to prevent supply disruption to such customers. Certainly, a commitment to more economic solidarity and cooperation among OECD countries would be difficult to reconcile with threats to unilateral disruptions in food shipments. Economic considerations—the importance of the USSR in setting the conditions for a lucrative international grain market and the benefits from a trade surplus with it— make it a problematic target for severe supply disruption, at least given present relations. Most discussions of coercive food power in fact tacitly consider it most useful in dealing with LDCs which import grain.

How sensitive an importing LDC is to changes in international grain

302

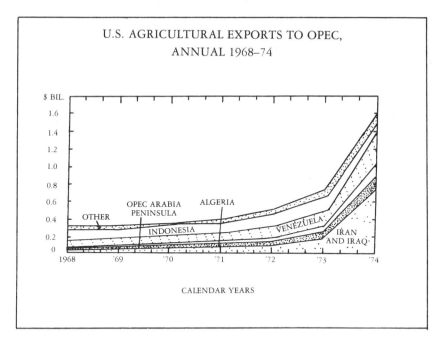

Figure 2

Source: USDA, ERS. *Foreign Agricultural Trade of the U.S.* March, 1975.

least developed countries (with per capita GNP less than $200) and many of the nations designated by the U.N. as most seriously affected by higher oil import costs, fall into this category. Here the question of physically restricting food shipments may not be as germane as changing the financial terms for imports. Dramatic increases in import costs may effectively reduce supplies. In many nations with significant portions of the population at subsistence levels, reduced supplies may translate into starvation or severe malnutrition.

Recent projections for the lower income developing countries' future dependence on food imports strongly suggest vulnerability for many countries *unless* their food production policies change substantially for the better, or new domestic and international structures for distributing food come into being. The International Food Policy Research Institute's study on future food needs in LDCs concluded that:

> Unless the trend of production in DME (Developing Market Economies) improves in the future, production of cereals, the major food in most developing countries, will fall short of meeting food demand in food deficit countries by 95–108 million tons in 1985/6

depending on the rate of economic growth. This compares with shortfalls of 45 million tons in the food crisis year 1974/5, and an average of 28 million tons in the relatively good production period 1969/71.[29]

The magnitude of the projected food deficits could be put into perspective by realizing that the average level of U.S. grain exports from 1966–76 was about 51 million metric tons.[30]

Several points should be made. First, there will not be a "food deficit" per se. Production shortfalls, relative to increasing food consumption needs, will translate into poorer diets or starvation for *some sectors* of the population in food deficit developing market economies. Second, the food needs of the developing market economies will be *higher*, if present relationships between income and diet hold, as economic development occurs within a market framework. This implies that there will be, at least within food deficit developing market economies, greater tension between the desire of those earning more money to consume more costly animal protein and attempts to meet the *minimal* nutritional needs of poorer people. The tension is likely to become more acute in many countries where economic development programs have increased economic inequality without providing significant employment opportunities for the poor.[31] Third, the growing "food deficit" and the poverty of the "food deficit" groups within developing market economies are a chronic problem. Hunger, malnutrition, and even starvation will not be "caused" by crop failures (although crop failures will certainly make them worse) but by inadequate growth in production—itself often a consequence of economic, political, and social disincentives to production within the affected countries.

The magnitude of the projected gap between prospective food demand and local production for developing market economies requires that the position of individual countries be analyzed *in the context* of the greatly increased needs of the countries as a whole. The greatest "food gaps" are projected for low-income countries (those with per capita income less than $200 in 1972), including India, Bangladesh, Indonesia, Sri Lanka, and a large portion of sub-Saharan Africa. This group of states accounts for over 60% of the total population of developing market economies. The implication of these projections is that individual poor countries may increasingly be competing against each other for what may be relatively uncertain quantities of low-cost, special-credit food supplies. If these countries have to make purchases at full commercial prices, it is unlikely that anything like the projected deficit will actually be imported. The effects of less than adequate supplies will have to be distributed (economically and politically) among groups within poor countries. If past distribution patterns continue, it is likely that poor people will bear the heaviest burden in all but a few countries.

It is difficult to escape the conclusion that hunger and undernutrition will become even starker characteristics of many poor LDCs than they have been in the past, unless improvements are made in food production or food distribution. Increasing hunger may become a security threat for some LDCs as much because it can generate domestic instability as because it can work to reinforce the international economic weakness of such nations. In most cases, however, coercive food power does not have a larger domain than American economic power in general. By and large, food power could be used, at relatively low cost to the United States, primarily to deal only with nations over which the United States already has substantial economic leverage. In addition, unless the United States has the capability to offer benefits, or rewards, to such countries on the basis of its food resources, attempts to use food resources to threaten or punish may be relatively indistinguishable from what "normal market forces" would do in times of increased scarcity.

In the discussion thus far, it has been more or less presumed that a consistently tight food market would enhance the ability of food exporters to exercise food power. Clearly, the economic costs of interrupting supplies would be less if increasing scarcity made it less likely that such actions might trigger reduced markets in the future. Yet, this may not be a safe assumption. Food power (coercive as well as non-coercive) can be undertaken only with *politically* available resources. The food resources which policy-makers might be able to use internationally in tight markets will be, in part, a function of the *domestic response* to tighter markets, and hence, higher consumer prices when domestic arenas are sensitive to international transactions. This response, in turn, will depend on the political voice of consumers within the country, the extent to which protecting domestic consumption is incompatible with manipulating international food transactions, the role of the government specified by agricultural policies, and the political and moral *values* that emerge regarding food. It is possible that much tighter markets could result in a decreased ability to use food as a resource for behavioral power: either the politically available resources might decline, or a domestic consensus on the inappropriateness of using food in this way might emerge.

In part, the recent history of American food policy at least suggests that tighter markets may encourage limitations on the use of food resources for political or military purposes. First, as a result of the decline in publicly held reserves, the effects of international sales have been reflected domestically. Questions of food policy now involve a much heavier weighting of consumer and inflationary impacts. Whether such political forces would become more potent if markets were consistently tight is unknown at present, but strong domestic pressure on behalf of consumers (and efforts to control the domestic economy) could result in substantially greater restrictions on food exports. Secondly, increased food shortages could contribute to changing values on the *appropriate* use of food entering international channels. Tighter food supplies in 1972–73 coincided with Congressional actions to make the allocation of commodities through P.L. 480 more responsive to nutritional and economic needs. More serious shortages of food could result in an even stronger expression of the principle that internationally available food be used to relieve hunger and malnutrition among the most needy, not to extract political or military concessions. A genuinely tight market might also put a higher priority on using whatever food resources were available to take actions which might reduce the likelihood of greater scarcity—including contributing to the ability to increase food production and aid in its effective storage and distribution.

The effect of domestic interests on the ability to exercise food power is worth exploring a bit further, for it emphasizes the complexities which actually surround the idea of American food power. When food is not scarce vis-à-vis commerical international markets, surplus disposal becomes an important objective of concessional sales. This may increase the "bargaining power" of countries that might otherwise have been purely passive beneficiaries of American food assistance. For example, by mid-1976, when American rice stocks were high and there was pressure from rice producers to increase concessional sales to reduce stocks, Indonesia held out for better repayment terms—indicating that it might *refuse to take the surplus rice.*[32] Nations with large food needs and relatively low income, like India, Bangladesh, Indonesia, and Sri Lanka are important to American policymakers trying to dispose of surpluses under provisions which require most of it to go to low-income countries. Only a few countries with per capita GNP below $300 can absorb large shipments. These countries, in the most precarious position when production was low, may not always be the passive targets of American food power.

Additional Ways of Using Food Resources

Thus far the focus has been on relatively coercive means for using food resources and doing so primarily to affect the behavior of others. There are, however, other possibilities: the option of using food resources to reward others, to strengthen them, and to achieve structural goals (such as more stable international markets).

Food resources may be used to reward other actors for cooperation and to help build new relationships. Hence, in waiving the restriction on shipping P.L. 480 commodities to nations which traded with Cuba or North Vietnam, (i.e., Syria) President Ford defended the sales as contributing to the national interest of the United States because:

Syria is a key to our efforts to achieve a just and lasting peace in the Middle East. Our success will depend in part on Syrian confidence in our intention to develop a broad and constructive bilateral relationship with that country. Concessional sales of agricultural commodities to Syria constitute a tangible demonstration of our intended role in that regard.[33]

It is difficult to argue that the $19 million in commodities could be used as an effective "lever" on Syrian policy. Alternative funding sources are available, and food was not scarce in 1976. However, providing such shipments could help set the "tone" of a new relationship.

Food resources may also be used to increase a government's ability to carry out policies in keeping with American interests, as well as to foster cordial relations. Providing Egypt with over $80 million in P.L. 480 commodities (primarily wheat) undoubtedly contributed to managing a difficult food situation in Egypt.[34] While it is unlikely that American food aid has increased Sadat's interest in a negotiated settlement in the Middle East, it may have helped provide resources to sustain such a commitment.

American food resources may also be used to provide reassurance to politically important nations. In the aftermath of uncertain food supplies, the United States concluded long-term agricultural trade agreements with Japan, Israel, South Korea, and Taiwan.[35] At one level, the agreements provide greater import security. In part, however, they reassure allies (Japan, Israel, South Korea, and Taiwan) that their well-being is an American priority worth reaffirming. This was particularly important in the aftermath of the Soviet-American five-year trade agreement, whose primary purpose was market stabilization, but which was open to interpretation by allies as a signal of American foreign policy foci. Similar guarantees have been provided for in programming P.L. 480 commitments.[36]

American food resources have also been used to manage the effects of international transactions on the United States and wider international markets. The trade agreement concluded with the USSR was an attempt to smooth out Soviet purchases, making them less disruptive to the American economy and to market prices in general. The fact that the United States export volume was large enough to make meaningful guarantees and still not excessively constrain other export options allowed it to use a *bilateral* agreement to achieve this objective.

America's importance as a market for agricultural commodities, as well as an exporter, opens another option for strengthening other nations or fostering new relations. The United States is a major market for many foodstuffs which provide significant export earnings for LDCs. These include products not produced in the United States—such as coffee, tea, cocoa, and bananas—as well as some which may compete with domestic production, such as sugar and vegetable oils. In some cases, providing preferential access to American markets can increase the export earnings of LDCs, providing them with greater purchasing power for a range of goods. Some minimal trade adjustments along these lines have been made.

Where others' agricultural exports compete with domestic production, the difficulties in granting such income-increasing access are more serious. In some cases, the costs to the United States as a diversified economy are relatively small, while the benefits to LDCs are large. For example, as a number of LDCs have begun to produce palm oil as a way of diversifying traditional exports, access to American (and European) markets is very important. Malaysia, the largest exporter, for example, diversified to counter falling rubber export prices and now has sufficient production to need the large markets America and Europe provide. Attempts to push for import quotas to protect U.S. soybean oil production failed, primarily because palm oil imports account for less than 8% of U.S. edible oil consumption.[37] On the other hand, when the world price of sugar dropped, and competition from foreign producers appeared to threaten domestic production, the import duties were tripled—imposing great costs for LDCs dependent on sugar for the bulk of their foreign exchange earnings.[38]

Strategies for Relating Food Resources to National Security

How much emphasis is placed on developing the ability to exercise coercive food power, maximize revenue from international food sales, or solve chronic problems of malnutrition and hunger will have important implications for the type of national food structure which seems desirable, as well as for the international food regime toward which the world moves. Placing top priority on the ability to exercise coercive food power, for example, would imply changing American domestic structures to insulate the domestic economy from the effects of international food transactions and to increase governmental control over the disposition of food supplies. At the international regime level, it would imply a more cohesive bloc of exporters—perhaps even a cartel. Maximizing revenue from international sales, on the other hand, would imply minimal governmental involvement—except to promote market development—and an internal structure capable of creating a good balance between supply and demand. At the regime level, it would imply liberalized agricultural trade in basic foodstuffs such as grains. A primary commitment to reducing malnutrition and hunger would imply redistribution, either of purchasing power or of food resources, and international institutions designed to minimize the opportunities for speculation and instability. In reality, no single interest would be overriding, but it is useful to characterize the alternatives carefully to see the different conceptions of security they contain, as well as the foregone possibilities once any one scheme is adopted.

312

Insulating the American domestic economy more effectively from the effects of international events would require relatively large public stocks. Large stocks are implied because, under a food power strategy, they would have to cover both variations in supply and in demand. Most discussions of reserves consider only fluctuations in supply—primarily as a result of weather changes. In order to protect the domestic market from changes in international production, the United States would need to stabilize a significant portion of global supply fluctuations unilaterally, as it did before the recent drawdown of stocks. The U.S. Department of Agriculture has estimated that covering roughly two-thirds of the fluctuations would require about 26 million metric tons of grain, 15 million of them foodgrains. This is roughly comparable to American stock levels before the Soviet grain deal. Simulation results for market operations with stocks between 1976–1982 suggest that slightly smaller stocks (23 million metric tons) would have storage and interest costs averaging $293 million per year.[39] However, insulating the United States domestic market from demand fluctuation as well could require higher stock levels. Speculation or panic buying can trigger demand fluctuations which are larger than those in supplies, as the experience of 1972–75 indicates. Since maximizing coercive food power would imply avoiding bilateral agreements to stabilize demand, such as that between the U.S. and USSR, the U.S. would have to assume much of the stabilization burden single-handedly. The need to do so is predicated upon the desirability of being able to reward countries with large sales if they are needed as well as to coerce by curtailing supplies.

How much such a stocks program would actually cost to operate would depend upon how much general market conditions, or the exercise of coercive food power, would make it necessary to support farm prices. When public stocks must insulate domestic farmers from lower prices, the costs of stock programs may be high, as they were for Commodity Credit Corporation (CCC) stocks throughout the 1950s and 1960s. The cost of CCC stocks, independent of other farm programs or export subsidies, averaged about $312 million per year, 1954–72.[40]

Greater government control over commercial sales would also be necessary. This could be achieved, to some extent, by institutionalizing in a licensing system the less formal procedures of oversight the General Sales Manager's office in USDA exercised when supplies were tight and exporters, required to report by telephone their plans to make large sales, were asked to hold back on some sales until more information about supplies was available.[41] However, it is important to remember that the bulk of American-grown grain is marketed by companies which operate transnational marketing networks. This has two implications. First, in the short run, the United States government cannot completely control another country's imports—except in terms of prohibiting sales of American grain to make it impossible to get necessary quantities. Second, in the medium run, companies with such networks may find (or invest to produce) alternative sources of supply and new marketing patterns.

This, of course, does not make coercive food power useless. Restricted supplies to the USSR, for example, will make things harder there. But it does mean that there may be substantial economic costs in the intermediate run (3–5 years) which could affect the American position in the export market. Countries fearing coercive food power may be willing to give preference in purchases to new suppliers to encourage diversification. Similarly, governments in newly exporting countries may be willing to provide export subsidies to make their commodities economically competitive, as does Brazil. Such conditions could diminish the American share of good commercial markets.

The prospect of more coordination among the really large grain exporters—the United States, Canada, and Australia—could also change the capability to exercise coercive food power. Together, these countries control more than three-quarters of world grain exports. Acting in concert, they would certainly have a strong basis for exercising food power. Acting together to exert political influence, as opposed to simply coordinating to change world food prices, requires a shared political interest. It was the OAPEC countries, with a common interest in the outcome of the 1973 war between Egypt and Israel, as well as agreement on the importance of Arab-Israeli relations as a policy issue, that instituted the oil embargo. Without a shared interest in exercising coercive food power, some members of this group might, nevertheless, refrain from interfering with one member's attempt to do so. If, for example, an effective agreement to sustain international grain prices were in effect, members might be reluctant to undermine it for fear of destroying the basis of the agreement. The United States, as the largest exporter, would be in the best position to obtain such tacit consent, since without its participation a price stabilization or price setting agreement could not operate.

Maximizing Revenue from International Food Sales

The $10–11 billion balance of trade surplus in the agricultural sector has been important in America's overall balance of payments. If dependence on oil imports continues and prices remain high, sustained gains from agricultural exports will continue to be important. Sustaining or increasing earnings from agricultural exports requires continued access to commercial markets, and when possible, their expansion. The present emphasis on improving diets in Eastern Europe and the USSR opens lucrative new markets. Having these markets has made unrestricted agricultural production

314

possible and has similarly made less government involvement in costly farm programs a viable option. The large balance of trade surpluses the United States runs with the USSR are primarily the result of large grain sales.

In the last few years, sales to the USSR have come primarily in response to weather—imports cover production shortfalls and make the slaughter of cattle less necessary. However, future sales may not be so dependent on weather. Soviet livestock production has not yet become the scientific operation it is in the United States or Europe. There is a potential market in products and technology which makes large-scale feedlots possible. Shifts toward feedlot production, in turn, will stimulate a greater demand for feedgrains as well as protein used in more efficient livestock feed. A large, unmet desire for meat suggests that the demand for feed-related imports could grow much faster than feedgrain production—even if planned increases in production are not frustrated by bad weather.

In addition, the type of market development required to take advantage of this new source of revenue is easier to bring about than is large-scale market development in most poorer LDCs. Demand does not have to be "created." Neither do sales depend on attempting to create new production techniques "appropriate" to situations where economies of scale cannot be achieved or concentrated agricultural operations create unacceptable social consequences.

Using food exports to enhance America's international economic strength would require few changes in domestic agricultural policy. Minimizing threats of political leverage would be important, however. Foreign fears about exploitable dependence could result in a reluctance to be involved in international agricultural trade over and above levels made necessary by production shortfalls. Greater confidence about the essentially economic character of trade, on the other hand, could produce a willingness to use it to move more quickly into meat production than attempts to rely on domestically produced inputs would permit. Long-term purchasing contracts might be used more extensively to minimize the impact of international sales on domestic consumer prices. Stocks of some form would be required, but with markets stabilized by purchasing agreements, they would only have to cover fluctuations in supply and would not require unilaterally stabilizing as large a share of the market as under the "food power maximizing" strategy.

The "revenue maximizing" strategy would place greatest emphasis on economic coping as a means of promoting national security. Food would be used to hedge against income threats, primarily those related to oil imports. The operation of a "revenue maximizing" strategy would probably make the USSR and Eastern Europe more sensitive to disrupted food supplies. It would also, however, make it more costly for the United States to disrupt them—unless international markets were very tight. While the strategy

315

would imply less than optimal conditions for exercising coercive food power, it might actually enhance American ability to use relatively non-coercive means to influence Soviet policy on food-related issues. For example, it might be much easier to get the USSR to assume a greater responsibility for sharing the costs of managing international food transactions.

Maximizing Nutritional Improvement

Using food resources to reduce hunger and malnutrition would imply quite different policies and institutions. Malnutrition, poverty, and inadequate agricultural production are chronic problems in many LDCs. The humanitarian concern for coping with these problems is clear. To the extent that the United States sees its leadership tied to the ability to create international structures capable of handling global problems in less threatening ways, nutritional improvement may become a security concern as well.

As the earlier discussion of food power indicated, poorer LDCs provide the most likely targets of successful food power. Yet these countries are also those with the most serious food problems. If they are unable to solve them, or at least cope with them, their coping failures may become important sources of international instability. While coercive food power (curtailed supplies or higher prices) could inflict damage, it is unlikely that simply refraining from coercive food power will stabilize or improve the situation in countries with serious problems. More positive policies are required.

The United States could exercise leadership in improving global nutrition in a variety of ways. First, it could guarantee the imports required by LDCs to begin or maintain nutritional assistance programs. Such programs might reasonably be tied to "self help" provisions, as are P.L. 480 sales currently. Guaranteeing import levels under the present programs would involve changing the requirement that concessional shipments be made only from the "surplus" remaining after domestic needs and commercial commitments had been met. Since it is difficult to envision a situation where requirements to meet domestic needs would be dropped, the commitment to nutrition programs would come at the expense of export earnings from commercial sales, assuming paying markets were available for agricultural products. Earmarking established quantities of food for nutritional programs, not for sale on the domestic market of the recipient country, would be a major step toward making American food resources a base for reducing hunger. As such, however, it might come at the expense of programs to use food as a way of providing additional revenue to friendly governments or as a means of relatively indiscriminate surplus disposal. Clearly, there would be costs vis-à-vis the "food power maximizing" or the "revenue maximizing" programs.

Second, the United States might take steps to establish global food

316

reserves—both to share the costs of making food available over fluctuations in weather and to provide a wider base for nutrition aid programs. Global reserves could be used to provide nutritional assistance independent of, or in conjunction with, programs to stabilize the fluctuations in world market prices. Achieving either of these objectives at the global level would require both American leadership and some constraints on the United States' ability to control its donated food resources. As such, it could not readily use "food power" to influence national behavior on issues of political importance to Americans only. On the other hand, the ability to shape national policies on food production, attention to nutrition, and population control might be increased under such a program.

Third, American resources might be used to establish international programs to reduce the risks inherent in expanding food production in poorer LDCs. Hopkins has suggested, for example, that an international crop insurance program be established.[42] The program would be capitalized by a wide range of producing and exporting countries to cover crop failures in poor producing countries. Payments made under the program would permit these countries to replace their production on the commercial market until the crisis passed. This could be meshed with nutritional aid programs, operating at established levels, to distribute the costs of shortfalls in LDCs to those able to bear them without undergoing severe malnutrition.

Such programs could provide governments *willing* to make a transition to more labor-intensive strategies of development assistance the ability to do so. Such development strategies, based on agricultural production, appropriate technology, and labor-intensive production could provide a viable alternative to more politically radical strategies for solving problems of hunger, unemployment, and low productivity. They would also provide a foundation for integrating poorer LDCs into the world economy on terms which would be better for both rich and poor countries alike.[43] Again, however, removing such programs from threats of political leverage would be necessary, especially in issue areas unrelated to food.

The two strategies discussed earlier would have detrimental implications for global nutrition. Maximizing food power would imply more systematic attempts to link food resources to a range of other political issues. It is very easy for a concern with hunger and nutrition per se to erode under such an orientation. Even worse, political manipulation of food resources, or growing fear that this may happen, may actually exacerbate hunger and malnutrition, leading either to a gross misallocation of resources in attempts to become artificially "self-sufficient" or attempts to shift the immediate costs and risks of a serious problem to different social groups without laying a foundation for solving the problem itself.

Maximizing revenue could also have serious nutritional implications. If paying demand in new commercial markets, like Eastern Europe or the

USSR, expanded very rapidly while food needs grew in other parts of the world, an even greater portion of international food transactions would be directed toward enhancing diets that are nutritionally adequate. Without great adjustments within poorer countries, this would translate into greater difficulty in meeting basic nutritional needs.

Clearly, however, some attention must be given to political, economic, and nutritional goals in developing a strategy for linking food to national security as well as developing the means for making food resources usable. For example, provisions to channel the bulk of P.L. 480 sales to poorer countries without alternative means for handling U.S. "surplus" production and without iong-term programs to utilize considerable volumes of food, have led to unsatisfactory outcomes for all concerned. There is hunger in many countries where per capita income is above the arbitrary cutoff, especially where the income distribution is heavily skewed. Food resources cannot be made available. At the same time, poor countries with bumper crops consider U.S. aid efforts "dumping" operations, with potentially serious effects on local production.

A more adequate strategy for linking food and national security might incorporate several premises. First, given the present and projected food problems in many LDCs, food production, nutrition, and rural employment are going to become more pressing development issues. The failure to find "market" solutions to such problems will make it even more difficult than it is now to legitimate Western economic values. Second, structures which directly and immediately trade-off revenue and nutritional improvement will make it politically and economically difficult to provide assistance when it is most needed. Attempts to stabilize markets and tie such stabilization to assistance genuinely oriented toward more sustainable development would be an important step toward making long-term improvement compatible with short-term requirements. Third, political differences will remain, and will undoubtedly continue to shape the use of food resources. However, such uses should be bounded—permitting influence on governments without using the most vulnerable groups within a society as the levers for exerting such influence.

The idea that America has great "food power" is both true and false. The ability to use coercive food power to influence all but the poorest nations is limited to situations where food is genuinely scarce. Even then, however, using food power may have significant costs. On the other hand, there is potential to use food as a leadership resource and as a means for solving chronic nutritional problems. Except under the starkest scenarios, the American interest in fostering stable international economic structures and avoiding crises would imply greater attention toward positive, rather than punitive uses of its food resources.

Footnotes

1. Lester Brown an i Erik Eckholm, *By Bread Alone* (Elmsford, New York: Pergamon, 1972). Contemporary neo-Malthusians, like Malthus himself, may find their predictions falsified by dramatic changes in production—whether as the result of new technology, greater emphasis on agriculture, or changes in social structures.
2. Francis Moore Lappe, *Diet for a Small Planet* (New York: Ballantine Books for Friends of the Earth, 1971).
3. For a discussion of food as a constraint to development and means for altering the situation, see John Mellor, *The New Economics of Growth* (Ithaca, New York: Cornell University Press, 1975).
4. For a discussion of the direct and indirect links between rural discontent and violence, see Jeffery M. Paige, *Agrarian Revolution* (New York: Free Press, 1975).
5. The distinction between sensitivity and vulnerability follows that made by Robert O. Keohane and Joseph S. Nye, "World Politics and the International Economic System," in *The Future of the International Economic Order: An Agenda for Research*, ed. C. Fred Bergsten (Lexington, Mass.: Lexington Books, D.C. Heath and Company, 1973), p. 124.
6. The idea of a food embargo against OAPEC countries was considered specifically in Congressional Research Service, *Data and Analysis Concerning the Possibility of a U.S. Food Embargo as a Response to the Present Oil Boycott, prepared for the Senate Committee on International Affairs* (Washington, D.C.: 1973). A more general discussion of food power is provided in Emma Rothchild, "Food Politics", *Foreign Affairs*, 52:4 (January 1976): 285–307.
7. Central Intelligence Agency, Office of Political Research, *Potential Implications of Trends in World Population, Food Production, and Climate* (Washington, D.C.: Government Printing Office, 1974): pp. 2–3.
8. *Washington Post*, 10 January 1976.
9. The definition follows Klaus Knorr, *The Power of Nations* (New York: Basic Books, 1975), p. 4.
10. The questions are adapted from Hayward Alker, "On Political Capabilities in a Schedule Sense: Measuring Power, Integration and Development" in *Mathematical Approaches to Politics*, ed. Hayward Alker, Karl Deutsch and John Stoetzel (New York: Elsevier, 1973).
11. United States, Department of Agriculture, Economic Research Service, *Reserve Stocks of Grain: A Review of Research* (Washington, D.C.: Government Printing Office, 1975), p. 1.
12. United States, Department of Agriculture, Economic Research Service, *The World Food Situation and Prospects to 1985* (Washington, D.C.: Government Printing Office, 1974), p. 22.
13. Ibid., p. 21.
14. *1974 Annual Report on Public Law 480: Food For Peace* (Washington, D.C.: Government Printing Office, 1976), p. 66.
15. Ibid., p. 66.
16. For a general description of changes in food aid provisions, see Ibid., pp. 6–16.
17. Ibid.
18. United States, Department of Agriculture, Economic Research Service, *U.S. Agricultural Exports Under P.L. 480* (Washington, D.C.: Government Printing Office, 1974), p. 1.
19. The value of agricultural exports to Europe for fiscal 1976 is estimated to be about $7 billion; exports to Japan are about $3.2 billion. Together these two markets account for half the value of U.S. agricultural exports. See United States, Department of Agriculture, Economic Research Service and Foreign Agricultural Service, *Outlook for U.S. Agricultural Exports* (19 May 1976), pp. 7–8.
20. For a discussion of Brazilian export programs and their impact on American agricultural

319

exports, see United States, Department of Agriculture, Economic Research Service and Foreign Agricultural Service, *Foreign Agricultural Circular: Oilseeds and Products*, (April 1976).

21. 80% of U.S. grain exports are handled by five major companies: Louis Drefus, Continental Grain Company, Cook Industries, Cargill, Inc., and Bunge Corporation. See Cheryl Christensen, "The Political Economy of Food" (prepared for the International Studies Association meetings, February 1975).

22. *Feedstuffs*, 15 March 1976.

23. See statements by then President Ford and Jimmy Carter, *Washington Post*, 28 May 1976.

24. Elizabeth Farnsworth, "Chile: What Was the American Role? More than Was Admitted," *Foreign Policy, 19* (Fall 1974): 127–41; for a slightly different perspective, see "Chile: What Was the American Role? Less than Charged," *Foreign Policy, 19* (Fall 1974): 142–56.

25. The discussion of Indonesia follows C. Peter Timmer, "The Political Economy of Food: Indonesia," *Food Research Studies* XIV:3 (1975): 197–231.

26. See, for example, United States, Department of Agriculture, Economic Research Service, *Canada's Export Market Development for Agricultural Products* (Washington, D.C.: Government Printing Office, 1975).

27. Computed from unpublished computer printout made available by the Economic Research Service of the United States Department of Agriculture.

28. Ibid.

29. International Food Policy Research Institute, *Meeting Food Needs in the Developing World: the Location and Magnitude of the Task in the Next Decade* (Washington, D.C.: IFPRI, 1976), p. 1.

30. Ibid., pp. 1–2.

31. See Hollis Chenery et al., *Redistribution with Growth* (Oxford: Oxford University Press for the World Bank and the Institute of Development Studies, 1974).

32. *Washington Post*, 20 May 1976.

33. The White House, "Memorandum for the Secretary of State and Secretary of Agriculture," Presidential Determination, 76–79, Washington, D.C., 2 March 1976. (Typewritten.)

34. *Quarterly Report of the General Sales Manager* (Washington, D.C.: Office of the General Sales Manager, United States Department of Agriculture, July 1976), Table 8.

35. Ibid., p. 16.

36. Ibid., p. 7.

37. United States, Department of Agriculture, Economic Research Service, *Analysis of the U.S. Fats and Oil Industry to 1980* (Washington, D.C.: Government Printing Office, 1976), p. 11.

38. *Wall Street Journal*, 21 September 1976.

39. Rodney Walker, Jerry Sharples, and Forrest Holland, "Grain Reserves for Feed Grains and Wheat in the World Grain Market," in *Analysis of Grain Reserves: A Proceedings*, ed. David Eaton and W. Scott Steele (Washington, D.C.: Economic Research Service, United States Department of Agriculture, 1976), p. 128.

40. Computed from figures provided in Willard W. Cochrane and Mary E. Ryan, *American Farm Policy, 1948–1973* (Minneapolis: University of Minnesota Press, 1976), pp. 316–55.

41. Interview with Mr. Elmer Klump, Foreign Agricultural Service, United States Department of Agriculture, May 1976.

42. Raymond Hopkins, "Global Food Regimes: Overcoming Hunger and Poverty" (prepared for the 1980's Project of the Council on Foreign Relations, nd.), pp. 35–37. (Mimeographed.)

43. Ibid.

The Authors

CHERYL CHRISTENSEN is assistant professor of government and politics at the University of Maryland, College Park. In 1976 she was a Foreign Affairs Fellow of the Council on Foreign Relations, attached to the United States Department of Agriculture, Economic Research Service. She has contributed chapters to many books and is the author of a forthcoming book on the international political economy of food (Free Press).

ROBERT G. GILPIN, JR. is professor of politics and international affairs at the Woodrow Wilson School, Princeton University. He is the author of several books, including *American Scientists and Nuclear Weapons Policy* (Princeton: Princeton University Press, 1965); his most recent is *U.S. Power & the Multinational Corporation* (New York: Basic Books, 1975).

JANET KELLY is assistant professor of political science at the University of Massachusetts, Boston, and Research Fellow at the Center for International Affairs, Harvard University. She has published in the fields of international banking and monetary relations and her recent book is *Bankers and Borders: The Case of American Banks in Britain* (Philadelphia: Ballinger, 1977).

KLAUS KNORR is William Stewart Todd professor of public affairs, Woodrow Wilson School, Princeton University. Among his recent books are *Historical Dimensions of National Security Problems* (Lawrence, Ks.: University Press of Kansas, 1976), *The Power of Nations* (New York: Basic Books, 1975), and *Military Power and Potential* (Lexington, Mass.: D.C. Heath and Company, 1970). He is also an editor of *World Politics*.

STEPHEN D. KRASNER is assistant professor of political science at the University of California, Los Angeles. He has contributed chapters on international raw materials markets and world economy to several books. His most recent title is "State Power and the Structure of International Trade," *World Politics* (April 1976).

HANNS MAULL is the European Secretary of the Trilateral Commission, based in Paris. During 1975–76 he was a Research Fellow with the Centre for Contemporary European Studies of the University of Sussex. He has contributed numerous articles on international problems to many English and German periodicals, and his book, *Europe and International Energy Politics*, is forthcoming.

RONALD I. MELTZER is assistant professor of political science, State University of New York at Buffalo. His research interests are in the areas of international economic relations, U.S. foreign trade policy, and U.S. foreign policy-making. He has published an article, "The Politics of Policy Reversal," in *International Organization* (Autumn 1976).

CLARK A. MURDOCK is associate professor of political science, State University of New York at Buffalo. He recently spent a term as visiting senior lecturer in political science at the University of South Africa, and while there, presented a paper, "The Role of South Africa in Future U.S. Foreign and Defense Policy," at the South African Institute of International Affairs. He is the author of *Defense Policy Formation* (Albany: State University of New York Press, 1974).

FRANK N. TRAGER is professor of international affairs and director, National Security Program, New York University; and director of studies, National Strategy Information Center. He has written numerous books, articles, and monographs on Asian and National Security topics and is the general editor of the *National Security Studies Series*.

Index

Christensen, Cheryl, 14, 16, 79, 216
Chromium, 89
CIEC. *See* Conference on International Economic Cooperation
City of London, 37–39, 50, 54, 55
Clausewitz, Karl von, 63
Clean float, 234
Cobden, Richard, 20
Coca-Cola Bottling Co., 80
Coercive economic power, 99, 101–03, 109–10; and control over supply, 103–05; and demand intensity, 105–06; bases of, 110–13; costs of compliance with, 106–09; costs of use of, 113–14; use in high vs. low conflicts, 108–09, 118–19; and counter-coercion, 112–13; and U.S. food exports, 302, 309–10, 313–14
Coffee, 89
Collective cognizance, 202
Collective economic security: achievement of, 202–04, 206, 224; obstacles to, 204–06, 224; and safeguarding and adjustment assistance, 216; and export controls and access to supplies, 221–22
Collective self-reliance, 150
COMECON. *See* Council for Mutual Economic Assistance
Command economy, 47, 49, 163
Commodity agreements, 11, 147, 148, 152–53, 221
Commodity Credit Corporation (CCC), 313
Communist economies, 62
Communist regimes: and interdependence, 10; as strong states, 162–63, 178, 198; monetary system of, 252–53. *See also* individual names of, e.g. Soviet Union
Compact of iron and rye, 41
Comparative advantage, 36, 40
Condliffe, John, 42, 49
Conference on International Economic Cooperation (CIEC), 150, 204, 222, 277
Congress of Vienna, 31
Connally, John B., 78
Continental Blockade, 103
Cooper, Richard N., 75, 207, 256
Coping capability, 75–78, 118–19
Coping mechanisms, 74–76, 215
Corn, 300–05 (table)
Corn Laws, 36
Corruption, 161, 164, 178
Costs: interdependence, 204–05; of compliance with economic coercion, 106–09; of defiance, 107–08; of using economic coercion, 113–14
Council for Mutual Economic Assistance (COMECON), 10
Counterpart funds, and P.L. 480, 297–98
Crop insurance programs, 317
Cuba, 103, 104, 106, 125

Daimler-Benz (Company), 254
Debt, foreign, 96
Defense Production Act (1950), 143
de Gaulle, Charles, 245
Dependency theory, 43, 44, 45, 73
Dirty float, 210, 235
Dollar. *See* United States dollar
Dollar glut, 243
Dollar overhang, 252

East-West trade, 10, 162, 171–74, 207, 253, 295–96, 311
Echeverria, Luis, 124
Economic issues: politicization of, 6–7, 59, 67–68, 70–72; and security issues, 67–72
Economic nationalism: origins of, 39–42; during interwar period, 50–52, 55; resurgence of, 57, 61, 225. *See also* Protectionism
Economic power: active vs. passive, 114–16; and monopolistic market control, 99–100, 118; and use of foreign aid, *see* Foreign aid; as coercive threat, 99–119; utility of, 99–101; and vulnerability, 78–81; vs. military power, 3, 110, 116–18. *See also* Coercive economic power
Economic threats, 72–74
Economic warfare, 100–02, 107, 116, 121. *See also* Embargoes
EEC. *See* European Economic Community
Egypt, 184, 187, 311; and Arab-Israeli Conflict, 265–66, 269, 284; relations with Soviet Union, 124, 125, 187
Embargoes: effectiveness of, 103–05, 121; by U.S., against Communist states, 121, 174, against Cuba, 103, 104, 106, 125, against England, 101–02, 103; against Rhodesia, 105; on food exports, 299, 302. *See also* Oil embargoes
Engels, Friedrich, 42–44
England, 49, 114, 177, 186, 271; during 19th century, 9, 30–39, 101–02, 133, 134, 188, 197, 241; during 20th century,

47–48, 51–54, 197; monetary problems in, 94–95

ENI, 271

Environmental Protection Agency (EPA), 175, 177

Environmentalists, and energy crisis, 174–75, 177

Ethiopia, 105

Eurocurrency market, 136

Eurodollars, 245, 247, 248, 250, 252

Europe: dependence on Arab oil, 142–44, 262–63 (table), 265, 268 (table), 274 (table). *See also* European Economic Community

European Economic Community (EEC), 2, 3, 13, 205, 219, 236, 274 (table); economic power of, 110, 111, 114, 115, 118; trade by, 83, 84; and Arab-Israeli Conflict, 269–72

Exchange rates: fixed, 3, 56, 233–34, 244, 251; floating, 61, 210, 232, 233–34, 248–50, 251–52; adjustments in, 94–95

Export Administration Act (1969), 220

Export controls: and national security, 218–20; and collective economic security, 221–23

Export-Import Bank, 173

Exports, growth in, 206

Exxon. *See* Standard Oil of New Jersey

Faisal, King, 266

Federal Reserve Board, 169, 170

Fels, Gerhard, 214

Feudalism, 23

Fichte, Johann, 41

Food for Peace. *See* Public Law 480

Food resources: scarcity of, 289–93, 307–08; and nutritional assistance programs, 316–18; sales of, and revenue maximization, 214–16, 317–18; non-coercive use of, 310–13; of U.S., 293–96; and U.S. foreign policy, 79–80, 296–302, 308–10. *See also* individual names of, e.g. Grain, Wheat

Ford Administration, 214

Ford, Gerald R., 69, 115; and U.S. agricultural export policy, 81, 114, 263, 302, 310

Foreign aid; purposes of, 100–02, 122, 123–24; and P.L. 480, 297–99

Foreign Assistance Act, 298

Foreign Investment: by England, 36–37; by

U.S. 52–53, 80–81; and vulnerability, 92–94

Foreign Trade and Investment Act (1972; Burke-Hartke bill), 209

Founding Fathers (U.S.), 170–71

France, 87, 122, 186, 205, 219; during 19th century, 30–31; domestic political structure of, 77; energy policy of, 177, 271; monetary policy of, 245, 250–51, 255

Free trade: origins of, 36–39; collapse of, 51; multilateral, 54, 55–56; and U.S. tariff policy, 53–54

French franc, 74, 94

Fuel, 85–86 (tables)

Gambia, 164

Gandhi, Indira, 124

General Agreement on Tariffs and Trade (GATT): goals of, 1, 54, 55, 207, 218; inadequacies of, 207–10, 203, 220, 223; Article 11 of, 220; Article 19 of, 212–13. *See also* Kennedy Round, Tokyo Round

German Historical School, 41–42

German mark, 233, 235, 244

Germany, 118, 122, 205; economic growth in, 3, 78, 188; economic nationalism in, 41–42, 50–52, 55; business-government relations in, 77–78; monetary policy of, 95, 248; and Arab-Israeli Conflict, 271

Ghana, 164, 201

Gilpin Robert G., Jr., 14, 68, 80, 92, 133, 137, 148, 200, 206, 208, 235

GNP, 162; and foreign trade, 81–84, 90, 117; and military expenditures, 184 (table), 195; and R & D, 188–89 (table)

Gold, 233; standard, 37–39, 50, 51, 53, 232, 238, 241; two-tier market for, 246

Gosovic, Branislav, 148, 151

Grain, 115, 263, 293–96, 298–302

Great Society Program, 244

Greece, 124; ancient, 22, 24

Gross National Product. *See* GNP

Group of Seventy-seven: and NIEO, 60, 146–49; commodity stabilization program of, 152–53, 155, 156; demands for guaranteed markets, 147; diplomatic gains by, 153–54; OPEC as exemplar for, 149–50; solidarity of, 150–52, 155

Group of Twenty (IMF), 206

Gulf Oil Corporation, 139–40

Guyana, 112

324

and food scarcity, 289–93; and national will, 16–18

National Stripper Well Association, 174

National will, 9, 111, 161, 224; and military strength, 191–98; and national security, 16–18. *See also* Political culture

NATO, 194

Nazi Germany, 116

Navigation Acts, 29

Neo-colonialism, 44–45

Neo-Marxism, 43, 45

Neo-mercantilism, 8, 39–42

Netherlands, 153–54, 174, 266, 267–68, 271, 284

New Economic Policy, 57

New International Economic Order (NIEO), 130, 133; demands for, 4, 10–12, 60, 63, 100, 111, 120, 138, 146–57; Swedish and Dutch support of, 153–54; U.S. attitude toward, 148, 150; and oil link, 149–50, 218

Nigeria, 265

Nisbet, Robert, 59

Nixon, Richard M., 57, 68, 115, 169, 173, 248–49, 266

Non-discrimination, 208, 212

Non-proliferation treaty (1968), 121

North Sea, 265, 285

Norway, 114

Nuclear Regulatory Commission, 175

Nuclear weapons, 121

Nye, Joseph S., Jr., 69–70, 201, 202

OAPEC. *See* Organization of Arab Petroleum Exporting Countries. Occidental Petroleum Corporation, 145

OECD. *See* Organization for Economic Cooperation and Development

OEEC. *See* Organization for European Economic Cooperation

Oil: as a weapon, 259, 265–72, 280–81; and Arab-Israeli Conflict, 265–72; and producer-consumer trade relations, 261–64; and producer power, 277–79; international distribution system for, 275–79; bilateral supply arrangements for, 276–77

Oil and Gas Associations, 174

Oil embargo, 7, 73, 118, 119; and Arab-Israeli Conflict (1967), 261; and Arab-Israeli Conflict (1973), 3–4, 71, 90, 104, 105, 106, 110, 146, 218, 261, 262–63,

272–75; against Netherlands, 266, 267–68, 271, 283–84

Oil prices, 260, 273; rise in and OPEC, 60, 100, 156, 175, 259–60

Oil production, 130, 133, 265; oligopolistic control of, 137–41, 174; U.S. government involvement in, 141–42

Okinawa, 169

OPEC. *See* Organization of Petroleum Exporting Countries

Open international economic system. *See* Liberal economic system

Optimal currency area, 234

Orders-in-Council, 102

Organization for Economic Cooperation and Development (OECD), 137, 157; and oil resources, 204, 261, 271, 277; and trade, 202, 222

Organization for European Economic Cooperation (OEEC), 143

Organization of Arab Petroleum Exporting Countries (OAPEC); and oil embargo, 5, 149, 266–68, 284, 293, 314; solidarity of, 283–84, 285, 286

Organization of Petroleum Exporting Countries; 291; and oil embargo, 4, 5, 71, 174, 218; and oil prices, 60, 100, 136, 144–46, 156, 174, 175, 259–60; and oil resources 134–35, 273, 275 (table); support of NIEO, 120, 138; as exemplar, 149–50, 218, 219; and leapfrogging, 144–46; and restructuring, 155–57; agricultural imports by, 305, 307 (figure); monetary power of, 253–54; solidarity of, 260, 283–84, 285, 286; and U.S. energy policy, 175–77

Ottawa Agreements (1932), 51

Pahlevi, Mohammed Reza, Shah of Iran, 145

Palm oil, 312

Palmerston, Lord Henry, 35

Paraguay, 115

Paris Conference (1975). *See* Conference on International Economic Cooperation

Participation agreements, 146

Patron-client relationship, 104, 107, 116, 125

Pax Americana, 47, 54

Pax Britannica, 27, 38, 42, 47, 52, 54; and rise of liberalism, 30–31

People's Republic of China, 49, 62, 83, 110, 187; and Soviet-Albanian relations, 107;

foreign aid, 102, 103, 105, 106, 107, 122; and international monetary system, 252–53; grain production in, 115, 263; influence in Middle East, 100, 264, 284; passive economic power of, 114–15; relations with Yugoslavia, 102, 103, 105, 106, 107; trade with West, 10, 105–06, 162, 171–74, 207, 253, 311; wheat imports by, 10, 111, 172–73, 295–96, 299, 302

Soybeans, 218, 291, 299, 312

Spain, 135

Special Drawing Rights (SDRs), 232, 246–48, 249

Special International Fund, 147

Sri Lanka, 304, 308, 310

Stalin, Joseph, 48

Standard Oil of California (SOCAL), 140, 141

Standard Oil of New Jersey (Exxon), 139–140, 145

State-centric system, 3, 12

Statecraft: skill in, as base for coercive economic power, 111–12; military, 189–91, 193

Stevenson, Adlai, E., III, 173

Strategic Arms Limitations Talks (SALT), 68

Strategic goods, 121, 174

Sudan, 291, 304

Suez Canal, closing of (1967), 143–44, 261, 262, 265

Suez Crisis (1956), 143–44, 236, 261, 262

Sugar, 312

Supplies, access to; and national security, 218–20; and collective economic security, 221–23

Swap network, 250

Sweden, 154, 186

Switzerland, 92, 186

Syria, 187, 265, 266, 284, 310–11

Taiwan, 123

Tanker fleets, 277–78, 279

Tanzania, 112

Teheran Agreement (1971), 146

Texaco (Company), 141

Texas Railroad Commission, 174

Third world, threat from 151–53. *See also* Less-developed countries

Threats: economic, 72–74; military, 192–94, 197; perception of, 8, 16; to core values, 69–72, 127

Togo, 164

Tokyo Declaration (1973), 210, 211, 218

Tokyo Round: background of, 209–10; safeguarding negotiations at, 211–17; export controls negotiations at, 218–23; objectives of, 223–24

Trade, 40, 81–84, 90, 117, 206; in mercantile era, 28, 29, 36; and collective economic security, 202–06, 216; and interdependence, 36–37, 201, 206–07; and national security, 200–02; liberalization of, 208–09; politicization of, 207–10, 213; and vulnerability, 81–92. *See also* East-West trade; Free trade; Protectionism

Trade Act (1974), 106, 173, 213, 214, 220

Trager, Frank N., 69

Trans-Arabian pipeline, 265

Transnationalism, 3

Transportation, 19th century revolution in, 33–34

Tripartite Agreement (1936), 54

Tripoli Agreement (1971), 146, 265

Tunisia, 266

Turkey, 124

Turkish Petroleum Company, 139

UNCTAD. *See* United Nations Conference on Trade and Development

United Arab Emirates, 273

United Brands (Company), 164

United Nations, 112, 122; General Assembly Sixth Special Session, 150; General Assembly Seventh Special Session, 147, 151; Resolution 242, 106, 269, 270

United Nations Conference on Trade and Development (UNCTAD), 151, 152, 207, 214, 222

United States, 101, 193; as food power, 293–302, 309–18; as weak state, 169–71, 174; business-government relations in, 170–71; economic aid to Latin America, 100, 125; economic power of, 47, 52–56, 61–62, 79–81, 133, 134, 188, 206; embargoes against Communist nations, 103, 104, 106, 111, 112, 121, 122, 123, 125; energy crisis and policy of, 115, 171, 174–77, 260; foreign investments by, 52–53, 80–81, 92–94; foreign trade of, 53–54, 79–84, 263, 305–07 (table); Middle East policy, 264, 268–69, 271, 293, 311; military expenditures by, 184, 192, 194, 195; mone-